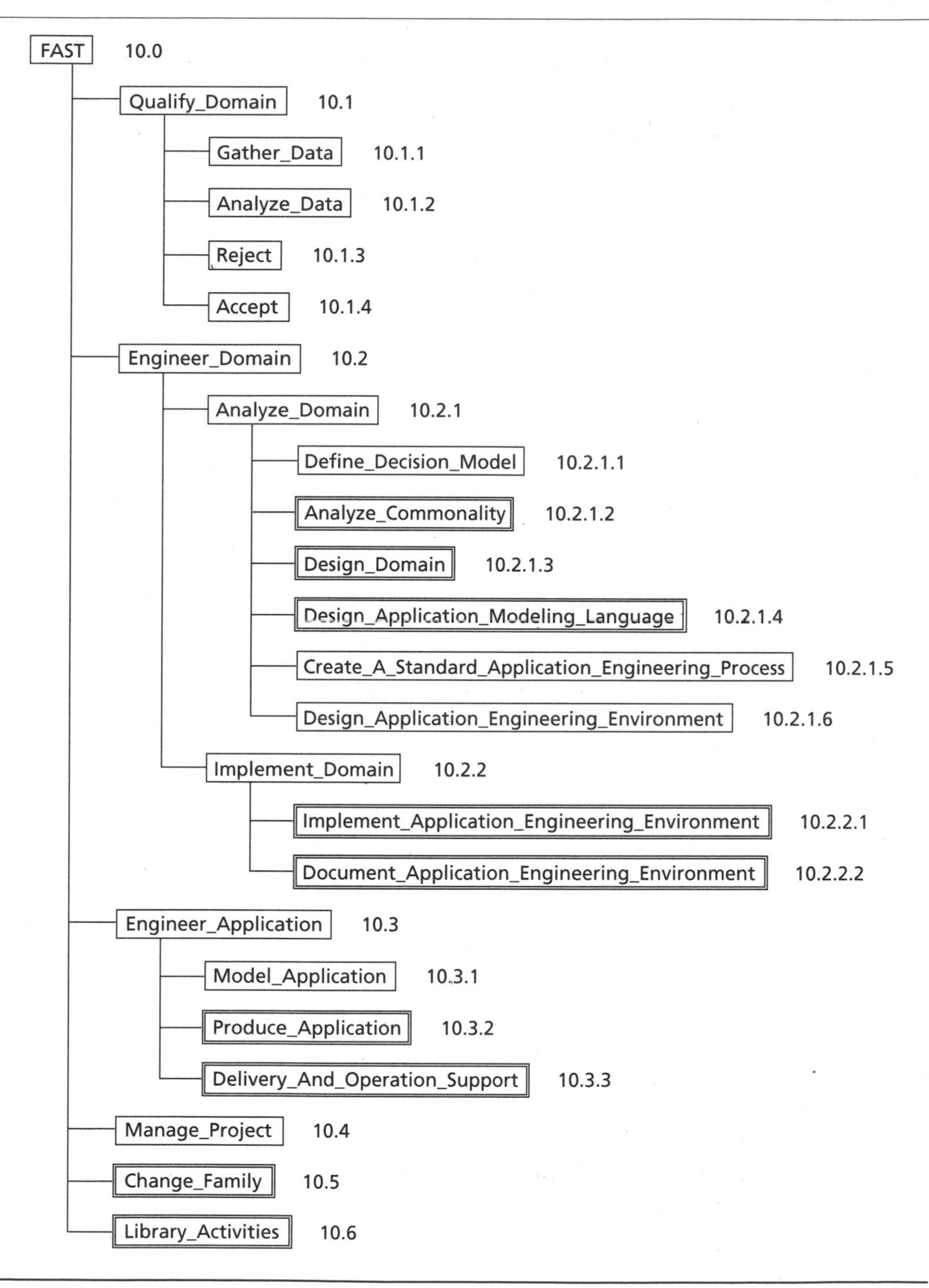

The FAST Activity Tree

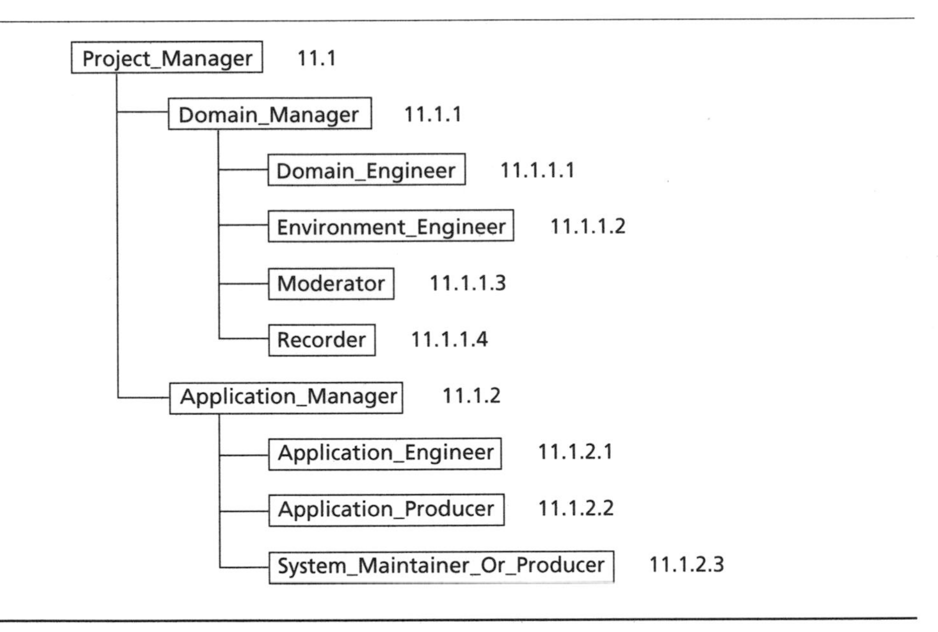

FAST Role Tree

Software Product-Line Engineering

Software Product-Line Engineering

A Family-Based Software Development Process

David M. Weiss
Chi Tau Robert Lai

ADDISON–WESLEY

An Imprint of Addison Wesley Longman, Inc.
Reading, Massachusetts ◆ Harlow, England ◆ Menlo Park, California
Berkeley, California ◆ Don Mills, Ontario ◆ Sydney
Bonn ◆ Amsterdam ◆ Tokyo ◆ Mexico City

Many of the designations used by manufacturers and sellers to distinguish their products are claimed as trademarks. Where those designations appear in this book, and Addison Wesley Longman Inc. was aware of a trademark claim, the designations have been printed with initial capital letters or in all capitals.

The authors and publisher have taken care in the preparation of this book, but make no expressed or implied warranty of any kind and assume no responsibility for errors or omissions. No liability is assumed for incidental or consequential damages in connection with or arising out of the use of the information or programs contained herein.

The publisher offers discounts on this book when ordered in quantity for special sales. For more information, please contact:

AWL Direct Sales
Addison Wesley Longman, Inc.
One Jacob Way
Reading, Massachusetts 01867
(781) 944-3700

Visit AW on the Web: www.awl.com/cseng/

Library of Congress Cataloging-in-Publication Data

Weiss, david, 1945-
Software product-line engineering : a family-based software development process / David Weiss, Chi Tau Robert Lai.
p. cm.
Includes bibliographical references and index.
ISBN 0-201-69438-7
1. Computer software—Development. I. Lai, Chi Tau Robert. II. Title.
QA76.76.D47W454 1999
005.1—dc21 99-21056
CIP

ISBN 0-201-69438-7
Text printed on recycled paper
1 2 3 4 5 6 7 8 9 10–CRW–0302010099
First printing, July 1999

Contents

Foreword

MOST SOFTWARE PROFESSIONALS BEGIN AS NOVICE PROGRAMMERS, people who have learned little more than how to write functioning programs in some programming language. As they ripen into experienced developers, they go through several clearly recognizable stages. Understanding the steps they go through provides us with useful insight into the problems we continue to experience in software development.

Novice programmers believe that once they get their program working neither they nor anyone else will ever have to change it again. For them, nothing matters except that the program seems to work and they get the answers they expect. They consider their job done when the code compiles and passes a few basic tests.

A major step forward comes when novice programmers recognize that if they are successful in their efforts, they are writing not a single program but the first of a long sequence of programs. They start to realize that (a) the program won't be perfect when they write it, and (b) the requirements will change with time. This leads them to start thinking about various aspects of designing software so that it will be easier to make the changes that will inevitably follow. For example, more advanced programmers think about providing detailed design documentation and encapsulating or hiding design decisions that are likely to change. As their understanding grows, they spend more of their time on design and documentation and proportionally less on the code itself.

At first, software designers work in an *ad hoc* way with design-for-change principles applied haphazardly whenever opportunities present themselves. As experience grows, they learn that the principles should be applied in a systematic way and that an effort should be made to be sure that no likely change is overlooked. At this stage, designers try to anticipate possible changes, and they compile lists of potential changes that are to be used when designing and, later, when reviewing a proposed design.

Many experienced designers view change as a kind of unpredictable, undesirable, but unavoidable phenomenon. They believe that if only they had enough foresight, they would be able to get a program right the first time and further change would not be necessary. They subsequently learn that a set of similar programs may be needed; that is, it is not always desirable or appropriate to produce and maintain only one version of a program. Within a single system, there may be a need for many subprograms that share some algorithms, data structures, and other elements but that also differ in important ways. Moreover, not all users of a product have the same requirements and desiderata. A market may exist for a set of products with many things in common but with important, *user-visible* differences. In other words, there may be a market for a software product line.

Very sophisticated designers know that they can take advantage of the fact that many similar programs will be needed, and they use the similarities, together with an understanding of the differences, to reduce development costs, maintenance costs, and user confusion. In this context, design for change is not viewed as a defensive move but as an aggressive tactic that will increase software quality while reducing cost. To do this, programmers and designers must learn to view their work not as designing a single product that might have to be changed but as designing a generic product or a product-generator, so that their organization will be able to adapt quickly to new market realities by bringing out new versions.

Programmers with experience in developing program families soon recognize the need for a systematic, formal design process with well-defined milestones and product-evaluation criteria. They know that if they simply rely on their intuition, they will overlook some of the possible variations within a family, but sometimes they do not notice exploitable similarities and therefore introduce unnecessary variation into their products.

With more experience, programmers learn that in most cases software designers do not have enough information to design a family properly. Some of that information may be known only by specialists within their own organizations, their customers' organizations, or their suppliers' organizations. These designers require guidance in gathering and documenting the information they need to design a good program family. Recognizing that designing such a family is not the work of a single individual, they also look for information about the organization of the work force and examples of how to document the results of each information-gathering stage.

Eventually, experienced software family designers want to go beyond simply recording information for use by program designers; they know that, in many cases, it is possible to embed what they have learned (about the commonalities and differences in a program family) in specialized program-generation tools that can be used to speed up the process of producing new members of a family.

David Weiss and Robert Lai have provided a book that can accelerate the maturation process just described. Based on many years of industrial software design experience, they have written a book that explains the importance of developing program families, shows how to do it, and provides concrete examples. It is in the "how to do it" part that this book excels, because it illustrates a process that has been successfully applied to reduce costs for organizations that develop large programming systems. This process takes into account both the design aspects and the organizational issues. To date, relatively few programmers have passed through all the maturation stages outlined here. With the help of this book, many more can learn how to exploit the idea of program families and bring about a substantial improvement in the state of practice in the software industry.

David Lorge Parnas
Director of the Software Engineering Program
Department of Computing and Software
McMaster University

Preface

INDUSTRIES AND MARKETPLACES OFTEN SUFFER RADICAL CHANGES in seemingly brief periods of time. The software development industry, in all its forms, has the opportunity to undergo such a change now. The hallmark will be a conversion from software development processes that are characterized by developing an individual system and then creating variations of it, to software development processes that create product lines and families of systems. Creating variations on individual systems takes continual investment in understanding new requirements, and in redesign, recoding, and retesting. Creating product lines and families, on the other hand, invests in support for understanding new requirements and rapidly creating new family members with little or no redesign and recoding and with reduced retesting. Changing from the first strategy to the second means changing the software development techniques that you use and changing your organization. Fortunately, you can make both changes incrementally if you know what you are trying to achieve.

We wrote this book to show you what we think your target in improving your software development process should be: a software development process focused on building families. The process we describe is based on our experience with creating software families, experience that extends back to the middle 1970s. Most recently we have seen improvements from applying family-based processes at Lucent Technologies, showing decreases in development time and costs for family members of 60%–70%. Our comparison is based on measuring the time and effort to create variations on a product before a family-based process is introduced and again after it is used.

Our intent is to identify the key ideas whose combination can radically alter the way software developers do their jobs, with attendant major gains in their productivity and in the quality of their products. By focusing software developers on building software families, these ideas can be woven into a process for software development that is much more effective than the processes in common use today. The result is a paradigm shift in software development that involves creating two new types of organizations: one devoted to defining families of programs and creating facilities needed for rapidly producing family members and a second one devoted to rapidly producing family members by using those facilities. Creation of members of a family is akin to a production process and is enabled by an investment in tools and processes for the entire family. The result is to make it possible to create high-quality software applications much faster than with current processes.

Most of the ideas we use—such as abstraction, separation of concerns, information hiding, formal specification, and model building—have permeated the research literature in software engineering for many years but have not been widely applied in engineering practice. A process that incorporates these ideas into a practical, family-oriented software production process was introduced at AT&T in 1992 by David Weiss; its roots can easily be traced back through 30 years of research in software engineering conducted by a variety of people. Called the Family-Oriented Abstraction, Specification, and Translation (FAST) process, it is now in use at Lucent Technologies, where its evolution is continuing. Because of its focus on producing family members, we often refer to FAST as a software production process rather than a software development process.

This book introduces the ideas that software development organizations need to know to evolve into software production organizations. Such an evolution is easiest if an organization can create for itself a software production process. Accordingly, the FAST process is really a pattern for doing so, and we think of any process that conforms to that pattern as a FAST process. Put another way, FAST processes form a family. Within Lucent we have created several members of the FAST family of processes, using variations on the basic pattern as people and circumstances demand. With the help of this book we hope that you can begin to create your own FAST processes.

Planning and structuring for change is a central theme of FAST processes. It has also been a key theme in software engineering for many years. Characteristic of this theme is a continuing search for better abstractions. Finding and applying appropriate abstractions in software design and in programming languages has been a major tool for software engineers. FAST processes further develop the theme of abstraction by asking software engineers to find, for each family, abstractions that are useful in defining the family and describing its members. For each family we incorporate such abstractions into a language for specifying and modeling family members. The description of a family member in the language can be analyzed for completeness, consistency, and other properties, and, with a sufficient investment, engineers can build tools that generate the software for the family member from its description. The ability to perform each of these steps represents a further step in an organization's evolution from a software development organization to a software production organization. The ability to do all of them represents a step in the evolution of the software engineering community to use abstractions to better advantage.

As an organization evolves from software development to software production, so will its FAST processes evolve. We have started this evolution within Lucent Technologies.

To understand and track our progress, we need a way of precisely describing the processes we are using and have used. Our mechanism for doing so is the Process and Artifact State Transition Abstraction (PASTA) process description method.

PASTA allows us to describe the artifacts that we use in our process, the activities that are performed during the process, the operations that we use to manipulate the artifacts, and the roles played by people during the process. It allows us to describe activities that may proceed concurrently and activities that must be performed sequentially as well as situations when backtracking may occur. A PASTA model of a process is also a good basis for developing automated support for the process.

This book contains a PASTA reference model for FAST processes. Having such models gives us a record of the evolution of FAST. The nature of PASTA and its supporting tools help us to understand the possible effects of a change to FAST and make it easier for us to make changes to the model. PASTA thereby facilitates changes to the FAST process. We have left certain aspects of the model incomplete because they vary considerably from one organization to another. For example, the configuration management process is usually highly specialized for an organization.[1] We have done no more than sketch how change reporting might be handled for a family. We hope that you will use the model in this book as a starting point for creating your own reference model for your own FAST process.

We live in a time when business enterprises of all sorts appear to be undergoing continuous change. Such change usually relies on altering the processes that the enterprise uses. In manufacturing industries, the idea of redesigning product lines and processes so that a product is easy to produce using its production process is known as concurrent engineering. Both product and process are designed together. FAST and PASTA together can be viewed as concurrent engineering for software: FAST processes help software engineers to design both a family whose members are based on predicted changes and a process for producing those members based on the predictions. PASTA helps a software development organization to deploy and enact FAST as a production process, providing a way to create guidebooks and toolsets to support the process.

A variety of industries have adopted the notion of continuous change in the interest of gaining a competitive advantage—namely, to be able to produce customized products rapidly. The software development industry is no different. Competitive demands are pushing software developers to create products in greater variety faster than ever before. FAST is designed to help software engineers respond to this trend and, by appropriate investment and planning, to take advantage of it.

1. See R. E. Grinter, "Recomposition: Putting It All Back Together Again," ACM Conference on Computer Supported Cooperative Work (CSCW '98) (Seattle: November 14–18, 1998), for an interesting view of how configuration management varies among software development organizations.

Acknowledgments

This book was in the planning, creating, and re-creating process for an agonizingly long time. We thank our wives—Joanne Glazer Weiss and Ya Chien Chuang—for their patience and willingness to delay other projects in favor of the book. We also thank Deborah Lafferty for her patience and encouragement through many missed deadlines. Many people helped to shape the ideas that underlie FAST and PASTA and worked to polish them enough so that they were ready for use. Prominent among them are David Parnas, Grady Campbell, Stuart Faulk, Rich McCabe, James Kirby, Jr., James O. Coplien, Omer Aiken, and Steve Yau. We would never have had the confidence to write this book without the assistance and support of many people who were willing to experiment with FAST and PASTA and who helped to shape them into their current working form. Prominent among these people are David Cuka, Mark Ardis, Lloyd Nakatani, Bob Olsen, Lynn Paulter, Paul Pontrelli, Doug Stoneman, Richard Braatz, Lizette Velazquez, Jan Sharpless, Ivy Mackowiak, Steven Nolle, Carl Chang, Wei Tek Tsai, Tom Case, Ken D. Shere, Lina-Na Hwa, Martha Lin, Chu-San Sam Shen, C. W. Chen, Ya-Chien Chuang, and Herman Chuan-Ming Hsiung. Art Pyster, Eric Sumner, Jan Sharpless, and Mary Zajac provided management support and encouragement. Deserving of special mention are David Cuka, who did much of the development work on the SPEC example and who has been an early and tireless advocate of FAST within Lucent, and Dan Hoffman, who did much of the development work on the Floating Weather Station example. James O. Coplien occupies a special niche in our thoughts, first for his encouragement to us to write this book and second for his explorations of the ideas of commonality and variability and how to use them to create a multiparadigm approach to software development. These explorations are captured in his own book, which we commend to your attention. Special thanks to Tina Murthy for helping to create the FAST PASTA model and to Ching-Peng Chu, Chung Hong Chien, Ting-Shun Cuang, Jimmy Truong, Tong-Gao Tang, and Wei-Li Johnson Liu for helping to implement the PASTA toolset, which we used to create the FAST PASTA model. Joanne Glazer Weiss helped with the tedious task of verifying table formats.

David dedicates this book to Jack and Bertha Weiss. Robert dedicates this book to Tsung-Yen and Chiu-Lan Lai.

David Weiss
Lucent Technologies
Naperville, IL

Chi Tau Robert Lai
International Software Process Constellation
Reston, VA

February 1999

1 Introduction: The Need for Families

THIS CHAPTER EXPLAINS THE CENTRAL DILEMMA OF SOFTWARE engineering and outlines why family-based software development processes can be a remedy for it. It introduces the notions of families and domains, product lines, the term *domain engineering*, and the FAST software production process, which is based on domain engineering. It also discusses our expectations for what you will learn from this book.

The Dilemma of Careful Engineering and Rapid Production

As software engineers, we face a continuing dilemma. On the one hand, we are asked to create software that attracts customers with its functionality, ease of use, and reliability and that is easy to enhance and evolve as customer needs and technology change. Meeting this demand requires careful engineering. On the other hand, we are pressured to produce software so that it can be marketed ahead of the competition. Unfortunately, the pressure for rapid production is often the enemy of careful engineering. We frequently sacrifice to schedule pressures the engineering activities that contribute to more than getting a single product out the door as fast as possible. By failing to pay attention to activities that promote faster development of other versions of the same product, or of similar products, we repeat the same sacrifice for each new version or similar product.

Attaining resolution between schedule pressure and careful engineering is rarely a consideration in current software development processes. We describe a software development process in this book that is designed to help practicing software engineers to resolve the dilemma of simultaneous careful engineering and rapid production. We suggest both a general approach to software production and a specific software production process. Both elements are intended to help resolve the tensions generated by the dilemma. Software engineers who achieve resolution give their companies and themselves a competitive edge: they can capture, keep up with, and even lead an ever-changing marketplace.

Engineers in other fields experience the same pressures and often manage to respond to them. In fields such as aerospace engineering, automotive engineering, and computer engineering, methods of rapidly producing carefully engineered products have long been explored and continue to improve. Many of these methods are based on the idea of developing a family of products that can be produced with one production facility. A *family* is a set of items that have common aspects and predicted variabilities, such as a common chassis but different engines and transmissions.

In many cases, each member of a family is a complete product, such as a family of automobiles in which each automobile is a member of the family and is a complete product in itself. In other cases, each item is part of a product and is intended to fit into a larger family, such as a tire for an automobile. We call a family of products designed to take advantage of the common aspects and predicted variabilities a *product line*. Although software development is quite different from development of airplanes, automobiles, or computers, software engineers can benefit significantly from applying family-based production strategies. This book's purpose is to show, by principle and example, from experience and measurement, how you can apply such a strategy to software production.

Our goal is to provide you with a systematic approach to analyzing potential families and to developing facilities and processes for generating family members. The result is a carefully engineered environment for rapidly producing family members. Similar approaches are in use in a variety of places, and common terminology is for the engineered families to be known as *domains*. Figure 1-1 depicts a common pattern for these approaches. Here, the software engineer's role is split into two parts: the domain engineer, who defines a family and creates the production facilities for the family, and the application engineer, who uses the production facilities to create new family members. Correspondingly, the two parts of the approach are known as domain engineering and application engineering. Our approach for developing families is known as Family-Oriented Abstraction, Specification, and Translation (FAST). As we progress through our discussion of FAST, we refine the descriptions of the activities that the domain

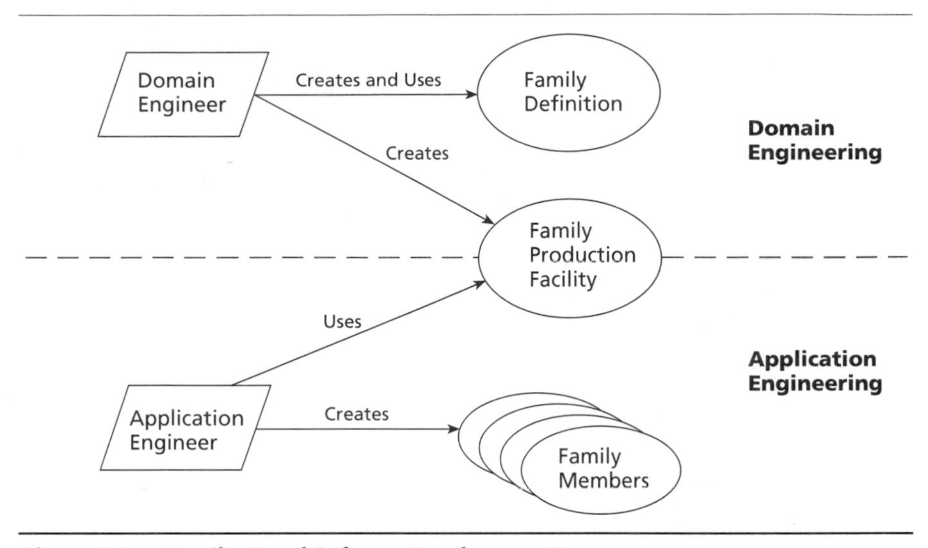

Figure 1-1. *Family-Based Software Development Processes*

and application engineers perform and of the artifacts that they produce, providing you with a description of FAST as a software development process.

1.1 Problems FAST Addresses

FAST, like other family-based approaches, is designed to attack the major problems that lead to increased software development intervals and inhibit attention to careful engineering. These problems include the following.

- Ill-defined and changeable requirements, especially in two situations: one in which your customers may be uncertain about their needs but can describe the ranges of choices for the decisions they are considering; the other in which developers are uncertain about the exact demands of a market but can predict market trends.
- Confusion of requirements, design, and code, especially difficulties created when the requirements for a program are described with statements such as "It must behave just like our existing program except in certain ways."
- The need for rediscovery and reinvention, especially in situations in which developers must locate and interview people who are the experts about one part of a system in order to understand the consequences of making a change elsewhere in the system.

- The need to adapt legacy software to new technology and new requirements, especially when the software does not accommodate change well, the code is the only trustworthy documentation, and the knowledge needed to change the code safely resides only in a few peoples' heads.
- Redundant specification, especially when the information that you need and use to describe and develop a system is described in one place and one notation during requirements determination and is described again in another place and another notation during design, and again during coding, and again during testing.

These problems make the software developers' task a lengthy and costly one, often requiring developers to iterate many times among design, code, and testing to determine the acceptability of a new system or a new version of an existing system. Much engineering is repeated each time, and the pressure to develop the new system or version quickly does not allow for the care needed.

To alleviate these problems, FAST includes a phase in the development process that focuses on defining a family and carefully engineering an environment for very rapid production of family members. The FAST software production paradigm gives developers and customers a chance for early, quick evaluation of different members of a family by making it easy to describe members of the family and rapidly produce them from their descriptions. In particular, we seek to provide the software developer with the capability to do the following:

- Bring the customer into the production loop for the purpose of validating requirements
- Separate the concerns of determining and validating requirements from the concerns of designing, coding, and testing
- Respond rapidly to changes in requirements
- Model a system so that its characteristics can be quickly explored
- Rapidly generate deliverable products, including code and documentation, from a model of a system

Our target improvement in the time interval and cost for software production is a factor of between 5:1 and 10:1. Our comparison is between (1) using the FAST process to generate family members and (2) producing systems by writing or rewriting code in high-level languages such as C, C++, Java, Ada, COBOL, or FORTRAN. The target is derived from our early experiences with FAST, primarily in telecommunications domains.

The FAST strategy is based on investing in production facilities for a family. The investors expect that the cost of the investment will be repaid by enabling rapid and inexpensive production of a variety of family members. Put another way, the investment in production facilities is amortized over the set of family members that are produced, with the expectation that the speed of and variety in production will provide the investors with a competitive advantage. The investment in careful engineering for the family is repaid with the ability it provides for rapid production, helping to resolve the software engineer's dilemma.

1.2 Applications of FAST

The FAST process was developed and is in use within Lucent Technologies. The domains vary considerably in application, scope, and complexity. A few examples from Lucent experience are command recognition, database views, and runtime equipment reconfiguration. For example, the domain of command recognition consists of thousands of commands and the software that recognizes each one when it is invoked. In addition, the software produces the customer documentation for each command in a standardized format. This domain is one of many embedded in a software product line. The code produced for family members is targeted for different members of the product line. For some of our domains, the family definition has been used across different product lines, with different production facilities for different products built on different platforms.

1.3 Benefits of FAST

Family-based processes such as FAST, in which the knowledge needed to produce family members rapidly is packaged for widespread and efficient use and reuse without abuse, are worth creating because successful software systems inevitably evolve into families. FAST provides the following benefits in this evolution.

- More-efficient production of family members. FAST makes the production of family members more efficient, and this means that they can be produced in less time and cost than if FAST is not used.
- Ability to support a greater variety of family members. FAST permits the production and support of more family members than can be done without a family-based process.
- Graceful aging. The use of FAST leads to a family that ages gracefully.

- Improved quality. Improvements in common designs and code lead to improvements in all family members, thereby allowing you to leverage quality improvements across the family. We expect an additional gain from commonalities across families, wherein the use of designs and code shared by families leads to improvements across many families.
- Competitive advantage in domains of application. Organizations that adopt the family approach gain a competitive advantage in the domains where they apply it. They can adopt a business strategy of developing a family for the purpose of rapidly producing many variations on a product at low cost with high quality.

1.4 What Can Readers Expect?

This book gives readers who would like to use FAST a working knowledge of the FAST process. It is intended to provide a series of successively more detailed and more formalized descriptions of FAST, interspersed with examples. It is not intended to survey domain engineering development processes, to compare FAST with other software development processes, or to describe our experiences in applying FAST in a variety of domains.

In the early chapters we provide you with the underlying motivations and principles along with an example, drawn from the command recognition domain, that describes the products of using FAST in a real domain. This example does not give much detail on how those products were created. In later chapters we give both informal descriptions of each major step in the FAST process and a detailed example of the application of those steps to an example, the Floating Weather Station (FWS) domain. The example shows you how the product of each step was created, and it includes the code for generating members of the FWS domain. We have run the resulting code on a variety of platforms using a standard Web browser.

In the final chapters we give a more precise description of FAST by exhibiting a model of the FAST process. The model is formalized as a set of state machines. For each step in the process, the model provides at least a definition of the output of the step, the prerequisites for performing the step, the activities that take place within the step, the roles of the people who perform the activities, and the resources needed to accomplish the step. For some critical activities we also give a detailed description of how to perform the step.

Each activity and each artifact produced or used during the performance of FAST activities has an associated state transition machine. As domain engineers and application engineers progress through the process, the artifacts that they create or modify become progressively more complete and trigger state transitions in the activities. Typical artifacts are design documents, code, and test specifications. For example, a process might enter a test state, In_Test, when a unit of code has been inspected and its test specification has been baselined.

Because we use process and artifact state transition abstractions, our process modeling approach is known as PASTA. Our PASTA model of FAST serves to explain FAST in more detail, to help us to improve FAST, and to help us to develop automated support for FAST.

The process we describe is an ideal FAST process; our experience shows that people follow it to the extent that they find it useful. We provide a reference process and guidance on how to produce software, but you may want to substitute your own methods to achieve the objectives of the process, or you may use only parts of it to achieve your specific objectives. For example, an early activity in the FAST process is to define the family of programs that you expect to produce. You may decide that initially this is all you want to do. FAST provides you with a method for doing it, but you may decide to use some other method. The determining factors are what works well in your organization and your domains. As advocated by J. Coplien, a multiparadigm approach to software design fits well with the idea of family-based development. You must choose the paradigms that work well for you.

Readers who are interested only in understanding the goals and benefits of FAST, the ideas on which it is based, and examples of its application can find them in Chapters 1 through 5. This knowledge is sufficient for you to understand the conditions under which FAST can be used and the benefits it brings. These chapters also convey sufficient understanding so that you could observe the methods and outputs produced by a group of software developers and decide whether they are using FAST. In particular, you should know what questions to ask a group of software developers in order to make such a decision.

Readers interested in the formal process model of FAST, and in the PASTA process modeling approach that we used in constructing it, should read Chapters 6 and 7. The FAST process model appears explicitly in Chapters 9–13. It is the foundation for the description of FAST in all chapters of this book.

We wrote this book because we think that there is enough industrial experience with FAST so that we can be confident that it works. In other words, if you have a family you can use FAST to produce the facilities that you need to produce members of your family rapidly.

1.5 Summary

FAST is intended to satisfy the following concerns in improving the efficiency with which variations on complex systems can be produced.

1. Designing for change. FAST is based on techniques that are specifically intended to solve the problem of designing for change.[1]
2. Systematizing the process of producing systems that are members of a family. Learning to use FAST requires learning how to design processes for producing family members. In this respect it is similar to concurrent engineering—that is, designing and developing a product includes designing the process for producing the product.
3. Systematizing knowledge capture. FAST uses a systematic approach for identifying the information necessary for production of family members so that it can be encoded in toolsets used to model and generate family members and so that it can be used to train new domain and application engineers. Because the FAST process requires the documentation of such information, it does not leave the organization when people depart.
4. Supporting rapid software production. The goal of FAST is to provide automated generation of family members as an integral part of the application engineering process.
5. Improving software quality. FAST achieves software quality improvements by sharing of requirements, design, and code throughout families. When an improvement is made to shared code, all family members benefit in all families that use the code or will use the code in the future.
6. Facilitating economic analysis. FAST includes an analysis of the costs and paybacks for its application in a domain.

In addition to FAST there are other domain engineering processes that you may want to consider or whose activities you may want to substitute for FAST activities.

1. Techniques developed during the Software Cost Reduction project are one example. See [1], [2], [7] in Section 1.7.

1.6 Nomenclature Introduced

Application engineer Engineer responsible for understanding a customer's requirements for a family member, creating a specification for it, and using the production facilities for the family to produce the new family member.

Application engineering A process for rapidly creating members of a family (applications) using the production facilities for the family.

Domain Family that has been engineered to make production of family members efficient.

Domain engineer Engineer responsible for creating a set of production facilities for a family to make the production of family members efficient.

Domain engineering A process for creating the production facilities for a family.

Family A set of items that have common aspects and predicted variabilities.

FAST A process for developing software families. Acronym for Family-Oriented Abstraction, Specification, and Translation.

PASTA A state-based approach to process modeling. Acronym for Process and Artifact State Transition Abstraction.

Product line A family of products designed to take advantage of their common aspects and predicted variabilities.

1.7 Readings for Chapter 1

[1] Alspaugh, T., Faulk, S., Britton, K., Parker, R., Parnas, D., and Shore, J. *Software Requirements for the A-7E Aircraft.* Washington, D.C.: Naval Research Laboratory, 1978.

See Chapter 8 (Required Subsets) and Chapter 9 (Expected Types of Changes) for an example of how you might incorporate into a requirements document predictions about expected changes and potential family members.

[2] Clements, P. *Software Cost Reduction through Disciplined Design.* Washington, D.C.: 1984 Naval Research Laboratory Review. Available as National Technical Information Service order number AD-A1590000, pp. 79–87, July 1985.

A description of a methodology for creating program families and the benefits of so doing.

[3] Coplien, James. *Multi-Paradigm Design for C++*. Reading, MA: Addison Wesley Longman, 1998.

An insightful book that explains the idea of multiparadigm design with focus on its application to C++. The discussions of analyzing commonality and variability for the purposes of constructing families provide insight on the FAST commonality analysis process described in our later chapters.

[4] Neighbors, James M. "The Draco Approach to Constructing Software from Reusable Components." *IEEE Transactions on Software Engineering* SE-10 (1984): 564–574.

An early explanation of the idea of domain engineering, including the creation of domain-specific languages and an approach to building generators based on them.

[5] Parnas, D.L. "Software Aging." Invited plenary talk, Proc. 18th Int. Conf. Soft. Eng., Berlin, June 1994.

A discussion of the characteristics of software as it ages and some of the reasons for such aging.

[6] Parnas, D.L. "On the Design and Development of Program Families." *IEEE Transactions on Software Engineering* SE-2 (March 1976): 1–9.

This paper defines and elaborates on the idea of program families and discusses methods for their definition and design.

[7] Parnas, D.L., and Clements, P.C. "A Rational Design Process: How and Why to Fake It." *IEEE Transactions on Software Engineering* SE-12, 2 (February 1986): 251–257.

An explanation of why it is important for you to have in mind and to try to follow an ideal design process, and what to do when you can't follow your ideal process.

2 Family-Oriented Software Production

THIS CHAPTER DESCRIBES THE FUNDAMENTAL IDEAS UNDERLYING a family-oriented software production process in general and FAST in particular. It discusses the underlying strategies for developing families using those ideas.

Basic Assumptions

Three assumptions underlie our approach to family-oriented software production. Phrased as hypotheses, they are as follows.

- The redevelopment hypothesis. Most software development is mostly redevelopment. In particular, most software development consists of creating variations on existing software systems. Usually, each variation has more in common with other variations than it has differences from them. For example, the different versions of a telephone switching system that accommodate different customers' requirements still have in common many requirements and much design and code. The versions may differ in the algorithms that they use to compute telephone bills or in some of the specialized features that they offer to the end user, but all of them may offer the same features for processing calls and may use the same type of equipment.
- The oracle hypothesis. It is possible to predict the changes that are likely to be needed to a system over its lifetime. In particular, we can predict the types of variations of a system that will be needed. Manufacturers of telephone switches know from experience that different customers will want to use different billing algorithms. It is a pattern that governs their business.

- The organizational hypothesis. It is possible to organize both software and the organization that develops and maintains it so as to take advantage of predicted changes. In particular, the software and its developers can be organized so that a change of any predicted type can be made independently of changes of other types and so that making such a change requires modifying at most a few modules in the system. The task of producing a new version of the software then consists of making relatively independent changes in different modules. For example, experienced manufacturers of telephone switches try to design their software so that the billing algorithm can be changed independently of other aspects of the system, such as the way calls are routed.

The redevelopment hypothesis suggests that we find a way to avoid redeveloping the common aspects of our software. The common aspects become the basis for identifying a family and in some way are embedded in each family member.[1] The oracle hypothesis suggests that the variable aspects are predictable—in other words, that we can predict the family members that we will need. The organizational hypothesis suggests that software developers can take advantage of the predictability. Together, these hypotheses suggest that you should often make a family the unit of software development; you identify the set of programs that constitutes the family by defining a set of commonalities and variabilities that determine what is in the family and what is not.

Family-oriented software development was suggested as early as 1968. More recently there have been several suggestions for engineering families based on the idea of identifying abstractions that are common to a family and using them as the basis for designing a specification language for describing family members. A variety of technologies can then be used to implement a translator for such a language. The general goal of all these approaches is to make software development more efficient by specializing for a particular domain the facilities, tools, and processes that you use to produce software. You make an investment in specialized facilities, tools, and processes that you might otherwise not make, but your investment is repaid many times over in increased efficiency in your software development process.

1. In later chapters we show some of the ways to embed common aspects in family members.

2.1 FAST Strategies

Making families the units of software development means adopting strategies that take advantage of the commonalities and variabilities that define the family. These strategies help you move from a collection of programs that seem to have some common aspects to a well-defined, carefully engineered family whose members you can produce rapidly. We think of this evolution in four stages.

1. Potential family. A set of software for which one suspects that there is sufficient commonality so that it is worth studying the common aspects of the software
2. Semifamily. A set of software for which common and variable aspects have been identified
3. Defined family. A semifamily for which an economic analysis has been performed to establish that it is worth investing in means to exploit the commonalities and variabilities in creating family members
4. Engineered family. A defined family for which an investment has been made in processes, tools, and resources for rapidly creating family members. When each family member is a complete product, we call an engineered family a product line

FAST uses the following strategies for creating engineered families.

- Identify collections of programs that can be considered families. A family is a set of programs that have enough in common that it is worthwhile to base the production of family members on a set of common assets.
- Design the family for producibility—that is, design a process for producing family members concurrently with creating a common design for family members. The idea is to make it easy to produce any family member by following the process, which includes steps for applying the common design.
- Invest in family-specific tools to make the production of family members rapid using the production process.
- For each family, create a way to model family members for two purposes:
  1. To help the developer to validate the customer's requirements by exploring the behavior of the model
  2. To provide a description of the family member from which the deliverable code and documentation for the family member can be generated

Because we generate the deliverable code directly from the model of the family member, we know that the behavior of the deliverable code corresponds to the behavior of the model.[2]

Note that no one type of model is appropriate for all families; for each family we use a type of model that is suited to the family. The model is expressed in the form of a language, which we call an application modeling language (AML) to emphasize its role in modeling the behavior of the applications that we want to generate from it.[3] Our AMLs, which vary considerably in form from one family to another, include

- Textual specification languages
- Graphical representations of decision trees
- Tables
- Data flow diagrams

Figure 2-1 shows the results of integrating these strategies to create a domain and produce domain members. Domain engineering has two major outputs: an environment that includes an AML and associated tools for creating domain members and a process for using the environment to create domain members. The output from application engineering is domain members.

Figure 2-2 shows a FAST process with domain engineering as the investment activity and application engineering as the payback activity. To keep the process under control, there is a feedback loop between the two. The result of domain engineering is the production facility for the family, here shown as an environment for performing application engineering. The output from application engineering is the applications that are produced for customers.

Organizations that use a family approach have a competitive advantage in the domains where they apply it. They can adopt a business strategy of developing a family for the purposes of reducing development costs for themselves and maintenance costs for their customers and also to consolidate their marketing

2. Knowing that the behavior of the model corresponds to its implementation is, of course, based on the assumption that our translator from model to code faithfully implements the semantics of the family. This is a similar problem to knowing that a compiler correctly implements the semantics of a programming language, but it is simplified because our modeling languages are usually very much simpler than general purpose programming languages.
3. Other terms frequently used for application modeling language are *domain specific* language and *application specific* language.

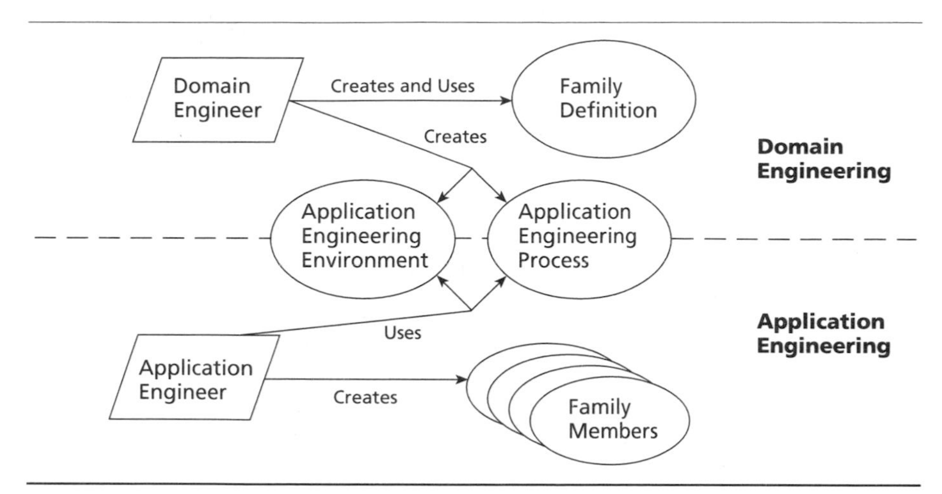

Figure 2-1. *Outputs from Domain Engineering and Application Engineering*

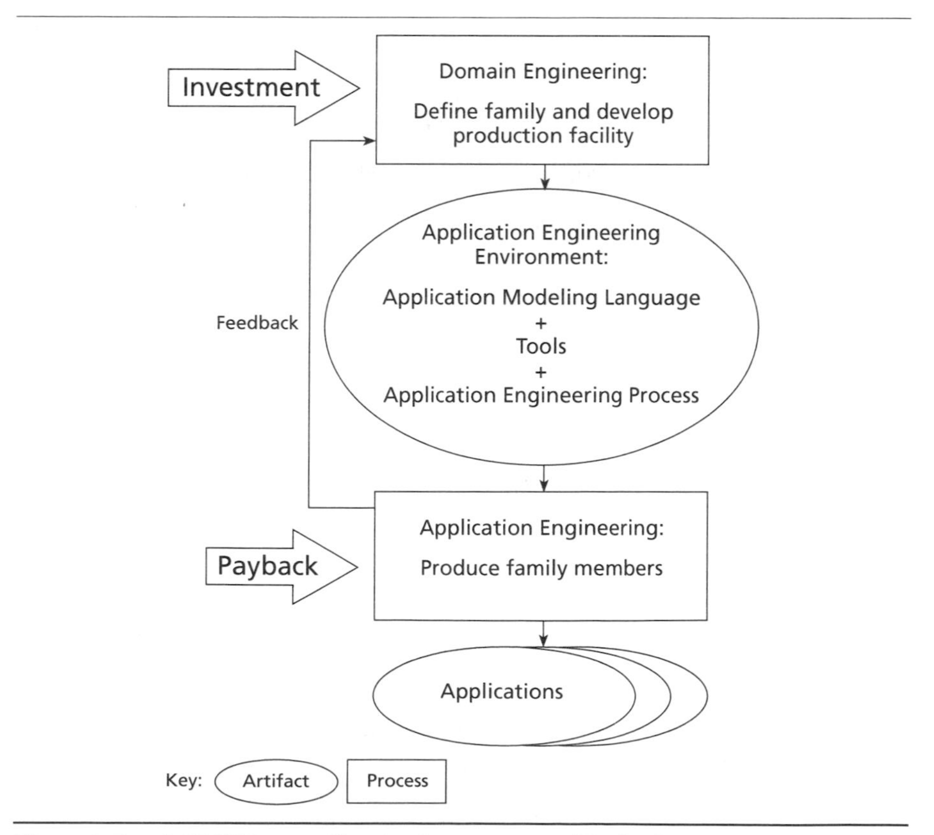

Figure 2-2. *A FAST Process Showing Investment and Payback*

strategy. Because it is a systematic process for defining a family and generating family members, FAST provides adopting organizations with an added advantage: it helps them to produce rapidly many variations on a product at low cost with high quality.

2.2 Foundations for Engineering Families

Software engineers have developed a variety of ideas and methods that make it feasible to adopt the FAST strategies. FAST is an integration of those ideas and methods into a software production process. The more important of them include the following:

- Predicting expected changes to a system over its lifetime
- Separating concerns
- Designing for change using abstraction and information hiding
- Formally specifying and formally modeling systems
- Creating application modeling languages for specifying family members
- Composing software from adaptable, reusable components
- Designing process and product concurrently
- Building compiler compilers
- Using template-based reuse
- Restricting variability to gain efficiency

FAST integrates these ideas and methods into a process for developing tools and assets that are tailored to the job of producing members of a family. Software engineering technology has produced a variety of tools suitable for automating the production of family members. Examples are tools such as YACC and lex, METATOOL, TEDIUM, Visual C++, SAP, and database schema design tools that are provided with database managers such as dBASE or ORACLE.

FAST encourages the application of such tools to the task of building the production facilities for a domain. It makes more systematic the process of constructing domain-specific tools and the processes by which they're used. It makes the domain-specific tools and the code that they generate more efficient by restricting the variations that they must handle and by exploiting the commonality in the family.

The first three ideas on our list—predicting change, separating concerns, and designing for change using abstraction and information hiding—are key to FAST and are worth further discussion.

2.2.1 The Role of Abstractions in Identifying and Designing Families

FAST relies heavily on abstractions to achieve its intent. It uses and reuses them in a variety of ways—for example, to identify and specify variability and commonality in software systems and to represent processes for producing such systems.

FAST takes the view that an abstraction is a many-to-one mapping—in other words, that there are many different ways to implement an abstraction. If an abstraction represents a decision to be made, such as how to implement communications with a device, then the choice for the decision may be hidden by the abstraction. The creator of the abstraction provides a standardized interface to its users that conceals the implementation and still provides the necessary services. For example, a virtual device is an abstraction that conceals the details of how to control a device while still providing access to the services and data provided by the device. One key to designing successful software systems that are maintainable and customizable is to choose a good set of abstractions to represent the system.

Choosing a good set of abstractions is at the heart of many of today's software engineering methods. Object-oriented analysis and design methods make finding abstractions the first or a very early step in their processes. So does FAST. FAST also imposes the restriction that the variability represented by each abstraction be explicitly bounded. This restriction eases the domain engineers' job by allowing them to take advantage of the bounds to make the tools and the processes they design more efficient. Knowing the domain and range of the many-to-one mapping represented by each abstraction gives the domain architects a considerable advantage in deciding how to generate the family members in the domain.

Figure 2-3 indicates a major way that abstractions are used in an instance of the FAST process. Domain engineers create abstractions for the family that are used both in the design of the application modeling language for the domain and in the design of the family for the domain—that is, in the architecture for the domain. These abstractions can be used to create a library of adaptable components for the domain, which are used in generating family members.

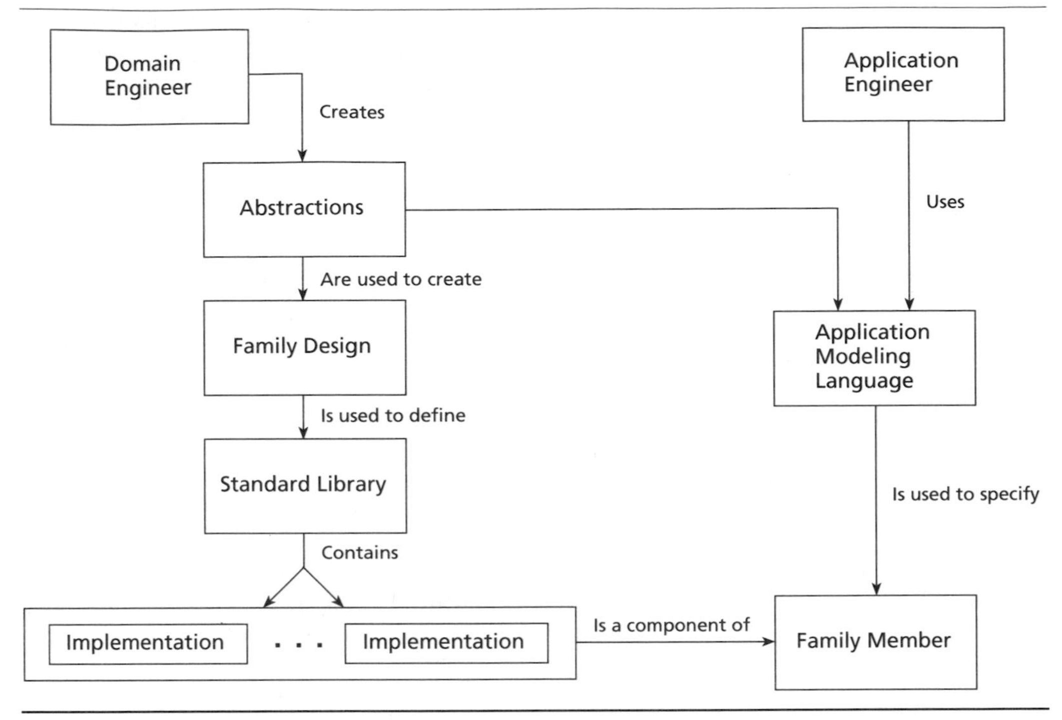

Figure 2-3. *Use of Abstractions in the FAST Process*

2.2.2 The Role of Information Hiding and Separation of Concerns

The information hiding principle tells us that a key set of abstractions in software design comprises those abstractions that can be used to conceal the decisions most likely to change. In the parlance of D. L. Parnas, the way that each decision is implemented becomes the secret of an information hiding module.[4] The module offers its users an abstract interface by which they can use its services. The abstract interface separates the concern of which services the module offers from the concern of how those services are implemented within the module. The abstractions that are central to supporting the variabilities for a family

4. Parnas defines a module as a work assignment for a programmer or a small team of programmers. For an information hiding module, an important aspect of the assignment is how to implement the module's secret.

form the basis for constructing the information hiding modules from which family members can be built.[5]

The oracle hypothesis suggests that it is possible to predict the decisions that are likely to change from one family member to another—the *variabilities* for the family. Applying the oracle hypothesis and the information hiding principle together provides us with an approach for finding architectures suitable for creating assets common to a family. FAST is built on this approach.

2.2.3 Predicting Change

Clearly, your ability to predict change is a critical component in constructing families. Predicting change is not an all-or-nothing proposition. The better you are at it, the easier it will be for you to produce family members that meet customers' needs now and in the future. Your confidence in your ability to predict change also influences the investment you should be willing to make in the production facilities for your family. Sometimes it's better to invest little initially in tools for generating family members and wait to see how well your predictive powers are working. As you gain confidence, you can return through the feedback loop shown earlier in Figure 2-2, increasing your investment in your production facilities each time. When we do this, we find that our system becomes more robust even to unpredicted changes.

We find that a reasonably good guide to future change is past change. If you have existing software that will form the basis for a family, its change history is one starting place for prediction. Examining the recent change history also tells you what parts of your software are currently undergoing the most change. They may be your ripest targets for domain engineering because they most likely reflect both the parts of the software that are generating the most revenue and the bottlenecks to faster software development. They represent revenue generation because they are the places where new features are being implemented to sell to customers. They represent bottlenecks because they are where most of the effort in change is being invested. Indeed, it is likely that the most rapidly changing parts of the software have acquired a reputation for being trouble spots. Most people in your organization probably already know where they are.

In addition to trying to predict future changes from past changes, you should consult people whose business it is to predict marketplace and technological changes. Marketing organizations are one fertile source of such predictions, and

5. In the language of object-oriented design, the information hiding modules are embodied as classes and the abstract interface includes the public class methods.

your marketers should be part of your process for predicting change. Early adopters of technology are another potential source and should be brought into your process. Perhaps the best source is developers who have worked a long time with the software and are familiar with the domain—if you can find them.

FAST explicitly identifies a step in the process and an artifact produced during that step whose purpose is to define a family through identifying commonalities and variabilities: what is not likely to change and what is likely to change. We call that step *analyzing commonality,* and the associated artifact is a *commonality analysis document.* Such a step distinguishes family-oriented development processes from other software development processes, and it should be a key part of your efforts to apply a family-oriented process. Commonality analysis helps provide a systematic basis for creating families.

Software engineers are struggling to produce customized products that will capture wider markets and to produce them quickly. Introducing a systematic process based on the idea of designing for change is essential to winning this struggle. When a production process lacks systematization, it is easy to lose control of possible product variations, with an attendant increase in cost and time to customize.

2.3 Organizational Considerations

The previous sections have focused on technological ideas that underlie family-oriented development. Organizational considerations are also important. Conway's law tells us that the structure of a system mirrors the structure of the organization that builds it. If you reorient your software development process around domains, you also may need to change your software development organization. You may decide to have a development organization that owns each domain and an organization that is responsible for integrating the domain members to form a system.

For example, one approach is to create a product line organized around domains. The product line may be too large and complex to be considered a single domain, so you may decompose it into subdomains and apply FAST to each subdomain. For example, you might have a device subdomain, a display subdomain, a database subdomain, and a variety of others. You then build each member of the product line by building one member from each subdomain and then integrating the members. In this way you build a device component, a display component, a database component, and all the other components that you need to produce a member of the product line; then you integrate them. Each component is built to meet the needs of the particular product line member. Figure 2-4 shows three members of a product line, each one built for a different customer. Each product line member is composed of members of different subdomains, with subdomain 1 members labeled in the diagram.

Layered architectures, such as protocol stacks, use this approach. Each layer in the stack may have a different implementation for different platforms and requirements. Creating a complete protocol stack consists of choosing an implementation for each layer and integrating them. Each layer has an abstract interface to those above and below it, allowing the different layers to be implemented independently.

Organizationally, a different development organization may own each subdomain. There may be a separate organization that is responsible for integration, and integration may also be treated as a subdomain. Taken together, the development organizations form the development organization for the product line. The extent to which you are able to create such an organizational structure depends both on your ability to create subdomains and on how sophisticated

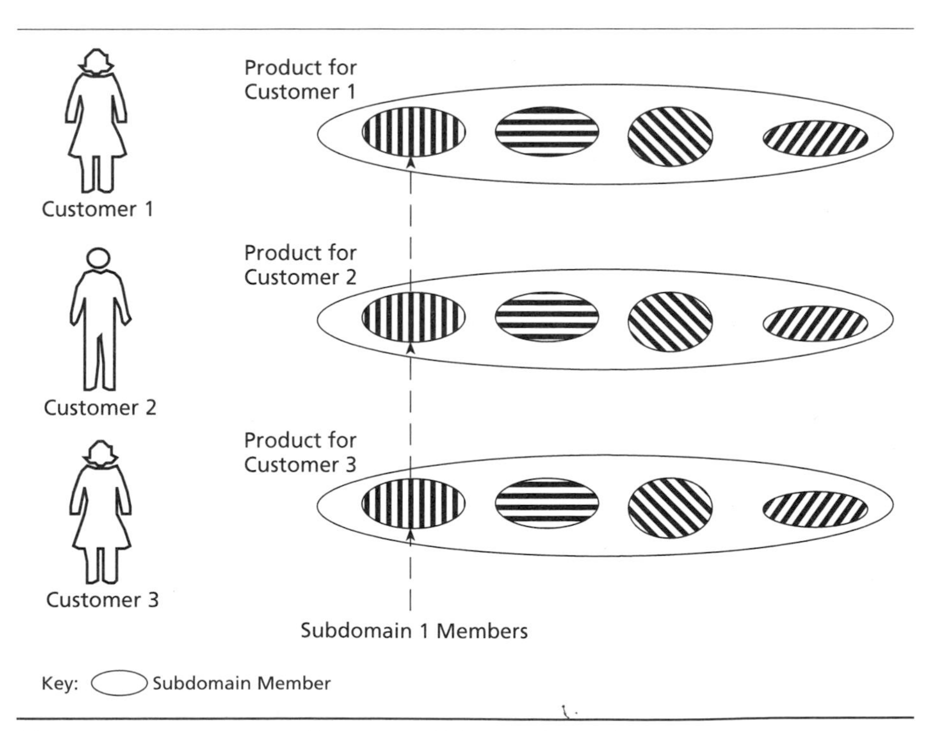

Figure 2-4. *Product Line Members Built from Subdomains*

and disciplined your organization is. Particularly well-disciplined organizations may find that they can create and maintain subdomains that are used in a variety of product lines, thereby gaining additional leverage from each subdomain.

2.4 Summary

FAST is based on the assumption that most of our software development effort is redevelopment and that we can identify those aspects of the software that we continually redevelop as well as predict those aspects that are likely to change. When there is sufficient commonality among software that we expect to develop, we can define a family and invest in tools and methods for rapidly producing family members. The technology for developing such tools and methods already exists.

Key to the FAST approach are ideas such as explicitly predicting changes and using abstraction, information hiding, and separation of concerns to create architectures, components, tools, and processes to take advantage of our predictions. The process for creating an environment for producing family members is domain engineering. The process for using the environment is application engineering. A central part of the environment is an application modeling language that is used to create models of family members along with tools that allow us to produce rapidly any family member from its model.

An organization that adopts FAST, or any other family-oriented approach, may have to restructure itself to take advantage of the efficiencies gained.

2.5 Nomenclature Introduced

Abstract interface For information hiding modules, an interface that provides access to the services of the module but hides how the secret of the module is implemented.

Application modeling language A language for modeling a member of a domain with the following attributes.

1. The language allows you to specify a domain member by the requirements that distinguish it from other domain members; common requirements need not be specified.
2. The language allows you to analyze the behavior of a domain member.

AML Acronym for Application Modeling Language.

Commonality Assumption that is true for all members of a family.

Information hiding module A work assignment for a programmer or group of programmers that embodies a decision that is likely to change independently of other decisions. See [10], [11] for further explanation and examples.

Interface The set of assumptions that the programmers of one module may make about another module.

Variability An assumption about how members of a family may differ from one another.

2.6 Readings for Chapter 2

[1] Bentley, J.L. "Programming Pearls: Little Languages." *Communications of the ACM* 29, 8 (August 1986): 711–721.

An explanation of what little languages are and why they are useful. In FAST, such languages are called application modeling languages.

[2] Britton, K., and Parnas, D. "A-7E Software Module Guide." NRL Memorandum Report 4702. Washington, D.C.: Naval Research Laboratory, December 1981.

This design document contains a good explanation of the principle of information hiding and an example of its application to the design of a real-time system.

[3] Britton, K.H., Parker, R.A., and Parnas, D.L. "A Procedure for Designing Abstract Interfaces for Device Interface Modules." *Proc. 5th Int. Conf. Software Eng.* (1981): 195–204.

This paper describes a practical approach for designing abstractions that are used in creating a family. It shows how to create and use abstractions that represent and are implemented by devices and the software that monitors and controls them. Each device has an associated abstract interface that presents the device's abstractions to its users.

[4] Campbell, Grady H., Jr. "Abstraction-Based Reuse Repositories." REUSE_REPOSITORIES-89041-N. Herndon, VA: Software Productivity Consortium, 1989.

This paper briefly discusses the idea of storing abstractions of components in a reuse library and creating instances of them, automatically adapted, as they are needed to build members of families.

[5] Campbell, Grady H., Jr., Faulk, Stuart R., and Weiss, David M. "Introduction to Synthesis." INTRO_SYNTHESIS_PROCESS-90019-N. Herndon, VA: Software Productivity Consortium, 1990.

An overview of a process that was a forerunner of the FAST process and that uses the same patterns of domain engineering and application engineering as FAST.

[6] Cleaveland, J. Craig. "Building Application Generators." *IEEE Software* (July 1988): 25–33.

This paper shows, by example, the technology available for building generators for family members that are described using application modeling languages. The basic technology relies on the use of templates and on automatically generating parsers and parse tree manipulation tools for constructing generators.

[7] Conway, M. "How do committees invent?" *Datamation* (April 1968): 28–31.

An investigation of how and why the structures of systems come to reflect the structures of the organizations that build them.

[8] Dijkstra, E.W. "Notes on Structured Programming." In *Structured Programming,* edited by O.J. Dahl, E.W. Dijkstra, and C.A.R. Hoare. London: Academic Press, 1972.

See Dijkstra's chapter for a discussion about separation of concerns and designing for change, and a brief discussion of program families.

[9] Ladd, D.A., and Ramming, J.C. "A*: A Language for Implementing Language Processors." *IEEE Transactions on Software Engineering,* SE-21 (November 1995): 894–901.

An example of technology that can be used for creating code generators for application modeling languages.

[10] Parnas, D.L. "On the Criteria to Be Used in Decomposing a System into Modules." *Comm. ACM* 15 (December 1972): 1053–1058.

This paper contains the first published explicit description of the principle of information hiding and gives an example of the benefit of its application to the design of software.

[11] Parnas, D.L., Clements, P.C., and Weiss, D.M. "The Modular Structure of Complex Systems." *IEEE Transactions on Software Engineering* SE-11 (March 1985): 259–266.

This paper gives a refined, systematic approach to the application of information hiding to the design of families of real-time systems. It builds on the work described in [2], [3], and [10].

3 AN EXAMPLE: FAST Applied to Commands and Reports

ONE OF OUR APPLICATIONS OF FAST HAS BEEN TO THE FAMILY of commands and reports used by technicians to monitor the operation of a telecommunications switch. This chapter describes the analysis of the family and the form and capabilities of the resulting language and application engineering environment.

The Commands and Reports Family

The commands and reports family is part of the software for a telecommunications switch. Such a switch enables telephone subscribers to place calls and can be viewed as a large computing system. An example is Lucent's 5ESS switch, which can handle millions of calls per hour and whose software contains millions of lines of code. To monitor and maintain the switch, technicians use an interface that allows them to issue commands to the switch and to receive reports on its status. As with other command systems, there is voluminous documentation that explains the meaning and use of each command and report. The commands, their associated reports, and the accompanying customer documentation form a software family within 5ESS software; henceforth we call this family the C&R family.

In applying FAST to the C&R family, we viewed a 5ESS switch as a machine that accepts commands, takes an action, and produces reports, as shown in Figure 3-1. The switch contains descriptions of valid command and report types and information about how to process each command type and how to format

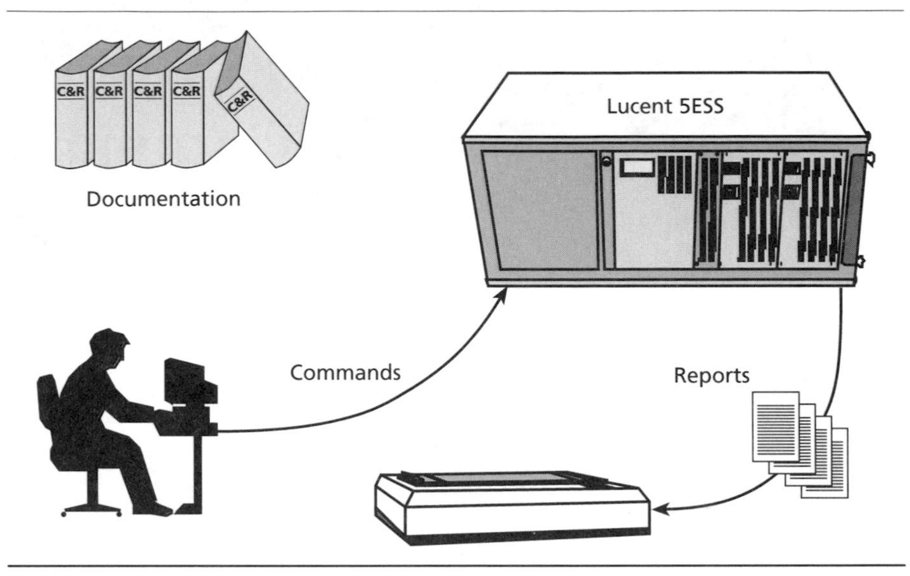

Figure 3-1. *A 5ESS Switch*

each report. A command recognition program checks commands for validity when they are issued by a technician and uses the processing information to decide what to do when it receives a valid command. A typical command set must conform to industry standards and includes thousands of commands and report types. Customers must be given documentation that describes the use of the commands and the format and meaning of the reports. The software for the C&R family consists of the descriptions of the command and report types maintained in the switch as well as the customer documentation for them.

We followed the standard FAST process in applying FAST to C&R, as sketched in Figure 3-2. We analyzed the family and used the results to define a language, called SPEC (Specification of Executable Commands), for specifying family members. We also developed a toolset, called ASPECT (a SPEC translator), for analyzing SPEC specifications, for generating the C&R descriptions maintained in the switch, and for generating the customer documentation.

Our purpose in engineering the C&R domain was to give 5ESS software developers a specification language and an application engineering environment that provided the following capabilities.

- A way of specifying for any input command, in one place, the following:
    - The syntax of the command, including its name (known as the command code) and the names and types of its parameters

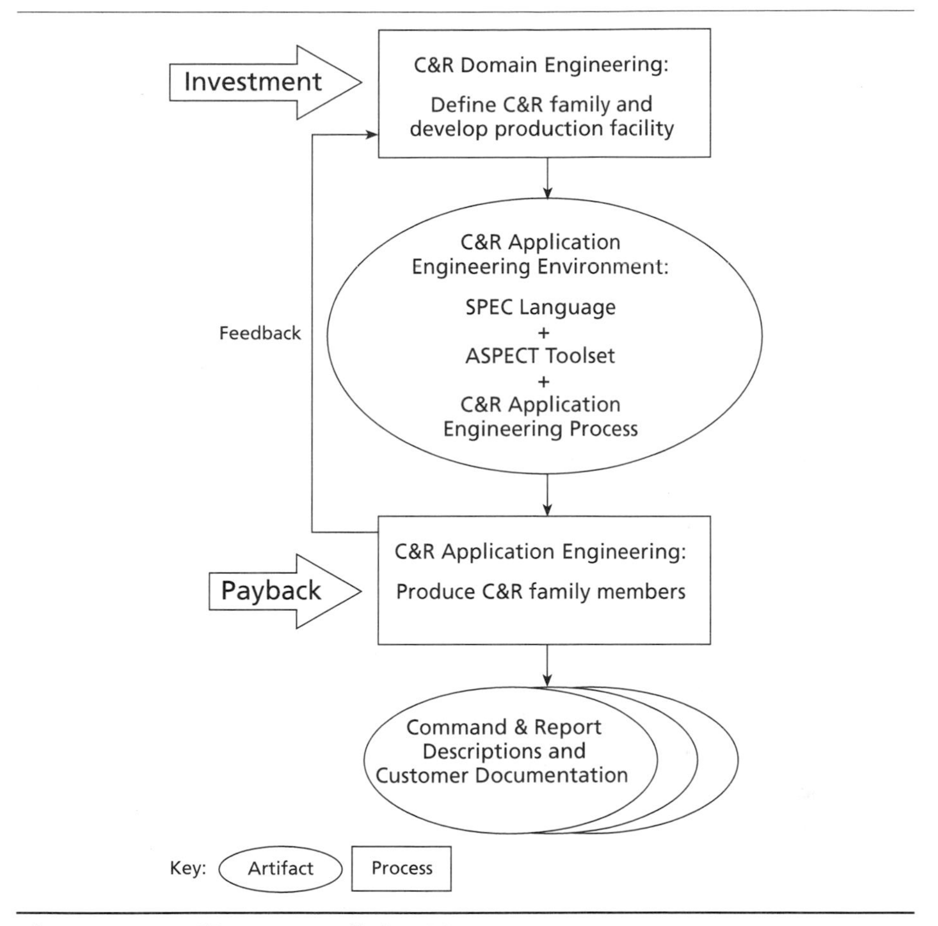

Figure 3-2. *FAST Process Applied to C&R*

- The identity of the program to be used to process the command
- Various administrative information about the command, such as the name of the data structure used to store information about the command
- The terminal acknowledgment—that is, the immediate response received by a technician to acknowledge that a command has been invoked
- The format of the report produced as a result of executing a command
- The associated customer documentation
- Any English text that must be translated to other languages to provide support for technicians when English is not their primary language

- A way of generating the files used by the 5ESS software to recognize and process input commands and generate output reports. (The code that we generate is loaded into a database at the time the software for the switch is built and is used at runtime to recognize commands and to format reports.)
- A set of support tools that helps automate documentation production and performs consistency checks on the specification of a command and on the specification of its associated report. The tools help guarantee that documentation is consistent with command usage and with report formats and guarantee that the same format is used in all documentation, making it easier for technicians to read and understand the documentation.

A key part of the specification for a command or report is the customer documentation for using the command or understanding the report. One of our objectives was to make the specification of the customer documentation an integral part of the C&R specification. This approach promotes consistency between the software and the customer documentation. It also makes it easier for developers to write consistent and complete documentation and allows the customer documentation to be generated from the specification.

The primary benefit of the FAST process as applied to C&R is that it decreases significantly the time and effort needed to specify a command and its associated report and documentation; it also improves the quality of the documentation. Secondary benefits are that developers now have tools available to aid them in improving the quality of their specifications. The primary disadvantage is the cost in time, effort, and facilities needed to develop and apply the generator and support tools. "Apply" here means everything needed to make the generator and support tools a standard part of the process and environment used by software developers in creating C&R. Although we treated both commands and reports as members of the same family, our description here focuses primarily on commands; reports are treated in the same way as commands in our specification language and its environment.

As part of the FAST process, we attempted to forecast the future family members that would be required, and we designed our language and toolset to accommodate the changes that would be necessary to generate these family members. Our forecasts have already paid off by enabling us to easily add to the toolset features that are compatible with recent advances in technology, such as generating HTML so that the documentation of commands can be read by a Web browser.

The benefits of FAST are gained at the expense of performing the analysis and development needed to create the language and toolset. We consider this cost to be amortized over all the code that is generated by software developers using the toolset.

3.1 Defining the C&R Family

Defining the C&R family means identifying potential family members and characterizing what they have in common and how they differ. Each command used by the office technicians who maintain a 5ESS switch consists of a command code followed by a set of parameters. Each command code consists of an action and an object, such as reporting the status of a line connected to the switch. In this example, the action is reporting and the object is the line. All members of the family of 5ESS commands have this structure. On the other hand, the particular actions, objects, and parameters used in commands vary over reasonably well-defined sets, and there are certain combinations that are not included in the family. For example, removing the clock is not a command that is included in the family because it would not make sense. However, the command that sets the clock is a member of the family. The FAST activity of deciding what family members have in common and how they may vary is called a commonality analysis; the results of the analysis are captured in a document designed for the purpose.

The C&R commonality analysis follows the standard form for a FAST commonality analysis, including the following sections.

- Introduction. Describes the purpose of the commonality analysis.
- Overview. Gives a brief overview of the C&R domain.
- Dictionary. Defines technical terms for the C&R domain that are used in the commonality analysis.
- Commonalities. Lists assumptions that are true for every member of the C&R domain.
- Variabilities. Lists assumptions about how members of the C&R domain may vary.
- Parameters of variation. Specifies the value space for each variability and the time at which the value of the variability must be fixed.
- Issues. Describes issues that arose during the analysis and how they were resolved.

Figure 3-3 shows excerpts from the C&R commonality analysis dictionary. Defined terms appear in italics wherever they are used throughout the document.

Command code	Unique identifier of an *input command*, consisting of a *verb* and an *object*.
Input command	A command entered by an office technician that acts as a stimulus to the 5ESS to perform tasks. Such tasks include changing the state or reporting the state of the 5ESS.
Input command definition	A specification of all the information needed to identify and produce an *input command* or a set of *input commands* with common structure and contents.
Input command manual page	Documentation of an *input command* for the customer's use.
Output report	An information message that is printed on an output device.
Output report definition	A specification of all the information needed to identify and produce an *output report* or a set of *output reports* with common structure and contents.
Purpose	*Customer documentation* that describes the use of an *input command*.
Verb	The name of the action indicated by an *input command*.

Figure 3-3. *Excerpts from Dictionary in C&R Commonality Analysis*

Figure 3-4 shows excerpts from the commonalities section of the C&R commonality analysis. The commonalities are organized according to the structure of the domain, as determined by the domain experts. Figure 3-5 contains excerpts from the variabilities section of the C&R commonality analysis. The variabilities section uses the same organization as the commonalities section. The complete analysis contains 54 definitions, 50 commonalities, and 28 variabilities. A team of five domain experts, led by a moderator, worked part-time to produce the document over an interval of about three months. The total effort was about 20 staff weeks.

We used the C&R commonality analysis to guide the design of a language for specifying family members, known as the specification of executable commands (SPEC) language. The requirements for the language are defined by the commonality analysis, but the analysis specifies only what the language must express and not how it must be expressed. SPEC specifications include definitions of commands and reports and their documentation. For example, commonality C6 requires that the description of an input parameter for a command include the parameter name and the set of values that can be assigned to the parameter. As you will see later, the SPEC language provides a way to do this using a property list. The existence of an input parameter description as part of every command definition in SPEC can be traced directly to the commonality analysis.

The SPEC translator produces command and report definitions used by the 5ESS software to recognize commands and generate reports at runtime. It also

COMMONALITIES

The following are basic assumptions about the domain of *input commands, output reports,* and customer documentation.

INPUT COMMANDS

C1. Each *input command* is uniquely determined by its *command code*. When an *input command definition* is used to define more than one *input command*, it defines multiple *command codes*, all of which share the same set of *input parameters*.

C2. Each *input command* is described on exactly one *input manual page*.

C3. The following *administrative data* are required in an *input command definition: msgid, process, ostype, schedule,* and *auth*. Each *input command* has exactly one value for each of these fields.

C4. A *verb* is an *alpha-string* with a maximum length.

C5. There is a fixed maximum number of *input parameters* permitted for *input commands*.

C6. An *input parameter description* consists of a *parameter name* and a *value specification*. The *value specification* defines the range of values that an office technician may use for the *input parameter*.

OUTPUT REPORTS

C7. *Output reports* appear in three different contexts as follows.

a. Runtime: At runtime an *output report* may appear on an output device, such as the printer.

b. Report definition: The set of *output reports* that a 5ESS switch may produce at runtime, and the meaning of each possible *output report*, must be defined before building the software for the switch.

c. Output report documentation: Each *output report* must be documented for customer use. The documentation of *output reports* must include all the information that the office technician needs to know to understand the report and determine the reason for its appearance at runtime.

C8. An *output report* contains the report type—*spontaneous* or *solicited*—and the text of the report.

C9. There is a fixed maximum number of characters in a line of an *output report*.

C10. Each *output report* is described on exactly one *output manual page;* however, an *output manual page* may describe more than one *output report*.

C11. An *output report definition* is a sequence of *text block definitions*.

DOCUMENTATION

C12. An (*input command* or *output report*) *manual page* consists of several fixed sections. It may also reference an *appendix*.

C13. An (*input command* or *output report*) *manual page* documents one or more *input commands* or *output reports*.

SHARED COMMONALITIES

C14. All the information needed to define an *input command*, the associated *solicited output report*, and the associated *manual pages* must be describable as one specification. It must be possible to generate from such a specification all the files and data needed to process *input commands* and produce *output reports* at runtime and to generate either (1) the *input command* and *output manual pages* or (2) files and data that can be used to generate the *input command manual pages* and *output manual pages*.

Figure 3-4. *Excerpts from the Commonalities Section of the C&R Commonality Analysis*

VARIABILITIES

The following statements describe how *input commands*, *output reports*, and *customer documentation* may vary.

INPUT COMMANDS

V1. The maximum length of a *verb*, *object*, *parameter name*, or *enumeration* value.

V2. The domain for *verbs*.

V3. The maximum number of *input parameters*.

V4. The *Csymbol* used to designate a *msgid*.

OUTPUT REPORTS

V5. The maximum number of characters in a line of an *output report*.

DOCUMENTATION

V6. The representation of an *input command* on an *input manual page*, particularly the following in the syntactic template for the *input command*:

a. The separators used between the *command code* and the list of *input parameters*
b. The terminator for the representation of the *input command*
c. The separator used between the *verb* and the *object*

Typical *input command* representations appear as follows:

<command code rep><separator1><input parameter rep><input terminator>

<command code rep><input terminator>

<verb><separator 2><object>

V7. Typographic distinguishers for command templates.

Figure 3-5. *Excerpts from Variabilities Section of C&R Commonality Analysis*

produces the customer documentation for the commands and reports. For example, a template for the usage of a command and a description of the command's purpose are included with the command's specification. The SPEC translator incorporates both the template and the purpose into the customer documentation for the command. An example of such a template, taken from a sample SPEC specification, is shown in Figure 3-6.

The application engineering environment for a family consists of all the procedures, tools, and artifacts needed to produce family members. Those who use the environment follow a process specified by its developers. For 5ESS C&R, the SPEC language and its translator are the central part of the environment.

```
COMMAND {
  TEMPLATE {
     abt-task:tlws;
     purpose: "Aborts an active trunk and line workstation (TLWS) maintenance task.";
     warning: "Once this command is entered, the consistency of all hardware states
                and data in use by the task is questionable.";
     }
  }
```

Figure 3-6. *Sample Command Template*

3.2 Using the C&R Application Engineering Environment

The C&R application engineering environment is designed to help its users to generate members of the C&R family rapidly and accurately. Users of the environment can specify particular family members by specifying the variations considered during the definition of the family. For example, they can specify the command codes, parameters, and associated documentation for members of the 5ESS C&R family. The language allows them to do so in a way natural to the family: using the abstractions that are used to define the family, such as actions and objects. The environment provides users with facilities for verifying the choices they have made, such as verifying that the command code is valid for 5ESS. It also checks the completeness of the specification, such as verifying that the purpose of each command has been specified and that each parameter has been documented.

The C&R application engineering environment embodies the process for creating family members envisioned during the definition of the family and provides the tools, procedures, and artifacts needed to carry out that process. Its users create a model of the family member that they would like to produce and then generate the family member from the model, which is a specification expressed in SPEC. Users generate the family member by supplying the specification to the SPEC translator, which performs completeness and consistency checks and generates the appropriate code and customer documentation.

3.3 The SPEC Language and Its Translators

The primary language construct used by SPEC is a property list. A property list contains a set of properties and zero or more nested property lists. Each property is expressed as a property name and a value for the property. For example, a property list for the *abt-task* (abort task) command contains the command code, parameters, and documentation for the command, as shown in Figure 3-6.

The command code, *abt-task*, and its parameter, *tlws*, are shown as they are used on the 5ESS. Furthermore, the documentation for the command is defined as a property of the command template and is free of any formatting codes. The documentation text is formatted by tools that are designed to produce correctly structured and organized documentation pages.

The idea of including documentation in source code is not new. In SPEC we have taken this idea a step further by making documentation keywords part of the language. We generate documentation from two sources within the specification of a command and its associated report: information associated with documentation keywords and information about the command and report contained in the specification. In Figure 3-6, the keywords *purpose* and *warning* are documentation keywords; the information associated with them is reformatted and used to generate user documentation. The definitions of the command code and its parameter are also used in generating the documentation as well as in generating the code for the command. Furthermore, the documentation text is semantically analyzed to apply documentation formatting rules to ensure its correctness. Figure 3-7 shows the documentation generated from the complete version of the SPEC fragment shown in Figure 3-6.

Figure 3-6 shows that the *abt-task* command has one parameter, *tlws*. All the information needed to define the command's parameters is defined in a PARAM property list, including the type of the parameter (defined in the TYPE property list as numeric, with a minimum value of 0, maximum value of 15, and default value of 0), documentation for the parameter (defined as the string associated

---

ABT-TASK:TLWS=a;

Warning: Once this command is entered, the consistency of all hardware states and data in use by the task is questionable.

• Purpose

Aborts an active trunk and line workstation (TLWS) maintenance task.

• Explanation of Parameters

a = Task identifier given to active TLWS maintenance tasks by the OP-JOBST command.

•Responses

Only standard system responses apply.

Figure 3-7. *Example of Formatted Generated Documentation*

```
COMMAND {
  TEMPLATE {
      abt-task:tlws;
      purpose: "Aborts an active trunk and line workstation (TLWS) maintenance task.";
      warning: "Once this command is entered, the consistency of all hardware states
               and data in use by the task is questionable.";
      }

  PARAM tlws {
      TYPE {
            domain: num;
            min: 0;
            max: 15;
            default: 0;
            }
      desc: "Task identifier given to active TLWS maintenance tasks
             by the OP-JOBST command.";
      csymbol: task_id;
      }
  }
```

Figure 3-8. *Sample Parameter Definition*

with the *desc* property), and storage for the parameter's runtime value (defined as the symbol *task_id*), as shown in Figure 3-8.

SPEC allows parameters used in more than one member of C&R to be defined once and then referenced when needed. This arrangement allows the SPEC user to define a set of commonly used parameters, reducing the effort involved in defining new family members and ensuring that the documentation is consistent both within the scope of a family member and between family members. For example, if the *tlws* parameter were used frequently, its definition could be parameterized and reused in any command or report as shown in Figure 3-9.

```
PARAM lib_tlws( x ) {
    TYPE {
          domain: num;
          min: 0;
          max: 15;
          default: 0;
          }
    desc: "Task identifier given to active TLWS maintenance tasks
           by the OP-JOBST command.";
    csymbol: x;
    }
```

Figure 3-9. *A Parameterized Version of TLWS*

Given this new definition of the parameter *tlws*, the definition of the *abt-task* command is shortened significantly, as shown in Figure 3-10. The value of the *csymbol* property is now a parameter to the definition of *tlws*, allowing reuse of the parameterized version in different specifications.

Although frequently used with parameters, the constructs for reuse are general and can be used with any property list in the SPEC language. Because documentation is frequently part of a property list, consistent reuse also helps ensure consistent documentation. For example, the description of the parameter *tlws* will be the same in the documentation of all commands that use the library definition of the parameter.

Collections of SPEC property lists are called libraries. Any property list that is used more than once is a candidate for inclusion in a library. A specification that is composed using predefined library property lists can be written much more quickly than one in which all property lists must be newly composed.

The structure of the SPEC language and the design of its environment reflect commonalities and variabilities described in the commonality analysis. For example, one of the variabilities identified during the commonality analysis for C&R was that the representation of the output could vary. Accordingly, the environment allows for multiple documentation formats, such as TROFF, HTML, and postscript. Figure 3-11 illustrates this capability. Because of this variability, the SPEC translator toolset (ASPECT in the figure) is designed so that extending the set of output formats requires only that a new (small) software module be coded to produce a new format. In general, the variabilities identified during the commonality analysis drove the modularization of the translator.

Also, because the documentation is encoded as part of the command specification, standards for the use and appearance of the documentation can be

```
COMMAND {
  TEMPLATE {
      abt-task:tlws;
      purpose: "Aborts an active trunk and line workstation (TLWS) maintenance task.";
      warning: "Once this command is entered, the consistency of all hardware states
                  and data in use by the task is questionable.";
      }

  PARAM tlws use lib_tlws( task_id )

  }
```

Figure 3-10. *An Example of Reuse in SPEC*

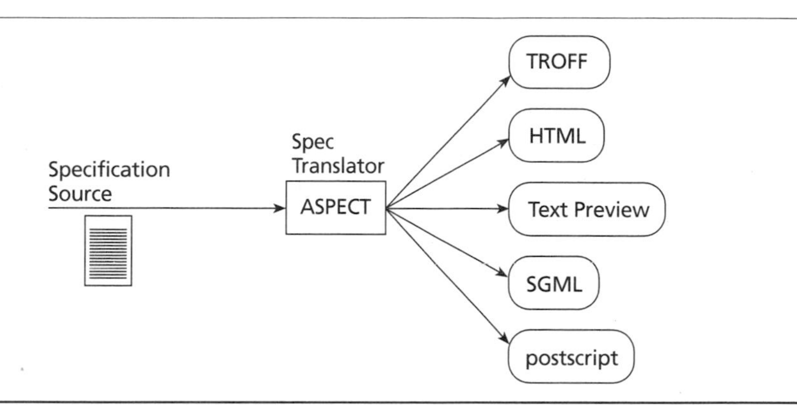

Figure 3-11. *Producing Multiple Documentation Formats*

applied automatically. This integration of documentation into the command specification yields a "single point of truth" for developers so that changes to the command and its documentation go hand-in-hand.

Tools for the SPEC language consist of a SPEC translator (ASPECT) and a set of programs that analyze a specification, produce different views of it, and generate code for it. For example, the documentation-generator tool produces output (as text, TROFF, postscript, or HTML) that defines a manual page for the C&R manual. Figure 3-7 shows the manual page generated for the *abt-task* command described in Figure 3-10.

The ASPECT toolset is a family of tools. All ASPECT tools operate on specifications written in SPEC, but vary in the form and type of the output that they produce. We expected that there would be continuing demand for new tools and modifications of existing tools. Our design for the toolset had to take this expectation into account.

3.4 Designing the Translators

We applied the principles of software family development again during the development of ASPECT. The ASPECT toolset was designed and implemented using existing parsing technology combined with the Software Cost Reduction (SCR) design process, which is based on the idea of designing software families. A minimal toolset for ASPECT includes four translators: a command translator, a report translator, and two documentation generators (one for commands and a second one for reports). It was clear that much of the functionality of the translators would overlap. For example, all translators parse the same syntax and generate consistent error messages; both command and report documentation share a common formatting language; parameters are shared among all translators, and so on. The translators also share a similar runtime sequencing into processing steps, as shown in Figure 3-12. Each translator must build a parse tree, preprocess the tree, build a symbol table, and traverse the tree to generate output.

These commonalities were part of the input for the design process for the toolset. The result was a set of information hiding modules from which individual translators are composed.

In accordance with the SCR development process, the architecture of the ASPECT family is embodied in an information hiding hierarchy described in a module guide and a uses relation. The module guide describes ASPECT as a collection of information hiding modules. The modules are organized into a hierarchy, and the module guide describes the secret that each module hides from other modules. Figure 3-13 shows the modular decomposition embodied in the module guide for the ASPECT family.

As you traverse the module hierarchy from its root downward, the granularity of the hidden information becomes finer. For example, our Device Drivers module hides the details of output formats from other modules. It is decomposed into individual modules, each one hiding the details of a single output format.

The uses relation between modules (Figure 3-14) describes which other modules are required for a given module to operate. For example, the Output Format Drivers use the Device Format Drivers, which use Error Reporting. Uses is another view of the architecture shared by all ASPECT processors. Each tool has a behavior-hiding module that controls its user-observable behavior. All tools have access to the same verification utilities, the same output format drivers, the same device format drivers, the same access and to operations on the

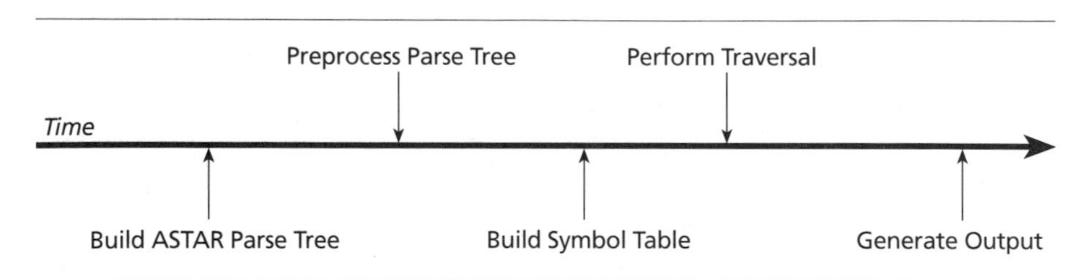

Figure 3-12. *Common Tasks of ASPECT Processors*

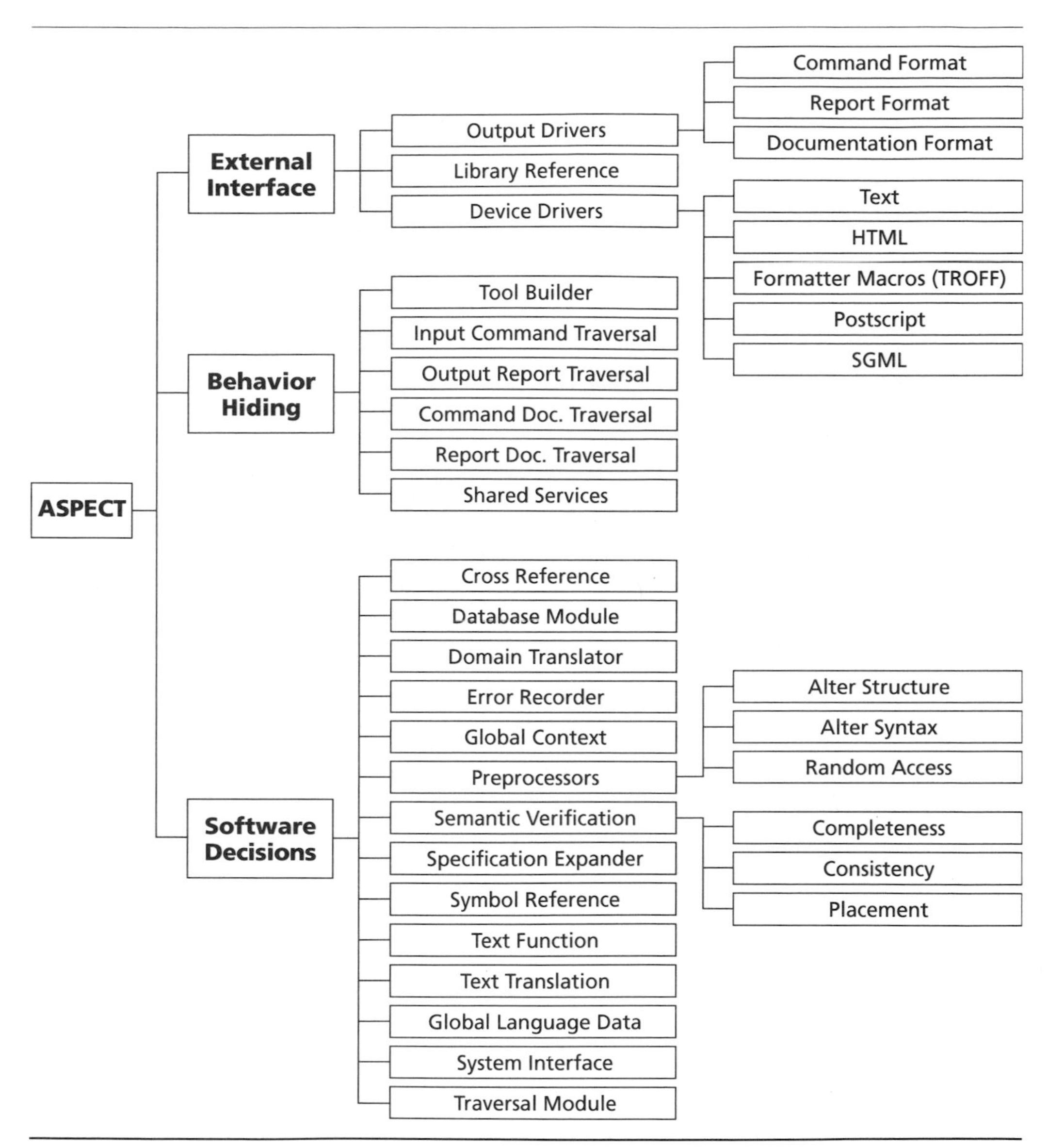

Figure 3-13. *The ASPECT Modular Decomposition*

parse tree, and the same error-reporting mechanisms. The result is substantial code reuse among ASPECT tools and consistency of their operation and output.

You create new tools in ASPECT by developing new behavior-hiding modules and new format driver modules, if necessary, and composing them with the rest of the system.

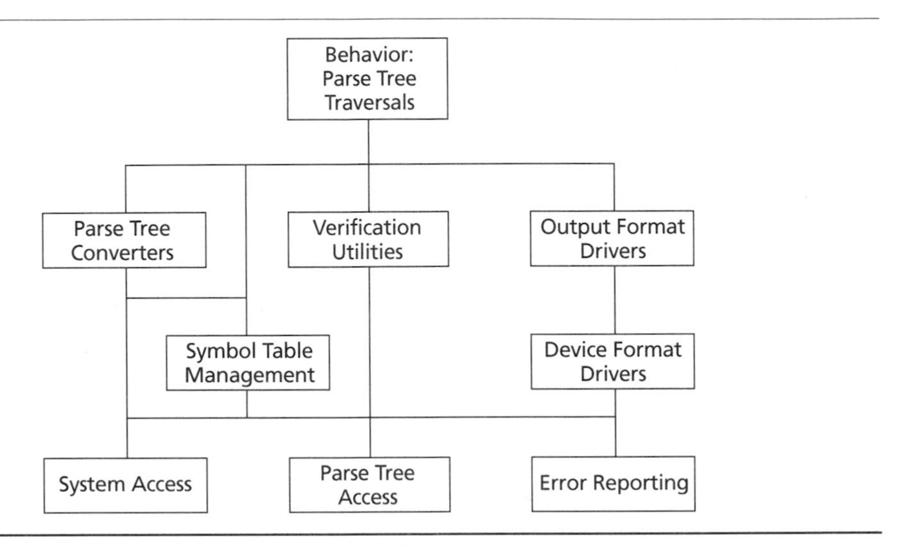

Figure 3-14. *Uses Relationship for ASPECT Modules*

The family approach to developing ASPECT paid off well when we needed to add new translators. Enhancing the toolset to generate HTML required the addition of a new device driver module to hide the details of generating appropriate HTML tags, and the HTML module was immediately available to all translators to generate HTML output. Further benefits are evident in the maintenance of the tools. Because all HTML output is produced in a single module, any errors in the HTML tags can be traced back to that module.

3.5 Summary

The SPEC language permits us to define a command, its user documentation, its associated report, and the report's user documentation in one place in a compact way. The structure of the language allows its users to share common definitions and allows us to create programs that can check the completeness and consistency of specifications. The syntax and semantics of SPEC use abstractions familiar to people who work in the C&R domain. As a result, writing the C&R specifications is easy and fast, and they are short. They can be checked for the kinds of completeness and consistency that are important to the end users of the commands and reports. For example, every command's purpose is described. (The toolset does not pretend to check that the descriptions correctly describe the commands and their parameters; that still requires human review.) These benefits are the result of viewing C&R as a family and applying the FAST process to analyze the family and create the SPEC language and the ASPECT application engineering environment.

In addition to engineering C&R as a family, we developed the ASPECT toolset as a family. We now have members of the ASPECT family that use technologies, such as HTML, that did not exist when we designed ASPECT but are specific examples of the kinds of changes that we predicted we would want to accommodate. HTML had not been invented when ASPECT was designed, but we planned the easy addition of new forms of documentation representation. The SCR design method helped us to create a design that easily accommodated our predicted changes.

C&R was one of the first domains that we engineered. We focused our attention on and reaped the benefits from thinking about C&R as a family, and we used technology we had at hand to build the application engineering environment for it. The approach of understanding the principles first and finding or building the tools to support them second has served us well in C&R and subsequent domains.

3.6 Nomenclature Introduced

C&R Acronym for commands and reports.

Commands and reports Domain whose members are definitions of executable commands, definitions of the reports associated with commands, and the customer documentation for them.

Commonality analysis Process for defining a family. Also, artifact resulting from a commonality analysis process. Key components of a commonality analysis document are a dictionary of terms, a list of commonalities, a list of variabilities, a list of parameters of variation, and a list of important issues that arose during the process.

Parameter of variation Quantification of variability, including the decision represented by the variability, the range of values allowed in making the decision, the time at which the value for the decision must be fixed, and a default value for the decision.

SCR Acronym for Software Cost Reduction.

Software Cost Reduction A family-oriented method for developing software that includes formal requirements specification and the use of information hiding, the uses relation, and cooperating sequential processes as key elements of software design. SCR was developed at the Naval Research Laboratory. See Chapter 2, reference [2], for an overview.

SPEC Acronym for Specification of Executable Commands. SPEC is the application modeling language for the commands and reports domain.

3.7 Readings for Chapter 3

[1] International Telegraph and Telephone Consultative Committee (CCITT) Yellow Book, Volume VI—Fascicle VI.7 Recommendations Z.311–Z.341, Geneva: 1981.

The international standard that governs the syntax of commands for telecommunications switches and the format of their documentation.

[2] Ladd, D.A., and Ramming, J.C. "A*: A Language for Implementing Language Processors." *IEEE Transactions on Software Engineering* SE-21, 11 (November 1995): 894–901.

A description of the parsing technology used in the ASPECT toolset to construct abstract parse trees.

[3] Perlman, G. "An Overview of the SETOPT Command Line Option Parser Generator." *Proceedings USENIX* (1985): 160–164.

An example of embedding documentation with source code so that either manual pages or executable code can be generated from the source.

4 An Overview of FAST

THIS CHAPTER INFORMALLY DESCRIBES THE ACTIVITIES USED IN the family of FAST processes and the artifacts used and produced during those activities. It discusses the economic justification for family-oriented production processes and gives a characterization of the family of FAST processes.

The Structure of FAST

FAST is a pattern for software production processes that strives to resolve the tension between rapid production and careful engineering. A primary characteristic of the pattern is that all FAST processes are organized into three subprocesses: one whose purpose is to identify families worthy of investment (qualifying the domain), a second whose purpose is to invest in facilities for producing family members (engineering the domain), and a third whose purpose is to use those facilities to produce family members very rapidly (engineering applications). Figure 4-1 shows this separation of concerns. Each subprocess has its own characteristic pattern of activities. Although we view FAST as a pattern for processes—allowing for considerable variability in individual FAST processes—for convenience and brevity we usually refer to FAST as if it were a single process.

Domain qualification consists of an economic analysis of the family and requires estimating the number and value of family members and the cost to produce them. Domain engineering makes it possible to generate members of a family and is primarily an investment process; it represents a capital investment in both an environment and the processes for rapidly and easily producing family members using the environment. Application engineering uses the environment

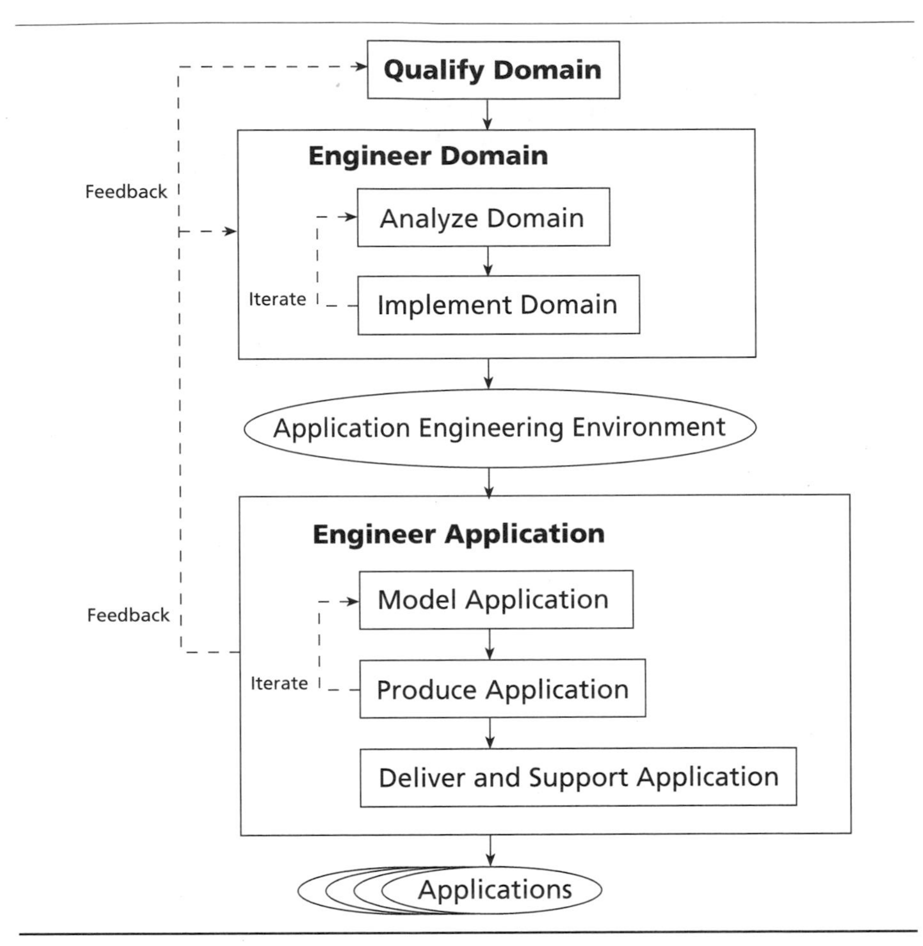

Figure 4-1. *The FAST Process Pattern*

and processes to generate family members in response to customer requirements. It is primarily a production process made efficient by the investment in domain engineering, and it is here that the payback from the investment occurs.

A characteristic of software development processes that are based on domain engineering is that producing an environment requires considerable careful engineering, and that may delay the time to production of the first family member. The FAST process seeks to reduce this time by introducing systematic methods for defining a family, for creating a way to describe family members, and for generating family members from their descriptions. Figure 4-1 shows the FAST top-level domain engineering and application engineering activities: analyze domain and implement domain, and the major artifacts involved in the process, the application engineering environment, and applications. We explore these elements in more detail later.

Families evolve as customer needs change, as new ideas for products emerge, and as new technologies appear. To direct and support the evolution of a family, domain engineering must be an iterative, continuing process. Feeding this process is information about how well family members fit customer needs and how well the application engineering environment for the family meets the needs of application engineering. Application engineers are a major source of such information because they have at hand considerable information about customer requirements and about the environment's usefulness in producing applications that meet those requirements. Accordingly, FAST processes have feedback loops between domain engineering and application engineering so that there is continual communication between the two, as shown in Figure 4-1.

There are a variety of approaches to domain engineering and application engineering, but as long as you follow the FAST pattern we consider the process to be a FAST process. Remember that the pattern is intended to help resolve the problem of rapidly producing high-quality software. One reason that we think of FAST as a pattern for processes is that we want to have sufficient flexibility to allow the use of different methods in different domains.

One way to recognize the flexibility of FAST processes is to realize that a FAST domain engineering process produces both an application engineering environment and the process for using it; each domain has its own application engineering process. In this book we describe several variations for enacting a FAST process. They differ in the way the application engineering environment is implemented but are alike in other respects.

Later in this chapter we look more closely at the elements of domain engineering and application engineering. To make clearer the intent and results of applying FAST, we discuss application engineering first and domain engineering second. First, however, we consider the economics of family-oriented software production.

4.1 The Economics of FAST

The basic economic assumption underlying FAST is that investment in engineering a family will be paid back by more-efficient production of family members. We start by distinguishing between two cases: one in which you pay little or no attention to domain engineering, and a second one in which you engineer the domain with the intent of making production of family members more efficient.

4.1.1 Case 1: No Domain Engineering

Assume, for simplicity, that the cost of producing a new member of the family without domain engineering is approximately constant; denote it by C_T. This is the typical case today. (If the assumption of constancy bothers you, assume that C_T is the average cost over the family members that will be produced.) Then the cost for producing N family members is N^*C_T. In Figure 4-2, this is shown as line A.

4.1.2 Case 2: Domain Engineering

Assume that the cost of domain engineering is I, representing the investment in producing family members more efficiently. Further assume that a result of this investment is that the cost of producing a family member is C_F. Then the cost for producing N family members is $I + N^*C_F$. If the domain engineering is successful, then $C_F < C_T$, and the resulting savings per family member, without considering the investment I, is $S_F = C_T - C_F$. For N family members, the savings is $N^*(C_T - C_F)$. To pay back the investment in domain engineering, N must be large enough so that $I < N^*(C_T - C_F)$. In Figure 4-2, line B shows the case in which the payback occurs after production of three family members, a realistic estimate based on our experience.

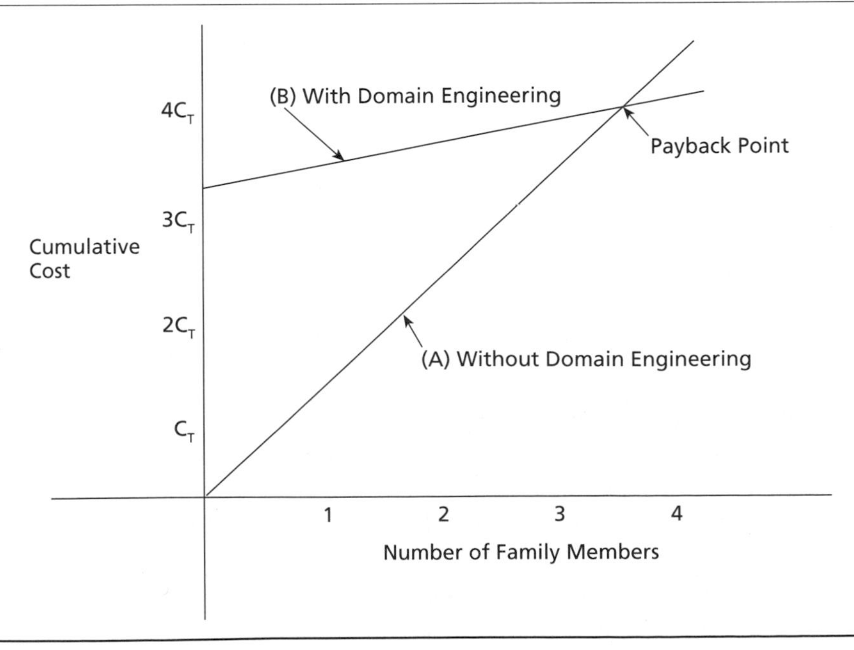

Figure 4-2. Cost of Producing N Family Members

4.1.3 The Fundamental Law of Family Production

Figure 4-3 shows another way to look at the savings from applying domain engineering. For each family member that you produce there is an increment in savings, S_F. The line in the figure shows the cumulative savings, with the payback point where the line crosses the X-axis. This is the point at which the initial investment in domain engineering is repaid. This line represents the fundamental law of family production: if S is the cumulative savings from investing in domain engineering, then

$$S = N^*(C_T - C_F) - I$$

Figure 4-2 and Figure 4-3 are representative; the slopes and intercepts of the lines they show depend on the particular family and the organization that produces it. Different families represent different technical challenges in applying the FAST process. For some domains, the result of the domain engineering process enables greater automation in the production of family members than other domains, resulting in different values for S_F.

Different organizations learn how to apply the process at different rates and configure themselves to apply it differently, resulting in different values for I. Some organizations may find it worthwhile to engineer domains that are specific to particular product lines, gaining a return on investment from the variability of domain members used within the product line. For example, you might treat signaling software within a telecommunications switch, navigation software

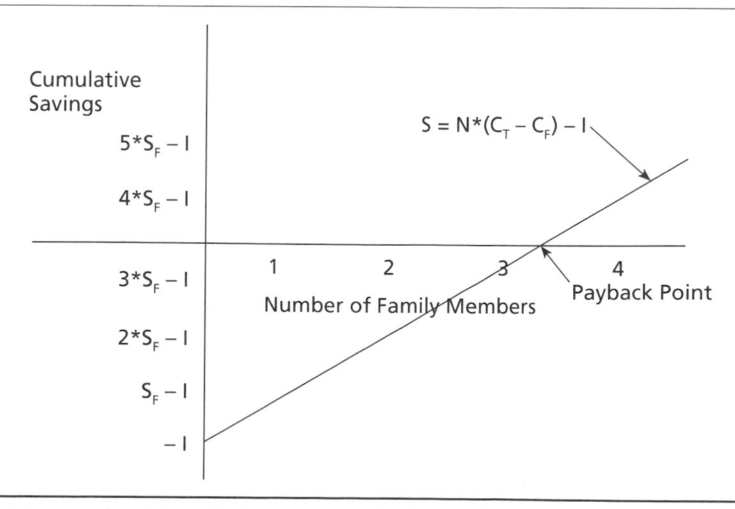

Figure 4-3. Payback from Using Domain Engineering

within a family of aircraft, sensor drivers for a particular line of weather sensors, or Hypertext Markup Language (HTML) interpretation within a Web browser as domains within products or product lines. Other organizations are able to take advantage of domains that can be used across a wide range of products and product lines, increasing the number of family members for which the results of domain engineering are used and enabling the organizations to invest more in domain engineering.

4.1.4 Risk Versus Automation

The size of S_F generally depends on how much automation results from the investment in domain engineering. Some families lend themselves well to automation, eliminating much of the effort associated with coding and unit testing. On the other hand, some parts of application engineering will never be automated. For example, the application engineer must interact with the customer to determine the requirements for a new family member and must be able to demonstrate to the customer that those requirements have been met. The application engineering environment is designed for this purpose and should drastically reduce the time and effort needed for requirements determination and validation, but some parts of those activities will always require human thought and creativity and cannot be automated.

We have found that even when little automation is achieved, the cost of domain engineering is repaid in both time and effort because the result is a domain that is better structured to accommodate change. In these cases, application engineering is closer to the traditional ways of developing software except that the software is better designed for change.

In every application of domain engineering there is a risk of failure; despite the investment, the domain accommodates change no better than if typical software development techniques had been used. A major intent of FAST is to ameliorate that risk by making domain engineering systematic and staged. FAST provides for incremental investment in domain engineering, with the early stages costing less and yielding less automation. For example, analyzing commonality can typically be accomplished by several domain experts in about three weeks, a relatively modest investment in time and effort.[1] Such an analysis usually yields sufficient insight to give you improvements in software development for the

1. We find that three to five domain experts led by a moderator experienced in the process usually works well.

domain, and it establishes the basis for automating some of the development process for the domain. Creating an initial application engineering environment, a later stage in the process, typically takes two staff years of effort but gives you the capability to generate most of the code for members of the domain.

As your experience with application engineering grows for a particular domain, you can incrementally increase your investment in domain engineering for that domain, as suggested by the feedback lines in Figure 4-1. Similarly, as your organization's experience with domain engineering grows, you can incrementally increase your investment in domain engineering across your organization. When successful, each incremental increase in investment is paid back either in more-efficient production of family members, in improvement of the quality of the family members, or in broadening of the scope of the family so that it can accommodate more customers.

You could make our simple economic model considerably more sophisticated by taking into account factors such as net present value of the domain engineering investment and payback, by varying the cost to produce family members as experience with the application engineering environment grows, and by varying the investment cost with the number of family members to allow proportionally larger investment in families that have greater expected payback. The underlying point remains the same, however: early investment is paid back in savings over a number of family members.[2] To see how that investment is paid back, we next look at the application engineering process.

4.2 Application Engineering

The purpose of application engineering is to explore very quickly the space of requirements for an application and to generate the application. Application engineers use the production facilities for the family to produce new family members that satisfy customer requirements. They may work directly with customers to understand and validate requirements, or they may receive the requirements from salespeople, system engineers, or others who are closely connected to customer needs. Customers may be external or internal, and requirements may be established by contract or by informal discussion.

2. Note that we could have done the same analysis for time savings with the same results; time spent in engineering a family is repaid in the time needed to produce individual family members.

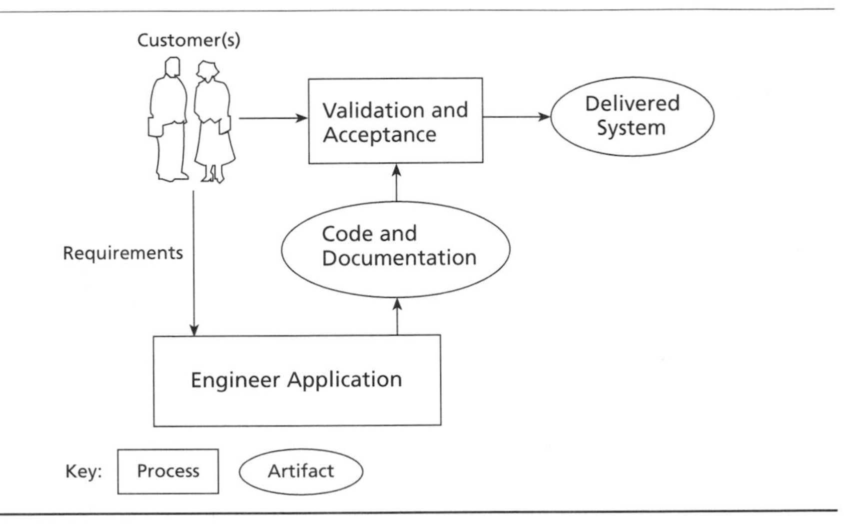

Figure 4-4. *Ideal Application Production Process*

In trying to understand and validate customer requirements, the application engineer can create a number of different models of the family member, analyzing them in various ways, before deciding to generate the code and documentation for the family. The production facilities must support this approach to engineering the family member; hence, we call these facilities an application engineering environment, and the applications are the generated family members.

Figure 4-4 shows an idealized view of the complete production process. It consists of analyzing a customer's requirements for a family member, engineering the application (including generating the family member), delivering the code and documentation for the application to the customer for validation and acceptance, and providing delivery and operational support for the family member.[3]

Engineering the application is an iterative process that makes heavy use of the analysis and generation tools provided by the application engineering environment, as shown in Figure 4-5. In the commands and reports (C&R) domain discussed in Chapter 3, application engineering consists of specifying commands and reports and their documentation using the SPEC language and generating the code for command recognition and report formatting. The process is iterative because the application engineer and the customer rarely establish satisfactory requirements on the first try.

3. Figure 4-4 is an idealized version of the process because actual processes rarely follow such simplified descriptions. The same is true for Figure 4-5 and Figure 4-6.

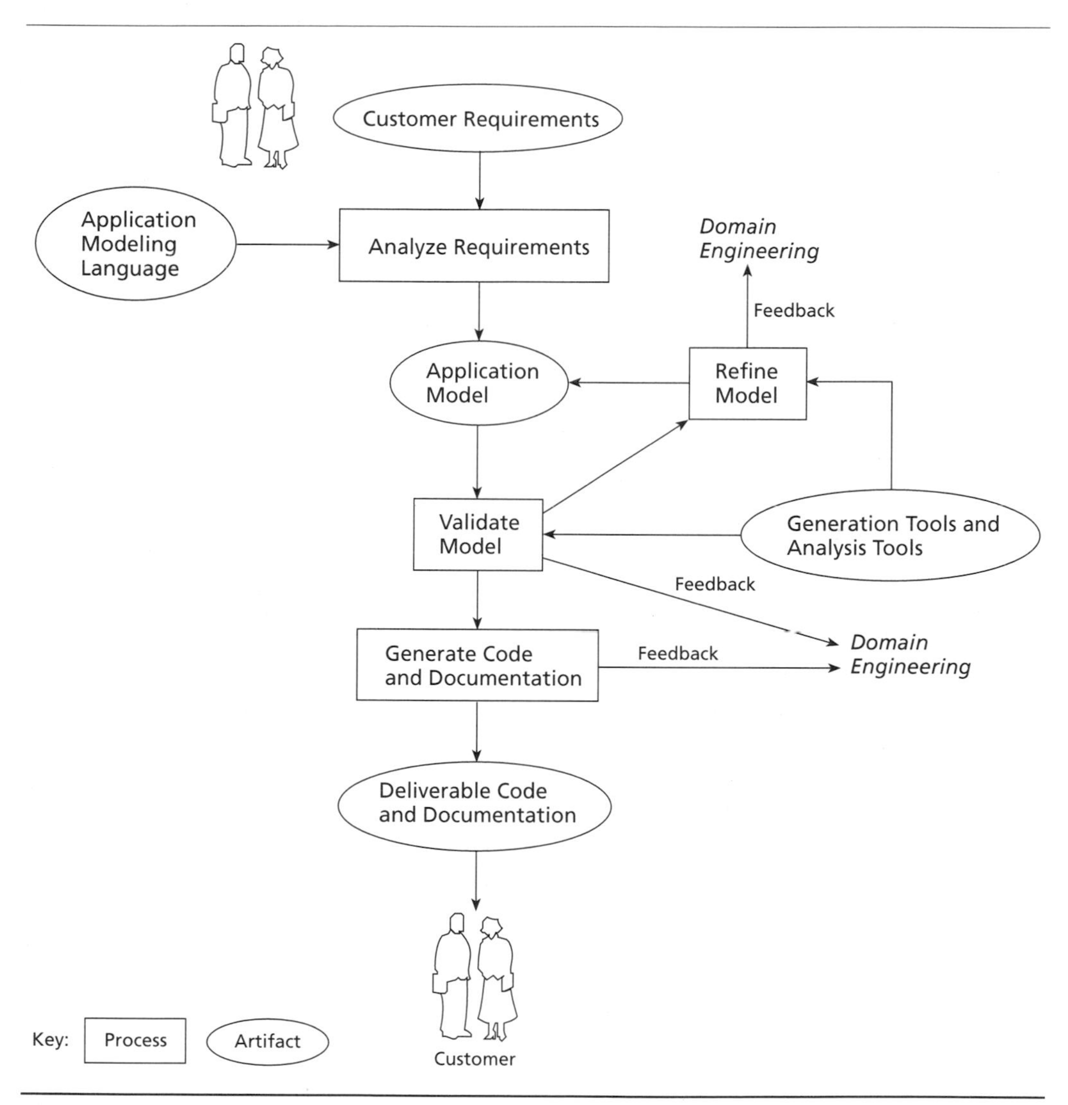

Figure 4-5. *Ideal Application Engineering Process*

The intent of application engineering is for application engineers to use facilities that help them to focus on understanding requirements without having to delve into the concerns of designing and coding. Freed from such concerns, the engineers can better interact with customers so that all of them gain better understanding of requirements. In C&R, the application engineer is free to concentrate on the concerns associated with resolving requirements for a command, such as

- Deciding what the action and object of the command are and how they should be named
- Deciding what parameters the command takes and how they should be named
- Deciding how to describe to the users the purpose of the command, its effect when invoked, and its parameters and their values

A key part of the application engineering environment is the application modeling language (AML) that is used to specify family members. We call it a modeling language to emphasize that specifications written in the language should be models—that is, they should be abstractions of the application that are guaranteed to have certain properties and to be analyzable in ways that are important in the domain. The environment provides capabilities for analyzing specifications written in the AML. Equally important, it should be possible to generate code from the model—that is, to map the abstraction into an efficient implementation.[4]

In the C&R domain the ASPECT toolset analyzes command specifications for completeness—for example, to determine whether all parts of the command have been specified and documented. In other domains, other types of analyses are important. For example, suppose that a domain has constraints on relationships among elements of the domain, such as a requirement that every hardware device have a backup that can be put into service if the primary device fails. In that case, the environment should give the application engineers the ability to determine, from their model of the application, whether or not the constraint is met. Other typical analyses might include constraint checking for transaction-oriented domains, deadlock and livelock analyses for domains that permit concurrency, and timing analyses in domains where meeting real-time constraints is important.

4.2.1 Application Engineering Artifacts

In an ideal application engineering process, as depicted earlier in Figure 4-5, the application engineer creates or refines the following artifacts.

4. In an actual application engineering process, it may not be desirable or possible to generate all the code and documentation for an application. Cost and implementation efficiency may lead you to generate most of the code and documentation for most applications. When you apply the economic model that is part of the FAST process you should include an analysis of where generation is most cost-effective.

1. A model of the application, which is created by the application engineer in the AML
2. Deliverable code for the application, which is typically generated from the model of the application by the application engineer through the use of tools in the application engineering environment
3. Customer documentation for the application, which is typically generated from the model of the application by the application engineer through the use of tools in the application engineering environment

4.2.2 Application Production Activities

In an ideal application production process using application engineering, the following key activities take place, as depicted in Figure 4-5.

1. The customer identifies or refines the requirements for the application.
2. The application engineer represents the requirements for the application as an application model.
3. The application engineer analyzes and refines the model until he or she is satisfied that it meets the customer's requirements. The application engineer can then generate a deliverable set of code and documentation from the model.
4. The customer inspects the application as the application engineer has modeled it, either by viewing the results of analyses or by testing the application as generated from the model.
5. The customer either accepts the generated application or returns to step 1.

Note that these activities terminate only when the customer is sufficiently satisfied with the application to accept it or is sufficiently dissatisfied with the process and those performing it that he or she stops participation.

4.3 Domain Engineering

The purpose of domain engineering is to make it possible to generate members of a family. To do so, domain engineers must accomplish the following.

- Define the family (also known as the domain).
- Develop a language for specifying family members (the application modeling language).

- Develop an environment for generating family members from their specifications (the application engineering environment).
- Define a process for producing family members using the environment (the application engineering process).

Domain engineering is an iterative process; its result is the creation or refinement of an application engineering environment and a process for using the environment. It consists of subprocesses for analyzing and implementing the domain, as shown in Figure 4-6.

Regardless of how you amortize your investment in domain engineering, you must have confidence that there is enough commonality to make it worthwhile to build a family. An early step in engineering the domain is to perform an analysis to gain such confidence. We call such an analysis a commonality analysis: characterizing a family by identifying both common and variable aspects of

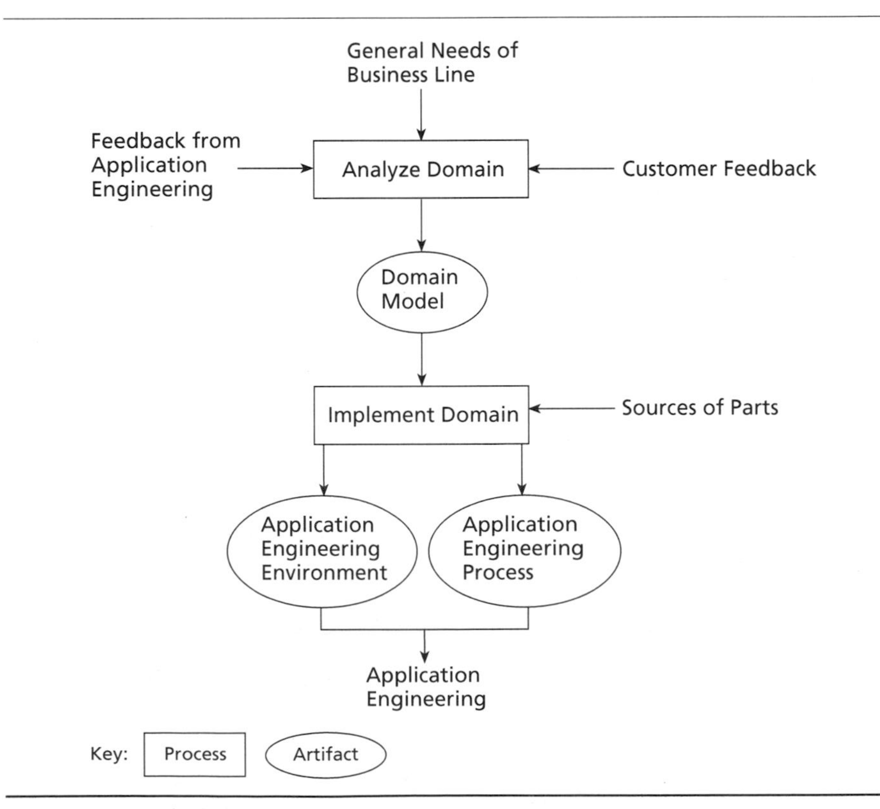

Figure 4-6. *Ideal Domain Engineering Process*

the family. Analyzing commonality and variability reduces the risk of building systems that are inappropriate for the market, and it increases the likelihood of finding a design for the family that takes advantage of both the commonalities and variabilities among family members. In the FAST process, commonality analysis is a key part of analyzing the domain and is the first step in automating the production of family members.

The purpose of analyzing the domain is to produce or refine a specification for the application engineering environment. From this specification the environment is developed. We call such a specification a domain model. Implementing the domain consists of developing or refining an environment that satisfies the domain model. We emphasize refinement because we expect that domains and their application engineering environments will evolve iteratively, with later iterations refining the results of earlier ones.

A key part of the domain model is the AML. FAST uses either of two approaches for generating family members from the AML: compilation or composition. For some domains, we find it easier to write a compiler for the AML. In others, we create a modular design for the family, implement each module as a template, and develop a composer that generates family members by composing completed templates. The templates used for a particular family member are determined by its specification in the AML.[5] Ideally, the application engineer who uses the AML need not know which approach has been used.

4.3.1 Domain Engineering Artifacts

In an ideal domain engineering process, as shown in Figure 4-6, the domain engineers create or refine the following artifacts.

1. An economic model of the domain based on the analysis described in Section 4.1.
2. A definition of the family, which identifies standard terminology for the family and assumptions that characterize what is common to all members of the family and how family members may vary.
3. A description of the decisions that must be made and the order in which they are made to produce an application, known as a decision model for the domain.

5. In principle, the compiler and composer approaches are not very different; only the scale of the templates changes.

4. A specification of the AML that is sufficient to implement either a compiler or a composer for it.
5. When the compositional approach is used:
   a. A design, known as the family design, that is common to all family members and forms the basis for generating family members.
   b. A specification for a mapping between the AML and the family design that is used to implement generation of family members by composition. We call this a composition mapping.
6. A design for the toolset that forms the application engineering environment.
7. A library of templates used to create code and documentation for applications.
8. Tools used to generate code and documentation for applications; the documentation for those tools.
9. Tools used to analyze application models to help the application engineer validate the models; the documentation for those tools.
10. A description of the application engineering process used to model and generate applications.
11. The documentation needed to understand how to use the application engineering environment.

4.3.2 Domain Engineering Activities

In an ideal domain engineering process, the following key activities take place. We group them into two categories: analyzing the domain and implementing the domain.

- Analyzing the domain
  1. Estimate or refine an estimate of the economic value of applying the FAST process; decide whether there are sufficient potential family members to justify the investment in domain engineering and to what extent it pays to generate family members. You can perform such an estimate using the fundamental law of family development (see Section 4.1.3).
  2. Create or refine a commonality analysis for the family. This document defines the members of the family by identifying what they have in common and how they may differ.

3. Establish or refine a decision model for the domain. This document defines the decisions that you must make to specify a member of the family.
4. Design or refine an AML for the domain.
5. Decide whether to use a compositional approach or a compiler approach to generate family members from specifications created in the AML.
6. For a compositional approach, develop or refine a family design and a composition mapping.
7. For a compiler approach, design the compiler.

- Implementing the domain

8. Create or refine a standard application engineering process.
9. Develop or refine an application engineering environment that supports the application engineering process. For the compositional approach, this includes at least implementing the family design and composition mapping. For the compiler approach, it includes at least developing a compiler for the AML. For both approaches, it includes developing analysis tools as well as the composer or compiler. Such tools can be designed to appear to the application engineer as an integral part of the compiler or composer.

At the end of an iteration of the domain engineering process, the application engineering environment and the process for using it are ready for use or improved for use in application engineering. Figure 4-7 shows a version of the FAST process that may be appropriate for you if you have not previously tried a domain-engineering-based process and your goal is to achieve automation in a domain with which you are very familiar. It includes the task of designing an AML but does not include the development of additional analysis tools.

4.4 Organizational Roles

Many of the activities and artifacts that are part of the FAST process are the same as or similar to those used in other software development processes. A few, such as the definition of the family, are unique to FAST. The order in which artifacts are produced and used varies significantly from those of software development processes that are not family-oriented. Accordingly, FAST uses roles and organizations that also vary significantly from those of such processes. An organization

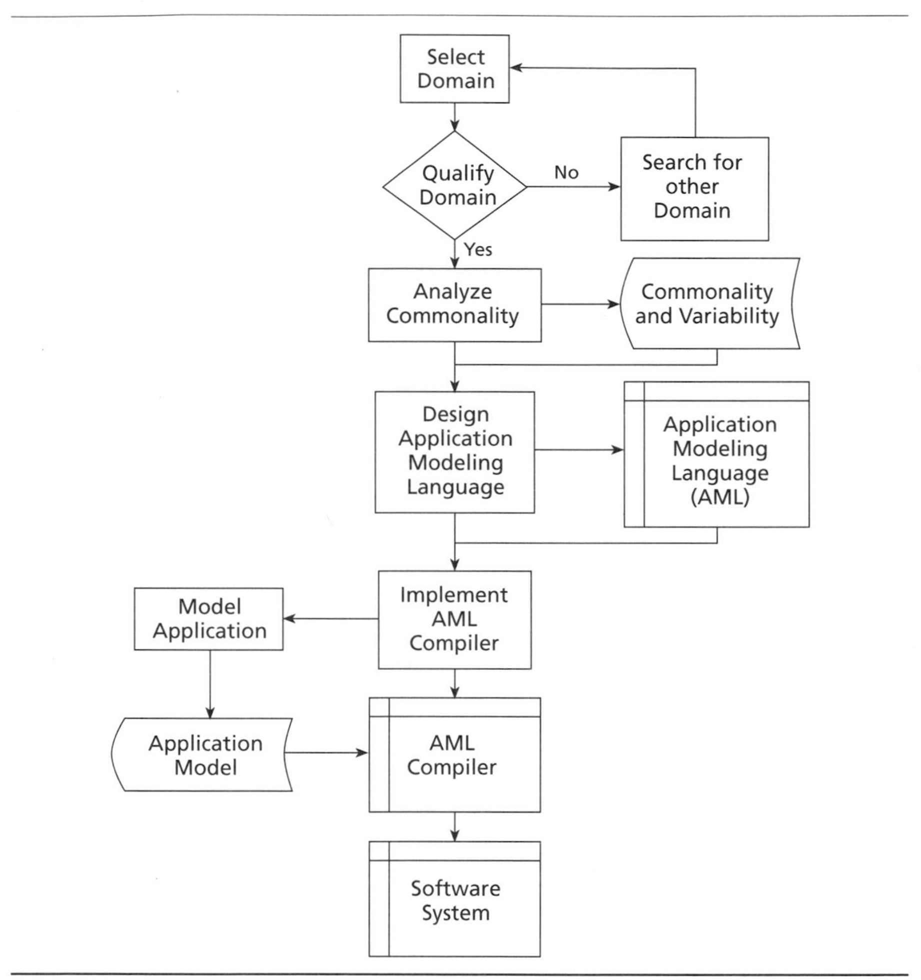

Figure 4-7. *Start-up Version of FAST*

that adopts FAST will have one group of engineers performing domain engineering and another group performing application engineering. Domain engineers are responsible for the continued evolution of the family and for ensuring that the investment in the family continues to be worthwhile. They are primarily organized according to domain, and their efforts span many projects.

Application engineers are responsible for producing family members that satisfy contracts with customers or that appeal to commercial markets. They are primarily organized according to project.

Figure 4-8 shows a suggested set of roles for use with FAST processes. The roles are arranged in a hierarchy that can be used as the start for a template for

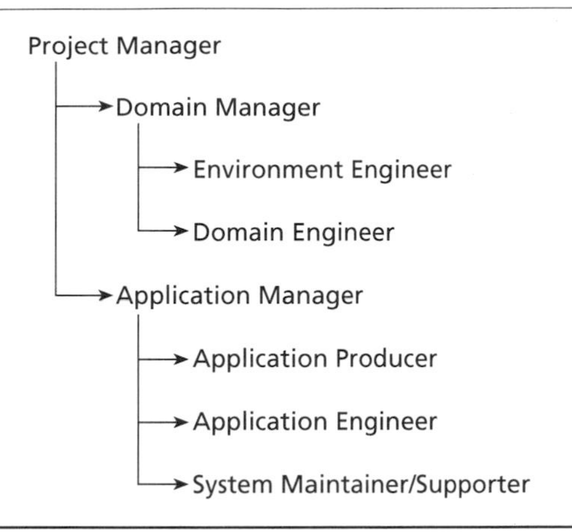

Figure 4-8. *FAST Roles*

an organizational hierarchy. An organization that adopts FAST may not adopt this hierarchy immediately, but it should expect to evolve into a similar one over time. Our experience indicates that you can start with a conventional software development process and rather slowly move to a process organized around domains.

Just as the FAST roles are organized into a hierarchy, we can arrange the FAST activities and artifacts into hierarchies that help to explain what the people who play different roles must do, what they must produce, and when they must produce it. Figure 4-9 shows the first few levels of a hierarchy of FAST artifacts. Each artifact in the hierarchy is composed of those below it; for example, an application consists of an application model and the documentation and code produced from the model. Note that the hierarchy of artifacts is similar to the hierarchy of roles. Indeed, the two hierarchies are constructed so that there is a clear relationship between them. For example, a FAST manager has responsibility for the production of the FAST artifact, and a domain engineer has responsibility for the production of the domain model. In later chapters we describe the FAST artifact hierarchy and these relationships in greater detail in the FAST PASTA model.

Similarly, the hierarchy of FAST activities is constructed so that there is a clear relationship among roles, artifacts, and activities. Figure 4-10 shows the first few levels of FAST activities. Performing an activity that is not a leaf node in the hierarchy consists of performing the activities below it. The sequencing among activities is defined by the prerequisites (the entry conditions) for the activities.

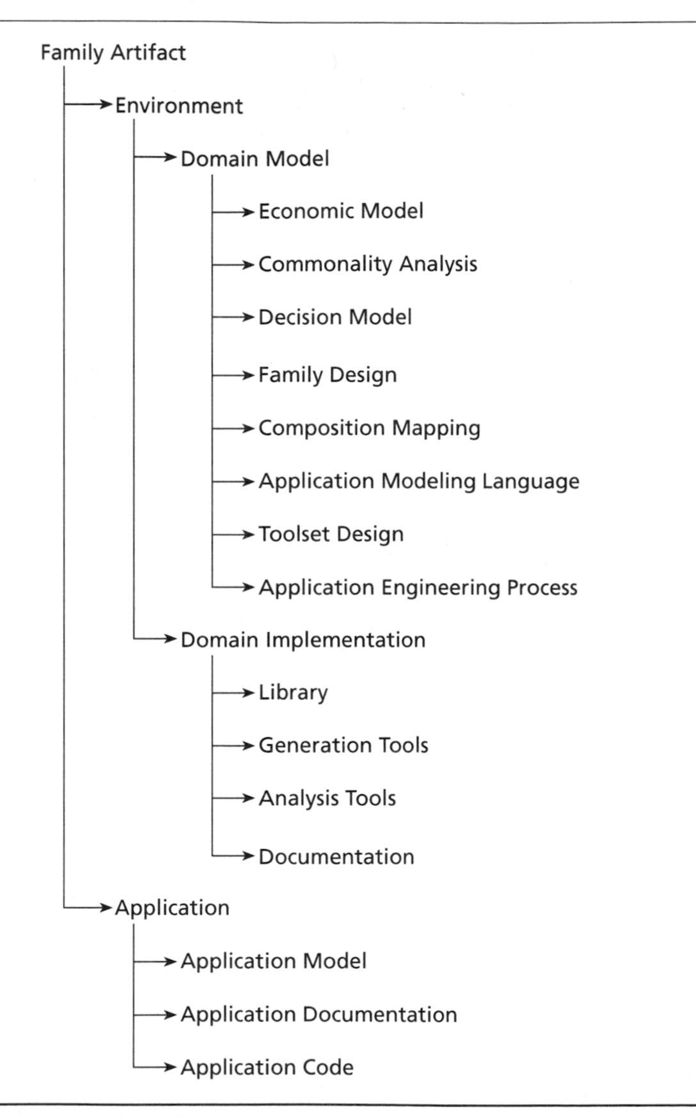

Figure 4-9. *FAST Artifact Hierarchy*

Our entry conditions are defined in terms of the states of artifacts. For example, a condition for proceeding with the design of an AML is that the commonality analysis document has been reviewed. The entry and exit conditions for activities are not shown in the activity tree but are specified elsewhere in the model, as discussed in Chapter 7 and shown in Chapter 10 in the activities section of the FAST PASTA model.

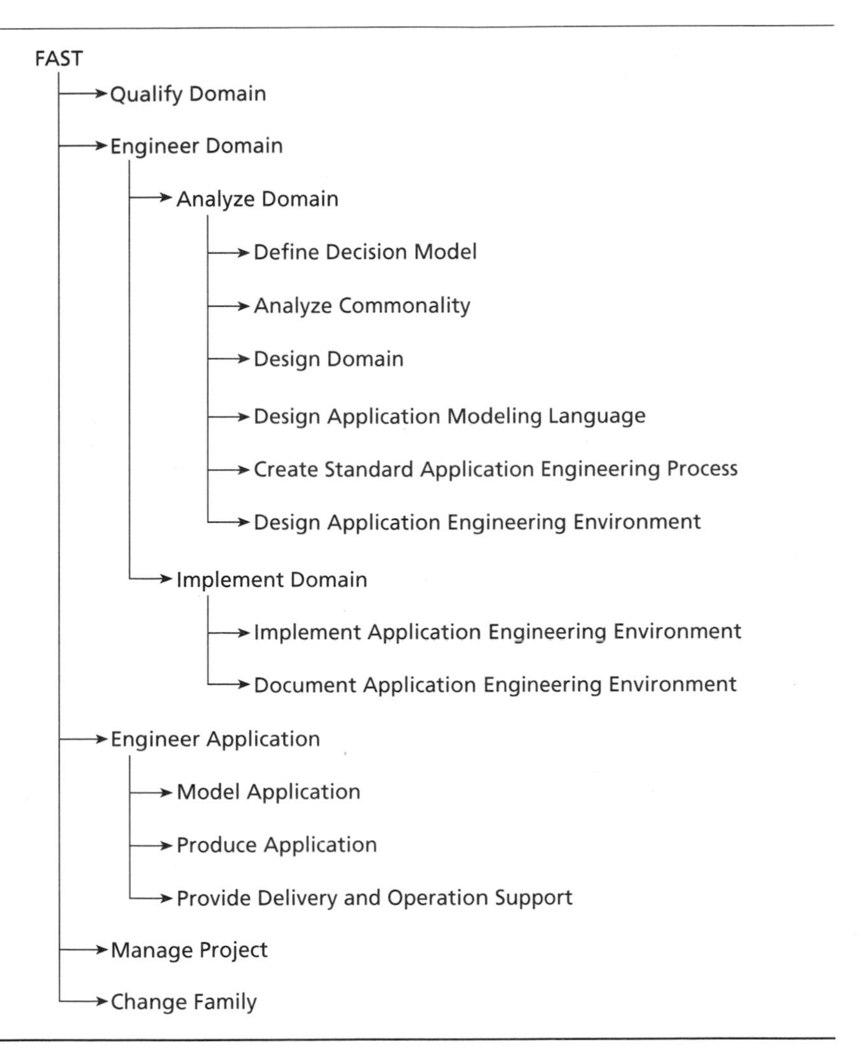

Figure 4-10. *FAST Activities*

Some activities may proceed concurrently, others in a particular required sequence. For example, Engineer Domain and Engineer Application can proceed in parallel; domain engineers may be refining parts of the application engineering environment while application engineers are using parts of it to model an application. The FAST PASTA model specifies the sequencing among activities in more detail.

4.5 Variability in the FAST Process

After you make the initial investment in domain engineering—that is, after you have created your application engineering environment—the time required to produce family members is quite short. However, creating the environment is not an all-or-nothing proposition. You can create it incrementally, adding capability to it as you better understand the family. If you are initially unsure about how many family members you may want to produce or if you are uncertain about how much commonality and variability there is in a family, you can make a small initial investment in the environment, with a correspondingly modest payback in time and effort to produce family members. As you come to understand the family better, you can invest more heavily in the environment. The result is that you can choose how to amortize the time and cost of producing your environment over a number of family members, possibly at the risk of increasing the production costs of later family members.[6]

FAST encourages you to both iterate on the development of your application engineering environment and use only the parts of the FAST process that you think are relevant to your situation. Both the systematic nature of FAST and the capabilities provided by using the FAST PASTA model help you to make decisions about how to invest in the FAST process. Because FAST is systematic, you can identify the activities to be accomplished and the artifacts to be produced at each step of the process. The FAST PASTA model gives you a clear, hierarchical view of the process. This view allows you to identify the parts of the process that you want to use and the capabilities that you will gain from using them. You can use the model to design your own member of the FAST process family that is tailored to your purposes.

Different domains and organizations offer different opportunities for finding and expressing common aspects of a family. Our standard technique is to start with written lists of assumptions about what is required in common among family members and how requirements for family members may vary as well as a set of standard terms used in discussing and describing family members—that is, a prose commonality analysis. We augment these commonalities and variabilities and the terminology with a variety of types of information and artifacts as we plan and create a family design and a generator for family members. We may vary the form of this information according to the needs of the domain and the organization that is engineering it.

6. Some of the approaches described in [1] in Section 4.8 suggest ways to do such amortization.

For some domains we use an information hiding hierarchy as the basis for the family design. Such a design identifies modules that are the same for all family members along with modules that must vary for different family members. The common modules need be implemented and verified only once for the family. To produce a family member, the code for the common modules is composed with the code for the variable modules.

Often, the variable modules may be implemented as templates, and much of the code of these templates is reused in producing different family members. The specification of the family member in the AML guides both the choice of variable modules to be included for that family member and the variations on the variable modules that are used to create the code for the family member. You create the code for the variable modules by supplying values corresponding to the variations as parameters to the templates. By a variety of mechanisms, the code for instances of the variable modules is then created from the templates and composed with the code for common modules to form the family member. Figure 4-11 shows the process for creating the code and documentation for a family member in three steps:

1. Select the templates needed for the family member by examining its description.
2. Create the code and documentation for the variable parts of the family member by creating instances of the templates.
3. Integrate the template instances with the common modules.

Chapter 5 gives a detailed example of this strategy.

In some of our new domains we are considering the use of design patterns to represent commonalities in the family design and of use cases to represent common services required of family members. Our rule is to use the paradigms that make sense for the domain and to keep languages, designs (including architectures), processes, and related artifacts and activities as simple as possible (but no more so).

4.6 Summary: The FAST Family of Processes

A FAST process is any systematic process for the construction of software systems as instances of a family of systems having similar descriptions. FAST is a family of processes. The hallmarks of a FAST process are as follows:

- The separation of domain engineering and application engineering into distinct, systematic processes

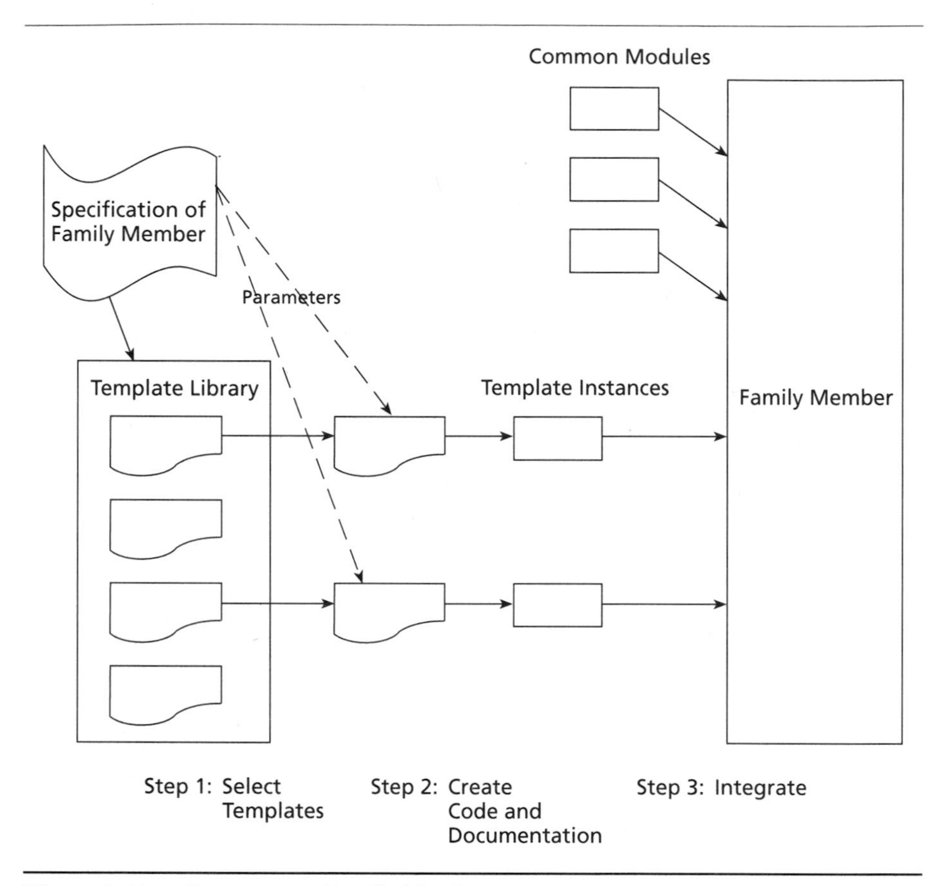

Figure 4-11. *Composing a Family Member*

- The explicit definition of the family based on commonalities and variabilities for predicted family members
- The capability to specify family members by the ways they differ from one another and the capability to analyze such specifications for desired properties
- Generation of all or most of the code and documentation for all or most family members

The most significant differences among FAST processes lie in the methods used for defining the family and the methods used for generating code and documentation. The FAST process model that we describe in the remaining chapters suggests methods but omits specific details of how to apply the methods. In most cases, these details can be found elsewhere.

When you apply FAST in a particular domain, you should pick methods that are suited to the domain and to the skills and backgrounds of the domain engineers. Keep in mind that domain engineering is an iterative process: your domain engineers will not find an optimal solution on the first iteration. Furthermore, improvements—in the application engineering environment for a particular domain and in the domain engineering and application engineering processes that they use—suggest themselves as the engineers become more experienced with applying FAST.

Our experience is that the benefits of applying FAST vary with the domain, but typically they are factors of 3 to 5 improvement in productivity, taken as either a decrease in development interval, a decrease in effort, or a combination of the two. As we gain more experience with FAST, we expect the benefits to improve typically to a factor of 10 or more.

4.7 Nomenclature Introduced

Analyze domain To create or refine the specification and design of an application engineering environment for a domain.

Application engineering environment Set of tools used for rapidly producing members of a domain from application models. The toolset is specifically designed for the domain.

Application engineering process Process for using an application engineering environment to produce members of a domain. The process is designed specifically for the domain.

Application model Model of a domain member in an application modeling language.

Artifact Work product of an activity in a software development process.

Composer Tool for generating members of a domain based on the composition and instantiation of templates.

Composition mapping A mapping from an application modeling language to a family design that specifies how to create a domain member from its specification in the AML.

Decision model A document that defines the decisions that must be made to specify a member of a domain.

Domain model Specification and design of an application engineering environment.

Domain qualification Activity to decide whether it is worth applying FAST to a family.

Entry condition Condition that must be true before an activity can be performed in a PASTA process model.

Exit condition Condition that must be true before an activity can be completed in a PASTA process model.

Family design A design that accommodates rapid production of members of a family, usually by taking advantage of the common and variable aspects of the family members.

Fundamental law of family production A law that states that the savings resulting from domain engineering are directly proportional to the number of domain members produced using the investment in the family, less the investment in the family. The constant of proportionality is given by the average cost savings per domain member.

FAST PASTA model Model of the FAST process using the PASTA process modeling approach.

Implement domain To implement the specification and design of an application engineering environment for a domain.

4.8 Reading for Chapter 4

[1] Parnas, D.L. "Designing Software for Ease of Extension and Contraction," *IEEE Transactions on Software Engineering* SE-5 (March 1979): 128–138.

This paper gives a technique for designing families that allows you to create new family members either by omitting components from the family design or by adding new components to the family design. It includes a small but detailed example.

5 AN EXAMPLE: The Floating Weather Station Family

THIS CHAPTER PROVIDES A DETAILED EXPOSITION OF THE application of FAST to a simplified version of a real-time system. For each step of the process it explains the decisions that are made and the rationale for them. It shows you how the whole process fits together and gives you insight into the thinking that goes on at every step. The addenda give you examples of the artifacts of the process.

The Floating Weather Station Family

Floating weather stations (FWSs) are buoys that float at sea and are equipped with sensors to monitor wind speed. Each FWS has an onboard computer that maintains a history of recent wind speed data. At regular intervals the buoy transmits the wind speed using a radio transmitter.

The FWS buoys are a potential family because all of them have certain requirements in common but can be configured in a variety of ways, including different types and numbers of wind speed sensors and the length of time covered by the history of wind speed readings that they maintain. Here, we apply the FAST process to the software that resides on the FWS onboard computer and operates the buoy. Our goal is to generate members of the family.

To provide a complete, detailed example of the application of FAST, we have simplified and abstracted FWS from a number of reactive, real-time systems.[1] Some of the simplifying decisions we have made are as follows.

- The variation in the FWS family has been kept small; for example, we deal with only one type of sensor. Equipment used by actual floating weather stations varies considerably more than in this example.
- We describe only one pass through the FAST process, and the result is a prototype for what an actual application engineering environment might be. In particular, we give some indication of what a full-fledged application modeling language might be and how it might be implemented, but we implement only a simple generator. One result is that the environment has little modeling capability, although it could easily be extended to have more.

  This simplification is realistic for an organization that is trying the FAST approach for the first time and wants to be cautious in approaching unfamiliar issues. We find that many software development organizations are wary of language design and want to be sure that they understand other aspects of the FAST process before designing an application modeling language.
- Generation of family members is accomplished primarily in three ways:
  - By defining a set of constants whose values are determined by the generator and inserted into the code for the family member before compilation
  - By selecting the appropriate classes from a library of FWS classes to be included in the set of code to be compiled
  - By inserting a few lines of code into predetermined locations

  In a more complicated family, the library would likely also contain parameterized templates; the generator would create instances of those templates using appropriate values for the parameters.

In addition, we have used the Software Cost Reduction (SCR) method in the design of the family because the SCR design principles are consistent with those needed to apply FAST and because the method allows observers to understand the basic design without needing to read the code. All the design artifacts that you need in order to understand the design are included either directly in the description of the example or in the addenda at the end of the example. You do not need prior understanding of the SCR methods to understand the FWS example.

1. The FWS family is a much simplified version of the HAS buoy family, which typifies the problems encountered by designers of real-time systems and which first appeared in [13].

One benefit of using SCR is that the design can be implemented in any of a number of languages; we have used Java here not only because it is currently fashionable but also because the mapping from the design to the language is relatively easy.

Figure 5-1 shows the FAST domain qualification and domain engineering activities applied to the FWS domain. The following sections describe those activities, mostly from the viewpoint of the FWS domain engineers. Each activity in the figure is annotated with the corresponding section number. Most of our time is spent on the more complex activities involved in engineering the FWS domain (those in Section 5.2). Because of the technical complexity of this activity, the FAST process model structures it into the subactivities, Analyze FWS Domain, described in Section 5.2.1, and Implement FWS Domain, described in Section 5.2.2. Each of these activities, in turn, is structured into subactivities. For FWS we have decided not to impose a standard set of activities beyond the levels shown in Figure 5-1. The steps in the activities that we use for the FWS family

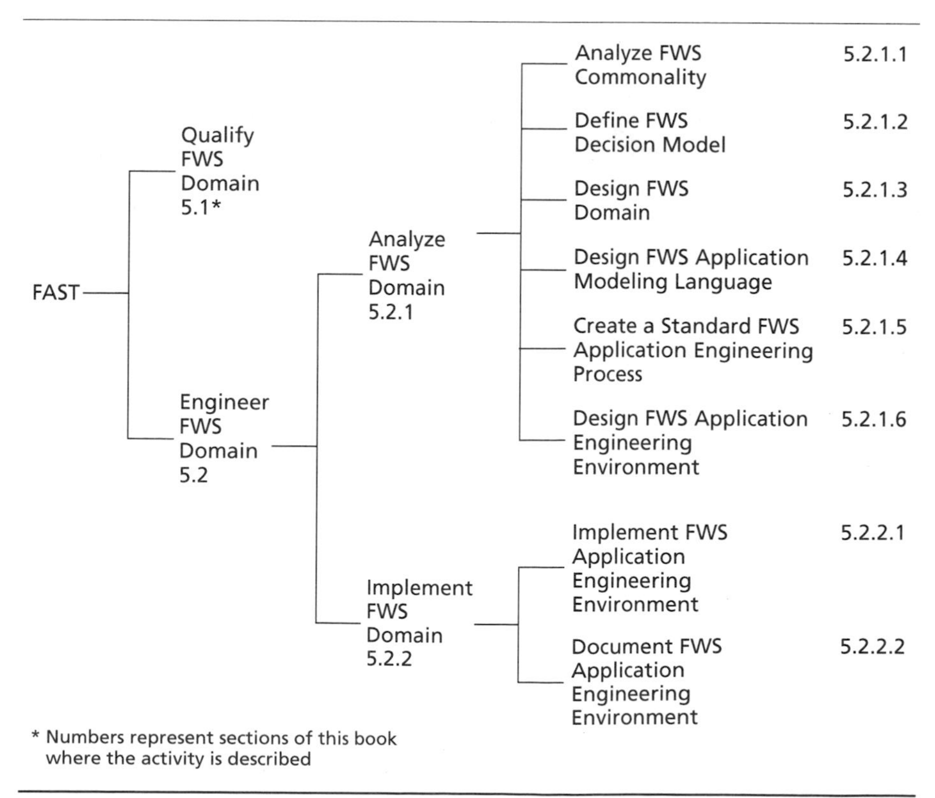

Figure 5-1. *FAST Domain Engineering Activities for the FWS Family*

beyond those levels are indicated by unnumbered section headers. For example, in Section 5.1, Qualify the FWS Domain, we include the steps Estimate Effort for the Current Process, Estimate Effort for the New Process, and Construct the Economic Model.

5.1 Qualify the FWS Domain

We start the FAST process for the FWS family by answering the question "Is the FWS family economically viable?" To do so, we create an economic model for it. Our participants in this activity are a group of domain engineers who currently produce the FWS systems; they are guided by a moderator experienced in the FAST process. As part of the qualification activity, the engineers consult sales and marketing people, who can provide data on customer needs and expected sales for the next year or two.

Estimate Effort for the Current Process. Our domain engineers estimate that the effort of producing a new member of the FWS family without domain engineering—that is, by their current process—is approximately six staff months for the average new family member. This effort includes all the typical tasks associated with software development, such as determining the requirements, understanding how to modify the design, identifying the code that must be changed, making and debugging the changes, integrating the code, acceptance testing, and documenting. Table 5-1 is a detailed categorization of the effort.

Table 5-1. *Effort for the Current FWS Process*

Activity	Cost
Understanding the new requirements	Six staff weeks (two people, three weeks)
Understanding the design implications of the new requirements	Six staff weeks (two people, three weeks)
Changing the code (includes debugging)	Three staff weeks (senior developer, one week, junior developer, two weeks)
Integration testing on software simulator	Four staff weeks (senior developer, two weeks, junior developer, two weeks)
Integration testing in the laboratory with actual hardware	Two staff weeks (two people, one week)

continued

Activity	Cost
Documenting	Four staff weeks (one technical writer, two weeks, one developer, two weeks)
Acceptance testing by the customer	One staff week (one person, one week)
Total Effort	26 staff weeks

Estimate Effort for the New Process. As a group we estimate that we can completely or partially automate the following activities if we can generate the code and documentation for FWS family members.

- Understanding the design implications. Savings: six staff weeks (two people, three weeks).
- Changing the code (includes debugging). Savings: three staff weeks (senior developer, one week, junior developer, two weeks).
- Documenting. Savings: four staff weeks (one technical writer, two weeks, one developer, two weeks).

Furthermore, our group believes that we may be able to eliminate integration testing on the software simulator because this activity is used primarily by individual developers to test the integration of their changed components with the rest of the software. Acting conservatively, we agree to decrease the effort for simulator testing by one week, to three staff weeks. We estimate a savings of 13 staff weeks depending on how much integration testing we can eliminate.

Our group also considers whether we will add new activities to the process of producing new FWS buoys. If we follow the FAST paradigm completely, our requirements for each FWS will be expressed in a new language. The amount of effort required to use such a language is unknown to the team, but they guess that it may make it somewhat easier to understand the requirements, perhaps reducing this part of the process by one staff week. Nonetheless, again acting conservatively and guided by the moderator's experience, they estimate that the effort in getting the requirements right in the new language will be one staff week, so the cost of understanding and modeling the requirements will be the same as the current effort for understanding the requirements. Furthermore, they believe that the generated documentation may require some review and revision, and they allocate two staff weeks to this job. This reduces our effort savings to about 12 staff weeks, as shown in Table 5-2.

Our moderator suggests that it may take about one staff year of effort to develop an application engineering environment for our domain. After some discussion,

Table 5-2. Effort for the New FWS Process

Activity	Cost
Understanding the new requirements (includes modeling in the new language)	Six staff weeks (two people, three weeks)
Integration testing on software simulator (may be greatly reduced or eliminated)	Three staff weeks (senior developer, one week, junior developer, two weeks)
Integration testing in the laboratory with real hardware	Two staff weeks (two people, one week)
Reviewing and revising generated documentation	Two staff weeks (one technical writer, one week, one developer, one week)
Acceptance testing by the customer	One staff week (one person, one week)
Total Effort	14 staff weeks

we put confidence bounds of 10 to 16 staff months on the estimate. Our estimate is based primarily on the moderator's experience and is preliminary; we will revise it as we proceed.

Construct the Economic Model. We can now construct a simple economic model for the FWS domain, shown in Figure 5-2. The three lines labeled A show the effort to produce FWS family members with our current process. We use a range of lines to indicate the uncertainty in our estimate. The bold lines are the nominal cost estimates. The dashed lines indicate the upper and lower bounds of the estimates. Similarly, the three lines labeled B indicate the effort we expect after we have engineered the domain; they include the cost of producing the application engineering environment. The shaded area represents the area in which we start to obtain a return on our investment in domain engineering. The return may come as early as the second FWS family member we produce using our application engineering environment, or as late as the fourth family member. We note that on the nominal lines we get a savings in effort of about 46% (12 staff weeks in 26) for each FWS system that we produce.

Based on consultations with our sales and marketing people, our team forecasts that we will need at least six new FWS family members to meet market demands in the next 18 months and that we will sell about 18 new FWS systems: three of each of the six new types.

Our team summarizes the results of the domain qualification in a business case that identifies the market needs, the resources needed to do the domain engineering, and the return on the domain engineering. Figure 5-2 plays a key role in the business case. The vice presidents of marketing and of research and development

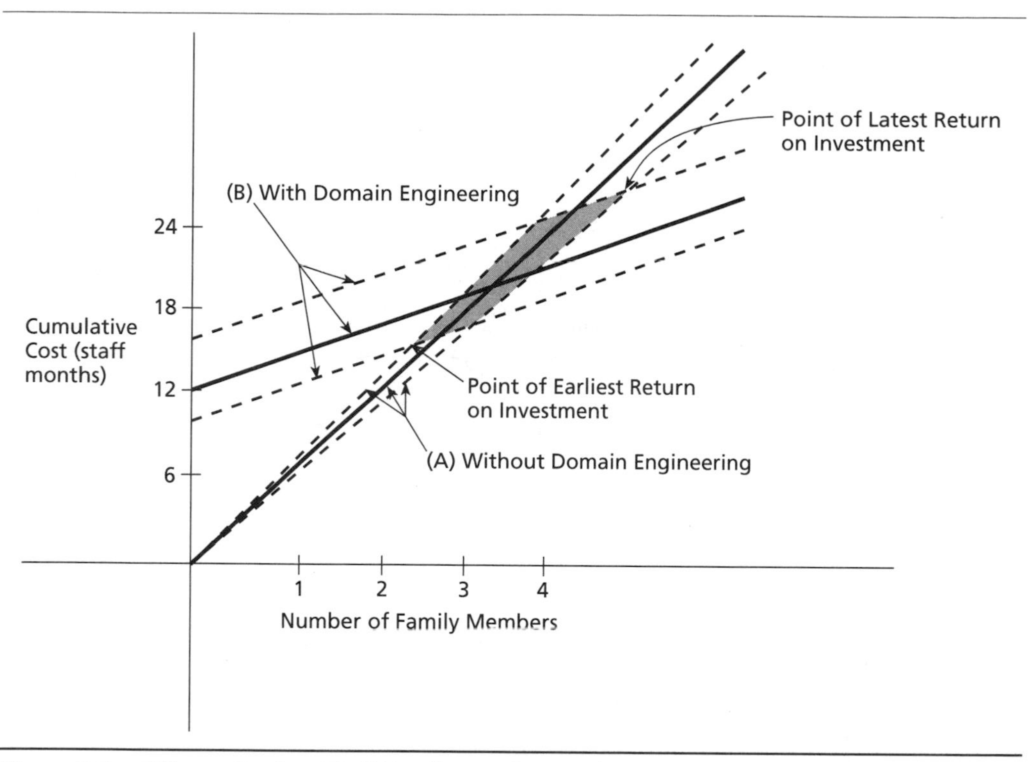

Figure 5-2. Effort to Produce FWS Family Members Both With and Without Domain Engineering

agree that the domain engineering should proceed, and they commit the necessary resources. We have now made considerable progress in defining our family.

5.2 Engineer the FWS Domain

We engineer the FWS domain to make it possible to generate variations of the software that controls an FWS—that is, to generate members of the FWS domain. Engineering the domain consists of two major steps: analyzing the domain and implementing the domain.

5.2.1 Analyze the FWS Domain

Table 5-3 shows the four activities that constitute FAST domain analysis, with a corresponding set of questions that characterize each domain analysis activity. The following sections show how we perform these activities for the FWS family.

Table 5-3. Domain Analysis Questions and Activities

Activity	Question
Analyze FWS commonality	What do members of the FWS family have in common, and how do they vary?
Define the FWS decision model	What decisions must be made to identify an FWS family member?
Design the FWS domain	What is a good way to organize FWS software to take advantage of the commonality and to accommodate the variability in the family?
Design the FWS application modeling language	What is a good way to model an FWS family member?

5.2.1.1 Analyze FWS Commonality

Now that we have management approval and support, the next step is to define precisely the family of FWS systems. Based on our domain qualification discussions, we have some notions of how many family members we may have and what some of our customers' needs may be. We define our family more precisely by performing a commonality analysis. The analysis consists of defining standard terminology for discussing FWS family members, deciding what is common to family members—that is, identifying their commonalities—and deciding how family members may vary—that is, identifying their variabilities. We also parameterize the variabilities and document any important issues that arise during the analysis.

Our moderator initiates the commonality analysis by spending a day with one of our domain experts to develop a straw commonality analysis. This straw analysis identifies the objectives of the analysis, briefly identifies the domains with which the FWS family must interact, defines a few terms relevant to the domain, lists a few commonalities, a few variabilities, and a parameter of variation, and identifies an issue. It uses the standard organization for commonality analysis documents and will be the starting point for the complete document.

The straw analysis is sent to a group of four domain experts, most of whom participated in the economic analysis for the domain. Among them, these domain experts cover all aspects of FWS systems, including sensors, radio transmission, power engineering, and data collection, storage, and analysis. These four people, together with the expert who helped produce the straw commonality analysis and the moderator, form the commonality analysis team. As before, we expect that sales, marketing, and other people will be available as we need to call on them during the analysis. Our group of domain experts, guided by the moderator, then begins developing a complete commonality analysis.

During structured discussions over three weeks, our domain engineers complete the commonality analysis. The discussions range over marketing issues, such as what capabilities customers are likely to want in the future, and engineering issues, such as feasibility, or how difficult it will be to provide for proposed future capabilities. The team tries to take into account constraints imposed by the existing implementations, opportunities for reuse of existing design and code, and known troublesome aspects of the existing software.

After an internal review by the team, the analysis document is reviewed by other domain experts, the document is revised based on their feedback, and a completed version is issued, as shown in Addendum A.

Note the structure of the document in the commonality, variability, and parameter of variation sections. In particular, commonalities and variabilities are organized according to whether they deal with behavior or with devices. Sections A.8 and A.9 contain additional useful information. Finally, several key issues that arose during the analysis of the family are documented to provide guidance for later phases of domain engineering and also for future evolution of the family.

Now that the commonality analysis is complete, we are ready to define the decision model.

5.2.1.2 Define the FWS Decision Model

The FWS decision model is the first step in creating a new process for producing FWS family members. The model indicates the decisions the FWS application engineer must make—and the order in which he or she makes them—to produce a new member of the FWS family. The FWS decision model is implicit in the table of parameters of variation of the FWS commonality analysis in Addendum A, Section A.6. Because most of the FWS decisions are independent of one another and because most of them consist of choosing a single value for a parameter, the FWS decision model is simple. Table 5-4 is a tabular representation of the decision model. The first column contains brief descriptions of the decisions to be made; they are taken from the table of parameters of variation in the commonality analysis. The second column indicates a partial ordering of the decisions. Those labeled 1, which we call first-phase decisions, must be made before those labeled 2, which we call second-phase decisions. The first-phase decisions seem likely to change less often than the second-phase decisions, and it is convenient to think of them, when made, as defining a subfamily of FWS.

Table 5-4. *Decision Model for FWS Family*

Decision	Order (Phase)
Maximum number of sensors on board an FWS	1
Maximum sensor period	1
Maximum transmission period	1
Minimum number of low-resolution sensors	1
Minimum number of high-resolution sensors	1
Type of message that will be transmitted	2
Weight applied to high-resolution sensor readings	2
Weight applied to low-resolution sensor readings	2
Length of the history of the sensor readings that will be used to calculate the weighted average of sensor readings	2
Number of wind speed sensors	2
The resolution of each sensor	2
Sensor period	2
Transmission period	2

We could design a family of translators that correspond to these subfamilies, with a single translator per subfamily, or we could design one translator that would handle all subfamilies. In the former case, the first-phase decisions become parameters to a translator generator. In the second case, we could have two sets of data to be input to the translator: one set for the first-phase decisions and a second set for the second-phase decisions. During the design of the application engineering environment we will determine the design of the translator and other tools.

Because much of the work was done during the commonality analysis and because of the nature of the FWS domain, defining the decision model has taken our team less than a day. Our potential family is now defined, and we are ready to proceed with the next domain engineering activities. Two people from our commonality analysis team express particular interest in designing the AML and the application engineering environment. They are dedicated to these activities, with continuing consulting from the moderator. The other team members return to their usual work assignments, with the promise that they will be available for occasional discussion sessions and for later reviews.

5.2.1.3 Design the FWS Domain

The FAST process model permits AML design and domain design to proceed concurrently. As we discuss work assignments, the question arises of whether to take a compiler or a composer approach to building our translator. We briefly review the two approaches. Building a compiler means creating a parser for the AML, creating a semantic analyzer for the parsed form, and building a code generator. In this approach, our generated code could be high-level (such as C or Java), machine code, or some other alternative.

Building a composer means creating a design, deriving a set of templates (possibly classes) from the design, and creating a mapping from the AML to the templates that uses instances of the templates to generate code. The mapping from the AML to the templates would probably still require parsing the language. In this approach our generated code is determined by our choice for the templates. If we use Java classes, our generated code will be Java.

The issue of compiler or composer seems initially to be premature because we have not yet designed our AML, but several points in the discussion show its relevance.

1. Building a compiler may not require us to have a design for our family, but building a composer requires it.
2. At a minimum, we must have enough of a design to show how our interfaces to other domains will work.
3. If we have difficulty in designing a language, having a design will still enable us to produce new family members rapidly and effectively. It might enable us to gain most of the advantages of domain engineering, defer language design, and reduce the cost and time to produce our first family member using the results of domain engineering.
4. If we build a compiler successfully and use only the minimum family design necessary, we may get to our first family member with less time and cost than if we created a complete design.

One of our team members notes that points 3 and 4 are the same arguments for two different alternatives. Both argue that there may be time and cost savings in getting to the first family member, but one argues for the composition approach and the other for the compiler approach. We need to know the relative risks of each alternative before we can proceed.

The senior architect on our team points out that we have never tried to design a language or a compiler, but we have lots of experience designing FWS systems. This suggests that language design is the greater risk when coupled with a compiler approach. Composition seems to be a moderately risky approach with a potentially high payoff. Omitting the AML seems to involve less risk, but also a lower payoff.

Our team decides that we will continue with both language design and family design, expecting to take a compositional approach to translator implementation. The family design will also represent a fallback in case we cannot design a satisfactory language. Excited at the prospect of using a new language, our team also decides that we will try to generate Java programs. The templates we use for composition will be written mostly or entirely in Java, and our composer will generate Java code.

Our FAST consultant (formerly our moderator) reminds us that the FAST process model allows us to work concurrently on the design for the domain and the design for the AML. He strongly recommends that we do so.

The FAST process partitions the design of the domain into two subactivities: developing a family design and developing a composition mapping. Because the target of the composition mapping is a set of templates derived from the family design, we work on the family design first.

Develop the Family Design. We have become accustomed to thinking of our FWSs as a family in which different family members result from making different choices for the same set of decisions. The family as a whole must accommodate and embody changes to different classes of decisions. Our design strategy must be compatible with this approach; we must be able to structure the software into modules, each of which implements a decision. This seems to be a good application for the information hiding principle, and we decide to start with that as our central structuring principle. We will begin by organizing our software into modules, each of which will be a work assignment whose purpose is to implement a design decision. The way the decision is implemented will be the secret of the work assignment, so our work assignments are information hiding modules.

The Information Hiding Structure for the Family. Our consultant suggests that it would be useful to create a module guide to describe the organization of our system as a hierarchy of information hiding modules. Each module in the hierarchy corresponds to a class of decisions. Subdividing a module corresponds to subdividing its class of decisions. We subdivide a module when we can subdivide its class of decisions so that each subclass is changeable independently of the others.

At the bottom level of the hierarchy we have modules, each of which is suitable as a work assignment for a programmer or a small team of programmers; the module's decision class cannot be subdivided further into independent decisions. The way in which a module's decision is implemented is the secret of the module. The services offered by a module are accessible only through the module's interface.

For example, we identify one class of decisions as decisions that define the behavior of an FWS: what outputs it produces and when it produces them. We call this the behavior-hiding class of modules. It is further structured into three submodules:

- The Controller module, whose secret is how the services provided by other modules are used to start and maintain the proper operation of a running FWS
- The Message Generation module, whose secret is how to use services provided by other modules to obtain averaged wind speed data and transmit it at a fixed period
- The Message Format module, whose secret is how to create messages in the correct format for transmission

Our module guide is shown in Addendum B; Figure 5-3 is a graphical overview of the module structure that shows which parameters of variation and variabilities are encapsulated in the leaf modules of the hierarchy. Composing the implementations of the leaf modules will produce an FWS system. Our process to

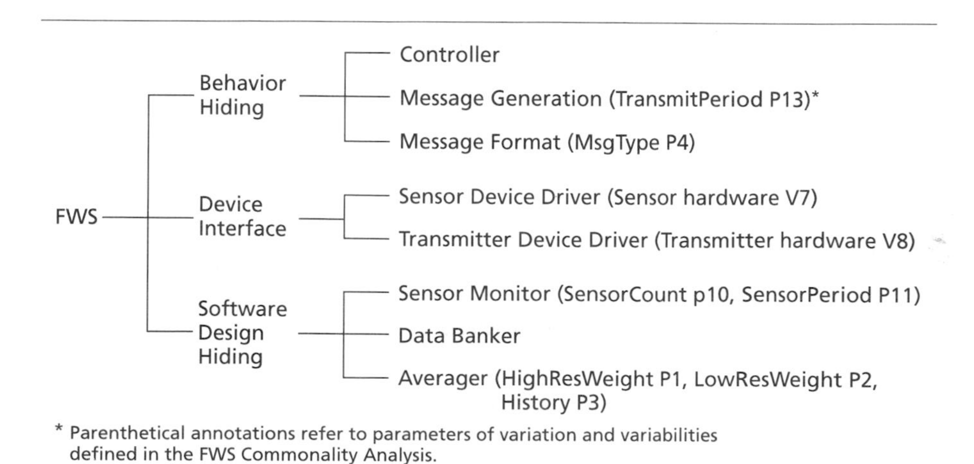

Figure 5-3. *Graphical View of the Floating Weather Station Module Hierarchy*

produce an FWS system is first to create instances of the Controller, Message Generation, Message Format, Sensor Device Driver, Transmitter Device Driver, Sensor Monitor, Data Banker, and Averager Modules. Then we compile them and create a set of executable code from the compilations.

Module Interfaces. The module guide tells us which modules we will have but says little about how each module will offer its services to its users, that is, what the module's interface will be. To remain consistent with the information hiding principle, we create an abstract interface specification for each module. Such a specification gives a black-box description of the functions that a module offers its users, including the syntax for each function and the externally observable result of invoking the function (including any exceptions that can result). Figure 5-4 is an abbreviated form of an abstract interface specification for the Message Format module. It defines a single access program, called *create*, for the module. Invoking *create* returns an output message in a format valid for transmission.

The collection of abstract interface specifications for the FWS modules tell the implementor of any FWS module the services that are offered by other modules, the syntax for invoking those services, and the meaning of using such a service.

Abstract Interface Specification for Message Format Module

1. Introduction

The Message Format module creates a message in the appropriate format to be transmitted. Implementations of this module must be able to handle long-form messages and short-form messages.

2. Access Program Table

The following programs provide access to the services provided by the module to its users. They are the only way to use the services provided by the module.

Access Program Name	*Parameters; input/output*	*Value*	*Exceptions**
create	message; output	*output message*	None

*In addition to standard exceptions

3. Local Data Types

message	For short messages, vector containing a single non-negative integer. For long messages, vector containing two elements (m,n), where m is a non-negative integer mod 256, n is an integer, and m is as follows: initially, m = 0; on the kth invocation of create, m = k mod 256.

4. Terms

output message A message in a valid format for transmission.

Figure 5-4. *Abbreviated Abstract Interface for the Message Format Module*

The abstract interface specification for a module also tells the implementor of the module which services he or she must provide for other modules—without having to know anything about those modules—and what specification the implementation must meet. When we later consider the implementations of the FWS modules, you will see that you can write the implementation of a module such as the Message Generation module without knowing the implementation of the Message Format module—as long as the abstract interface for the Message Format module is available to you.

The Process Structure for the Family. In addition to the information hiding structure, we need a design that can process different streams of events concurrently—that is, a design that decouples data transmission rates from data collection rates. In this way, data can be collected and prepared for transmission concurrently with the transmission of previously prepared data. To do so, we organize our design into a set of processes that can communicate and synchronize with one another. Because writing the code for each process is a work assignment, the code that controls each process is a part of one of the information hiding modules. We show the relationship between the modules and the processes by indicating for each process the module in which its controlling code resides.[2]

The complete set of processes for an FWS will not be determined until all our modules are implemented because some implementors may choose to organize the internal code of their modules into several processes. At the current design stage we do not yet know such decisions and cannot give a complete process structure. However, we can identify externally visible event streams that must be processed concurrently and start the process structure by associating processes with such streams. There are two types of such streams: output streams, such as wind speed transmission, and input streams, such as sensor readings. Because the input and output streams operate asynchronously, we decide to assign one process to the production of the wind speed transmissions.

For the input streams, we could have one process per sensor, or we could have one process that periodically reads all the sensors. The commonality analysis tells us that only one sensor period is specified; all sensors are sampled at the

2. Note that the term *process* here means a sequence of events performed by the FWS code. Previously we have used *process* to mean a set of activities performed by a set of roles to produce a set of artifacts, such as the FAST process. This double meaning for *process* conforms to common usage and prevails in part because both kinds of processes can be thought of as sequences of events.

same time. Accordingly, we decide to have one process that periodically reads all the sensors. This design reduces the process switching overhead at runtime and somewhat simplifies the calculations for estimating the amount of processor time used by each process.

These decisions complete the first of two phases of designing the process structure. We will complete the second phase during the implementation of the application engineering environment when the modules are implemented.

5.2.1.4 Design the FWS Application Modeling Language

Based on our commonality analysis—and confirmed by our modular design—we can see that a language for specifying FWS software will be a configuration language; we will use it to declare data that describe FWS configurations. This is evident from the parameters of variation and the decision model, which tell us that to define the software for a particular FWS we must decide on values for items such as the number of sensors, the type of each sensor, the period with which sensors are sampled, the weights assigned to each type of sensor for the purposes of averaging the sensor data, the period during which messages are transmitted, and the type of message to be transmitted.

Our language does not need control constructs because we do not have to describe algorithms, identify events and the responses to them, or define concurrent processes. All these elements of the FWS family are common to all family members and are fixed in the design.

Each specification (or program) in our language defines the configuration for one FWS. The language translator must check that the configuration is valid and must generate the code for the configuration. Some of the validity checks depend on some of the values supplied for the parameters of variation, such as the maximum number of sensors.

To specify an FWS family member, the language must include the parameters of variation that, when determined, fix a family member. Table 5-5, derived from the decision model by extracting all second-phase decisions from it and showing the associated parameters of variation, shows the parameters of variation that the language must be able to express. Note that we have excluded parameters that define a subfamily, such as the maximum sensor period; they will be included in the translator for the language.

As we consider how the language will appear to its users, we identify several alternatives.

1. A list of values, in fixed order, that contain the values for the parameters of variation.

Table 5-5. Parameters of Variation Expressible in FWS Language

Decision	Parameter of Variation
Weight applied to high-resolution sensor readings	HighResWeight (P1)
Weight applied to low-resolution sensor readings	LowResWeight (P2)
Length of sensor-reading history	History (P3)
Type of message that will be transmitted	MsgType (P4)
Number of wind speed sensors	SensorCount (P10)
Sensor period	SensorPeriod (P11)
The resolution of each sensor	SensorRes (P12)
Transmission period	TransmitPeriod (P13)

2. A table that is a simplified form of the table of parameters of variation, containing the name of each parameter and its value.
3. A free-form set of keyword-value pairs, with each keyword denoting a parameter of variation; for example, a pair of the form (TRANSMITPERIOD, 60) would specify a value of 60 seconds for the transmit period.
4. A set of graphical icons that together represent a configuration of an FWS and each of which has a way to let the user enter a value for the parameter of variation that the icon represents. For example, an icon representing a transmitter could have a place where a number for the transmit period could be entered. This alternative is the graphical equivalent of alternative 3.

Note that none of these alternatives resembles a traditional, general-purpose programming language such as C. The complexity and power of such languages seem unnecessary for our domain. In the interests of ease of use and flexibility for the user, we would like to adopt alternative 4. In the interests of time and simplicity of the language translator, we would like to adopt 1, but this approach seems a bit too rigid and user-unfriendly. (For the purposes of creating the list, or perhaps debugging, the user would have to remember the order.)

We decide that our first version of the language will use approach 2. After we have gained experience with an initial set of users, we will revise the language, with a graphical interface such as 4 as a target, and distribute it more widely. We expect that approximately three months of use of the initial language will be a good basis for a second pass through the domain engineering cycle and a major language revision, if necessary. We expect that our current major challenge will

```
LowResSensor(1)
LowResWeight(50)
History(3)
HighResSensor(1)
HighResWeight(100)
SensorPeriod(5)
TransmitPeriod(10)
MsgFormat(SHORTMSG)
```

Figure 5-5. *Sample FLANG Program*

be to develop the language translator using our family design. We call our language the FWS Language, or FLANG.

Figure 5-5 shows a sample FLANG program. Each parameter of variation consists of the name of the parameter and its value in parentheses. For example, *LowResSensor* has a value of 1, meaning that there is only one low-resolution sensor in this family member.

5.2.1.5 Create a Standard FWS Application Engineering Process

Now that we have a design for our family and a design for our language, we can think about how the language will be used to produce FWS family members—that is, what our application engineering process will be. We know that it will be derived from the decision model. The tools that support the process will be used to generate code based on the decisions identified in the decision model. Following the definition of our application engineering process we can define and implement an FWS application engineering environment. To help design the process, we take as input the table of parameters of variation from the completed commonality analysis (Section A.6, Parameters of Variation, in Addendum A) and the decision model shown in Table 5-4. We represent the FWS application engineering process in the style of a PASTA process model by describing the activities, artifacts, and roles that compose it. Figure 5-6 shows the FWS application engineering process.

Activities in the FWS Application Engineering Process

1. Determine the requirements for a family member.
2. Create the list of values that define an FWS family member: the decisions from the decision model shown in Table 5-4.
3. Run the composer to create the code for a new family member that conforms to the configuration defined by the list of values.

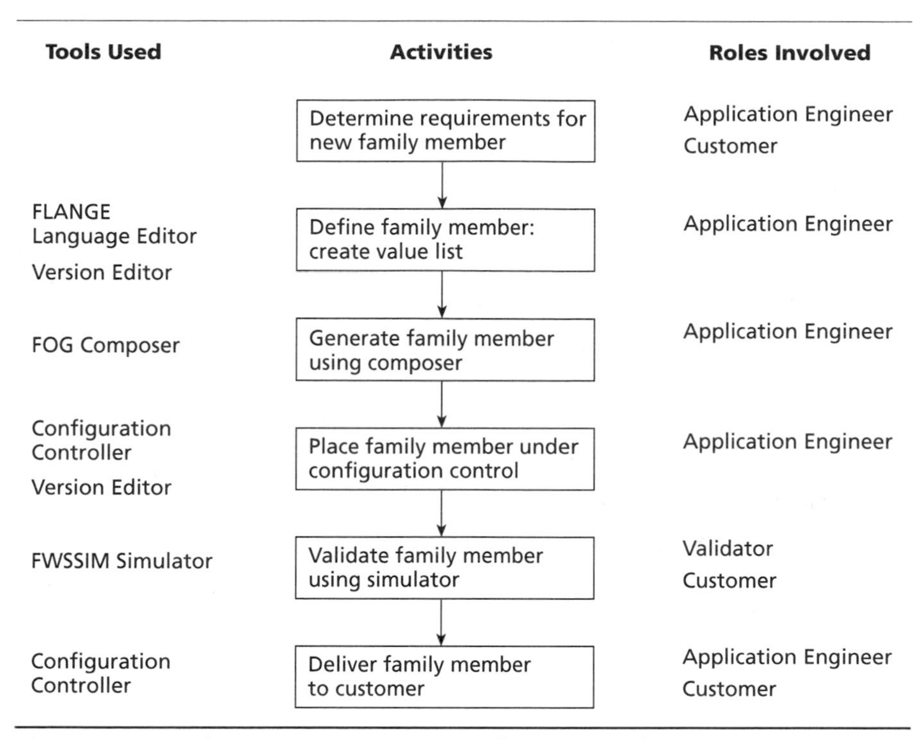

Figure 5-6. *Application Engineering Process for FWS Family Showing Tools Used*

4. Put the new family member under configuration control.
5. Test the new family member in a simulator.
6. Deliver the new family member when it has passed its validation tests.

Artifacts in the FWS Application Engineering Process

1. Table of values that define an FWS family member: an FLANG program.
2. Code for an FWS family member.
3. Validation data for FWS family member: data from validation of family member using simulator.
4. Language editor for the FWS language. Our first version is used to create lists of values that define FWS family members and is dubbed FWS Language Editor (FLANGE).
5. Composer, dubbed FWS Object Generator (FOG).
6. Library of templates used by the composer.

7. Configuration controller.
8. Simulator for validating FWS family members.

Roles in the FWS Application Engineering Process

1. Application engineer. Determines the requirements for a new family member; uses FLANGE to create an FLANG program to specify the family member and uses FOG to generate the family member.
2. Validator. Uses the simulator to validate FWS family members against their requirements.
3. Customer. Provides the requirements for FWS family member(s) and pays for family member(s) when they are delivered.

Comparison with the Decision Model. Note that all the decisions that must be made to specify a family member are included in the application engineering process, as indicated in activity 2.

5.2.1.6 Design the FWS Application Engineering Environment

We identify the activities in the application engineering process for which we would like to provide automated support. At a minimum, our toolset should help us to create new input files, generate the software for family members, allow us to validate family members, and help us to maintain control over the family members that we create. We think of a family member as consisting of an FLANG specification (a table of values for the parameters of variation that define the family member), the generated software for the family member, the inputs that were used to validate the family member, and the corresponding outputs.

The center of our environment is the FWS Object Generator (FOG), our family member generator. To help create the FLANG programs that are input for it, we can use one of our existing text editors with little or no modification; FLANGE's first version is just a text editor. To validate the software that FOG produces, we use our existing simulator, FWSSIM, which is already used for validating FWS software. We also use our existing configuration control and version control tool to manage the FLANG programs, the generated family members, and the validation scenarios. We call our environment the FWS Application Generation Environment, or FAGE.

FAGE consists of the following elements.

- Implementations of the modules and processes in our family design—that is, a library of templates used in composing family members.

- A composition program (FOG) to generate family members. This program takes as input an FLANG program that defines a family member and uses the library of templates to produce the family member.
- A tool (FLANGE) for creating the FLANG specification for a family member so that we have an easy way to create and edit specifications electronically. We use an existing editor to create a file that contains a table of values for the parameters of variation that define the configuration of a family member.
- A simulator to help validate the generated software for family members. We start with our current simulator, FWSSIM, but we may reimplement it in Java.
- A configuration control tool to maintain control over baselined versions of specifications, code, and documentation for family members.
- A version editor to allow us to keep track of the various family members that we have created and the relationships among them.

Figure 5-6 shows the activities in the FWS application engineering process and the tools that each activity uses.

5.2.2 Implement the FWS Domain

Now that we know the application engineering process and the tools that we need to support it, we can implement the environment. We use existing tools for the following:

- Creating and editing the specifications for family members
- Configuration-controlling family members
- Maintaining relationships among different family members
- Executing family members in a simulated environment

5.2.2.1 Implement the FWS Application Engineering Environment

Our primary new implementation work to create FAGE is to develop FOG, the generator for family members. Our first version of FOG generates code but not documentation. When we are confident that we can generate the code for family members, we will extend FOG to generate documentation for them as well. Figure 5-7 depicts the use of FOG to generate the software for FWS family members.

Implementing Generation: Designing the FWS Code Generator. Because FOG is a composer, we must create a mapping from FLANG programs to templates in the library that will be used to compose family members. We call this the *system*

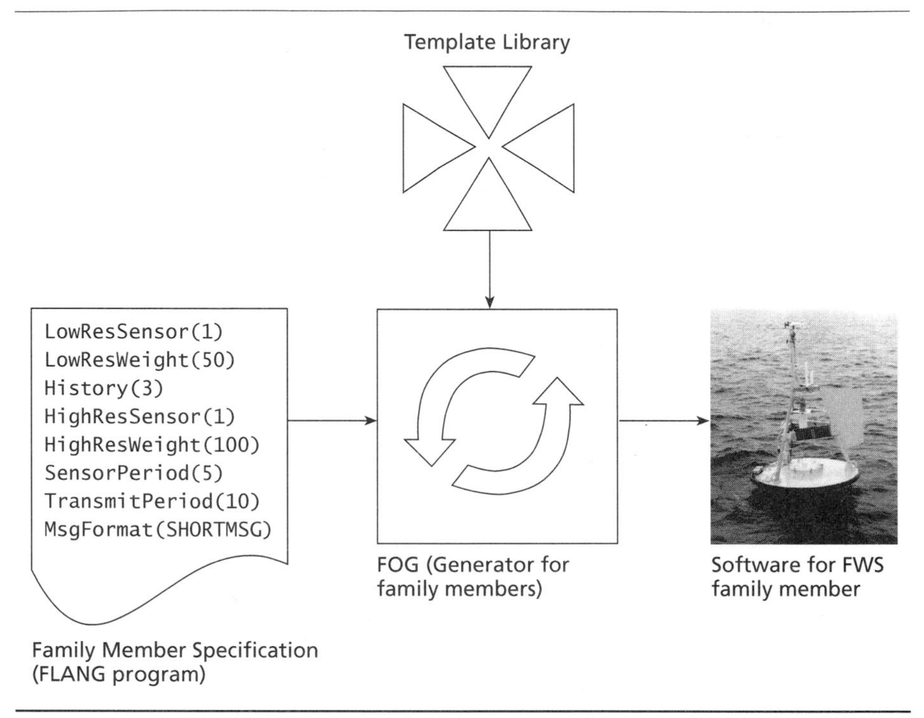

Figure 5-7. *Generating Software for FWS Family Members*

composition mapping. It describes, for each parameter of variation, the corresponding templates needed to implement the functionality represented by the parameter; it also embodies the rules for turning each template into code. FOG implements the system composition mapping by examining each value in an FLANG program, retrieving the corresponding templates as specified by the mapping, and following the rules for creating code from the templates. Figure 5-8 shows this strategy.

Correspondence between Parameters of Variation and Templates. Our design captures the variability in the FWS family in the information-hiding hierarchy. Each variability and parameter of variation that determines an FWS family member is assigned to a module, as described in the module guide and shown in Figure 5-3. If we implement each module as a template, then an initial correspondence between values defined in FLANG and templates is already decided. This correspondence may not be complete because some modules, such as the

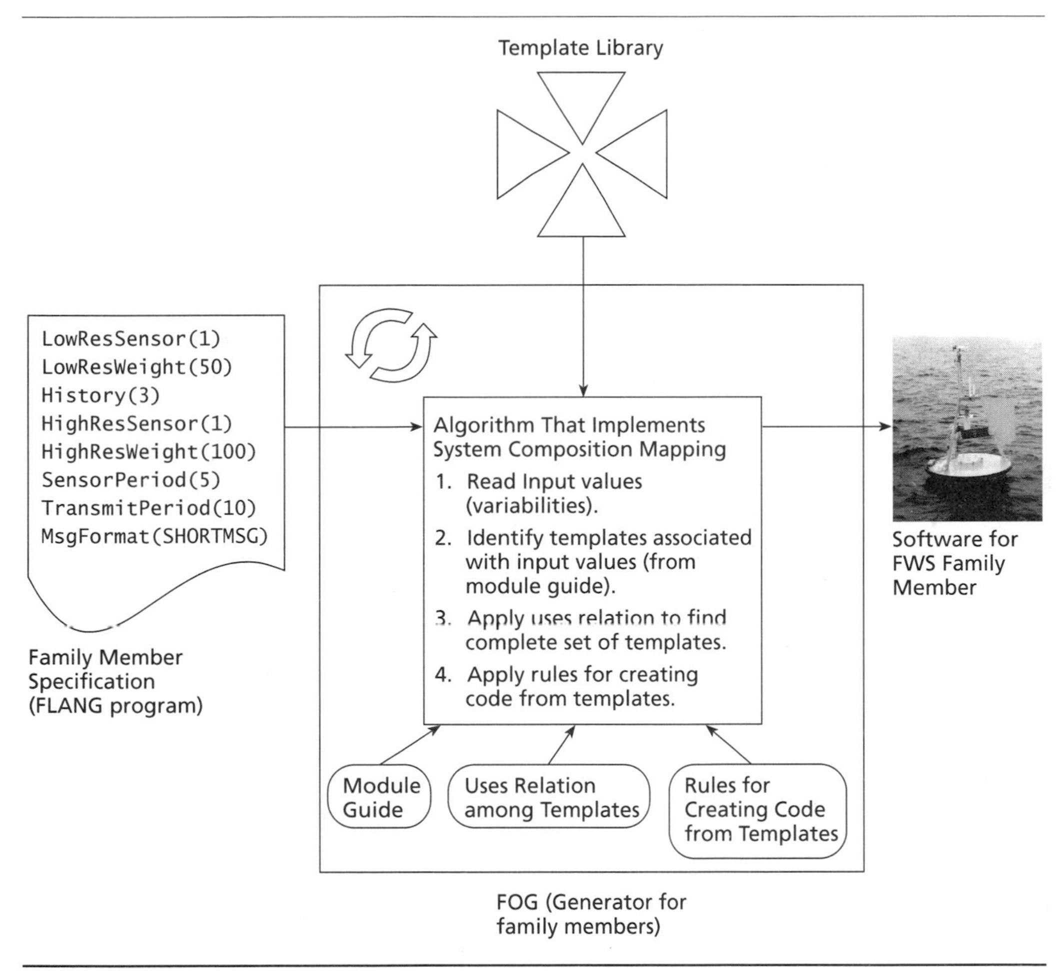

Figure 5-8. *FOG Generation Strategy*

Data Banker module, represent software design decisions that do not directly reflect variabilities.

To complete the correspondence, we must establish dependencies among the modules; that is, we define a uses relationship that shows, for each module, which programs in other modules it can use. For example, we might expect that programs in the Message Generation module will use programs in the Message Format module to enable properly formatted messages to be transmitted. The Message Generation module is also likely to use the Transmitter Device Driver and the Averager modules to perform its functions.

The Uses Relation. In constructing the uses relation we use the following guidelines.

- Programs that must be performed most frequently, such as reading external data that must be sampled often, should be at the bottom of the hierarchy. Often, such programs control or monitor hardware devices and cannot afford the overhead of invoking or waiting for other programs.
- Programs at higher levels in the hierarchy should run relatively less often than programs at lower levels.
- There should be no cycles in the uses relation. In that way, we can easily add or remove programs to create new family members.

The abstract interfaces for the FWS modules tell us which programs in the modules are available for use by programs in other modules. They give us the universe of programs from which the uses relation can be constructed.

Based on these guidelines, we decide that programs in the sensor device drivers and the transmitter device driver will not use programs in other modules because programs in the driver modules will probably execute more often than programs in most other modules. The Data Banker module also seems to be a module whose programs will execute often because data will be deposited into and removed from it often. Accordingly, we also place it at the bottom of the uses relation.

Note also that the sensor device drivers are supplied by the manufacturers of the sensors, and all of them obey the same abstract interface. The abstract interface provides only for reading data from the sensor, so another program must use the sensor device drivers and then deposit the data in the data banker. The module guide tells us that the secret of the sensor monitor module is "how to use the services provided by other modules to obtain wind speed data at a fixed period and store it for later retrieval." Accordingly, the Sensor Monitor module uses the sensor driver modules to read the sensor data and uses the data banker to store the data. Furthermore, the averager uses the data banker to retrieve the data and average it in preparation for transmission. Using similar kinds of reasoning, we place programs in the Message Format module at the bottom of the hierarchy, programs in the Message Generation module higher in the relation, and the Controller module at the top of the relation. Figure 5-9 shows this structure. Our uses relation follows the guideline that there should be no cycles in the relation, and therefore it forms a hierarchy.

One of our team members notes that the structure seems useful and reasonably clear for our FWS family, for which there is relatively little code, but wonders whether the technique will scale up to larger systems as the family evolves and grows.

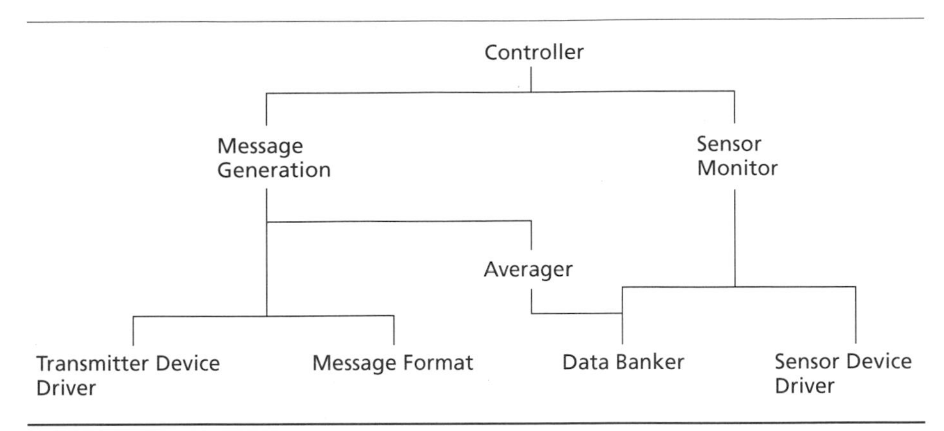

Figure 5-9. *Uses Relation among FWS Modules*

Our consultant points out that we have constructed the uses relation using programs in modules at the lowest level of our module hierarchy; we have abstracted it to the leaf module level, and we could abstract further to higher-level modules in the module hierarchy. He also notes that we can discern layers in the uses hierarchy. For example, the lowest level is a layer that provides access to the hardware as well as basic data storage and manipulation services. Such layering gives us another way to scale the uses relation for application in larger systems. We could design the relation as a series of layers and then identify the programs that will reside in each layer. In so doing, we can think of each layer as providing a virtual machine that provides services to layers above it and uses the services of the layers below it.

Applying the Uses Relation to Form the System Composition Mapping. Now that we have the module guide and the uses relation, we can create the system composition mapping. Our representation of the mapping is a table that shows for each parameter of variation the module(s) needed to provide the functionality it represents. The table is cast in a form derived from Table 5-5, showing the decisions that application engineers make in specifying an FWS family member, the corresponding parameters of variation, and the associated (leaf) modules. Table 5-6 shows the mapping. For example, the number of low-resolution wind sensors corresponds to parameter of variation P10, *SensorCount,* and is associated with the Sensor Monitor module, which uses the Data Banker and Sensor Device Driver modules (as shown in Figure 5-9). Note that the Controller module is not

Table 5-6. System Composition Mapping for FWS

Decision (Parameter of Variation)	Module(s)
Number of low-resolution sensors (LowResSensor, P10)	Sensor Monitor, Data Banker, Sensor Device Driver
Weight applied to low-resolution sensors (LowResWeight, P2)	Averager, Data Banker
Number of high-resolution sensors (HighResSensor, P10)	Sensor Monitor, Data Banker, Sensor Device Driver
Weight applied to high-resolution sensors (HighResWeight, P1)	Averager, Data Banker
Sensor period (SensorPeriod, P11)	Sensor Monitor, Sensor Device Driver
Transmission period (TransmitPeriod, P13)	Message Generation, Transmitter Device Driver, Message Format, Averager, Data Banker
Type of message that will be transmitted (MsgFormat, P4)	Message Format

included in the table because it is independent of any parameter of variation and is required in every family member.[3]

To verify that the correspondence between parameters of variation and modules is complete, we check that each parameter of variation expressible in FLANG is included in the composition mapping (compare Table 5-5 with Table 5-6) and that each leaf module is included in the uses relation (compare the leaf modules in the module guide, Figure 5-3, to the uses relation, Figure 5-9). To be sure that every module is used in a family member, for each module we invert the mapping and show that there is a parameter of variation expressible in FLANG that causes the module's template to be included in a family member. (Compare the set of modules in the composition mapping—the right hand column of Table 5-6—with the set of leaf modules described in the module guide, Figure 5-3, remembering that the Controller module is always included in the composition mapping.)

Now that we have created the system composition mapping, we must create the templates to be used in the mapping and the rules for creating code from the templates. Because the rules depend on the individual templates, we create rules and templates concurrently.

3. As it turns out, some version of every module is required in every FWS family member, but we did not know that when we started constructing the system composition mapping.

Implementing the Library of Templates. In creating templates we use a variety of strategies. For each module that has a parameter of variation associated with it, we use one or more of the following strategies to accommodate the variability.

- Parameterization. We parameterize the module; for example, we create parameters for *LowResWeight* and *HighResWeight*. They are used in the Averager module and determine the sensor weights to be used for calculating average values of sensor readings.
- Code modification. We designate a place in the module where lines of code can be inserted, deleted, or modified. For example, we leave a place in the Sensor Monitor module where lines of code can be inserted to obtain readings from sensors by invoking methods from various Sensor Reader modules, depending on how many of each type of sensor are included in the family member that is being generated.
- Alternation. We create alternative versions of the module (create a family of modules). For example, we create two different versions of the Message Format module: one for short messages and another one for long messages.

The following discussion identifies the strategies used for each FWS module. We are guided by the uses hierarchy and the process structure in creating templates. We have already decided that there will be two processes in FWS family members: one that handles the production of outgoing messages and a second one that handles sensor reading. Accordingly, we implement the Message Generation module and the Sensor Monitor module each as a process. In identifying strategies for template design, we start with the Sensor Monitor module and work down through the uses relation. We then do the same thing starting with the Message Generation module. Finally, we design the template for the Controller module.

Sensor Monitor Module. A simple design for the Sensor Monitor module is to implement it as a process that awakens after a sensor period has elapsed, reads the value of each sensor, writes the values into the data banker, and returns to sleep for another sensor period. We make the sensor period a symbolic constant, *SensorPeriod*, whose value is defined by FOG based on the value of the corresponding parameter of variation (P11, *SensorPeriod*); the first rule for creating code from the Sensor Monitor template is to supply it with the value of *SensorPeriod*. Because each sensor has a unique name, we can have FOG insert a line of code for sensor reading and data banker writing into the body of the Sensor Monitor module template. This means that the second rule for creating code

```
# First part of Sensor Monitor
class SensorMonitor extends Thread
{
    public void run()
    {
        while (true) {
#           Sleep for one SensorPeriod, where SensorPeriod is a constant
#           whose value is established by FOG at generation time.

            try { Thread.sleep(FWS.SensorPeriod); }
            catch (InterruptedException e) {}

# For each sensor included in the family member, one sensor read
# and one data banker write will be inserted here.

# Second part of Sensor Monitor
        }
    }
}
```

Figure 5-10. *Template for Sensor Monitor Module*

from the Sensor Monitor template is to insert a line of code for reading each sensor and writing its value to the data banker. This design ensures that all the sensors are read together and maintains the design of our process structure. Figure 5-10 shows an implementation of the template.

Sensor Device Driver. Because the sensor device drivers are supplied by the sensor manufacturer(s), we try not to adapt or change them in any way. For each sensor we have one driver that returns the value of the sensor. For purposes of simulation, we need versions of the sensor device drivers that run as part of FWSSIM and return values that can be displayed by FWSSIM. Figure 5-11 is a sample sensor device driver for a low-resolution sensor for use in FWSSIM.

Data Banker. Because the data banker is a data storage module, its adaptation strategy must ensure that its data storage facilities are large enough to hold the necessary data. The size of the storage needed is determined by the number of sensor readings that the data banker must store, so we parameterize it.

One way to do so is to create a runtime initialization routine that allocates the storage and initializes it. If *HistoryLength* defines the number of sensor readings that the data banker must store, we can make *HistoryLength* a symbolic constant whose value is defined by FOG based on the values of the corresponding

```
public class SensorDriver0
{
# This sensor driver works with the FWSSIM harness code. It returns a
# truncated integer value of a sensor reading provided by the harness.
   public static SensorReading get()
   {
      return new SensorReading(
         SensorReading.LowRes,
         (HarnessFrame.sensorValue / 5) * 5
      );
   }
}
```

Figure 5-11. *Sensor Device Driver Example for Low-Resolution Sensor for FWSSIM*

parameters of variation (P3, *History* and P10, *SensorCount*). Then the rule for creating code from the data banker template is to supply it with the value of *HistoryLength*. Note that *HistoryLength* is determined by multiplying the number of sensors on board an FWS by the number of sensor readings that are averaged to obtain a value to be transmitted. For example, if the readings are to be averaged over three cycles of sensor readings and there are five sensors on board, the data banker must be able to hold 15 readings.

The only complication in the data banker is that it must be accessed by two different processes, which might try to access it concurrently. Accordingly, reads from and writes to the data banker must be synchronized. Figure 5-12 shows an implementation of the template for the data banker.

Generated Code for SensorMonitor. Now that we know the form of the methods for the *SensorDeviceDriver* and *DataBanker* classes, we know what code must be inserted into the *SensorMonitor* class to implement its second rule for code generation. Figure 5-13 shows an example of a generated *SensorMonitor* class for a configuration with five high-resolution sensors.

Message Generation Module. The design for the Message Generation module is analogous to the design for the Sensor Monitor module: it is a process that awakens after a transmit period, uses the averager to get the current weighted average of sensor readings, uses the Message Format module to format the readings into a message, and uses the Transmitter Device Driver to transmit the message. We make the transmit period a symbolic constant, *TransmitPeriod,* whose

```
class DataBanker
{
   public static void init()
#  Initialization routine. Allocate and initialize a vector of length
#  HistoryLength, whose value is established by FOG at generation time.
   {
      for (int i = 0; i < FWS.HistoryLength; i++)
         v.addElement(new SensorReading(1,0));
   }
   public static synchronized void write(SensorReading r)
   {
      v.removeElementAt(0);
      v.addElement(new SensorReading(r.res,r.value));
   }
   public static synchronized Vector read()
   {
      return (Vector)v.clone();
   }
   private static Vector v = new Vector();
}
```

Figure 5-12. *Template for Data Banker Module*

```
Generated Code for SensorMonitor for an FWS Family Member with Five High-
# Resolution Sensors

class SensorMonitor extends Thread
{
   public void run()
   {
      while (true) {
         try { Thread.sleep(FWS.SensorPeriod); }
         catch (InterruptedException e) {}
DataBanker.write(SensorDriver5.get());
DataBanker.write(SensorDriver6.get());
DataBanker.write(SensorDriver7.get());
DataBanker.write(SensorDriver8.get());
DataBanker.write(SensorDriver9.get());
      }
   }
}
```

Figure 5-13. *Generated Code for the Sensor Monitor Module for a Sample Configuration*

value is defined by FOG based on the value of the corresponding parameter of variation (P13, *TransmitPeriod*). Because the Message Generation module is concerned only with a single transmitter and because all the decisions about the message type and averaging methods are hidden from it, message generation requires only that the value of the transmit period be supplied to it. It needs no other tailoring. The rule for creating code from the Message Generation template is to supply it with the value of *TransmitPeriod*. Figure 5-14 shows an implementation of the template for the Message Generation module.

Transmitter Device Driver. Because the transmitter device driver is supplied by the transmitter manufacturer, we try not to adapt or change it in any way. For simulation, we need a version of the transmitter device driver that runs as part of FWSSIM and returns values that can be displayed by FWSSIM.

Message Format Module. The Message Format module must accommodate two message formats but only one of the two for any given family member. A simple way to do this is to have two versions of the module and to have FOG select the appropriate version at generation time based on the value of the corresponding

```
class MessageGenerator extends Thread
#
# The message generator code is common to and the same for all family members.
# For each transmit period it uses the averager, message format, and
# transmit driver modules to create and transmit a new message.
#

{
   public void run()
   {
      while (true) {
#         Sleep for one TransmitPeriod, where TransmitPeriod is a constant
#         whose value is established by FOG at generation time.

          try { Thread.sleep(FWS.TransmitPeriod); }
          catch (InterruptedException e) {}
          TransmitDriver.send(MessageFormat.create(Averager.get()));
      }
   }
}
```

Figure 5-14. *Template for Message Generation Module*

```
class MessageFormat
{
   static public Vector create(int i)
   {
# For short messages, just send the value.
      Vector v = new Vector();
      v.addElement(new Integer(i));
      return v;
   }
}
```

Figure 5-15. *Message Format Module for Short Messages*

parameter of variation (P4, *MsgType*). The rule for generating code for the Message Format module is to pick the short message version if the value of *MsgType* is *SHORTMSG,* and the long message version if the value is *LONGMSG.* In this approach we need no constants, parameterization, or tailoring, but we must keep track of the additional version of the module as part of our configuration control data. Figure 5-15 shows an implementation of the short-format message version, and Figure 5-16 shows the long-format message version of the Message Format module. Note that both versions meet the abstract interface specification for the Message Format module discussed in the section titled Develop the Family Design.

```
class MessageFormat
{
   static public Vector create(int i)
   {
# For long messages, create a new message number in sequence and send the
# message number and the value.

      Vector v = new Vector();
      msgNum++;
      v.addElement(new Integer(msgnum));
      v.addElement(new Integer(i));
      return v;
   }
   static int msgNum = 0;
}
```

Figure 5-16. *Message Format Module for Long Messages*

Averager. We could implement the algorithm for computing the weighted average of the sensor readings in a number of ways, but all require the weights of the different sensor types (P1, *HighResWeight,* P2, *LowResWeight*) and the number of sensor readings (derivable from P3, *History* and P10, *SensorCount*). We can make *HighResWeight* and *LowResWeight* symbolic constants whose values are defined by FOG based on the values of the corresponding parameters of variation. Because the averager obtains the values of the sensor readings from the data banker, we can also get the number of sensor readings from the data banker when we read their values, avoiding the need for the averager's implementors to know about *History* or *HistoryLength* and how it is computed. This means that the rule for creating code from the averager template is to supply it with the values of *HighResWeight* and *LowResWeight.* Figure 5-17 shows an implementation of the Averager module.

```
class Averager
#
# The averager code is common to and the same for all family members; it
# figures out how many readings to average from the size of the data stored
# in the data banker. The weights it uses are defined as constants, derived
# from the FLANG file that is input to the FOG composer.
#
{
    static public int get()
    {
        Vector v = DataBanker.read();
        int valueSum = 0;
        int weightSum = 0;
        # Use data banker size to determine number of readings to average
        for (int i = 0; i < v.size(); i++) {
            SensorReading r = (SensorReading)v.elementAt(i);
            # SensorReading is a pair containing both sensor resolution and the
            # value of the reading.
            int weight;
            if (r.res == SensorReading.LowRes)
                weight = FWS.LowResWeight;
            else
                weight = FWS.HighResWeight;

            valueSum += r.value * weight;
            weightSum += weight;
        }
        return valueSum/weightSum;
    }
}
```

Figure 5-17. *Template for Averager Module*

We could also implement the averager as a process, averaging data as they appear in the data banker and then synchronizing with the message generation process as necessary. This approach seems overly complicated, introduces extra synchronization overhead, and buys us little, so we have chosen not to use it.

Controller. The Controller module is responsible for integrating the services performed by the other modules into an executing FWS family member. Included in such responsibilities is ensuring that any needed initializations are performed and that the processes implemented by the Message Generator module and the Sensor Monitor module are started. To simplify code generation in FOG, we also place in the controller the declarations for the symbolic constants used by the other modules. The rule for creating code from the Controller template is to insert into it the declarations of the constants for *SensorPeriod, Transmit Period, LowResWeight, HighResWeight,* and *HistoryLength*. Figure 5-18 shows an implementation of the template for the controller. Figure 5-19 shows an example of the generated code for a complete controller.

```
# First part of Controller
import java.util.*;

public class FWS
{

# Constants defining FWS configuration will be appended here, followed by
# the code that initializes and starts the MessageGenerator and
# SensorMonitor process.

# Second part of Controller
   public FWS()
   {

#      Initialize DataBanker
       DataBanker.init();
#      Start MessageGenerator and SensorMonitor
   MessageGenerator m = new MessageGenerator();
   m.start();
   SensorMonitor s = new SensorMonitor();
   s.start();
   }
}
```

Figure 5-18. *Template for Controller Module*

```
# Generated code for the Controller for the following configuration:
# 5 high-resolution sensors, sensors read every second, long messages transmitted
# every second
#
#Corresponds to the following input file:
#LowResSensor(0)
#LowResWeight(0)
#History(3)
#HighResSensor(5)
#HighResWeight(1)
#SensorPeriod(1)
#TransmitPeriod(1)
#MsgFormat(LONGMSG)

# First part of Controller
import java.util.*;

public class FWS
{
public static final int SensorPeriod = 1000;
public static final int TransmitPeriod = 1000;
public static final int LowResWeight = 0;
public static final int HighResWeight = 1;
public static final int NumSensors = 5;
public static final int HistoryLength = 3 * NumSensors;

# Second part of Controller
   public FWS()
   {
      DataBanker.init();
      MessageGenerator m = new MessageGenerator();
      m.start();
      SensorMonitor s = new SensorMonitor();
      s.start();
   }
}
```

Figure 5-19. *Generated Code for the Controller Module for a Sample Configuration*

Completing the Process Structure. In developing the family design (see the earlier section Develop the Family Design) we completed the first phase of the process structure. As a result of the decisions made there, the Message Generation and Sensor Monitor modules were implemented as processes. Any of the other modules could also have been implemented as processes, but we generally chose not to do so. See, for example, the discussion of the implementation of the Averager module. There seemed to be no opportunities for performance or other gains from doing so, and the additional complications would make testing and other forms of verification more difficult. Our process structure contains two processes whose points of synchronization are in reading from and writing into the data banker.

Implementing the FOG Composer: The System Composition Mapping. Now that we have a design for the system composition mapping and have created the templates, we can implement the system composition mapping. As shown in Figure 5-8, the implementation must perform the following actions.

1. Read the input values (variabilities)—that is, read the FLANG program for the family member.
2. Identify the templates associated with the input values (from the module guide).
3. Apply the uses relation to find the complete set of templates.
4. Apply the rules for creating code from the templates.

After creating the uses relation and the templates and rules for using them, we know that instances of all the modules will be used in every FWS family member. Furthermore, there is only one module, the Message Format module, for which there is a choice of alternative implementations. We organize the templates into a set of files that are read by FOG, are adapted according to the rules, and are written to a single file ready for compilation.

Figure 5-20 depicts the templates as a set of files. We implement the system composition mapping as a Perl program and can now be more specific about its actions.

1. Read the FLANG program for the family to be created.
2. Create an empty output file.
3. Append to the output file a copy of the first part of the controller: the file Code Base 0.
4. Create the declarations for the symbolic constants and append them to the output file.
5. Append to the output file copies of the second part of the controller, the data banker, and the first part of the sensor monitor: the file Code Base 1.
6. Append to the output file the methods invocations that read the sensor values and write them into the data banker.

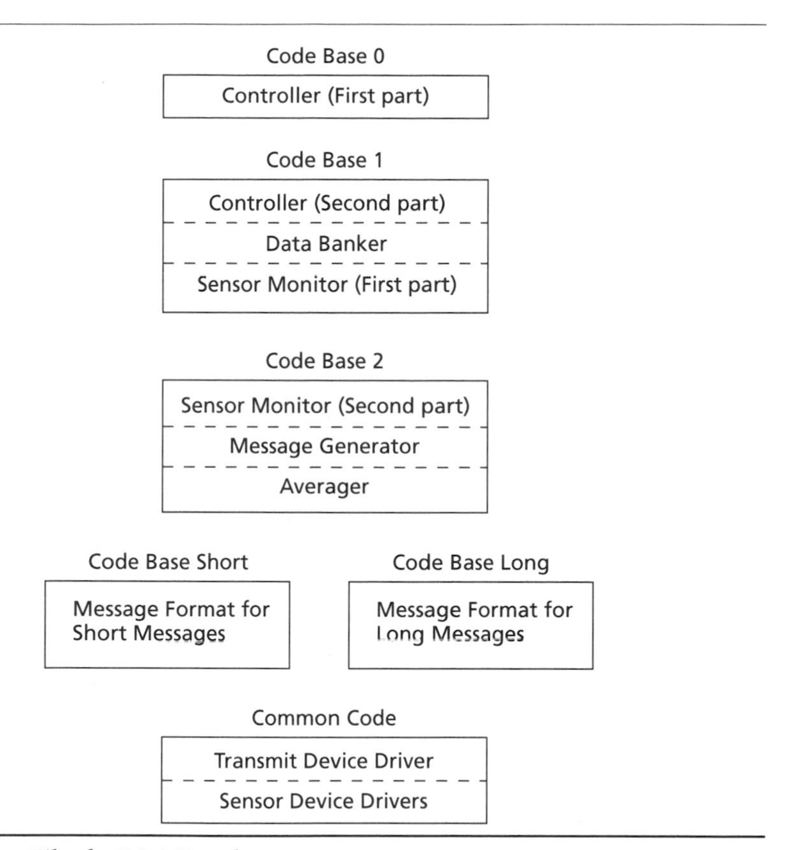

Figure 5-20. *Files for FOG Templates*

7. Append to the output file copies of the message generator and averager: the file Code Base 2.
8. Decide whether short-form or long-form messages are needed, and append to the output file a copy of the corresponding Message Format module: either the file Short or the file Long.

At the completion of this sequence of actions, the templates have been tailored to create the code for the required family member and the generated code is ready to be compiled and linked to the common code for all family members. Figure 5-21 shows an implementation of the control logic, and Figure 5-22 and Figure 5-23 show the utility functions used by the control logic to append the appropriate code to the output file.

Addendum D gives a set of generated code for a Floating Weather Station with five high-resolution sensors that reads the sensors every second and transmits a message every second.

```
# ------------------------------- FWS Family Object Generator (FOG) -----------------
#!/bin/perl
#***** load parameter of variation values, i.e., read FLANG program
open(PARMFILE,"$ARGV[0]") || die "cannot open $ARGV[0]";
$nn = 0;
while (<PARMFILE>) {
            $n++;
            if (/\s*(\w+)\s*\((\w+)\)/) {
                        # print "line $n: !$1!$2!\n";
                        $parms{$1} = $2;
            } else {
                        print "Format error. Parm file line $n\n";
                        exit(1);
            }
}
close(PARMFILE);

#***** generate the output file build/FWS.java
$BuildFileName = 'build/FWS.java';
unlink $BuildFileName;
open(BUILDFILE,">$BuildFileName") || die "cannot open $BuildFileName";

# Append Code Base 0, the first part of the Controller, to the output file
&appendFile("codeBase/FWS0.java");

# genConstants generates the symbolic constants and appends them.
&genConstants();

# Append the second part of the Controller, the DataBanker, and the first
# part of the SensorMonitor to the output file.
&appendFile("codeBase/FWS1.java");

# genDriverCalls generates the calls to the SensorDrivers and appends them
&genDriverCalls();

# Append the Message Generator and Averager to the output file.
&appendFile("codeBase/FWS2.java");

# Select the appropriate version of the Message Format module and append it
if ($parms{"MsgFormat"} eq "SHORTMSG") {
            &appendFile("codeBase/FWSShort.java");
} else {
            &appendFile("codeBase/FWSLong.java");
}

# Close the output file and we're done.
close(BUILDFILE);
```

Figure 5-21. *Control Logic for Implementation of the System Composition Mapping*

```
#***** Utility functions for FWS Family Member Generator

# Append the contents of file F to the build file
sub appendFile
{
        local($fileName) = @_;
        open(TMPFILE,$fileName) || die "cannot open $fileName";
        while (<TMPFILE>) {
                Print BUILDFILE;
        }
        close(TMPFILE);
}

# Generate symbolic constants and append them to the build file
sub genConstants
{
        print BUILDFILE
                "public static final int SensorPeriod = ",
                $parms{"SensorPeriod"} * 1000,
                ";\n";
        print BUILDFILE
                "public static final int TransmitPeriod = ",
                $parms{"TransmitPeriod"} * 1000,
                ";\n";
        print BUILDFILE
                "public static final int LowResWeight = ",
                $parms{"LowResWeight"},
                ";\n";
        print BUILDFILE
                "public static final int HighResWeight = ",
                $parms{"HighResWeight"},
                ";\n";
        print BUILDFILE
                "public static final int NumSensors = ",
                $parms{"LowResSensor"} + $parms{"HighResSensor"},
                ";\n";
        print BUILDFILE
                "public static final int HistoryLength = ",
                $parms{"History"} "* NumSensors",
                ";\n";
}
```

Figure 5-22. *Utility Functions for System Composition Mapping, Set 1*

```
#***** Utility functions for FWS Application Generation Environment

# Generate calls to Sensor Drivers and corresponding Data Banker writes
# and append them to the build file
sub genDriverCalls
{
        For ($i = 0; $i < $parms{"LowResSensor"}; $i++) {
                print BUILDFILE
                        "DataBanker.write(SensorDriver",$i,
                        ".get());\n";
        }
        for ($i = 0; $i < $parms{"HighResSensor"}; $i++) {
                print BUILDFILE
                        "DataBanker.write(SensorDriver",$i+5,
                        ".get());\n";
        }
}
```

Figure 5-23. *Utility Functions for System Composition Mapping, Set 2*

Implement Analysis Tools. The primary analysis tool in the initial version of FAGE is the simulator, FWSSIM. We implement it as a Java program that provides an interactive interface. The interface allows the user to enter wind speed values and see the resulting averaged value. FWSSIM is designed to work with any Java-enabled Web browser. Addendum E gives an implementation of FWSSIM.

Using the Analysis Tools. We would like to use the analysis tools for both validation and verification. The initial version of FWSSIM is a first step in that direction. For validation, it can be used to give a customer some picture of the operation of an FWS, including the data an FWS produces while it is operating.

For verification, FWSSIM allows black-box testing of an FWS; the inputs can be controlled and the outputs predicted and observed. However, FWSSIM must be instrumented to be of any use in clear-box testing and to be of any help in the thorny problem of ensuring that an FWS can meet its timing requirements. Indeed, by itself FWSSIM is not sufficient to address the timing problem. Having a process structure helps to create a model for investigating timing considerations, but we have not gone into the details of performing a timing analysis or applying tools such as a model checker.[4]

4. See [9] in Section 5.5 for a description of the capabilities of a model-checking tool.

As the FWS domain evolves and FOG becomes more sophisticated (if it does), we may want to build special analysis tools to help in its testing and debugging.

5.2.2.2 Document the FWS Application Engineering Environment

The commonality analysis serves as the basis for the requirements for the FWS family. The module guide, uses structure, process structure, abstract interfaces, and system composition mapping description are the design documentation.

Missing from our documentation set is the user documentation. Just as we have designed FOG to generate code, we can use a similar design to generate documentation for a particular family member. The documentation generator uses text templates that are parameterized for the parameters of variation, and it generates documentation that is specific to the family member with respect to the number and weight of high-resolution sensors, the number and weight of low-resolution sensors, the history used in averaging sensor readings, the sensor reading period, and the message transmission period. It takes as input the same FLANG programs that FOG uses and generates as output any one of a number of representations of the documentation, such as text, HTML, SGML, TROFF macros, and postscript.

5.3 Summary

The FWS domain is a simplified family, but it illustrates the techniques used for more-complex families. The domain engineers face many of the same issues that they would face with conventional development techniques, but the way in which they view those issues and their relative importance is different. Domain engineers are driven more by the need to create a variety of family members over an extended time than by the need to create a single family member as quickly as possible. FAST has given them a systematic approach for dealing with this problem, causing them to engage in different activities than they otherwise might at different times in the development cycle. Our discussion focuses on the more novel of these activities, such as identifying variabilities and commonalities early and modularizing to deal with the variability and take advantage of the commonality.

FAGE, as we leave it, is not yet a production-quality environment, although the foundation for building one is in place. In the interests of illustrating family development issues, we omit concerns and capabilities such as the following.

- Error checking. FOG in its current state is only a prototype. It lacks sufficient error checking, and the first-phase decisions from the decision model have not been incorporated into it.
- Analysis. FAGE has little built-in analytical capability. It needs better instrumentation as well as the incorporation of tools such as configuration managers and performance analyzers. Support for timing analysis, a key issue in the design of concurrent real-time systems, is also missing.
- Testing. We have incorporated some limited means for black-box testing but none for clear-box testing and debugging. Note, however, that FOG is much like a compiler in that after you have confidence that FOG works correctly, it is not necessary to test it or the generated code every time you use it. Validation of the generated system is a more important issue; FWSSIM is a primitive validator.
- Generating user documentation. We have only sketched a method for doing so. On the other hand, we have made a significant effort to include internal documentation, particularly design documentation.

The important points to remember about this example are as follows.

- The FWS family is simple, but it contains solutions to problems in contexts that are found in many domains. For example, the types of commonalities and variabilities in the family—such as variabilities that deal with differences in hardware devices—are found in many families. Emphasizing this type of variability often leads to an application engineering environment that is a *configurator*—a useful, reusable solution.[5] Remember to reuse knowledge, patterns, tools, and anything that can help you when you engineer a domain. Use—and reuse—what you know.
- FAST gave the FWS domain engineers a systematic process to use. While applying that process they simplified the problem as much as they could and also adapted the process to their own environment and needs. Both tactics were aimed at reducing the risks. The plan of the domain engineers is to make several passes through the domain engineering process, allowing them to build on existing solutions and to correct earlier mistakes. Remember to seek the simplest solutions that you can use, and expect to build on that simplicity. Our experience says that you will find unexpected and rewarding ways to do so.

5. See [8] and [14] in Section 5.5 for an example of another configurator.

- Two major benefits of following the FAST process are that we can maintain traceability of variabilities throughout the process and that we gain insight incrementally into our domain as we proceed through the process. Maintaining traceability helps to keep us focused on the goal of generating the family members that we expect to need, and it gives us confidence that we can generate them. We gain insight incrementally because we are asked to focus on different types of decisions at different times, such as what the variabilities for the family should be or what the modular structure of the software should be, and to justify those decisions. Remember to separate concerns, to focus on the right set of concerns at the right time, and to be aware of how a particular set of concerns helps you to meet your goals.
- We used a variety of techniques for different purposes at different stages—such as the SCR approach to family design—and several different approaches to creating templates. A number of other techniques would have worked as well. We used SCR because it focuses the domain engineers on the right set of family issues at the right times, because its documentation is well suited to describing and maintaining family designs, because it reduces integration time and effort, and because it is relatively language-independent but results in designs that map well to object-oriented languages that support modularity and abstraction. For languages that provide less support for modularity and abstraction, design documentation becomes more important. From our design documentation we could have mapped rather easily to Java, C++, C, or a number of other languages. However, producing SCR documentation requires that the domain engineers use more discipline than they may be accustomed to. Remember to choose methods within the FAST process that are well suited to your environment, people, needs, and goals.

5.4 Nomenclature Introduced

FAGE Application engineering environment for the FWS domain.

FLANG Application Modeling Language for the FWS domain.

FOG Code generator for the FWS domain, taking as input FLANG specifications and producing Java code as output. FOG works by instantiating and composing code templates.

FWS family A family of floating weather stations, each of which broadcasts the wind speed at regular intervals.

FWSSIM Acronym for Floating Weather Station Simulator.

5.5 Readings for Chapter 5

[1] Britton, K., Clements, P., Parnas, D., and Weiss, D. "Interface Specifications for the A-7E (SCR) Extended Computer Module." NRL Memorandum Report 5502. Washington, D.C.: Naval Research Laboratory, 31 December 1984.

A sample set of abstract interface specifications.

[2] Britton, K.H., Parker, R.A., Parnas, D.L. "A Procedure for Designing Abstract Interfaces for Device Interface Modules." *Proc. 5th Int. Conf. Software Eng.*, San Diego, CA, 1981.

A description of a method for designing abstract interface specifications.

[3] Britton, K., Parnas, D. "A-7E Software Module Guide." NRL Memorandum Report 4702. Washington, D.C.: Naval Research Laboratory, December 1981.

Module guide for the avionics software for the A-7E aircraft produced as part of the SCR project.

[4] Clements, P. "Software Cost Reduction through Disciplined Design." *1984 Naval Research Laboratory Review.* Available as National Technical Information Service order number AD-A1590000. July 1985: 79–87.

[5] Clements, P. "Interface Specifications for the A-7E Shared Services Module." NRL Memorandum Report 4863. Washington, D.C.: Naval Research Laboratory, 8 September 1982.

Another sample set of abstract interface specifications.

[6] Clements, P. "Function Specifications for the A-7E Function Driver Module." NRL Memorandum Report 4658. Washington, D.C.: Naval Research Laboratory, 27 November 1981.

Yet another sample set of abstract interface specifications.

[7] Clements, P.C., Parker, R.A., Parnas, D.L., Shore, J.E., and Britton, K.H. "A Standard Organization for Specifying Abstract Interfaces." NRL Report 8815. Washington, D.C.: Naval Research Laboratory, June 14, 1984.

A description of a standard format for specifying abstract interfaces, used in [1], [5], [6].

[8] Coglianese, L., and Tracz, W. "An Adaptable Software Architecture for Integrated Avionics," *Proceedings of the IEEE 1993 National Aerospace and Electronics Conference-NAECON 1993,* Dayton, OH, June 1993.

[9] Godefroid, P. "Model Checking for Programming Languages using VeriSoft." *Proceedings of the 24th ACM Symposium on Principles of Programming Languages,* Paris (January 1997): 174–186.

A description of a model-checking tool of the sort that might be included in FAGE to provide more analytical capabilities.

[10] Parnas, D.L. "On the Criteria to Be Used in Decomposing a System into Modules." *Comm. ACM* 15 (December 1972): 1053–1058.

Paper originally describing the information-hiding principle and its application to software design. Required reading for every software engineer.

[11] Parnas, D.L., and Clements, P.C. "A Rational Design Process: How and Why to Fake It." *IEEE Transactions on Software Engineering* SE-12, No. 2 (February 1986): 251–257.

A description of the design process used in the Software Cost Reduction methodology.

[12] Parnas, D.L., Clements, P.C., and Weiss, D.M. "The Modular Structure of Complex Systems." *IEEE Transactions on Software Engineering* SE-11 (March 1985): 259–266.

An example of the application of the information-hiding principle to the design of hard real-time systems, using the module structure from [3] as an example.

[13] "Software Engineering Principles." Course Notebook. Washington, D.C.: Naval Research Laboratory, July 1980.

Notes for a course that covers many of the ideas used in the FAST process. Includes the original description of the HAS buoy example, a more complex version of the FWS family.

[14] Tracz, Will. "LILEANNA: A Parameterized Programming Language." *Proceedings of the Second International Workshop on Software Reuse* (March 1993): 66–78.

ADDENDUM A
The Floating Weather Station Commonality Analysis

A.1 Introduction

Floating Weather Station (FWS) buoys are deployed at sea and periodically report the current wind speed via messages sent by radio. Each member of the FWS family contains an onboard computer that controls the operation of the buoy while it is at sea.

The purpose of this analysis is to provide the following capabilities for the FWS family of buoys:

- A way to specify the configuration of a particular buoy
- A way to generate, for a specified buoy configuration, the software that controls a buoy while it is at sea

Figure A.1 is a picture of a floating weather station.

A.2 Overview

This commonality analysis is concerned with the following issues.

- What equipment configurations should be accommodated?
- What computing platforms should be used on buoys?
- What capabilities will be needed to make buoys sufficiently reliable to perform their missions?

Interfaces to Other Domains

Floating weather stations interact with systems that are equipped to receive the signals transmitted by the onboard radio transmitter. Such systems may be shipboard, ground-based, or satellite-based. The software for the FWS domain interfaces with the sensors that the FWS uses to monitor wind speed and with the transmitter that the FWS uses to send messages. Figure A.2 shows these domains and gives a brief indication of the nature of the interface. For example, the sensor domain receives commands from the FWS software and sends data to it.

Figure A.1. Floating Weather Station

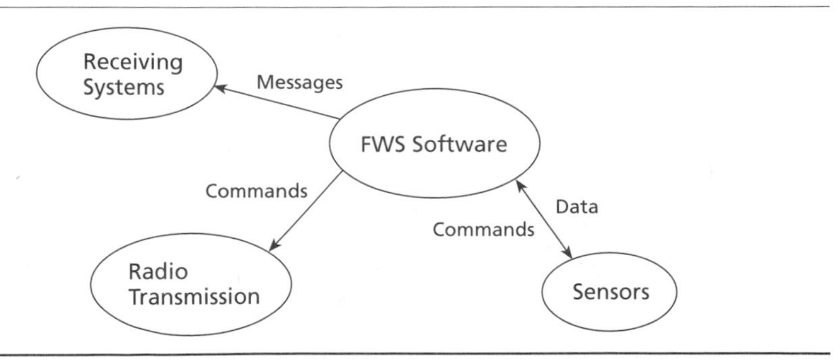

Figure A.2. FWS Software and Domains to Which It Interfaces

A.3 Dictionary of Terms

Sensor period The number of seconds between sensor readings

Transmission period The number of seconds between message transmissions

Weighted average Given a set of value/weight pairs:

$\{ (v_1,w_1), (v_2,w_2), ..., (v_N,w_N) \}$

where $w_i >= 0$ for all i in [1..N]

their weighted average is

$(v_1*w_1 + v_2*w_2 + ... + v_N*w_N) / (w_1 + w_2 + ... + w_N)$

Wind speed The speed of the wind in knots: nautical miles per hour

A.4 Commonalities

The following statements are basic assumptions about the FWS domain. They are true of all FWS systems.

Behavior

C1. At fixed intervals, the FWS transmits messages containing an approximation of the current *wind speed* at its location.

C2. The *wind speed* value transmitted is calculated as a *weighted average* of the sensor readings, calculated over several readings for each sensor.

Devices

C3. The FWS is equipped with one or more sensors that monitor *wind speed.*

C4. The FWS is equipped with a radio transmitter that enables it to send messages.

C5. Each sensor comes equipped with a software driver for it and a unique identifier. (See Section A.9 for association of sensors and identifiers.)

C6. Each sensor on board an FWS has a way to indicate its reliability.

A.5 Variabilities

The following statements describe how an FWS can vary.

Behavior

V1. The formula used for computing *wind speed* from the sensor readings can vary. In particular, the weights used for the high-resolution and low-resolution sensors can vary, and the number of readings of each sensor used (the history of the sensor) can vary.

V2. The types of messages that an FWS sends can vary according to both content and format. There are currently only two types of messages, which are described in Section A.8.

V3. The *transmission period* of messages from the FWS can vary.

Devices

V4. The number of *wind speed* sensors on an FWS can vary.

V5. The resolution of the *wind speed* sensors can vary.

V6. The *sensor period* of the sensors on an FWS can vary.

V7. The *wind speed* sensor hardware on an FWS can vary.

V8. The transmitter hardware on an FWS can vary.

V9. The method used by sensors to indicate their reliability can vary.

A.6 Parameters of Variation

Table A-1 shows the parameters of variation and their relationships to the variabilities. The table is organized according to behavior and devices.

A.7 Issues

Issue 1 What if one or more of the sensors fail?

Resolution: The FWS should ignore the values from bad sensors in computing the average of the sensor readings.

Issue 2 Should we allow for a variety of message types that would allow recipients of an FWS's messages to get data such as hourly averages of wind speed for the past 24 hours?

A1: Yes. This capability will widen the scope of services that we can provide to our customers. For example, as consumer boating systems become more sophisticated, we will be able to keep pace, gaining a competitive advantage.

Table A-1. *Parameters of Variation*

Parameter	Meaning	Value Space	Binding Time	Default
		BEHAVIOR		
P1: HighResWeight, V1	Weight applied to high-resolution sensor readings	[1..100]	Specification	50
P2: LowResWeight, V1	Weight applied to low-resolution sensor readings	[1..100]	Specification	50
P3: History, V1	Number of sensor readings used per sensor in calculating the weighted average	[1..10] 10 is maximum recommended by sensor manufacturer	Specification	5
P4: MsgType, V2	Type of message that will be transmitted	{SHORTMSG,LONGMSG}	Specification	SHORTMSG
		DEVICES		
P5: MaxSensorPeriod, V6	Maximum sensor period	[1 .. 600]	Translator Construction	600
P6: MaxSensors, V4	Maximum number of sensors on board an FWS	[2 ..20]	Translator Construction	20
P7: MaxTransmitPeriod, V3	Maximum transmission period	[1 .. 600]	Translator Construction	600
P8: MinLow, V4, V5	Minimum number of low-resolution sensors	[2 .. MaxSensors-2]	Translator Construction	2
P9: MinHigh, V4, V5	The minimum number of high-resolution sensors	[2 .. MaxSensors-2]	Translator Construction	2
P10: SensorCount, V4	Number of wind speed sensors	(LOW, HIGH), where LOW and HIGH are integers representing the number of low-resolution and high-resolution sensors respectively, such that Minlow ≤ LOW ≤ L Minhigh ≤ HIGH ≤ H L+H ≤ MaxSensors	Specification	1
P11: SensorPeriod, V6	Sensor period	[1..MaxSensorPeriod] sec.	Specification	5
P12: SensorRes, V5	The resolution of each sensor	For each sensor, one value in {LOWRES, HIGHRES}	Specification	LOWRES
P13: TransmitPeriod, V3	Transmit period	[1..MaxTransmitPeriod] sec.	Specification	10

A2: No. This capability requires too much additional software design to be worthwhile. We would have to incorporate a database system to hold the data and introduce additional threads to handle message creation and transmission. We would not gain sufficient new customers to pay back the cost.

Resolution: We will stay with two simple message types for now, but keep in mind that we may need to change our design in the future to accommodate additional message types. See V2.

Issue 3 Should we add additional sensor types to FWSs? We could add air temperature, water temperature, and other sensors that would give a more complete picture of the weather at the FWS location.

A1: Yes. This would broaden the appeal of the FWS to a much larger customer set. If we are careful about defining sensor types, we can easily add new types.

A2: No. This would complicate the software, extend the time and cost of domain engineering, and make it more difficult to achieve our objectives. The additional customer set would not be very large; we have very few customers asking for this capability now.

Resolution: Because this is our first pass through the domain engineering process, we should try to keep the family as simple as possible. Consequently, we will not add different sensor types. However, during the process of creating a family design, we should try to create a design that will enable us to evolve the family in this direction.

A.8 Message Formats

The FWSs currently use two message formats to transmit wind speed reports, as follows.

Let WS be the wind speed given as a non-negative integer value in knots (nautical miles per hour), represented in binary. For example, wind speed of 10 knots is represented as 110.

The two message formats are

- *ShortMsg:* One 8-bit byte containing WS.
- *LongMsg:* Two 8-bit bytes, the first containing a non-negative, integer message number, the second containing WS. Message numbers are generated in the sequence 0,1,2,3, ...

A.9 Sensor Driver Identifiers

Sensor drivers have unique identifiers, currently defined as follows.

- Low-resolution sensor drivers: *SensorDriver0, SensorDriver1, SensorDriver2, SensorDriver3, SensorDriver4*
- High-resolution sensor drivers: *SensorDriver5, SensorDriver6, SensorDriver7, SensorDriver8, SensorDriver9*

ADDENDUM B

The Floating Weather Station Module Guide

This guide to the modules of the Floating Weather Station family is patterned after the A-7E Module Guide [3] (Section 5.5) and uses the structuring principles described therein and in [12]. Accordingly, we quote, with suitable emendations, including the substitution of FWS for A-7, a section of the A-7 module guide to describe further the purpose of the FWS module guide. The FWS module guide provides an orientation for software engineers who are new to the FWS family, explains the principles used to design the structure, and shows how responsibilities are allocated among the major modules.

This guide is intended to lead a reader to the module that deals with a particular aspect of the system. It states the criteria used to assign a particular responsibility to a module and arranges the modules in such a way that a reader can find the information relevant to the purpose without searching through unrelated documentation.

This guide describes and prescribes the module structure. Changes in the structure will be promulgated as changes to this document. Changes are not official until they appear in that form. This guide is a rationalization of the structure, and not a description of the design process that led to it.

Each module consists of a group of closely related programs. The module structure is the decomposition of the program into modules and the assumptions that the team responsible for each module is allowed to make about the other modules.

Goals of the Module Structure

The overall goal of the decomposition into modules is the reduction of software cost by allowing modules to be designed, implemented, and revised independently. Specific goals of the module decomposition are as follows.

1. Each module's structure should be simple enough that it can be understood fully.
2. It should be possible to change the implementation of one module without knowledge of the implementation of other modules and without affecting the behavior of other modules.

3. The ease of making a change in the design should bear a reasonable relationship to the likelihood of the change being needed; it should be possible to make likely changes without changing any module interfaces; less likely changes may involve interface changes, but only for modules that are small and not widely used. Only very unlikely changes should require changes in the interfaces of widely used modules. There should be few widely used interfaces.
4. It should be possible to make a major software change as a set of independent changes to individual modules; except for interface changes, programmers changing the individual modules should not need to communicate. If the interfaces of the modules are not revised, it should be possible to run and test any combination of old and new module versions.

As a consequence of the preceding goals, the FWS software is composed of many small modules. They have been organized into a tree-structured hierarchy; each nonterminal node in the tree represents a module that is composed of the modules represented by its descendents. The hierarchy is intended to achieve the following additional goals.

5. A software engineer should be able to understand the responsibility of a module without understanding the module's internal design.
6. A reader with a well-defined concern should easily be able to identify the relevant modules without studying irrelevant modules. This implies that the reader be able to distinguish relevant modules from irrelevant modules without looking at their internal structure.

Design Principle

The FWS module structure is based on the decomposition criteria known as information hiding [10]. According to this principle, system details that are likely to change independently should be the secrets of separate modules; the only assumptions that should appear in the interfaces between modules are those that are considered unlikely to change. Every data structure is private to one module; it can be directly accessed by one or more programs within the module but not by programs outside the module. Any other program that requires information stored in a module's data structures must obtain it by calling module's programs.

Applying this principle is not always easy. It is an attempt to minimize the expected cost of software and requires that the designer estimate the likelihood of changes. Many of the changes that are accommodated by the module structure described in this document are guided by the variabilities described in the floating weather station commonality analysis shown in Addendum A.

Module Description

This document describes the module structure by characterizing each module's secrets. When it is useful, we also include a brief description of the services provided by the module. When a module's secret is directly concerned with a variability from the commonality analysis, we also identify the variability.

The remainder of this document consists of two parts:

1. A top-down overview of the module structure
2. A graphical depiction of the module structure (Figure B.1)

B.1 Behavior-Hiding Modules

The behavior-hiding modules include programs that must be changed if the required outputs from an FWS and the conditions under which they are produced are changed. Its secret is when (under what conditions) to produce which outputs. Programs in the behavior-hiding module use programs in the Device Interface module to produce outputs and to read inputs.

Controller

Service Provide the main program that initializes an FWS.

Secret How to use services provided by other modules to start and maintain the proper operation of an FWS.

Associated variabilities and parameters of variation None

Message Generation

Service Periodically retrieve data from the data banker and transmit it.

Secret How to use services provided by other modules to obtain averaged wind speed data and transmit it at a fixed period.

Associated variabilities and parameters of variation TransmitPeriod

Message Format

Service Support construction of an output message.

Secret How to create a message in the correct format for transmission.

Associated variabilities and parameters of variation MsgType

B.2 Device Interface Modules

The Device Interface modules consist of those programs that must be changed if there is a change to the input from hardware devices to FWSs or the output to hardware devices from FWSs. The secret of the Device Interface modules is the interfaces between FWSs and the devices that produce their inputs and use outputs.

Sensor Device Driver

Service Provide access to the wind speed sensors. There may be a submodule for each sensor type.

Secret How to communicate with—for example, read values from—the sensor hardware.

Associated variabilities and parameters of variation V7, the wind speed sensor hardware

Note that this module hides the boundary between the FWS domain and the sensors domain. The boundary is formed by an abstract interface that is a standard for all wind speed sensors. Programs in this module use the abstract interface to read the values from the sensors.

Transmitter Device Driver

Service Provide access to the transmitter.

Secret The details of the transmitter hardware.

Associated variabilities and parameters of variation V8, the transmitter hardware

Note that this module hides the boundary between the FWS domain and the radio transmission domain. The boundary is formed by an abstract interface that is a standard for all radio transmitters. Programs in this module use the abstract interface to send messages to the transmitter to be broadcast.

B.3 Software-Design-Hiding Modules

The software-design-hiding modules hide software design decisions based on programming considerations such as algorithmic efficiency. Both the secrets and the interfaces to this module are determined by software designers. Changes in these modules are more likely to be motivated by a desire to improve performance than by externally imposed requirements.

Sensor Monitor

Service Periodically retrieve data from the wind speed sensor(s) and deposit it in the data banker.

Secret How to use the services provided by other modules to obtain wind speed data at a fixed period and store it for later retrieval.

Associated variabilities and parameters of variation SensorCount and SensorPeriod

Data Banker

Service Store the most recent wind data.

Secret The algorithm and data structure used.

Associated variabilities and parameters of variation None

Averager

Service Process the current data banker data to produce a current wind speed estimate.

Secret The algorithm used.

Associated variabilities and parameters of variation LowResWeight, HighResWeight, and History

B.4 Issues

Issue 1 Should two decisions—how often to read sensors and how many sensors there are—be hidden in one module?

A1: No. These are two distinct parameters of variation that can change independently, and, as independent decisions, they should be hidden in different modules. In this structure we would have a Sensor Monitor module and a Sensor Reader module. (There could be one instance of the Sensor Reader module per sensor.) The Sensor Monitor module's responsibility is to inform the Sensor Reader module(s) what the *SensorPeriod* is. This could be done by the use of a SENSORPERIOD constant supplied at compile time to different instances of the Sensor Reader modules. Each instance could be implemented as a process. Each Sensor Reader module is then responsible for waking up at the specified period, reading its sensor, and storing its reading in the data banker for later retrieval. The Sensor Monitor module then becomes a module that runs at or before compile time.

A2: Yes. The decisions are not as independent as they appear. Because of timing constraints, adding sensors means that the program may not have time to read sensors as often. In this structure we would have a Sensor Monitor module and a Sensor Reader module. (There could be one instance of the Sensor Reader module per sensor.) The Sensor Monitor module's responsibility is to obtain sensor data from the Sensor Reader modules. The Sensor Reader module's responsibility is to provide sensor data when it is invoked.

Resolution: Alternative A1 would give us more independence in changing the values for *SensorCount* and *SensorPeriod* except that we would still have to recalculate the system timing when we changed either. It might require slightly less runtime code and would probably increase the amount of process switching overhead. Because *SensorCount* and *SensorPeriod* are not as independent of each other as we would like because of their joint effect on system timing, and because alternative A2 may require less process switching, we will choose A2.

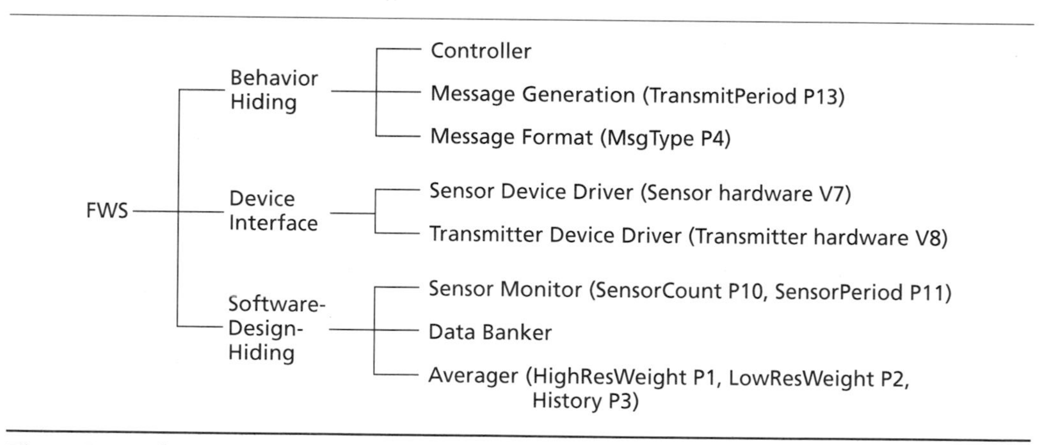

Figure B.1 *Floating Weather Station Module Hierarchy with Mapping to Parameters of Variation and Variabilities*

ADDENDUM C

The Floating Weather Station Application Generation Environment

C.1 Family Member Generator

```
#!/bin/perl

#***** load parameter of variation values

open(PARMFILE,"$ARGV[0]") || die "cannot open $ARGV[0]";
$nn = 0;
while (<PARMFILE>) {
    $n++;
    if (/\s*(\w+)\s*\((\w+)\)/) {
        # print "line $n: !$1!$2!\n";
        $parms{$1} = $2;
    } else {
        print "Format error. Parm file line $n\n";
        exit(1);
    }
}
close(PARMFILE);

#foreach $key (keys %parms) {
#   print "($key,$parms{$key})\n";
#}

#***** generate FWS.java
# Create the output file build/FWS.java
$BuildFileName = 'build/FWS.java';
unlink $BuildFileName;
open(BUILDFILE,">$BuildFileName") || die "cannot open $BuildFileName";

# Start with Code Base 0; append it to the output file
&appendFile("codeBase/FWS0.java");

# Call genConstants to generate the symbolic constants, insert them into
# the first part of the Controller, and append it to the output file
&genConstants();

# Append the second part of the Controller, the DataBanker and the first
# part of the SensorMonitor to the output file.
&appendFile("codeBase/FWS1.java");
```

```
# Call genDriverCalls to generate the calls to the SensorDrivers, insert
# them into the SensorMonitor, and append it to the output file.
&genDriverCalls();

# Append the Message Generator and Averager to the output file.
&appendFile("codeBase/FWS2.java");

# Select the appropriate version of the Message Format Module and append it to
# the output file.
if ($parms{"MsgFormat"} eq "SHORTMSG") {
   &appendFile("codeBase/FWSShort.java");
} else {
   &appendFile("codeBase/FWSLong.java");
}

# Close the output file and we're done.
close(BUILDFILE);

#***** utility functions

# appendFile(F)
#   append the contents of file F to the build file
sub appendFile
{
   local($fileName) = @_;
   open(TMPFILE,$fileName) || die "cannot open $fileName";
   while (<TMPFILE>) {
      print BUILDFILE;
   }
   close(TMPFILE);
}

sub genConstants
{
   print BUILDFILE
      "public static final int SensorPeriod = ",
      $parms{"SensorPeriod"} * 1000,
      ";\n";
   print BUILDFILE
      "public static final int TransmitPeriod = ",
      $parms{"TransmitPeriod"} * 1000,
      ";\n";
   print BUILDFILE
      "public static final int LowResWeight = ",
      $parms{"LowResWeight"},
      ";\n";
   print BUILDFILE
      "public static final int HighResWeight = ",
      $parms{"HighResWeight"},
      ";\n";
   print BUILDFILE
      "public static final int NumSensors = ",
      $parms{"LowResSensor"} + $parms{"HighResSensor"},
```

```
            ";\n";
        print BUILDFILE
            "public static final int HistoryLength = ",
            $parms{"History"}, "* NumSensors",
            ";\n";
}

sub genDriverCalls
{
    for ($i = 0; $i < $parms{"LowResSensor"}; $i++) {
        print BUILDFILE
            "DataBanker.write(SensorDriver",$i,
            ".get());\n";
    }
    for ($i = 0; $i < $parms{"HighResSensor"}; $i++) {
        print BUILDFILE
            "DataBanker.write(SensorDriver",$i+5,
            ".get());\n";
    }
}

# -------------------------- End Family Member Generator-----------------------------
# -------------------------- Code Base 0 ---- FWS0.java-------------------------------
# First part of Controller
import java.util.*;

public class FWS
{

# Constants defining FWS configuration will be appended here, followed by Code Base 1.
# -------------------------- Code Base 1 -----FWS1.java-------------------------------
# Second part of Controller
    public FWS()
    {
        DataBanker.init();
        MessageGenerator m = new MessageGenerator();
        m.start();
        SensorMonitor s = new SensorMonitor();
        s.start();
    }
}

class DataBanker
{
    public static void init()
    {
        for (int i = 0; i < FWS.HistoryLength; i++)
            v.addElement(new SensorReading(1,0));
    }
    public static synchronized void write(SensorReading r)
    {
        v.removeElementAt(0);
        v.addElement(new SensorReading(r.res,r.value));
    }
```

```
    public static synchronized Vector read()
    {
        return (Vector)v.clone();
    }
    private static Vector v = new Vector();
}

class SensorMonitor extends Thread
{
    public void run()
    {
        while (true) {
            try { Thread.sleep(FWS.SensorPeriod); }
            catch (InterruptedException e) {}

# For each sensor included in the family member, one sensor read and one data
# banker write will be appended here, followed by Code Base 2.

# ------------------------ Code Base 2 -------FWS2.java-------------------------------
        }
    }
}

class MessageGenerator extends Thread
#
# The message generator code is common to and the same for all family members.
# For each transmit period it uses the averager, message format, and
# transmit driver modules to create and transmit a new message.
#

{
    public void run()
    {
        while (true) {
            try { Thread.sleep(FWS.TransmitPeriod); }
            catch (InterruptedException e) {}
            TransmitDriver.send(MessageFormat.create(Averager.get()));
        }
    }
}

class Averager
#
# The averager code is common to and the same for all family members; it
# figures out how many readings to average from the size of the data stored
# in the data banker. The weights it uses are defined as constants, derived
# from the FLANG file that is input to the FOG composer.
#
{
    static public int get()
    {
        Vector v = DataBanker.read();
        int valueSum = 0;
        int weightSum = 0;
```

```
# Use data banker size to determine number of readings to average
      for (int i = 0; i < v.size(); i++) {
         SensorReading r = (SensorReading)v.elementAt(i);
# SensorReading is a pair containing both sensor resolution and the value of
# the reading.
         int weight;
         if (r.res == SensorReading.LowRes)
            weight = FWS.LowResWeight;
         else
            weight = FWS.HighResWeight;

         valueSum += r.value * weight;
         weightSum += weight;
      }
      return valueSum/weightSum;
   }
}
#
# Append here the code to create messages in the appropriate format, either
# short or long.
# ----------------- Code Base for Short Messages ---------FWSShort.java----------------
class MessageFormat
{
   static public Vector create(int i)
   {
# For short messages, just send the value.
      Vector v = new Vector();
      v.addElement(new Integer(i));
      return v;
   }
}
# ----------------- Code Base for Long Messages -----------FWSLong.java----------------
class MessageFormat
{
   static public Vector create(int i)
   {
# For long messages, create a new message number in sequence and send the
# message number and the value.

      Vector v = new Vector();
      msgNum++;
      v.addElement(new Integer(msgnum));
      v.addElement(new Integer(i));
      return v;
   }
   static int msgNum = 0;
}
# ----------------------------------------------------------------------------------
```

```
# ---------------------- Common code for all configurations -------------------------
# This code is designed to be used with the Harness simulator
#
import java.util.*;

public class TransmitDriver
{
   public static void send(Vector v)
   {
      for (int i = 0; i < v.size(); i++) {
         Integer x = (Integer)v.elementAt(i);
         Harness.display(x.intValue());
      }
   }
}

class SensorReading
{
   public static final int LowRes = 0;
   public static final int HighRes = 1;

   public SensorReading(int r,int v)
   {
      res = r;
      value = v;
   }

   public int res;
   public int value;
}

public class SensorDriver0
{
   public static SensorReading get()
   {
      return new SensorReading(
         SensorReading.LowRes,
         (HarnessFrame.sensorValue / 5) * 5
      );
   }
}

public class SensorDriver1
{
   public static SensorReading get()
   {
      return new SensorReading(
         SensorReading.LowRes,
         (HarnessFrame.sensorValue / 5) * 5
      );
   }
}
```

```
public class SensorDriver2
{
   public static SensorReading get()
   {
      return new SensorReading(
         SensorReading.LowRes,
         (HarnessFrame.sensorValue / 5) * 5
      );
   }
}
public class SensorDriver3
{
   public static SensorReading get()
   {
      return new SensorReading(
         SensorReading.LowRes,
         (HarnessFrame.sensorValue / 5) * 5
      );
   }
}

public class SensorDriver4
{
   public static SensorReading get()
   {
      return new SensorReading(
         SensorReading.LowRes,
         (HarnessFrame.sensorValue / 5) * 5
   );
   }
}
public class SensorDriver5
{
   public static SensorReading get()
   {
      return new SensorReading(
         SensorReading.HighRes,
         HarnessFrame.sensorValue
      );
   }
}
public class SensorDriver6
{
   public static SensorReading get()
   {
      return new SensorReading(
         SensorReading.HighRes,
         HarnessFrame.sensorValue
      );
   }
}
```

```
public class SensorDriver7
{
   public static SensorReading get()
   {
      return new SensorReading(
         SensorReading.HighRes,
         HarnessFrame.sensorValue
      );
   }
}
public class SensorDriver8
{
   public static SensorReading get()
   {
      return new SensorReading(
         SensorReading.HighRes,
         HarnessFrame.sensorValue
      );
   }
}
public class SensorDriver9
{
   public static SensorReading get()
   {
      return new SensorReading(
         SensorReading.HighRes,
         HarnessFrame.sensorValue
      );
   }
}
# --------------------End of common code for all configurations -----------
```

ADDENDUM D

A Generated Floating Weather Station Family Member

```
# ---------------------BuildFile---------------------FWS.java------------------------
# ---------------- Generated code for the following configuration: --------------------
# 5 high resolution sensors, sensors read every 1 second, and long messages transmitted
# every 1 second
#
#Corresponds to the following input file
#LowResSensor(0)
#LowResWeight(0)
#History(3)
#HighResSensor(5)
#HighResWeight(1)
#SensorPeriod(1)
#TransmitPeriod(1)
#MsgFormat(LONGMSG)

#
import java.util.*;

public class FWS
{
public static final int SensorPeriod = 1000;
public static final int TransmitPeriod = 1000;
public static final int LowResWeight = 0;
public static final int HighResWeight = 1;
public static final int NumSensors = 5;
public static final int HistoryLength = 3 * NumSensors;
   public FWS()
   {
      DataBanker.init();
      MessageGenerator m = new MessageGenerator();
      m.start();
      SensorMonitor s = new SensorMonitor();
      s.start();
   }
}

class DataBanker
{
   public static void init()
```

```
    {
        for (int i = 0; i < FWS.HistoryLength; i++)
            v.addElement(new SensorReading(1,0));
    }
    public static synchronized void write(SensorReading r)
    {
        v.removeElementAt(0);
        v.addElement(new SensorReading(r.res,r.value));
    }
    public static synchronized Vector read()
    {
        return (Vector)v.clone();
    }
    private static Vector v = new Vector();
}

class SensorMonitor extends Thread
{
    public void run()
    {
        while (true) {
            try { Thread.sleep(FWS.SensorPeriod); }
            catch (InterruptedException e) {}
            DataBanker.write(SensorDriver5.get());
            DataBanker.write(SensorDriver6.get());
            DataBanker.write(SensorDriver7.get());
            DataBanker.write(SensorDriver8.get());
            DataBanker.write(SensorDriver9.get());
        }
    }
}

class MessageGenerator extends Thread
{
    public void run()
    {
        while (true) {
            try { Thread.sleep(FWS.TransmitPeriod); }
            catch (InterruptedException e) {}
            TransmitDriver.send(MessageFormat.create(Averager.get()));
        }
    }
}

class Averager
{
    static public int get()
    {
        Vector v = DataBanker.read();
        int valueSum = 0;
        int weightSum = 0;
```

```
      for (int i = 0; i < v.size(); i++) {
         SensorReading r = (SensorReading)v.elementAt(i);

         int weight;
         if (r.res == SensorReading.LowRes)
            weight = FWS.LowResWeight;
         else
            weight = FWS.HighResWeight;

         valueSum += r.value * weight;
         weightSum += weight;
      }
      return valueSum/weightSum;
   }
}
class MessageFormat
{
   static public Vector create(int i)
   {
      Vector v = new Vector();
      msgNum++;
      v.addElement(new Integer(msgnum));
      v.addElement(new Integer(i));
      return v;
   }
   static int msgNum = 0;
}
# -----------------------------End of generated code --------------------------------
```

ADDENDUM E

The Floating Weather Station Environment Simulator

```
# ----------Harness to Simulate a Floating Weather Station and Its Environment----------
import java.awt.*;

public class Harness
{ public static void main(String[] args)
    {
        f.resize(363,267);
        f.show();
        FWS s = new FWS();
    }
    public static void display(int i)
    {
        f.displayMessage(i);
        f.repaint();
    }
    public static HarnessFrame f = new HarnessFrame();
}

class HarnessFrame extends Frame
{
    public HarnessFrame()
    {
        image = Toolkit.getDefaultToolkit().getImage("buoy.gif");

        Panel harnessPanel = new Panel();
        harnessPanel.setBackground(Color.red);
        harnessPanel.setLayout(new BorderLayout());

        Panel msgPanel = new Panel();
        msgPanel.add(new Label("Message. Num:"));
        numField = new TextField(3);
        numField.setBackground(Color.white);
        numField.setEditable(false);
        numField.setText("");
        msgPanel.add(numField);
        msgPanel.add(new Label("Value:"));
        msgField = new TextField(3);
        msgField.setBackground(Color.white);
        msgField.setEditable(false);
```

```
        msgField.setText("");
        msgPanel.add(msgField);
        harnessPanel.add("North",msgPanel);

        Panel sensorPanel = new Panel();
        sensorPanel.setLayout(new BorderLayout());
        sensorPanel.add("North",new Label("Current wind speed:"));
        Panel sensorButtonPanel = new Panel();
        sensorButtonPanel.add("West",new Button("down"));
        sensorField = new TextField(3);
        sensorField.setBackground(Color.white);
        sensorField.setEditable(false);
        sensorField.setText(Integer.toString(sensorValue));
        sensorButtonPanel.add(sensorField);
        sensorButtonPanel.add("East",new Button("up"));
        sensorPanel.add("South",sensorButtonPanel);
        harnessPanel.add("South",sensorPanel);

        add("East",harnessPanel);
    }
    public void paint(Graphics g)
    {
        g.drawImage(image,0,0,this);
    }
    public boolean handleEvent(Event evt)
    {
        if (evt.id == Event.WINDOW_DESTROY)
            System.exit(0);
        return super.handleEvent(evt);
    }
    public boolean action(Event evt,Object arg)
    {
        if (arg.equals("down")) {
            if (sensorValue > 0) {
                sensorField.setText(Integer.toString(--sensorValue));
            }
        } else if (arg.equals("up")) {
            sensorField.setText(Integer.toString(++sensorValue));
        } else {
            return false;
        }
        repaint();
        return true;
    }
    public void displayMessage(int m)
    {
        if (m < 0)
            numField.setText(Integer.toString(-m));
        else
            msgField.setText(Integer.toString(m));
    }
```

```
    Image image;
    TextField sensorField;
    public static int sensorValue = 0; // simulated value for drivers
    TextField msgField;
    TextField numField;
}

# --------------------------------- End of Harness ------------------------------------
```

6 Process Modeling

Everything should be as simple as possible, but not simpler.—Albert Einstein

THIS CHAPTER EXPLAINS WHY IT IS IMPORTANT TO HAVE A PRECISE model of the FAST process. We also describe the ideas underlying the PASTA modeling approach used to create the FAST process model.

Motivations for Process Modeling

A process is a sequence of decision-making activities. For any engineering process, the engineers need to know what decisions they can make, when they can make them, what the results mean, and how they should be represented. Developing software means making decisions about the requirements for the software, the programs that should implement the requirements, the required properties of those programs (including properties such as their structure, their interfaces, and their performance), ways to verify that the programs meet their requirements, and the structure of the development organization. Artifacts—such as requirements documents, code files, and organization charts—capture the decisions made. Describing FAST means describing the artifacts that the application and domain engineers (and their managers) produce and use, the sequences of activities that they use to produce them, and the roles people play in producing them. Such a description is a process model; it gives us a reference for the process and a reasonably complete and consistent way of explaining it.

To ensure that FAST is systematic and to talk and write about it in a systematic way, we use a way of describing it that allows us to manage its evolution and that helps you to use it effectively. A good description gives us confidence that we have adequately covered all the steps in software development and that we can adequately describe FAST. A good description also helps you to repeat the process for many different software development projects and gives you a reference for it that helps you to perform the process. The description lets us describe changes to the process so that we can record the use of the process in practice and understand the consequences of proposed changes. It provides us with a reference that we can use for comparison as the process evolves.

As systems become bigger and more complex, the process used to produce them must provide for well-defined steps in their production, and the precision of the process definition becomes more important. For example, the task of making a change to a complex system becomes difficult and time-consuming if the software developer cannot find a good source of information that describes where in the system various types of decisions are contained.[1] A process that results in the documentation of such information in an easily understandable and easily accessible way makes the developers' jobs simpler, faster, and less error-prone. To be effective, the process must define the contents of the documentation and specify when the documentation is created and updated, what the form of the documentation is, who is responsible for creating and maintaining it, and where it can be found.

PASTA is a way to model complex processes in a graphical, systematic, precise, and structured way. You can use it to give a brief overview of a process or to give a description sufficiently precise and detailed so that it is suitable for automation. The FAST PASTA model in Chapters 9–13 serves a reference model for the FAST family of processes.

Because of the complication in a process such as FAST and because of the amount of backtracking and invention involved, no formal model will completely and accurately describe software development. Furthermore, the developers will inevitably change the process as they use it. Our goal is to be accurate in describing the work products of the process, the tasks that engineers enacting the process can and cannot be working on at any time, and the criteria for completing the work products. The model is incomplete in that we do not attempt to prescribe a total ordering on the events. Rather, at points in the process we specify that any one of a set of activities can proceed next. The engineers choose which of those activities to pursue.

Just as software development is a complex process, so is designing a software development process. The process designers must have a way to organize the

1. Typical decisions are how you communicate with hardware devices, how algorithms are implemented, how and when outputs are calculated, and how data are represented.

process so as to manage its complexity and modularize it so that it can be read, understood, and changed one part at a time. Organizations that use a process will change it to accommodate their changing needs over time, and process designers will keep track of different versions of a process as it evolves. PASTA models provide the capabilities that process designers need to maintain intellectual control over a continuously evolving family of processes.

For a new process to be successful, its designers must be able to communicate it simply and precisely to its users. A PASTA model forms the basis for such communication. We believe in this so strongly that we provide a PASTA model of the FAST process as part of this book. We expect it to define what we mean by FAST to potential users of FAST.

6.1 A PASTA Model as a Communications Medium

Process designers, process environment developers, and software developers see the process model as serving different purposes. For the process designers, the model is a way to represent the process and to baseline its current design. The model gives them a reference that they can use to compare with the process as it is used. For those who develop the environment that supports the use of the process—the process environment developers—the model serves as a specification for the environment that they must develop.

For the software developers, the model serves as a guide for what they must do at each step, as a source of templates for the artifacts that they produce and use, and as a way of training developers who are unfamiliar with the process. It answers the questions

Who should do what?

When do they do it?

How do they do it?

What should they produce?

What resources do they need?

How do they know when they're finished?

The model serves as a focal point for communication among the software developers, process designers, and process environment developers, as shown in Figure 6-1. Each group provides the others with feedback about how well the model

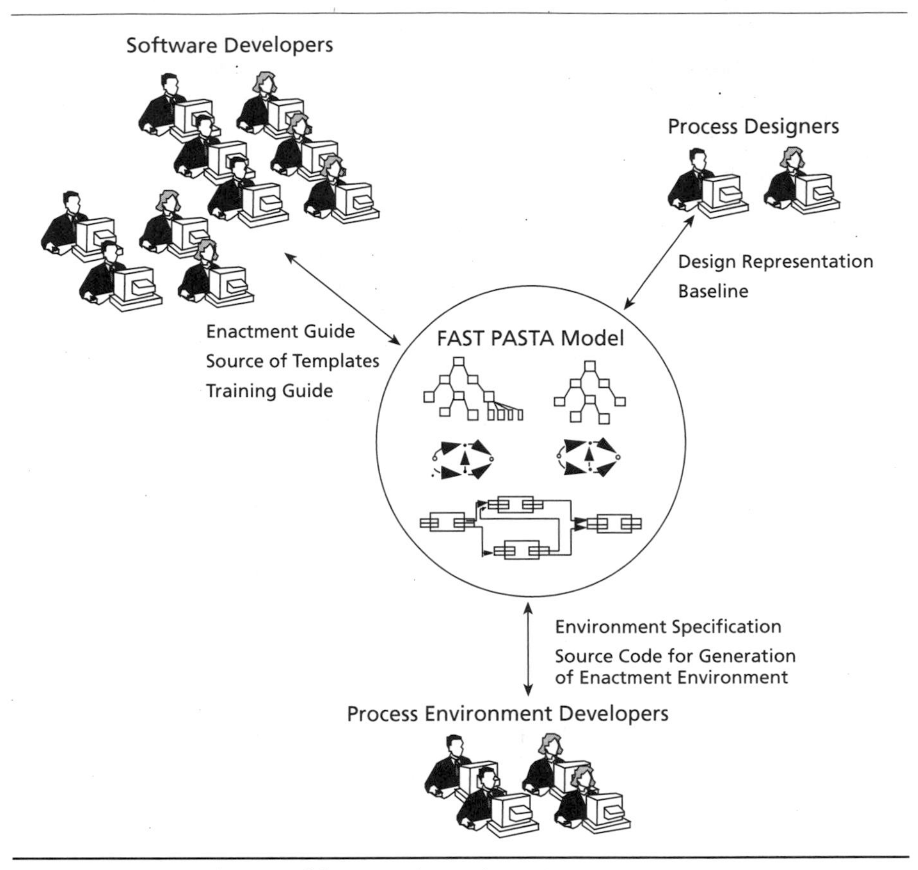

Figure 6-1. *A PASTA Model as Seen by Various Users*

serves their purposes, providing a mechanism for continuous process improvement. The situation is exactly analogous to a FAST process, as shown earlier in Figure 2-2, where the domain is process design, the application engineers are the process designers, the domain engineers are the process environment developers, and the customers are the software developers.

6.2 Elements of a PASTA Model

PASTA models are constructed using abstractions that are appropriate to process design and that enable the process users to answer the preceding questions. They are built from the following elements.

1. *Role:* A role can be used to represent a unit of responsibility, assignment, authority, or work force. Roles can be used to describe organizations and to give work assignments to people enacting a process. Roles indicate who can perform an activity.

2. *Artifact:* Artifacts represent final or intermediate work products or the information needed to produce them. Such work products may be documents, code, or various representations of information. For example, a set of data stored in a file may be an artifact. Artifacts indicate what must be produced.

3. *Artifact state:* An artifact state (A-state) is the condition of the artifact, usually an indication of the progress made toward completing the artifact. Artifacts change state as the result of activities performed during the process.

4. *Process state:* A process state (P-state) is a group of activities that is performed in a particular situation to satisfy a particular concern. For example, a design P-state might consist of a set of activities whose concern is how to organize software into meaningful chunks. The situation in which the P-state is performed (or active) is defined by an entry condition that must be satisfied before the P-state is entered. The effect of performing the P-state is specified by an exit condition. When the P-state is active and the exit condition becomes true, the process transitions out of the P-state. The entry and exit conditions for P-states are specified in terms of artifact states. The artifact states determine which P-states can be active at any time during enactment of the process.

   A P-state can be organized into substates each of which satisfies a subconcern or contributes to satisfaction of the concern of the P-state. Ultimately, each P-state is organized into operations on artifacts. P-states indicate what must be done to make progress, when it can be done, who can do it, and what the criteria are for completing an activity.

5. *Operation:* An operation is an activity that can be performed on one or more artifacts and that is not further organized into subactivities. Operations form the lowest level of the P-state hierarchy; a P-state that is completely decomposed into operations is not further decomposed. When performed, operations cause artifacts to transition from one state to another; operations' descriptions say how to perform them. Each operation has an entry and an exit condition that, respectively, define the condition that must be true before the operation can be performed and what must be true when the operation is complete. Operations indicate what must be done and who can do it.

6. *Analysis:* An analysis is an activity that provides information about the state of the process, its artifacts, and the roles of the people who are enacting it. Examples of information that might be provided by analyses include

- Which P-states are active
- What the current state of an artifact is
- How many people are currently enacting the process
- Which person is playing what role
- How many labor hours have been expended in enacting the process
- What defects have been found in a particular artifact
- How much code has been produced

   Analyses indicate what progress has been made, how fast it has been made, what resources have been used, and what the quality of the artifacts is.

7. *Relation:* Relations show relationships among process elements. The artifact, activity, and role hierarchies represent relations that are built into PASTA. You may need to add other specialized relationships, such as communications among roles, to model some processes. A process may impose a set of relations on artifacts for several different purposes, such as the following.
   - Completeness. For example, a design document may not be considered complete until the corresponding requirements document is complete.
   - Separation of concerns. For example, the information hidden in a module may be documented in a module guide, whereas the module's interface may be documented in an interface specification.
   - Chronological ordering. For example, a test specification may not be started until a requirements specification is baselined.

We often use relations to specify and implement analyses that perform completeness and consistency checks. We liken the key elements of PASTA to subjects, verbs, and objects; roles are the subjects, activities are the verbs, and artifacts are the objects. Figure 6-2 shows a domain engineer (role) qualifying a domain (activity) by using an economic model (artifact).

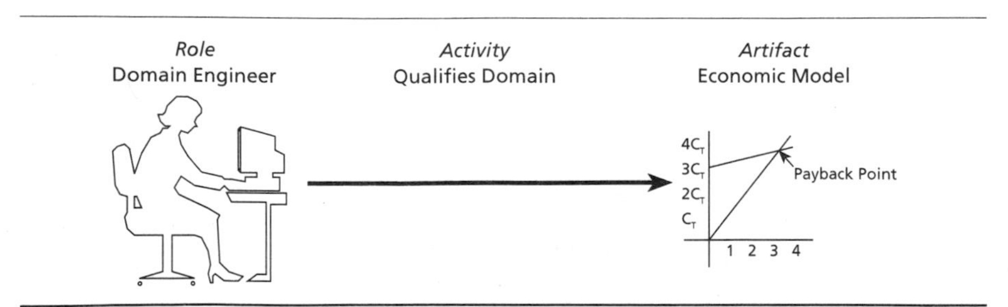

Figure 6-2. *Relationships among Role, Activity, and Artifact*

6.3 Process Activities as State Machines

PASTA assumes that the decision-making in a process can be characterized as a set of state machines that are executing in parallel, with each state corresponding to a set of activities to be performed by people enacting certain roles. PASTA uses state-based models of processes because the concurrency and backtracking that occur in complex processes such as software development can be directly mapped into a state model. In particular, a state model easily allows transitions to previously visited states, allowing us to represent backtracking. These transitions represent, for example, a designer redoing some or all of a design. Concurrency in the state machines allows progress in a number of different activities at the same time. An activity such as analyzing commonality is one of a number of states of the process that are possibly in progress.

A detailed model of FAST must be organized so that humans describing or reading about the process don't get lost in a sea of activity descriptions. The PASTA P-state hierarchy organizes activities so that we can describe and read them systematically. You define the hierarchy by decomposing each state machine for a PASTA activity into a set of substate machines so that the higher-level machine executes by executing the lower-level machines. For example, the activity representing the entire FAST process is organized into five substate machines: Qualify Domain, Engineer Domain, Engineer Application, Manage Project, and Change Family. Executing FAST means executing those five lower-level activities. Figure 6-3 shows this organization but does not specify the order of performance of the activities or the entry and exit conditions for each activity, all of which are described elsewhere in the model. The process modeler decides how deep the decomposition should be for any particular activity, so an activity such as Engineer Domain may have more levels in its decomposition than the activity Qualify Domain does. We have already seen the complete FAST activity hierarchy in Chapter 4 (shown in Figure 4-10) and a specialized version of it in Chapter 5 (shown in Figure 5-1).

We consider a P-state to be *elementary* if it has no substates, consisting solely of operations and analyses. A *composite* P-state is composed of substates. The P-state machine for a composite P-state consists of its substates and the transitions among them. We view all except the lowest-level activities as process states. When we say that a process state is composed of its substates, we mean that the lower-level states form a state machine that defines the upper-level state. The lowest-level activities are then operations that can be performed in their parent

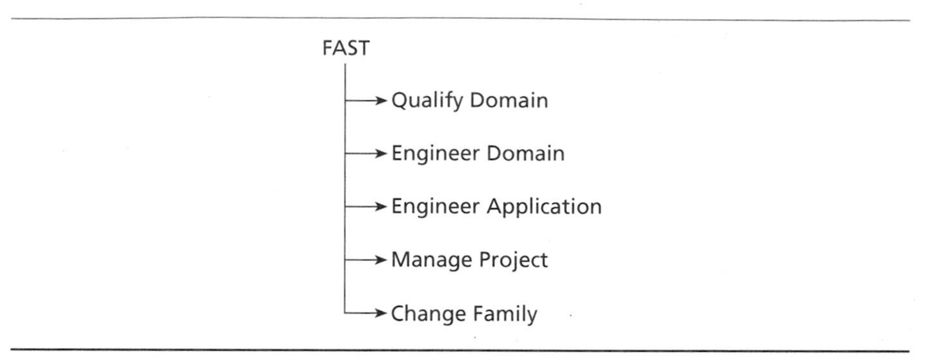

Figure 6-3. *FAST Activities*

states, subject to the entry and exit conditions for the operations and their parent state.

The root of the activity hierarchy is a single composite P-state whose entry condition is that the need exists to create the artifacts produced by the process and whose exit condition is that the artifacts have been produced. The bottom level in the hierarchy contains the set of operations that can be performed on artifacts during enactment of the process. Middle layers consist of composite P-states. Figure 4-10 shows the activity hierarchy for FAST. The root activity is FAST, and Analyze Commonality is one of the operations.

Using a state hierarchy helps the process modeler and the process user to keep track of where they are in the process, but it also permits the process states to be modeled at different levels of detail and permits the model to reflect the organization of the software developers. For example, organizing a set of states into a design state permits us to represent in a single abstract state both the unique characteristics of a design method and the activities performed by a design team. The substates of the design state give more detail about the method. In FAST, the state Implement Generation includes two variations for implementing a translator for an AML: either composition or compilation. When Implement Generation is decomposed further, the distinction between the two methods appears in possible alternative substates.

To describe the software development organization, we associate with each P-state the roles of people who can perform it, and we separately define the relationships among the roles. In this way the model dictates the organization of the developers.

6.4 Artifacts as State Machines

Artifacts are the work products of a software process and are typically documents or code. Most artifacts are composites, with their elementary building blocks defined at the lowest level of an artifact hierarchy. As with the activity hierarchy, the depth of decomposition is at the discretion of the process modeler. Figure 4-9 shows the FAST artifact hierarchy.

We usually define the states of the artifacts to correspond to milestones in the process of making key decisions, such as whether a family is economically viable, what the members of a family are, or what the application modeling language for a family should be. The results of these decisions are expressed as completions of milestones in the activities that create (or refine) the artifacts, such as analyzing an economic model, creating a commonality analysis, or defining the syntax and semantics for the AML.

As key decisions are made and milestones are completed, the states of one or more artifacts may change. From the artifact's view, during its lifetime it will sequence through various states as decisions are made. Often, making these decisions results in the artifact becoming closer to completion. Accordingly, we can associate a state machine with each artifact so that transitioning through the state machine represents making progress on completing the artifact.

For the FAST process, sample artifacts are the commonality analysis, the family design, and the application model. Typical states for these artifacts are the following.

- Referenced. An artifact has been referenced somewhere in the process, meaning that a need for it exists and that it must be created if it does not exist.
- Defined and Specified. The contents of the artifact have been defined and specified.
- Reviewed. The artifact has passed a review and has been accepted.

To identify clearly the names of states, we connect the components of a state's name with underscores. For example, Defined_And_Specified is the name of a state.

Table 6-1 shows some sample decisions, corresponding artifacts, and artifact states.

To characterize the state of a development, we characterize the state of the artifacts produced during the development process, the activities that are performed on artifacts (especially those that cause state changes in the artifacts), the

Table 6-1. Some Sample Decisions, Corresponding Artifacts, and Artifact States

Decision	Artifact(s)	States
Is the family economically viable?	Economic model	Referenced Started Reviewed
What are the members of the family?	Commonality analysis	Referenced Standard_Terminology_Established Commonalities_And_Variabilities_Established Variabilities_Parameterized Reviewed
How should family members be described?	Application modeling language	Commonality_Analysis_Reviewed Language_Type_Identified Language_Specified
How should the software for the family be organized to take advantage of the commonality among family members and the predicted variability in family members?	Family design	Referenced Defined_And_Specified Reviewed
What is the implementation of a component of the family design?	Code for the component	Referenced Designed Reviewed Tested
What progress toward engineering a domain has been made?	Report of milestones achieved and resources used	Referenced Delivered

conditions under which those activities are performed, and the roles of the people who perform them. For example, activities that might be performed on a commonality analysis include creating it, checking it for completeness and consistency, and conducting a formal review of it.

Just as we use a hierarchy to organize P-states for easier reading and writing, we use a hierarchy to organize artifacts. An artifact is elementary if it is not decomposed into other artifacts, and it is composite if it can be decomposed into subartifacts. Documents such as requirements specifications, design specifications, and test plans are usually composite artifacts. They are composed from sections that are intended to be read (and written) as a unit. Although each artifact must ultimately be composed of elementary artifacts, we do not limit the number of decomposition levels.

We use artifact hierarchies for several purposes, including identifying work assignments, monitoring progress, performing verification, building applications, and ensuring a technically sound solution to the problem of meeting requirements. There are a number of approaches to organizing systems hierarchically, such as the functional approach or the information hiding approach, each of which results in a different set of elementary artifacts. The set of artifacts to use and how they should be organized are process-dependent, and the decision is left to the process modeler. Artifacts in the FAST hierarchy include documents, tools, models, and code. As with state names, we use underscores to connect the components of artifact names.

Note that the code for a family member is an elementary artifact in the FAST PASTA model. We model code as elementary in FAST because it is generated and usually dealt with as a single entity. In a process in which code is composed by hand, we would probably model it as composite.

6.5 Prescribing the Order of Events

When necessary, the process designer can prescribe a particular sequencing of events. We think of this as enforcing a particular subprocess. For example, the formal review of a commonality analysis is always performed after the analysis has been checked for completeness and consistency; analyzing the commonality among family members always precedes designing the application modeling language. We believe that it is a major error to proceed with the language design before the domain is understood, and we encode this belief into the FAST process by prescribing the order in which the commonality analysis and language design activities can take place.

To prescribe the order of activities, PASTA uses the entry and exit conditions that specify when an activity can begin and what conditions must be true when it terminates. The entry and exit conditions are expressions on the states of artifacts. For example, the commonality analysis must be in the Reviewed state before the language design activity can start.

6.6 Prescribing a Methodology

Software processes vary in many ways, including the way the software is organized into parts, the relations used to define dependencies among the parts, and the artifacts produced and used during the process. (The two variations on the FAST domain engineering process—the compositional and compiler variations noted in Chapter 4, Section 4.3—are an example of process variation in which different activities and artifacts are used.) The process modeler specifies a methodology by prescribing the artifacts to be used, the activities to be performed and their sequencing, the roles that people play, the communications among the roles, and the relationships among the artifacts. The definitions of these elements of the process are the interpretation of the methodology. An engineer using the methodology follows the activities prescribed by the P-states to produce or refine the prescribed artifacts in the prescribed order. The greater the detail in the model, the more it tries to bind the engineer to a specific methodology.

6.7 The Role of Process Modeling in FAST

Process models play a multiplicity of roles in FAST. As shown in Figure 2-2, application engineering embodies the payback from using FAST. It is the process that the application engineer uses for producing family members using the production facilities for the family. As discussed in Chapter 2 and shown in Figure 2-1, both the application engineering process and the application engineering environment are products of domain engineering. Both are created by the domain engineer during domain engineering for use by the application engineer. Accordingly, the domain engineer must have some way of describing the application engineering process.

Defining the application engineering process, and the associated production facility, requires capturing knowledge (often known only to a few people) and incorporating it into a set of tools that can be widely distributed and used. Rather than being disseminated by word of mouth, the facts and assumptions needed to customize the software for the family are incorporated into an engineering environment and a process for using that environment. Because FAST requires the documentation of such facts and assumptions, they do not depart the organization when people leave. The domain engineer creates a model of the application engineering process to capture and document much of this knowledge.

We use process modeling as an activity outside the FAST process to describe FAST, and we use it as an activity within FAST to describe the application engineering process that is produced as part of domain engineering.

6.8 PASTA Abstractions

PASTA uses two state abstractions—one for artifact states (A-states) and a second one for process states (P-states)—and gets its name from its focus on process and artifact state transition abstractions. When a process is being enacted, we define its state to be the set of its active P-states, which in turn are defined by states of its artifacts. An enactment of the FAST process may be in the state Qualify_Domain when the artifact Economic_Model has been referenced. The need for the artifact has been recognized, but it has not yet been reviewed; it is still in the process of being defined, specified, and analyzed. The process may stay in the P-state Qualify_Domain as the Economic_Model transitions through the A-states Started, Defined_And_ Specified, and Reviewed. In this example, the P-state Qualify_Domain is defined to be the condition that the artifact Economic_Model is in one of the preceding A-states.

Activities performed by participants in the software process cause the state machines for the artifacts to transition from one A-state to another—that is, to become closer (or farther from) completion. Engineers use the A-states as a guide in making progress on artifacts. Indeed, we can generate from a PASTA process model a guide to tell the engineers who use the process what they can do at any point in the process, what artifact they should work on, what the form of the artifact is, what procedure they can use to produce it, and various other information to help them make progress through the process.

6.9 Creating PASTA Process Models

PASTA uses tree diagrams, forms, and state transition diagrams to describe process elements. The hierarchy of process states, the hierarchy of artifacts, and the hierarchy of roles are represented using trees. We use forms, represented as tables, to define process states and to define artifacts and their states. For process states, the forms specify state entry and exit conditions, state transitions, and the operations and analyses that can be performed in the states. We also use transition diagrams to describe the process state machines and the artifact state machines. PASTA provides a predefined set of tables and predefined semantics for the trees and diagrams it uses. Table 6-2 is the process state definition form for the P-state Qualify_Domain. Figure 6-4 is the corresponding P-state transition diagram, which shows the sub-P-states and gives an indication of the entry and exit conditions for the substates. For example, the entry to substate Gather_Data is a

Table 6-2. Process State Definition Form for Qualify_Domain

Process State Definition Form

Name	**Qualify_Domain**
Synopsis	Domain qualification is the process by which economic viability is determined for a domain. A domain is economically viable when the investment in domain engineering is more than repaid by the value obtained from domain engineering. The process consists of predicting the number of family members in the domain, the value of those family members, the cost of investing in domain engineering, and the cost of not investing in domain engineering. The result is an Economic_Model for the domain.
Main Role	Domain_Engineer, Domain_Manager
Entrance Condition	state-of(Economic_Model)=Referenced or state-of(Change_Report)=Domain_Change_Authorized
Artifacts List	Economic_Model
Information Artifacts	Environment
	OPERATION LIST
Name	**Gather_Data**
Synopsis	Gather the data needed to decide whether a domain exists and is worth engineering.
Name	**Analyze_Data**
Synopsis	Create an Economic_Model for the domain that can be used to evaluate the cost and time savings from applying domain engineering.
Name	**Reject**
Synopsis	The Economic_Model has been created and evaluated for the domain. It is not worth investing in the domain.
Name	**Accept**
Synopsis	Based on the evaluation of the Economic_Model for the domain, it is worth investing in the domain.
Exit Condition	state-of(Economic_Model)=Reviewed
Informal Specification	1. Gather data on the number of expected family members, current cost and time to develop family members. 2. Characterize process currently used to develop family members and identify potential savings in time and cost from automation. 3. Create an economic model that shows the difference in cost and time to develop family members using the current process and using domain engineering; include the cost of domain engineering in the model. 4. Use the model to decide whether the investment in domain engineering is worth the savings in cost and time for the domain.

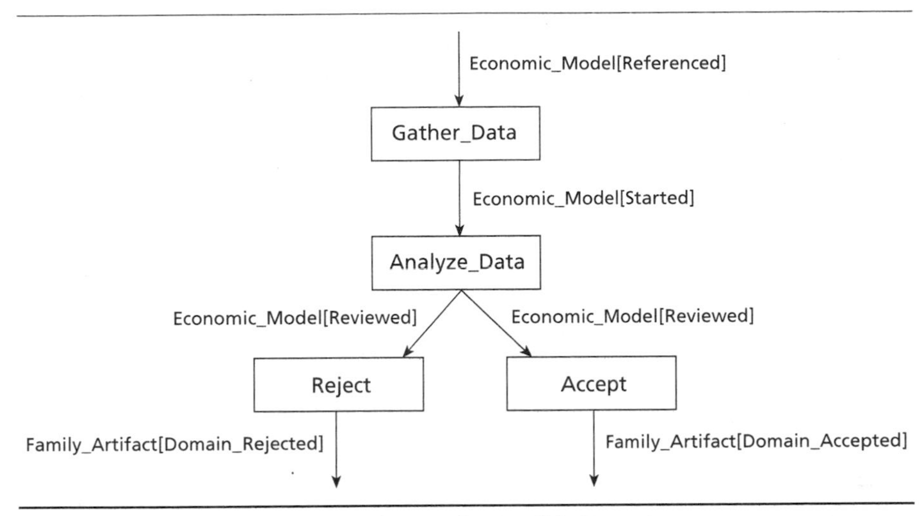

Figure 6-4. *P-State Transition Diagram for Qualify_Domain*

function of the artifact Economic_Model when its A-state is Referenced. The exact function is specified in the P-state definition form for Gather_Data (shown in Chapter 10).

We do not expect process designers, including ourselves, to create a satisfactory model in one pass. Rather, we develop a model, starting with simple versions of each of the artifact, process, and role trees and filling them out only to a few levels. We iterate several times on each tree, trying to get the structure of the activities and the artifacts right. As nodes in the trees are created, we record a short synopsis of each one. These synopses are used as the starting points for the artifact, P-state, operation, analysis, and role definition forms.

The completion of the definition forms and the state transition diagrams follows the development of the trees. Because the artifact state transitions can be effected only by operations that must appear in the P-state tree and because operations in the P-state tree must act on artifacts, we continuously check the consistency of the process as it is created.

To be more precise, the process engineer who uses PASTA to describe a process performs the following activities to create a PASTA process model. (Note that there is considerable iteration and concurrency in performing these activities.)

- Decide which artifacts are to be created, modified, and used during the process. Artifacts can be organized into subartifacts; for example, a document can be organized into sections, or code can be organized into modules. The complete set of artifacts is organized into a hierarchy, represented as a tree, that shows the decomposition of artifacts into their constituents. For example, a branch of the tree can show documentation organized into requirements documentation, design documentation, and test documentation. Each artifact in the tree is described in detail using a table. Figure 4-9 shows the top four levels of the artifacts for the FAST process, represented as a tree.

- Determine the states of the artifacts and the transitions among them. A state machine diagram is constructed for each artifact.
- Determine the states of the process. States can be organized into substates; for example, a design state could consist of a modular design state and an interface design state. The complete set of states is organized into a hierarchy, represented as a tree, that shows the decomposition of process states into their substates. We describe each process state in the tree in detail using a table and construct a state machine diagram for it. Figure 4-10 shows the top four levels of the process state tree for the FAST process. Note that it does not show sequencing or transitions among the states. Those concerns are addressed in the tables defining each state and in the state's transition diagrams.
- Determine the operations and analyses that can be performed in each state of the process. Each operation and analysis is described using a table.
- Determine the roles of the people who enact the process. Roles are arranged in a hierarchy represented as a tree. Each role in the tree is described using a table.
- Determine the relationships among the artifacts. Each relationship is described using a table.

To help in the creation of PASTA models, we use a PASTA editor that allows us to draw the tree diagrams and state transition diagrams and fill in templates for the forms. The semantics of PASTA models is built into the editor, allowing it to perform consistency checks between diagrams and trees, to fill in redundant information between trees and diagrams automatically, and to offer its users menus of existing process elements for reuse. For example, the editor maintains a list of all roles that the user has defined and allows the user to choose from the list when specifying roles to perform newly defined operations.

6.9.1 The Process User's Concerns

The preceding discussion focuses primarily on the concerns of the process designer. The users of the process—those who perform, or enact it—care about what they are required to do and how they are required to do it. To the extent that a process model makes their jobs easier, they will welcome it. To the extent that it makes their jobs harder, they will ignore, circumvent, complain about, and try to change it. No matter the case, it is unlikely that the same set of people will enact the same process in the same way twice in a row. Different situations will encourage or force them to change the process each time they enact it. To allow for differences in enactment, most process modeling techniques have an inherent flexibility. In PASTA this flexibility is manifested in a variety of ways. Each one allows the process designer to be as precise as necessary, from silence through machine-executable precision, in a variety of forms.

1. The artifact tree can be as detailed as necessary. The exact structure and form of each artifact can be prescribed in detail or can be left to the discretion of the enactors.
2. The P-state tree can be elaborated as much as necessary. Each P-state can be decomposed into a detailed set of substates or operations, with a prescribed sequencing among them, or it can be left elementary.
3. The precondition for entering a P-state or performing an operation or analysis can be relaxed or demanding in terms of the states of artifacts.
4. The operations to be performed in a P-state can be described with a precision that allows them to be automated, or they can be described in a way that allows the enactor considerable discretion in how to do the job.
5. The roles in the process can be many and narrowly focused or can be few of broad scope.

The initial version of a process model may have only a few levels in the P-state and artifact trees. As the uncertainty in the process decreases or there is greater willingness to invest more effort in process modeling, the trees can be further elaborated along with the descriptions of the P-states, operations, analyses, artifacts, and roles.

The representation of the process model to the process enactor is likely to be quite different from its representation to the process modeler. For example, the process enactor may see some combination of guidebooks, standard templates, on-line documentation, e-mail messages, and Web pages as the representation of the process that he or she is trying to enact. PASTA gives the process modeler flexibility in describing the interface to the process enactor, mostly through the definitions of the data types of artifacts, the form of the results of performing an operation or analysis, and the forms of communication used by people enacting different roles in the process. How the specifications from the process modeler are converted into the representation seen by the process enactor is beyond the scope of the process modeling concerns addressed by this book. We are here primarily concerned with how the process modeler describes the structure and behavior of a process such as FAST.

6.9.2 PASTA Models as Used by Process Environment Developers

A PASTA process model helps make clear which parts of the process can be automated and what automated support can be provided for the users of the process. For example, software development artifacts are usually written specifications, including requirements, designs, code, and documentation. A PASTA model of a software development process can clarify precisely the form of each specification, enabling the specifications to be stored electronically. Each specification can then be mapped to a file in a directory or perhaps to an object in a database. Because the model defines the allowable states of each artifact, the state of a specification also can be stored and can be tracked by developers and their managers. This approach makes most sense when the states correspond to progress in completing the specification so that the state transitions correspond to milestones in the development process.

PASTA models allow the process designer to be precise in defining state transitions, operations on artifacts, and analyses of the state of the process and of its artifacts. When the operations and analyses are automatable, their definitions in the model give the specifications for the programs that implement them.

An environment that supports the use of a process, when the process is defined in a PASTA model, provides capabilities such as the following.

- Electronically storing artifacts and their states and reporting on the states on request
- Performing analyses, as specified in the model, that provide the developers with information about the status of the project as it proceeds, including the status of artifacts, P-states, and operations, resources allocated and used, and quality of the code and documentation produced
- Executing automatable operations on artifacts
- Providing an on-line guide to the process definition for use by the process enactors and the process designers
- Providing on-line help for the process enactors, including suggestions for activities that can be performed next and help in performing them

It is also important to have the process definition available in electronic and hard copy forms for team members to reference.

6.10 Process Measurement Using PASTA

So far, our discussions have focused on the qualitative aspects of process modeling. A PASTA process model also lets you quantify the process so that you can know the resources needed to enact it, identify the degree to which activities may be bottlenecks, and quantify the effects of changes. Put another way, PASTA models provide you with a means to measure a process. PASTA gives you ways to think about measurement, including measures of the model and measures of the performance of the process as it is being enacted.

6.10.1 Measuring a Process Model

The measures you use to quantify a process model depend on your goals for creating the model. Measures might include estimators of process size and complexity, or predictors of resources needed to enact the process. For size and complexity measures you can use functions of the number of artifacts, P-states, and roles. However, such complexity measures are generally unsatisfactory because they depend on the decisions that the process modeler has made in decomposing the process into its elements. A different decomposition of the same process might give different values for the same complexity measure, suggesting that the complexity that you are measuring is the complexity of the representation and not the complexity of the underlying process. We know of no good way to resolve this problem, but we find that with time and experience we develop some understanding of the meaning of measures such as the number of artifacts or the number of artifact states.

6.10.2 Measuring Process Performance

Software developers are much more used to measuring the performance of a process as it is being enacted than measuring the complexity of a process. Many software development organizations use standard measures, such as the number of staff weeks to create artifacts such as files of code or design documents. Your organization's measures should depend on what's important to your organization. One way to define what you want to measure is to use the goal-question-metric approach.

PASTA models give you a context in which to define your measures. For example, each operation may have an associated estimate of the resources needed to perform it. You can define analyses for each P-state that calculate resources expended during the performance of the process while it is in the P-state. If your goal is to construct a process that optimizes the speed with which a new product is developed, you would define an analysis based on the time it takes to perform the operations in the process's P-states. If you are concerned with quality, you might define analyses that calculate various measures associated with defects.

Each analysis defined in a PASTA process model has an associated trigger event that causes the analysis to be invoked during the performance of the process. During the performance of a process, the results of the resource analyses can be compared against the predicted resource needs. This information can be fed back to the process modeler so that the model can be updated and fed back to the project manager. In this way, he or she can accurately track the progress of the project. Based on the results of the analyses, experienced project managers can change the process to improve its performance while it is being performed. As an organization collects data about its processes, the project managers can tailor the processes to their projects before the start of a project based on data from previous performances and on their experiences with the process.

6.11 Summary

PASTA models are based on the idea that processes can be represented as state machines. The state of the process is captured by two sets of state machines: those that represent the artifacts produced and used during the process, and those that represent the activities that take place during the process. The two kinds of state machines are closely related: the states of the artifacts determine the states of the activities. As engineers make decisions during the process, artifacts come closer to completion (sometimes farther from completion when a decision is made to return to a previous state) and transition through different states, usually arriving at a baselined or reviewed state. The state transitions on artifacts are caused by the completion of various activities, such as completing the list of commonalities in a commonality analysis or completing the construction of an economic model. Activities are performed by people assigned to certain roles, such as domain engineer or application engineer.

To help construct and understand a PASTA model, we arrange activities, artifacts, and roles in separate hierarchies. For example, the activity Engineer_Domain is organized into the subactivities Analyze_Domain and Implement_Domain. The sequencing among activities is determined by the entry and exit conditions for each activity, which are expressed in terms of the states of artifacts. In many cases, these conditions allow activities to proceed in parallel. An activity is specified by the following.

- Its place in the activity hierarchy
- A form that defines its entry and exit conditions, its subactivities, the people who can perform it (according to their roles), the artifacts that it can use, and an informal and a formal description of what it does
- A state transition diagram that defines its operation in terms of the operations of its subactivities and the artifacts on which they operate

Defining a process model helps you understand the process better. It forces you to be specific about activities, artifacts, and roles needed to enact the process. A PASTA model serves as a basis for changing a process to improve it and adapt it to changing needs.

From a PASTA model we can generate a guide for the people who use the process and a set of tools to help them. If the model includes analytical functions that define a set of measures, some of those tools can automate some of the data collection.

Having a precise process model provides the following benefits.

- It speeds technology adoption. The model can be used as a training aid and as a reference when the process is applied.
- It improves your understanding of the process. By forcing us to give a precise description of FAST, creating the FAST process model forced us to think through the FAST process.
- It gives users of the process a clear description of what they must do at all stages of enacting the process. It answers the questions

  What do I do next?

  How do I do it?

  How do I know when I'm finished?
- It provides a basis for automating support. The model gives guidance that could be used to build tools that support enactment of the process and that automate parts of the process; it is a source of requirements for automating the process.
- It provides a basis for measuring enactments of the process by defining the data that are collected during the process.
- It forms the basis for process improvement by providing the information that is needed to reason about the process. Variations on the process are easy

to describe using the PASTA notations and mechanisms; it is then easy to construct and perform scenarios that try out process variations.

- It forms the basis for process standardization by providing a standard way of describing processes.

The FAST process is a particularly apt target for process modeling because it can be described with relatively few process states. Its semantics are based on a particular approach to software production (the family approach), and it uses a specific set of artifacts. It also has sufficient complexity and variation to be a challenge for the modeler. In fact, the FAST PASTA model describes a family of processes, any of which could be called a FAST process.

The FAST PASTA model gives a standard, precise description of FAST. PASTA has also been used to model software inspection processes, the Booch software design method, a process for performing clinical trials of medical techniques, airplane design and assembly processes, and a nuclear waste handling process.

A PASTA model is a reference for a process. We do not view it as a static model but rather as a model that will change over time as the process that it describes evolves. The FAST PASTA model in this book is a reference model for the FAST process. Because FAST is really a family of processes, the model is there to help you understand FAST and to adapt it to your needs.

6.12 Nomenclature Introduced

Artifact hierarchy Hierarchy of artifacts defined by the relation "is a component of." B is a subartifact of A if B is a component of A.

Artifact state The condition of the artifact, usually an indication of the progress made toward completing the artifact. Artifacts change state only as the result of an operation.

A-state Abbreviation of artifact state.

Artifact tree Representation of the artifact hierarchy as a tree.

Process designer Person who defines a software development process.

Process environment developer Person responsible for developing the environment used to perform a process.

Process model A specification of a process.

Process state A group of activities that is performed in a particular situation to satisfy a particular concern. For example, a design process state may consist of a set of activities that are performed when a requirements specification has been completed and whose concern is how to organize software into meaningful chunks.

P-state Abbreviation of process state.

P-state hierarchy Hierarchy of process states defined by the relation "is a sub-activity of." P-state B is a substate of P-state A if B is an activity that can be performed as part of performing A.

P-state tree Representation of the P-state hierarchy as a tree.

6.13 Readings for Chapter 6

[1] Basili, V., and Weiss, D. "A Methodology for Collecting Valid Software Engineering Data." *IEEE Transactions on Software Engineering* SE-10, No. 6 (November 1984): 728–738.

A description of a measurement methodology based on the idea that software development measures should be directly related to software development goals, known as the goal-question-metric methodology.

[2] Cain, B., and Coplien, J. "A Role-Based Empirical Process Modeling Environment." *Proc. IEEE Second Int. Conf. Software Process*, Berlin (1993): 125–133.

An empirical approach to identifying the roles that people play in a software development process, accompanied by an informative visual technique for displaying the relationships among roles. The results are based on data gathered by interviews of software developers in a variety of organizations.

[3] Kirby, J. Jr., Lai, R.C.T., and Weiss D.M. "A Formalization of a Design Process." *Proc. 1990 Pacific Northwest Software Quality Conf.*, October 1990, pp. 93–114.

A description of the SCR design process using a method that was a forerunner to PASTA.

7 Representing a PASTA Model

THIS CHAPTER DESCRIBES THE VARIOUS FORMS THAT PASTA USES for describing process models. Each element of a model is specified using either a tree, a table, or a state transition diagram. We describe here the form and meaning of each type of representation.

7.1 Representations of PASTA Elements

The tree diagrams, forms, and state transition diagrams used by PASTA to describe process elements are standardized within PASTA and follow a prescribed format designed for describing elements of process models. Figure 7-1 shows the diagrams that PASTA uses for various process elements: trees for role, activity, and artifact hierarchies, and state transition diagrams for activity and artifact state machines.

Figure 7-2 shows the inverse view. For each type of representation it shows the process elements that use the representation.

The intent of the forms is to help a process modeler specify a process in a precise, concise, readable way as well as to provide a basis for measuring and automating some or all of the process (and the modeling process). Forms use a combination of informal (prose) and formal notations. For example, you can describe an analysis that is performed in a P-state using either English or a pseudocode notation. The latter could serve as the basis for writing a program that implements the analysis.

PASTA also uses diagrams to summarize information that would be tedious to extract from the forms, such as the hierarchies of P-states and artifacts. In

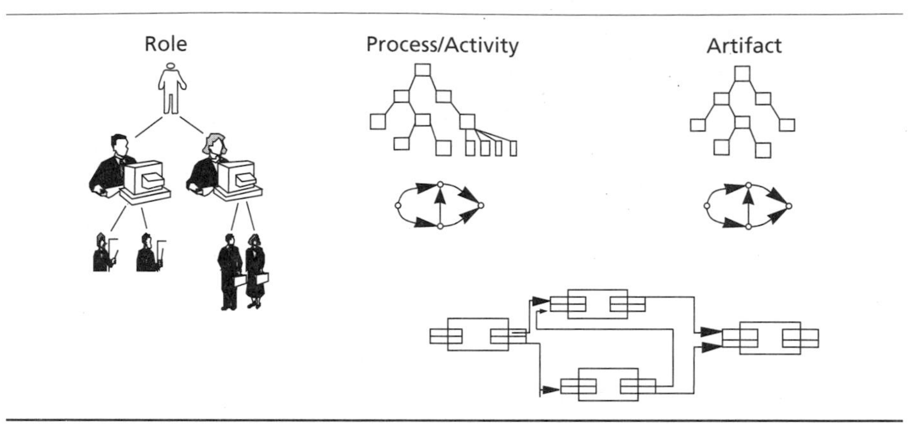

Figure 7-1. *Representations of Process Elements in PASTA*

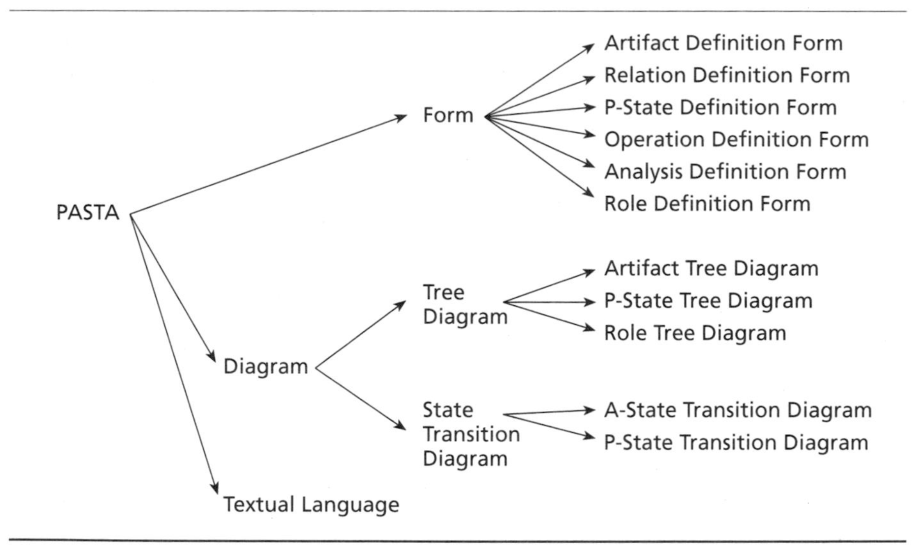

Figure 7-2. *PASTA Representations and Their Corresponding Process Elements*

general the forms are intended to define the complete semantics of the model. The diagrams summarize the forms and act as a visual complement to them. People who prefer visual representations may look at the diagrams first and the forms second; those who prefer textual representations may do the reverse. The remainder of this chapter describes the hierarchies (tree diagrams), forms (tables), and state machine diagrams used to represent PASTA models.

7.2 PASTA Forms

Table 7-1 summarizes the purposes of the forms that PASTA uses. Each of these forms is defined in greater detail in the rest of this section. You will notice that many of the forms contain redundant information. This is intended to help readability for the process designer. The redundancy is constructed in such a way that often an automated tool will be able to supply the redundant entries.

Table 7-1. *PASTA Forms*

Form	Purpose
Analysis Definition Form	Defines an analysis that can be performed in a P-state. Key elements include 1. How the analysis is triggered 2. The type of the result returned by the analysis 3. The artifacts used by the analysis 4. Specifications of the procedure used to perform the analysis
Artifact Definition Form	Defines the artifacts used by a process. Key elements include 1. Subartifacts, if any 2. States of the artifact 3. Relationships with other artifacts
Operation Definition Form	Defines an operation that can be performed in a P-state. Key elements include 1. Artifacts that can be changed by the operation 2. Entry and exit conditions for the operation 3. Specifications of the operation 4. People who can perform the operation (by roles)
P-State Definition Form	Defines a process state. Key elements include 1. People who can perform operations and invoke analyses in the P-state (by roles) 2. Artifacts that can be changed by operations in the P-state 3. Entry and exit conditions for the P-state 4. Substates 5. Operations and analyses that can be performed in the P-state
Relation Definition Form	Defines the relationships between pairs of artifacts. Used mostly when the state of one artifact may depend on the state of another artifact.
Role Definition Form	Defines a role used in a process. Key elements include 1. Subroles 2. Activities: operations and analyses that can be performed by the person enacting the role

7.2.1 Notational Considerations

Because we want the PASTA forms to be readable by humans and parseable by programs, names that consist of more than one word, such as Application_Modeling_Language, use underscores to connect the words to make parsing easier. Such underscoring applies to names of P-states, operations, analyses, artifacts, relations, and roles. In some places, such as entry and exit conditions for P-states, we use mathematical operators, such as state-of, with hyphenated names to distinguish them from the names of elements of the model.

We start with the artifact and process state definition forms because they are central to PASTA models.

7.2.2 Artifact Definition Form

Table 7-2 shows the Artifact Definition Form template used to record information about artifacts. An artifact has states, can have subartifacts, and can be related to other artifacts. The form is organized into sections.

- Description section. Contains entries for the name of the artifact; a brief synopsis of its purpose; its complexity, and the type of the data structure used to store information about the artifact.

  Artifacts that are decomposed into subartifacts are denoted as COMPOSITE. The artifact hierarchy tree, shown in Figure 4-9, shows the decomposition of FAST artifacts. For example, the domain model is defined as a composite artifact with the subartifacts economic model, commonality analysis, decision model, family design, composition mapping, application modeling language, toolset design and application engineering process. Artifacts that are not decomposed further are denoted as ELEMENTARY. In FAST, the application modeling language is an elementary artifact.

- State section. Defines the states of the artifact. For each state, this section contains a brief synopsis of the state and the condition that is true when the artifact is in the state. For elementary artifacts, there is no condition. For composite artifacts, the condition for each A-state is a logical function of the states of subartifacts; the A-states of a composite artifact are defined in terms of the states of its subartifacts. In the FAST PASTA model, the states of the domain model are defined in terms of the states of its subartifacts. Note that each subartifact is defined in its own artifact definition form.

- Subartifact section. Lists all the subartifacts of the artifact, including, for each subartifact, its name and a synopsis.

Table 7-2. *Artifact Definition Form Template*

Artifact Definition Form

Name	**Artifact name**	
Synopsis	Prose description of artifact	
Complexity Type	Either ELEMENTARY or COMPOSITE	
Data Type	Data type used to store information about the artifact, predefined or user-defined	
	A-STATE LIST	
Name	**The name of the state**	
Synopsis	Prose description of the meaning of the artifact state	
Condition	For artifacts that are ELEMENTARY—that is, not decomposed into subartifacts—this cell is blank. For composite artifacts, a logical function of the states of other artifacts	
	SUBARTIFACT LIST	
Name	**Subartifact name**	
Synopsis	Synopsis of the subartifact	
	RELATION LIST	
Relation Name	Names of related artifacts	Direction: To or From or both

- Relations section. Identifies all the relations between the artifact and other artifacts, including, for each relation, its name, the name of the other artifact involved in the relation, and the direction of the relation. We generally use such relations to indicate that the state of one artifact may change as a result of a state change in another artifact or to indicate that a change in one artifact may require a change in the other. If the relation between artifacts is asymmetric—for example, one artifact must change state before the other can—we indicate the direction of the asymmetry.

Table 7-3 and Table 7-4 are the artifact definition forms for the artifacts Decision_Model and Tool_Set_Design. The forms show that Decision_Model is an elementary artifact with states Reviewed, Defined_And_Specified, and Referenced. It is related to the artifacts Tool_Set_Design, Parameters_Of_Variation,

Table 7-3. Artifact Definition for Decision_Model

Artifact Definition Form

Name	**Decision_Model**	
Synopsis	The Decision_Model describes the decisions that must be made and the order in which they are made to produce an application. The decision model defines the primary concerns of the Application_Engineering_Process.	
Complexity Type	Elementary	
Data Type		
	A-STATE LIST	
Name	**Reviewed**	
Synopsis	The set of decisions has been reviewed to ensure that it captures all the variabilities defined in the Commonality_Analysis, that any ordering among decisions is necessary, and that every family member can be specified using the set of decisions.	
Condition		
Name	**Defined_And_Specified**	
Synopsis	The set of decisions for the domain has been identified. These decisions are used to specify family members. Making a complete set of decisions completely identifies a family member. The order in which decisions must be made to specify family members has been defined.	
Condition		
Name	**Referenced**	
Synopsis	A set of variabilities for the domain has been established as part of performing a commonality analysis.	
Condition		
	RELATION LIST	
Decision_Tool	Tool_Set_Design	From, To
Parameter_Decision	Parameters_Of_Variation	From, To
Decision_Process	Application_Engineering_Process	From, To

Table 7-4. *Artifact Definition for Tool_Set_Design*

Artifact Definition Form

Name	**Tool_Set_Design**	
Synopsis	The toolset consists of the tools that are part of the application engineering environment. They include tools for analyzing application models and generating applications from them. The toolset also includes supporting tools, such as editors. The Tool_Set_Design consists of the design for the set of tools, including at least a description of tools that are or will be included in the application engineering environment.	
Complexity Type	Elementary	
Data Type		
	A-STATE LIST	
Name	**Tool_Set_Designed**	
Synopsis	The tools needed to translate the Application_Modeling_Language and to provide any other support needed by the application engineers in generating family members are designed.	
Condition		
Name	**Tool_Family_Specified**	
Synopsis	The tools needed to translate the Application_Modeling_Language and to provide any other support needed by the application engineers in generating and validating family members have been identified, defined, and specified.	
Condition		
Name	**Language_Specified**	
Synopsis	The Application_Modeling_Language is in the language specified state; the syntax and semantics for the language have been designed and defined and the language has been reviewed.	
Condition		
	RELATION LIST	
Decision_Tool	Decision_Model	From, To
Tool_Implement	Analysis_Tools	From, To
Tool_Implement	Generation_Tools	From, To

and Application_Engineering_Process. In the FAST process, the decision model and the toolset design are related because each tool in the toolset supports making at least one decision in the decision model. Accordingly, the toolset design cannot transition to a state where it is fully specified (Tool_Family_Specified) until the decision model is in the state Reviewed. Furthermore, if the toolset design is changed so that it no longer corresponds to the steps in the decision model, then the decision model must change. The name of the relation is Decision_Tool, and the relation is symmetric; it is both from the decision model to the toolset design and from the toolset design to the decision model.[1]

7.2.3 A-State Machine Diagrams

In addition to the tabular description of the A-state machine for each artifact, PASTA shows the machine as a state transition diagram. Figure 7-3 shows the A-state transition diagram for the artifact domain-model for the FAST process. An A-state transition diagram is similar to a conventional state transition diagram; each arc represents an activity that causes an A-state change, and each node represents an A-state. For example, Figure 7-3 shows that the Domain_Model can transition from the state Referenced to the state Domain_Qualified when the operation Analyze_Data is performed. Each activity that appears on an arc must be an activity that is defined as part of the PASTA model for the process—that is, it must appear somewhere on the activity tree for the process. This constraint, and a corresponding constraint on P-state transition diagrams, allows you to cross-check for completeness between activities and artifacts.

7.2.4 Process State Definition Form

Table 7-5 shows the template for the Process State Definition form (PSDF) used to record information about process states. Table 7-6 shows the PSDF for the P-state Qualify_Domain. A P-state can have substates, operations that can change artifacts, analyses that provide information about artifacts but do not change them, and roles that can perform the operations and analyses (if an operation or analysis is automated, the role can invoke it). Each of these is listed in the PSDF but is defined in a separate form. For example, although the operations that can be performed in the P-state are listed in the form, each operation is defined in a

1. More precisely, there are two relations: one from Decision_Model to Tool_Set_Design and another one in the other direction. For convenience and simplicity, we condense them into one symmetric relation here.

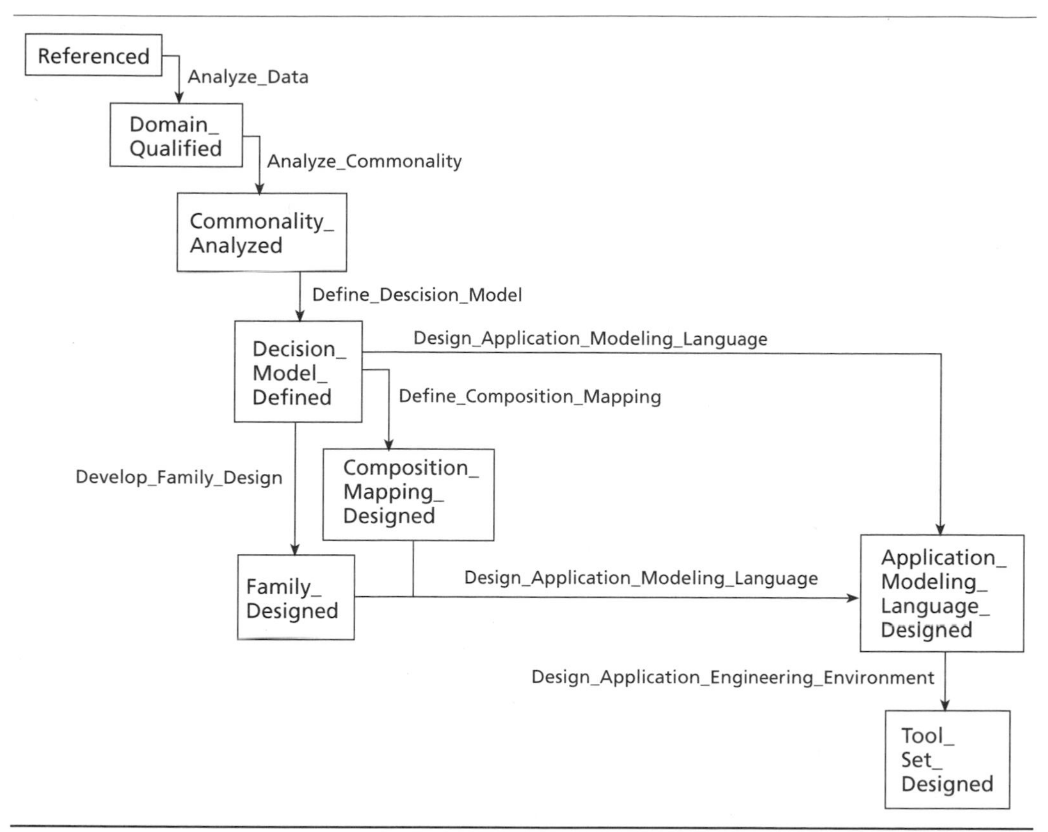

Figure 7-3. *A-State Machine for the Artifact Domain_Model*

separate operation definition form. The conditions for state entry and state exit are defined in the PSDF. Usually a P-state has either substates or operations but not both.

The PSDF is organized into the following sections.

- Description section. Entries for the name of the P-state, a brief description of the P-state, the roles that are concerned with activities in the state, and the entry condition for the P-state.
- Artifacts section. List of artifacts that are used in the state. Artifacts can be modified in the P-state or can be used only for information purposes.
- Substates section. List of the substates of the state. For each substate, this section includes the name and a synopsis of the substate. Each substate is defined elsewhere in its own PSDF.

Table 7-5. *Process State Definition Form Template*

Process State Definition Form

Name	**P-state name**
Synopsis	Prose description of process state
Main Role	Names of the roles principally concerned with activities in this state
Entrance Condition	Precondition for state entry
Artifacts List	List of artifacts used in the state: all artifacts that can be modified by an operation in the state.
Information Artifacts	List of artifacts referenced in the state: all artifacts that can be read but not changed by operations in the state.
	SUB-P-STATE LIST
Name	**Substate name**
Synopsis	Prose description of substate
	OPERATION LIST
Name	**Operation name**
Synopsis	Operation description
	ANALYSIS LIST
Name	**Analysis name**
Synopsis	Analysis description
Exit Condition	Postcondition at state exit
Informal Specification	
Formal Specification	

Table 7-6. Process State Definition Form for Qualify_Domain

Process State Definition Form

Name	**Qualify_Domain**
Synopsis	Domain qualification is the process by which economic viability is determined for a domain. The process consists of predicting the number of family members in the domain, the value of those family members, the cost of investing in domain engineering, and the cost of not investing in domain engineering. The latter is the cost of producing the family members without the use of an application engineering environment. The result is an Economic_Model for the domain.
Name	**Qualify_Domain**
Main Role	Domain_Engineer, Domain_Manager
Entrance Condition	state-of(Domain_Model) = Referenced
Artifacts List	Economic_Model
Information Artifacts	Environment
	OPERATION LIST
Name	**Gather Data**
Synopsis	Gather the data needed to decide whether a domain exists and is worth engineering.
Name	**Analyze_Data**
Synopsis	Create an Economic_Model for the domain that can be used to evaluate the cost and time savings from applying domain engineering.
Name	**Reject**
Synopsis	The Economic_Model has been created and evaluated for the domain. It is not worth investing in the domain.
Name	**Accept**
Synopsis	Based on the evaluation of the Economic_Model for the domain, it is worth investing in the domain.
Exit Condition	state-of(Economic_Model) = Reviewed
Informal Specification	1. Gather data on the number of expected family members, current cost, and time to develop family members. 2. Characterize process currently used to develop family members and identify potential savings in time and cost from automation. 3. Create an economic model that shows the difference in cost and time to develop family members using the current process and using domain engineering; include the cost of domain engineering in the model. 4. Use the model to decide whether the investment in domain engineering is worth the savings in cost and time for the domain.
Formal Specification	

- Operations section. List of the operations that can be performed in the state, with a synopsis of each operation. For each operation, this section includes its name and a synopsis. Each operation is defined elsewhere in its own operation definition form.
- Analysis section. List of the analyses that can be performed in the state. For each analysis, this section includes its name and a synopsis. Each analysis is defined elsewhere in its own analysis definition form.
- Exit condition. The condition that must be true to exit from the P-state.
- Specification section. Specification for performing the activity defined by the P-state. Both an informal specification and a formal specification may be supplied. We use informal specifications when the P-state is not automatable and use formal specifications when it is automatable. The formal specification defines for the environment engineer the effect of performing the P-state or an algorithm to be performed in the P-state.

Table 7-6 shows the PSDF for the P-state Qualify_Domain, an activity used to determine the economic viability of a domain. Domain engineers and domain managers perform the activities in this state. They use the artifact Economic_Model and change its state, and they refer to the artifact Environment.[2] The state is entered when the artifact Domain_Model is in the Referenced state, and the operations Gather_Data, Analyze_Data, Reject, and Accept can be performed in the state. The process exits the state when the Economic_Model is in the Reviewed state.

The informal specification outlines how to perform the activity but does not go into detail. More specificity is left to the state transition diagram and to the specifications of the operations in their own PSDFs. If the P-state could be automated, we would also supply a formal specification.[3] You can compare the process used in constructing the economic model for the floating weather station in Section 5.1 with the process described in the PSDF. The operations Gather_Data, Analyze_Data, and Accept are all performed. Although the states of the economic model are not explicitly identified in the example, you can still see that it passes through the states Referenced (when the Qualify_Domain P-state is first

2. Economic_Model is actually a subartifact of Environment, but changing the A-state of Economic_Model does not necessarily change the A-state of Environment. The use of Environment as an information artifact here means that parts of the Environment artifact other than Economic_Model may be used as information in performing the P-state.
3. Of course, we could also supply a formal specification even if the P-state is not automatable, but we have chosen not to do so here.

entered), Started (when the data needed to construct the model have been gathered), Defined_And_Specified (when the model has been constructed, as shown in Figure 5-2), and Reviewed (when the vice presidents agree that domain engineering should proceed).

7.2.5 P-State Machines

The process state definition form specifies the substates of the P-state but does not show the state transitions among them. PASTA uses a state transition diagram for this purpose. Figure 7-4 shows the P-state transition diagram for the P-state Qualify_Domain. For each substate and operation of the P-state, there is a rectangle in the diagram representing the substate and its entry and exit conditions. The representations of the entry conditions denote the artifacts and states used in defining the conditions, but they do not show the complete logical functions; they give only an indication of them. The complete functions are shown in the PSDF. For example, the entry condition for Gather_Data is that the state of the Economic_Model is Referenced. On exit from Gather_Data the state of the Economic_Model is Started.

Figure 7-4 shows the allowable state transitions. For example, starting in state Gather_Data the P-state can transition to Analyze_Data and then can go to either Accept or Reject. Transitions from these states transition the process out

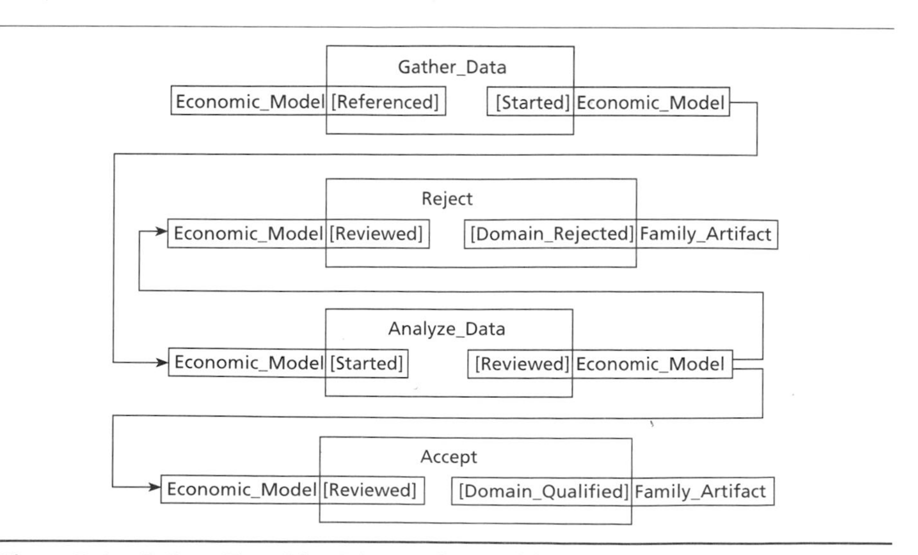

Figure 7-4. *P-State Transition Diagram for Qualify_Domain*

of the Qualify_Domain state. Note that operations in several P-states can change the state of an artifact. For example, both Accept and Reject can change the state of Family_Artifact, thereby affecting the P-state(s) for which the artifact state is a precondition. Also, a single A-state change can result in several P-state transitions, such as Economic_Model transitioning into the state Reviewed.

7.2.6 Relation Definition Form

Table 7-7 shows the template for the relation definition form, which is used to specify relations among artifacts. We consider each relation to be a set of ordered pairs. Table 7-8 shows the relations between the Tool_Set_Design and the Decision_Model. The synopsis defines the nature of the relation, and the list of

Table 7-7. *Relation Definition Form Template*

Relation Definition Form

Name	**Relation name**
Synopsis	Prose description of relation
POSSIBLE ARTIFACT PAIR LIST	
From:	Artifact name
To:	Artifact name

Table 7-8. *Relation Definitions for Decision_Tool*

Relation Definition Form

Name	**Decision_Tool**
Synopsis	Each tool in the toolset supports the making of a decision in the decision model. Note that some tools may provide indirect support for a number of decisions or for the decision model as a whole, such as tools that can be used to maintain the state of the application engineering process.
POSSIBLE ARTIFACT PAIR LIST	
From:	Family_Artifact.Environment.Domain_Model.Decision_Model
To:	Family_Artifact.Environment.Domain_Model.Tool_Set_Design
From:	Family_Artifact.Environment.Domain_Model.Tool_Set_Design
To:	Family_Artifact.Environment.Domain_Model.Decision_Model

ordered pairs shows that the relation is two-way: changes to the Decision_Model can affect the Tool_Set_Design and vice versa. Note that in this case we have used a fully qualified form of the name of each artifact to show how to define their positions in the artifact hierarchy unambiguously. Because the names are unique for this case, the full qualification is not strictly necessary.

7.2.7 Role Definition Form

Table 7-9 shows the template for the role definition form, and Table 7-10 shows the definition of the Domain_Manager role for FAST. Roles can be hierarchically structured to show organizational or project structure. For example, in the FAST process, the domain manager and application manager report to the project manager. The forms that define the P-states, operations, and analyses in which a role participates show all the roles that participate in the activity, thereby showing which roles cooperate on which activities. Each role in the hierarchy is defined in a role definition form, which is organized into the following sections.

- Description section. Gives the name and a brief synopsis of the role.
- Subrole section. Children of the role in the role hierarchy. The role hierarchy is often defined by the relation "reports to"; subroles report to their parent role. For example, in the FAST role hierarchy, shown in Chapter 4, Figure 4-8, the Domain_Engineer role reports to the Domain_Manager role.
- Activities section. For each activity that the role may perform, shows the name of the activity and a synopsis of it. The section is organized into no more than three lists: a P-state list, an operations list, and an analyses list.

Table 7-9. *Role Definition Form Template*

Role Definition Form

Name	**Role name**
Synopsis	Prose description of role
Member List	Roles that are children of the role
	P-STATE/OPERATION/ANALYSIS LISTS
Name	**Names of activities that the role can perform**
Synopsis	Prose description of activities

Table 7-10. *Role Definition for Domain_Manager*

Role Definition Form

Name	Domain_Manager
Synopsis	The domain manager manages the engineering of the domain, monitoring progress, setting priorities, and allocating resources to the domain engineering tasks.
Member List	Domain_Engineer, Environment_Engineer, Moderator, Recorder
	OPERATION LIST
Name	**Request_Family_Change**
Synopsis	Decide whether a proposed change is a domain change or an implementation change: either a change that will result in a change to the set of family members for the domain, or a change that will affect the implementation of the Application_Engineering_Environment but that will not affect the set of family members for the domain. A domain change is usually made in response to new, unforeseen customer requirements, and an implementation change is usually made in response to an application engineer's request to make the Application_Engineering_Environment easier or better to use.
Name	**Evaluate_Implementation_Change**
Synopsis	Evaluate a proposed implementation change to the family to determine whether it is worth making.
Name	**Evaluate_Domain_Change**
Synopsis	Evaluate a proposed domain change to the family to determine whether it is worth making.
Name	**Change_Family**
Synopsis	Make a change to the family that results in either a different set of family members for the family or different ways of generating family members. The change requires that the domain be reanalyzed or reimplemented, in part or in whole.
Name	**Reject**
Synopsis	The Economic_Model has been created and evaluated for the domain. It is not worth investing in the domain.

7.2.8 Operation Definition Form

Table 7-11 shows the template for the operation definition form. Operations can change artifacts, often resulting in an A-state transition, or can merely read them to obtain information needed to perform the operation. Each operation has an entry condition and an exit condition. The specification of an operation describes how to perform the operation and usually gives an algorithm for it in both informal and formal terms. Note that the specification is distinct from the

Table 7-11. *Operation Definition Form Template*

Operation Definition Form

Name	**Name of the operation**
Synopsis	Prose description of the operation
Role List	List of roles that can perform the operation
Entrance Condition	Precondition for performing the operation
Operation Type	Manual or Automated
Artifacts List	List of artifacts used by the operation—that is, all artifacts that can be modified by the operation (read-write artifacts)
Information Artifacts	List of artifacts referenced by the operation that can be read but not changed by the operation (read artifacts)
Exit Condition	Postcondition for the operation
Informal Specification	Prose description of the procedure used to perform the operation
Formal Specification	Formal description of the procedure used to perform the operation

postcondition for the operation, which describes its externally visible effect. The form is organized into the following sections.

- Description section. Contains entries for the name of the operation, a brief description of it, a list of the roles that can perform the operation, the entry condition for the operation, and the type of the operation (whether it is automated or is performed manually).
- Artifacts section. Lists the artifacts that are used by the operation. The artifacts are divided into two categories: those that can be modified by the operation (read-write artifacts), and those that provide information but cannot be modified (read artifacts).
- Exit condition. The condition that must be true to exit from the operation.
- Specification section. Specification for performing the operation. Both an informal specification and a formal specification can be supplied. We use informal specifications when the operation is not automatable and use formal specifications when it is automatable. The formal specification defines for the environment engineer the effect of performing the operation or an algorithm for performing it. The notation for both types of specifications is left to the discretion of the process designer.

Table 7-12 is an operation definition form used in the FAST model to define the operation for establishing a standard set of terminology for a family. This operation is part of the commonality analysis subprocess—that is, it is an operation within the P-state Analyze_Commonality. Its purpose is to define the significant terminology used by domain experts in discussing the domain. Also participating in the operation are the moderator and recorder roles. The operation is manual—it

Table 7-12. Operation Definition Form for Establish_Standard_Terminology

Operation Definition Form

Name	**Establish_Standard_Terminology**
Synopsis	Define all significant terms used by domain experts in discussing the requirements or engineering of systems in the domain.
Role List	Domain_Engineer, Moderator, Recorder
Entrance Condition	State-of(Commonality_Analysis) = Referenced
Operation Type	Manual
Artifacts List	Standard_Terminology
Information Artifacts	Domain_Model
Exit Condition	State-of(Standard_Terminology) = Reviewed
Informal Specification	Standard terminology for the domain consists of words and phrases that represent key ideas or abstractions in the domain. Such terminology is usually commonly used in discussing the domain. During the analysis of commonality for the domain, a dictionary of standard terminology is constructed as follows. 1. While creating a commonality analysis, domain experts frequently use a term, consisting of a word or a short phrase, to describe a key idea or abstraction in the domain, or a participant in the analysis identifies the need for a term to express some idea or abstraction. 2. Domain experts participating in the analysis identify possible definitions of the term. 3. Domain experts attempt to achieve consensus quickly on the definition of the term that best defines the key idea or abstraction. 4. If consensus is quickly achieved, the definition is entered into the dictionary section of the commonality analysis, and all uses of the term are italicized. 5. If consensus is not quickly achieved, defining the term is made into an issue and assigned to a domain expert. 6. As a homework assignment between meetings, the domain expert identifies alternative definitions of the term and recommends one. 7. The domain expert presents the alternative recommendations to the group of domain experts doing the analysis and recommends one. 8. The domain experts achieve consensus on the best alternative. 9. The definition is entered into the dictionary section of the commonality analysis, and all uses of the term are italicized.

cannot or has not been automated[4]—and it affects the state of the Standard_Terminology artifact and uses the domain model for information purposes. The operation can be performed when the artifact Commonality_Analysis is in the Referenced state, and it finishes when Standard_Terminology is in the Reviewed state. The informal specification for this operation is quite detailed, showing how the operation is to be performed step-by-step.

7.2.9 Analysis Definition Form

Table 7-13 shows the analysis definition form template. Table 7-14 is the definition of the FAST progress analysis. Analyses perform actions that provide information to the enactors of a process or to the tools that support the enactment of a process. They do not modify artifacts in the artifact hierarchy, but they can produce items such as reports, files, or e-mail messages that are not part of the artifact hierarchy for the process. One of their primary uses is to calculate the values of measures indicative of the state of the process and the artifacts produced

Table 7-13. *Analysis Definition Form Template*

Analysis Definition Form

Name	**Analysis name**
Synopsis	Prose description of the analysis
Information Artifacts	List of artifacts referenced by the operation
Analysis Function	Name of function to be invoked to perform analysis (if the analysis is automated)
Analysis Type	Management, quality, consistency, process_status, or user-defined
Informal Action	Prose description of the procedure used to perform the analysis
Formal Action	Formal specification of the procedure used to perform the analysis
Role List	List of roles that can perform the analysis
Trigger Type	Type of event that can trigger the analysis: state_entrance, state_exit, user, periodic, or operation invocation
Result Type	Form of the artifact that results from analysis: file, data_structure, diagram, table, text_report, or form
Action Type	Mode in which result of action is delivered: prompt_message, save_to_file, mail_to_role

4. Cannot be automated in this case.

Table 7-14. *Analysis Definition Form for Progress_Analysis*

Analysis Definition Form

Name	**Progress_Analysis**
Synopsis	This analysis generates a report on the progress of the project. The report describes what is next in the process and what is the current state of the active artifacts.
Information Artifacts	Family_Artifact
Analysis Function	Progress_calculation
Analysis Type	(management, process_status)
Informal Action	Note: The report produced by this analysis is called Progress_Report. It is a report on progress that identifies the existing P-states, the set of P-states that can become active next, the set of artifacts, their existing A-states and their next possible A-states. This information is stored in Progress_Report, in a form ready for presentation. Progress is calculated based on the following information: • The set of active P-states • The set of active artifacts • The set of current and possible next A-states for each active artifact • The set of P-states that could become active based on the next possible A-states of the active artifacts and the entry conditions for all P-states
Formal Action	1. Progress_Report.Current_Active_Artifact <- Identify_current_active_artifact() 2. Progress_Report.Current_Active_P-State <- Collect_current_active_P-State(Progress_Report.Current_Active_Artifact) 3. Progress_Report.Next_Possible_Active_P-State<- Collect_next_possible_active_P-State(Progress_Report.Current_Active_Artifact)
Role List	Project_Manager, Domain_Manager, Application_Manager
Trigger Type	(state_entrance, state-exit, user)
Result Type	(file:progress_file, table:progress_table)
Action Type	(prompt_message, save_to_file)

during the process, that is, to report on the progress of the enactment. For example, the FAST process includes a resource analysis that indicates the resources used during the process enactment. The analysis definition form is organized into the following sections.

- Description section. Contains entries for the name of the analysis, a brief description of it, the artifacts referenced by it, the name of a function that, when invoked, performs the analysis (for automated analyses), and the type of the analysis (management, quality, consistency, process_status, or user-defined).

- Specification section. Lists the actions taken by the analysis. As with operations, we include both an informal and a formal specification of the analysis.
- Roles section. Shows a list of the roles that can perform the analysis.
- Input/output section. Contains a list of the inputs and outputs for the analysis, including the type of events that can trigger the analysis (state_entrance, state_exit, user, periodic, or operation invocation), the type of the result of the analysis (file, data_structure, diagram, table, text_report, or form), and the mode in which the result of the action is delivered (prompt_message, save_to_file, mail_to_role).

The progress analysis specified in Table 7-14 generates a report on the progress of the project. It uses the Family_Artifact for information. The informal specification indicates the information reported by the analysis—namely, the sets of active P-states and artifacts, and the P-states and artifacts that could next become active. The formal specification describes an algorithm for performing the analysis based on the existence of a set of procedures that provide the data needed. The output of the analysis is a file and table. It is triggered by one of three conditions: entry to a state, exit from a state, or by request from someone performing one of the appropriate roles. When the analysis is completed, the analysis can send e-mail to the person who requested it and can save in a file an indication that the analysis is finished.

7.3 Summary

PASTA uses tree diagrams to provide a hierarchical view of the activities, artifacts, and roles in a process model, and it uses tables to define the individual P-states, operations, analyses, artifacts, roles, and relations used in a process model. It also uses state transition diagrams to describe the state machines for artifacts and P-states. The easiest way to get an overview of a PASTA model is to start with the trees that define the artifact and activity hierarchies. You can then use the tables and state transition diagrams to trace particular paths through the process and to find explanations and specifications for the operations and analyses performed as part of the process described by the model. Figure 7-2 and Table 7-1 show the set of forms and diagrams that PASTA uses.

7.4 Nomenclature Introduced

Analysis definition form Table used to specify a P-state that is an analysis.

Artifact definition form Table used to define an artifact.

Operation definition form Table used to specify a P-state that is an operation.

P-State definition form Table used to specify a P-state that is not an operation or analysis.

Relation definition form Table used to specify the existence of a relation between two process elements.

Role definition form Table used to define a role.

7.5 Reading for Chapter 7

[1] Harel, D. "STATECHARTS: A Visual Formalism for Complex Systems." *Science of Computer Programming* 8 (1987): 231–274.

Statecharts are a method of describing a process as a set of concurrent state machines, in the same spirit as PASTA.

8 An Overview of the FAST PASTA Model

THIS CHAPTER HELPS YOU TO NAVIGATE THROUGH THE FAST PASTA model. It explains the structure of the artifacts, activities, and roles in the model and gives a brief description of each element.

8.1 FAST Model Hierarchies

We find that PASTA models are easiest to understand if you begin with the activity, artifact, and role hierarchies. Figure 8-1 and Figure 8-2 are more detailed versions of the FAST artifact and activity trees than those shown in Figure 4-9 and Figure 4-10. The FAST role hierarchy is shown in Figure 8-3. (Note that the nature of the PASTA models allows you to examine the model to any depth desired; you may initially want to look only at the first two or three levels in the artifact and activity trees.) The FAST formal model shown here contains 10 roles that use 62 different activities on 38 different artifacts.

Together, the Commands and Reports family described in Chapter 3 and the Floating Weather Station family described in Chapter 5 provide examples of the use of most of these artifacts and activities. The next few sections describe the FAST artifacts, activities, and roles and provide references to their use in our two sample domains.[1] Chapters 9–13 contain the definition forms for the artifacts, roles, process states, operations, analyses, and relations for the complete FAST PASTA model.

1. In the following sections, notations such as EC 3.3 or FWS 5.1 refer to specific sections of the chapters describing the Executable Commands (Chapter 3) and Floating Weather Station (Chapter 5) examples.

8.2 FAST Artifacts

Figure 8-1 shows the FAST artifact hierarchy. Family is the root artifact; it represents all artifacts used in FAST. The artifacts are organized into three subgroups: environment artifacts, application artifacts, and change report artifacts.

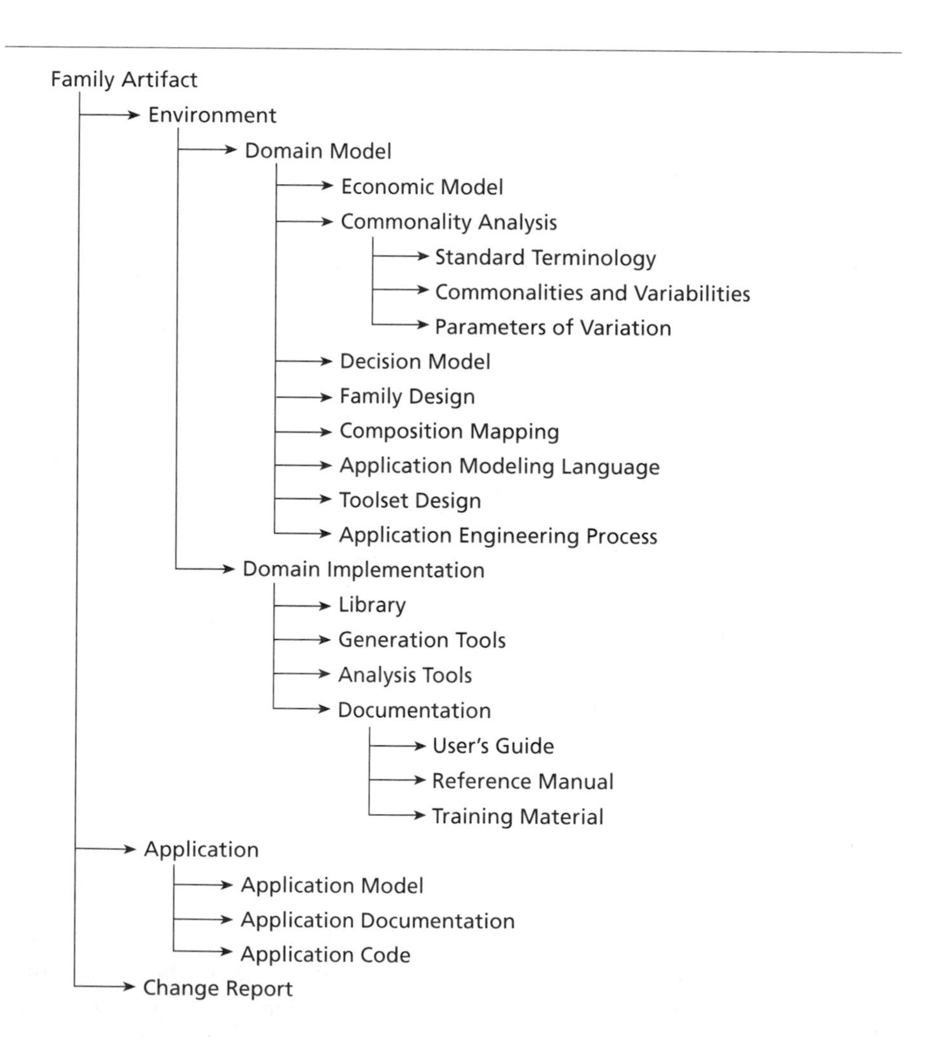

Figure 8-1. *FAST Artifact Tree*

8.2.1 Environment Artifacts

Environment artifacts are used to create and refine an application engineering environment. This group has five subartifacts: the domain model, the library, generation tools, analysis tools, and documentation. The library, generation tools, and analysis tools are the primary components of the application engineering environment.

8.2.1.1 Domain_Model

The Domain_Model consists of two kinds of artifacts: specifications for the contents and functions of various parts of the application engineering environment and the artifacts used in the analysis that produces the specifications. Domain_Model has the following subartifacts.

- Economic_Model. An analysis of economic viability for the domain over its life cycle. The analysis includes an estimate of the number of family members in the domain, the cost of producing the application engineering environment, the cost of producing applications using the environment, and the cost of producing them without the environment. (FWS 5.1)
- Commonality_Analysis. Definition of the family, containing both informal and formal descriptions. Primary elements are a set of terms that define a vocabulary for the family; a set of commonalities, in the form of assumptions, that are true for all family members; a set of variabilities, in the form of assumptions, that define how family members differ; and a set of parameters of variation that specify the range and decision time for each variability. (FWS 5.2.1.1, EC 3.1) Commonality analysis has three subartifacts.
    1. Standard_Terminology. Definition of significant terminology used by experts in discussing requirements and applications in the domain.
    2. Commonalities_And_Variabilities. A description of what is common to all systems in the domain and what varies among applications in the domain. Commonalities and variabilities are stated as assumptions.
    3. Parameters_Of_Variation. Each parameter of variation is a formalization of a decision that can vary to produce different family members. Parameters of variation are derived from variabilities so that each variability is specified by at least one parameter of variation.
- Decision_Model. The decisions that must be made and the order in which they are made to produce an application. The decision model defines the primary concerns of the application engineering process. (FWS 5.2.1.2)

- Family_Design. A design common to all family members. Such a design may consist of specifications for a set of abstract modules, relationships among them, and the parameters used in generating each concrete module from the corresponding abstract module. The family design is used with the compositional approach for implementing generation of family members. (FWS 5.2.1.3)
- Composition_Mapping. For each decision expressible in the application modeling language the composition mapping specifies the abstract modules in the family design that are needed to implement the decision. It specifies how decisions captured in an application model are used to provide values of the parameters used to instantiate abstract modules. The composition mapping is used in the compositional approach for implementing generation of family members. (FWS 5.2.2.1)
- Application_Modeling_Language. A specification language used to describe applications. The decisions that are identified by variabilities and their corresponding parameters of variation in the commonality analysis must be expressible in the application modeling language. A specification in the application modeling language is an application model and is used for generating the code and documentation for the application. It is also used as the basis for analyzing the characteristics of the application. (EC 3.3)
- Tool_Set_Design. A design that shows how the application engineering process is supported by a set of tools that form the application engineering environment, including tools for analyzing application models and generating applications from them. The toolset also includes supporting tools, such as editors. The toolset design consists of the design for the set of tools, including at least a description of the tools that are or will be included in the application engineering environment. (FWS 5.2.1.6)
- Application_Engineering_Process. The process used by application engineers to model applications and generate the code and documentation for them. The application engineering process is based on the decision model and the toolset design because it involves using the toolset to implement and record the decisions described in the decision model. (FWS 5.2.1.5)

8.2.1.2 Domain_Implementation

The Domain_Implementation consists of all the code and tools needed to produce family members.

- Library. A collection of component templates used to create code and documentation for applications. Such a library is usually needed in the compositional approach when applications are created by generating and integrating instances of templates stored in the library. (FWS 5.2.2.1, EC 3.4)

- Generation_Tools. Tools used to generate code and documentation for applications. (FWS 5.2.2.1, EC 3.4)
- Analysis_Tools. Tools used to analyze application models to help application engineers validate the models.
- Documentation. The documentation needed to understand how to use and maintain the application engineering environment, including a description of the application engineering process. Included are a user manual, a reference manual, and materials used for training for the environment. (FWS 5.2.2.2, EC 3.4)

8.2.2 Application Artifacts

Application artifacts consist of artifacts that are delivered as part of an application and supporting artifacts needed to produce the deliverable artifacts. This group has three subartifacts.

- Application_Model. A model of the application from which deliverable code and documentation for the application are generated. The application model is created by the application engineer using the application modeling language; he or she analyzes it to ensure that the customer's requirements are properly met. (FWS 5.2.1.4, EC 3.2)
- Application_Documentation. Customer documentation for the application. The decisions needed to generate the documentation are included in the application model; the application modeling language supports the specification of documentation. It may not be possible to generate all documentation for every application. Parts of the documentation that cannot be generated still transition through the same states as the documentation that is generated from the application model. (EC 3.4)
- Application_Code. Deliverable code for the application. The decisions needed to generate the code are included in the application model. It may not be possible to generate all code for every application. Parts of the code that cannot be generated still transition through the same states as the code that is generated from the application model. These states generally correspond to typical manual code development processes. (FWS 5.2.2.1)

8.2.3 Change_Report

Change_Report is used to request changes to the domain, including changes to the family brought on by changing marketplace trends and changes that make the application engineering environment more efficient and easier to use.

8.3 FAST Activities

Figure 8-2 shows the FAST activities hierarchy. The activity FAST is the root activity; it represents the collection of all the activities that take place during an enactment of the FAST process—that is, all activities needed to make it possible to generate applications as members of a family. FAST activities are organized into five subactivities: qualify domain, engineer domain, engineer application, manage project, and change family. Although our descriptions of these activities focus on creating new artifacts, they apply equally well to revising and refining existing artifacts.

8.3.1 Qualify_Domain

Qualify_Domain is the process for determining the economic viability of a domain. It includes analyzing the economics of the domain to be sure that it is worth engineering. (FWS 5.1)

8.3.2 Engineer_Domain

Engineer_Domain is the activity that creates and supports a standardized application engineering process and an application engineering environment that supports the process. Its two subactivities are analyze domain and implement domain. (FWS 5.2)

8.3.2.1 Analyze_Domain

Analyze_Domain is an activity for creating the specifications for an application engineering environment. Key parts of the activity include defining the family of which the domain is composed, designing an application modeling language in which to describe members of the family, and specifying the tools needed to analyze application models and to generate family members from application models. (FWS 5.2.1, EC 3.1) Its subactivities are as follows.

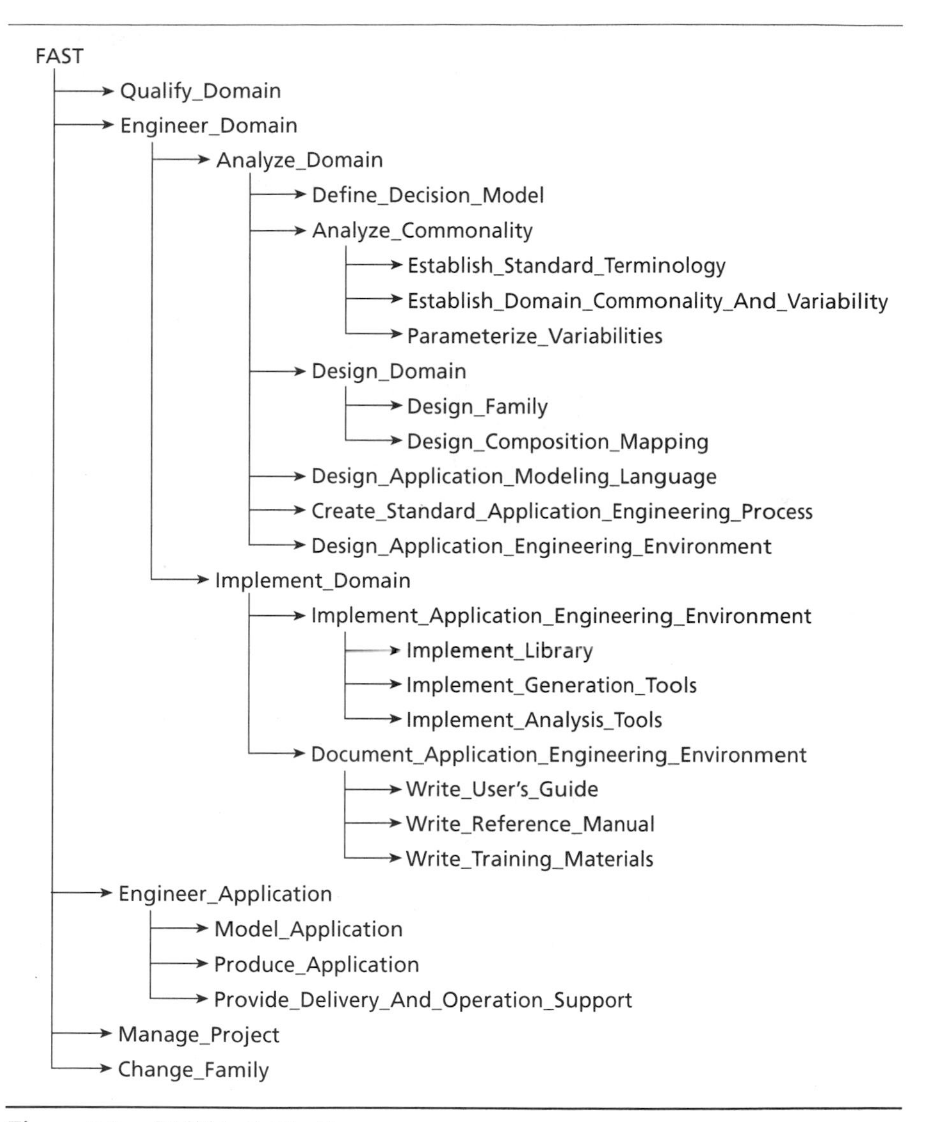

Figure 8-2. *FAST Activities Tree*

- Define_Decision_Model. Defining or refining a decision model consists of defining or refining the set of requirements decisions and engineering decisions that an application engineer must resolve in order to describe and construct a product. (FWS 5.2.1.2)

- Analyze_Commonality. Analyzing commonality consists of creating a commonality analysis that defines and bounds the family. (FWS 5.2.1.1) The activity includes the following.

  - Establish_Standard_Terminology. Define a set of standard terminology for the family.
  - Establish_Domain_Commonality_And_Variability. Identify assumptions that are common to all family members (commonalities) and identify assumptions that distinguish family members from one another (variabilities).
  - Parameterize_Variabilities. Define parameters of variation that quantify variabilities.

- Design_Domain. When the compositional approach is used for implementing the domain (see Chapter 4, Section 4.3), designing a family consists of creating or refining a design common to all family members, known as a family design, and creating a mapping, known as the composition mapping, between the application modeling language for the domain and the components specified in the design. When the compiler approach is used, the Design_Domain activity may not be used, although it is sometimes helpful in developing the compiler. (FWS 5.2.1.3) The subactivities are as follows.
  - Design_Family. Designing a family consists of creating a family design that can be used for generating members of the family. You can create such a design by organizing the software into information hiding modules; each module's secret is how to implement a parameter of variation.
  - Design_Composition_Mapping. The composition mapping provides automated traceability between specifications in the application modeling language and templates specified by the family design. You use the mapping to generate applications by mapping the values of parameters of variation expressed in the application modeling language into values of parameters to the templates specified in the family design. Then instantiate and integrate those templates.

- Design_Application_Modeling_Language. The application modeling language for a family is a language used for specifying family members. The language must be able to express the parameters of variation defined during the commonality analysis. Designing the language means designing the syntax and semantics to express the parameters of variation. The language designer uses the commonality analysis as the basis for the semantics. The abstractions identified in the commonality analysis often inspire the presentation of the language so that it appears natural for the application engineers. (FWS 5.2.1.4, EC 3.3)

- Create_Standard_Application_Engineering_Process. Creating the application engineering process requires the domain engineer to decide how the decisions to be made by the application engineers will be incorporated into a standard process for the domain, particularly how those decisions will be supported by the set of tools that will constitute the application engineering environment. Because the decisions are identified in the decision model, the domain engineer must map the decision model into a process. (FWS 5.2.1.5)

- Design_Application_Engineering_Environment. The application engineering environment consists of a set of tools that is used to analyze application models and generate code and documentation from them. Designing the environment means identifying the tools and deciding how they will support the application engineering process, including how they will communicate with one another and with the application engineers who will use them. It also includes designing the individual tools or identifying existing tools that can be used in the environment. (FWS 5.2.1.6, EC 3.3, 3.4)

8.3.3 Implement_Domain

The Implement_Domain activity consists of constructing the application engineering environment for the domain. The environment is built to the specifications determined during the analyze domain activity, which are expressed as the domain model. Implement_Domain's subactivities are as follows.

- Implement_Application_Engineering_Environment. This is the activity for developing the tools that form the application engineering environment. This activity is based on the Tool_Set_Design, the design of the Application_Modeling_Language, the Application_Engineering_Process, and the Domain_Design. (FWS 5.2.2.1)

- Document_Application_Engineering_Environment. This activity creates all the documentation needed to maintain and use the application engineering environment. The documentation includes user's manuals for the tools, training materials for the environment, and documentation needed to change the environment as the family evolves. The artifacts created during many of the domain analysis activities form part of the maintenance documentation for the environment. Of particular importance are the artifacts created when you design the domain, design the application engineering environment, create the application engineering process, and analyze commonality. (FWS 5.2.2.2, EC 3.4)

8.3.4 Engineer_Application

The Engineer_Application activity is an iterative process for constructing applications to meet customer requirements. Each application is considered a member of a family and is defined by an application model. An application engineering environment for the family is used to analyze application models and generate code and documentation from them. Engineer_Application has three subactivities.

- Model_Application. Modeling the application is the payoff activity in the FAST process. It consists of modeling a customer's requirements for an application as a specification in the application modeling language. The application engineer can analyze the model using the tools in the application engineering environment and then generate the code and documentation for the application from the model.
- Produce_Application. This activity produces the application and its documentation using the application engineering environment and the application model. When not all of the application can be generated, some parts of the application are developed manually.
- Delivery_And_Operation Support. This activity consists of delivering the application to the customer and providing operational support for it as agreed with the customer.

8.3.5 Manage_Project

Managing the project consists of managing the job of identifying and satisfying customer requirements using an application engineering environment. It includes the traditional tasks of management, such as scheduling, allocating, and monitoring resources. Managers can use traditional management techniques for application engineering projects provided that they understand the application engineering process. Consequently, the FAST PASTA model does not elaborate on the management aspects. You can tailor the model to create management activities specialized to your organization.

8.3.6 Change_Family

Successful software families evolve over time and need mechanisms to control and manage their evolution. Change_Family is the activity that provides the mechanism for changing a family, either to allow for changes in the set of family members that can be created with the application engineering environment or to make the generation of family members easier and more efficient with fewer defects. You can adapt standard change management techniques to FAST projects, so the FAST PASTA model does not elaborate on those aspects in any great detail. As with project management, you can tailor the model to create change management activities specialized to your organization.

8.4 FAST Roles

Figure 8-3 shows the role hierarchy for FAST projects.

8.4.1 FAST Manager

The FAST manager manages the engineering and evolution of the domain and the engineering of the applications in the domain. The application manager and the domain manager report to the FAST manager.

8.4.1.1 Domain Manager

The domain manager manages the engineering of the domain, including monitoring progress, setting priorities, and allocating resources to the domain engineering tasks. The domain engineer and the environment engineer report to the domain manager.

- Domain Engineer. Responsible for carrying out all activities needed to produce the domain model, to create a standard application engineering process, and to design the application engineering environment. He or she performs the last two activities in cooperation with the environment engineer.
- Environment Engineer. Responsible for carrying out all activities needed to implement the domain model.

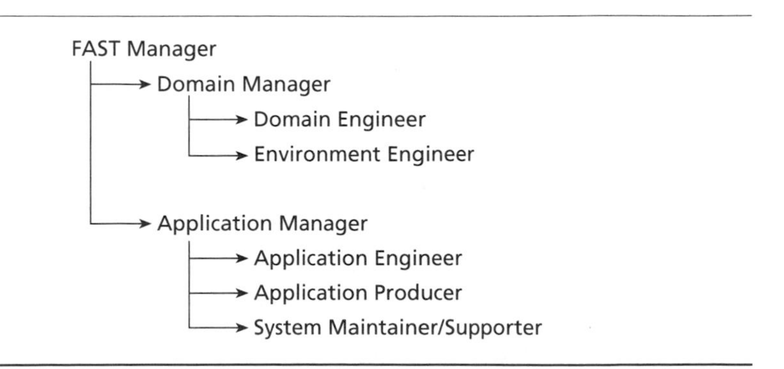

Figure 8-3. *FAST Roles*

8.4.1.2 Application Manager

The application manager is responsible for managing the production of applications, including monitoring progress, setting priorities, and allocating resources to the application engineering tasks. The application engineer, the application producer, and the system maintainer report to the application manager.

- Application Engineer. Responsible for performing the activities of engineering the application, which includes determining and validating customer requirements and generating applications using the application engineering environment.
- Application Producer. Responsible for integrating the system produced by application engineer(s) with any software that is not produced using the application engineering environment. This includes preexisting software that is being reused and that is not included in the environment's generational capabilities as well as software that is produced by a process other than application engineering. The application producer also assists the application engineer to model the application.
- System Maintainer/Supporter. Responsible for delivering the application to the customer and maintaining it after it is delivered. Such activities may be no different from those performed by the application engineer or may include both the application engineer's and the system producer's activities.

8.5 Gluing the Elements Together: The State Transition Diagrams

Understanding the P-states, artifacts, and roles is the first step in understanding a process such as FAST. They tell you the tasks that must be done, the form and meaning of what must be produced, and the people who must do it. The next key elements to understand are how you glue the P-states together—that is, in what order they can occur. The glue is embodied in the allowable P-state transitions, which are defined by the entry and exit conditions for each P-state. The P-state definition forms specify these conditions, as discussed in Chapter 7. The detailed FAST PASTA model given in Chapters 9–13 contains the forms that define all the P-states and their associated transitions as well as the forms defining the artifacts, the state transition diagrams for the P-states and the artifact states, and the forms defining the roles and relations for FAST. We suggest that you browse through them one P-state level at a time. Try to understand the sequencing among the top-level P-states before moving to the next level. Note that the process can enter a P-state as soon as its entry condition is satisfied so that a number of P-states can be in progress concurrently.

8.6 Typical Questions Answered by the Model

Chapter 6 (Section 6.1) indicates the types of questions that you may want to answer when using a PASTA model. Following are specific questions that may arise during the FAST process and ways you can use the model to answer them.

1. Who does what? For example, who performs Qualify_Domain?
   a. Search for the activity in the P-state hierarchy; you will find Qualify_Domain as a sub-P-state of the FAST P-state.
   b. Find the P-state definition form for Qualify_Domain. Look for the role(s) that perform it: Domain_Engineer and Domain_Manager.
   c. Find the artifact on which the P-state operates: Economic_Model.

   This sequence tells you that the Domain_Engineer and Domain_Manager create or modify the Economic_Model as part of the Qualify_Domain P-state.
2. When can we do that? For example, when can we perform Qualify_Domain?
   a. Search for the activity in the P-state hierarchy; you will find Qualify_Domain as a sub-P-state of the FAST P-state.
   b. Find the P-state definition form for the activity, such as for Qualify_Domain. Find the P-state entrance condition. Qualify_Domain can be performed when the Economic_Model is in the Referenced state.
   c. Find the artifact(s) you need in the artifact hierarchy. Economic_Model is a subartifact of Domain_Model, which is a subartifact of Environment, which is a subartifact of Family_Artifact.
   d. Find the artifact definition form for Economic_Model and note that it is an elementary artifact. Economic_Model is in the Referenced state when your organization recognizes that it may be worthwhile to apply FAST to a domain or to apply another iteration of FAST to a domain that has already been engineered but has not yet quantified the advantage it may get from doing so.

   This sequence tells you that you can perform Qualify_Domain when you first recognize that it may be worthwhile to engineer a domain: at the start of an iteration of the FAST process, when you are first creating or refining a domain, or when marketplace changes may warrant reengineering a domain.

3. How do I make this happen now? For example, how do I cause the activity Qualify_Domain to occur?

   a. Identify the resources needed to perform the activity. You will need a Domain_Engineer and a Domain_Manager to perform Qualify_Domain.

   b. Satisfy the entrance condition for the activity. For example, be sure that the Economic_Model is in the Referenced state.

   c. Perform the P-state. If the P-state has substates, they must be performed. If the P-state is an operation, perform the operation. From its P-state definition form, Qualify_Domain has four substates: Gather_Data, Analyze_Data, Reject, and Accept. Entry to each substate depends on the state of the Economic_Model. The state transition diagram for Economic_Model shows that Gather_Data must be performed first and can be performed when the Economic_Model is in the Referenced state: when you have decided that there may be an economic advantage to applying FAST to a domain or that you need to refine an existing Economic_Model. When this decision has been made, work on Qualify_Domain can start.

4. How do I do this? For example, how do I perform the operation Analyze_Data?

   a. Implement the specification for the operation described in the operation definition form for the operation. The operation Analyze_Data has both an informal specification and a formal specification. You can carry out either one.

5. What P-states can be performed in parallel? For example, while I am performing the operation Establish_Standard_Terminology (a substate of Analyze_Commonality), are there other operations that I or others could be performing concurrently?

   a. Look at the state transition diagram for the parent P-state, such as the state transition diagram for Analyze_Commonality. If there are no transitions from one substate to another, the substates can be performed in parallel. Note that the entrance conditions of each substate must still be satisfied before you perform them. The substates Establish_Standard_Terminology, Establish_Domain_Commonalities_And_Variabilities, and Parameterize_Variabilities can be performed in parallel after their entrance conditions are satisfied. The entrance condition for Establish_Domain_Commonalities_And_Variabilities is that the state of Standard_Terminology is Started. However, Standard_Terminology is not in the Started state until the operation Initialize_Dictionary has been performed. One way to see this is to examine the state transition diagram for Standard_Terminology. Another way is to examine the exit condition for Initialize_Dictionary.

6. Why is the process not progressing faster?

   a. Find all the P-states where progress could be made—that is, all P-states whose entrance conditions are satisfied. For these P-states, trace through their substates until you find the operations that could be in progress—that is, the operations whose entrance conditions are satisfied. For each such operation that is manual, find the role and the person playing that role and obtain the status of the operation.

   b. Based on the status obtained in the preceding step, identify the bottlenecks to completing each operation.

7. How can I speed up the enactment of the process?

   a. Apply the method described in the answer to question 6 to find bottlenecks in the process. Either add resources to operations that could make use of them or find alternative activities that can be enacted concurrently with those whose progress is slow.

      In the first case, find the resources needed and available by identifying the roles that can perform the operations and then by staffing those roles with available people. Find the roles by examining the operation definition form for the operation.

      In the second case, look at the parent activity of an operation to find child activities that can proceed concurrently with the operation, as discussed in the answer to question 5.

      In both of the preceding cases you may need to advance artifacts to states that help satisfy the entrance condition of a P-state, or you may need to determine how to make an activity occur, as discussed in the answer to question 3.

8.7 First Steps in Applying the Model

Suppose that you are a member of a software development team that wants to apply FAST. The next few sections explain how you might start to use the process.

8.7.1 Identifying Starting Activities and Roles

If you are unfamiliar with the FAST process but think that you might like to produce applications using it, a perusal of the P-states in the model shows you that there is a P-state called Engineer_Application that is a process for constructing applications. The entry condition for this P-state is that the Application_Engineering_Environment has been implemented. Looking at the artifacts in the model shows you that there is an artifact called Application that consists of an Application_Model, Application_Documentation, and Application_Code. The Application_Code and Application_Documentation are generated from the Application_Model. The Application starts in the Referenced state and is created by an Application_Engineer using the Application_Engineering_Environment. Your team must create such an environment before modeling the application.

The FAST P-state definition form shows you that there is a P-state called Engineer_Domain whose purpose is to create and support a standardized application engineering process and an application engineering environment that supports the process. You note that the entry condition for Engineer_Domain is that the environment is in the Referenced state; the need to produce an application engineering environment has been identified in response to the creation of a domain.

You wonder whether you need to create a domain, and you look again at the top-level FAST activities. There is an activity called Qualify_Domain that is a process for determining economic viability for a domain. This seems like a good start. You need a domain_manager and a domain_engineer to start. The first step is to gather data, and the second step is to analyze it. You note that the activities involved will result in the creation of artifacts and in state changes in those artifacts. There is also an algorithm for the key step of analyzing data to create an economic model to decide whether the domain is economically viable.

At this point you have determined the initial steps to take, the people you need to take them, the outputs they will produce, and the decision criteria for your next step(s). As you continue the process, you can use the model to guide you in deciding, at any point, what to do next, who should do it, what they should produce, and how they should produce it.

8.7.2 Other Scenarios

The preceding scenario assumes that you have only a copy of the model. If you have an environment for enacting the FAST process, the environment can guide your activities and decisions. For example, the environment may contain standard templates for artifacts such as environment models, and it may automate some of the algorithm for producing an economic model.

If you are familiar with the FAST process as a result of having previously used it, you may decide that you want to tailor it to your purposes. For example, you may decide that you do not need to qualify your new domain and that an informal decision to proceed with the domain engineering is sufficient.

If you have already performed one pass through domain engineering for your domain, you may decide to perform a second pass, during which you update only certain artifacts, such as the commonality analysis. Or you may decide to create some artifacts, such as the Application_Modeling_Language, that you did not create on the first pass.

The preceding scenarios are only a few that may occur as you use the process. In each scenario, you can use the FAST PASTA model as a guide. You can modify it according to your needs and automate activities that you understand well and perform often. The model can serve as a roadmap, a training aid, a basis for the development of an automated software development environment tailored to your organization and domains, and a guide to improving your software development process.

You now know enough about FAST and PASTA so that you can use the detailed model as a reference model for the FAST process. You may also want to consider creating your own PASTA model for other processes that you use or modifying the FAST process for your environment.

8.8 Readings for Chapter 8

[1] FAST Artifacts, Chapter 9.

The artifact tree, artifact definitions, and artifact state transition diagrams for the FAST PASTA model.

[2] FAST Activities, Chapter 10.

The activity tree, P-state definitions, and P-state transition diagrams for the FAST PASTA model.

[3] FAST Roles, Chapter 11.

The role tree and role definitions for the FAST PASTA model.

[4] FAST Analyses, Chapter 12.

The analysis definitions for the FAST PASTA model.

[5] FAST Relations, Chapter 13.

The relation definitions for the FAST PASTA model.

9 Artifact Definitions

THIS CHAPTER CONTAINS THE DEFINITIONS OF THE ARTIFACTS IN the FAST PASTA model. There is a section in the chapter for each composite artifact in the model and for most elementary artifacts. For some elementary artifacts, such as Standard_Terminology, the artifact definition form is omitted because the artifact is adequately described in the parent artifact definition form. For example, you can find the Synopsis for Standard_Terminology in the subartifacts section of the artifact definition form for Commonality_Analysis. Each section in the chapter contains the following elements.

- A tree diagram showing the artifact's subartifacts (if the artifact is composite)
- An artifact definition form for the artifact
- An artifact state transition diagram for the artifact

The organization and notations for these forms and diagrams are explained in Chapter 7. Figure 9.1 shows the FAST artifact tree. The nodes in the trees are labeled with the numbers of the sections in this chapter that contain their artifact definition forms and state transition diagrams. (For example, Environment is defined in section 9.1.) The CD-ROM that accompanies this book contains the complete FAST PASTA model shown in Chapters 9 to 13. It includes a browser that allows you to display and move easily among the different elements of the model, as well as an HTML version of the model that you can explore with a web browser.

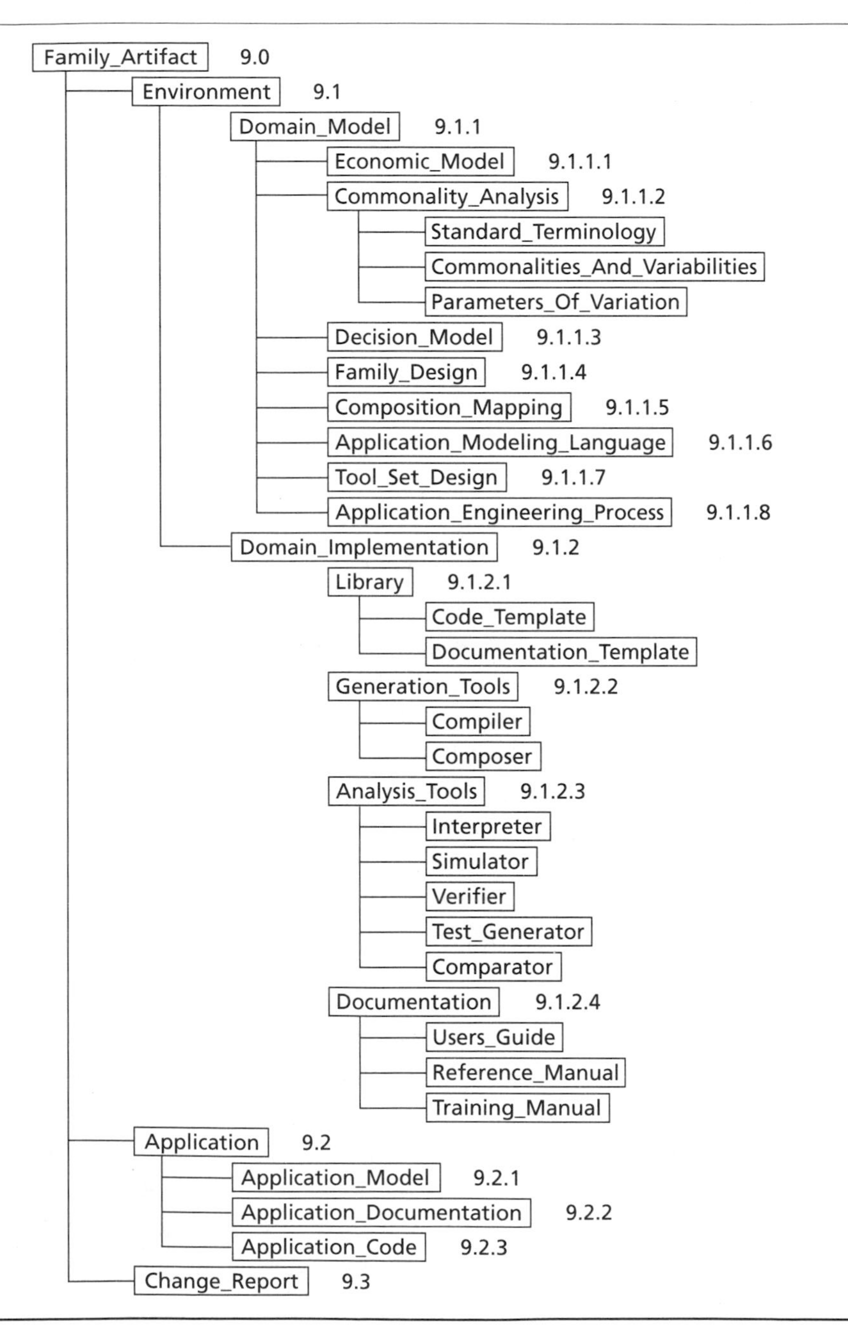

Figure 9-1. *The FAST Artifact Tree*

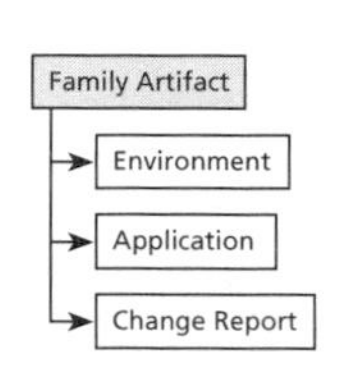

9.0 Family_Artifact

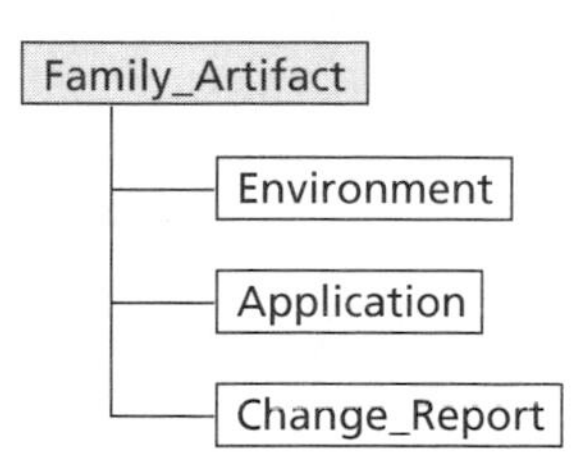

Artifact Definition Form

Name	**Family_Artifact**
Synopsis	Top-level artifact that contains all the artifacts for FAST.
Complexity Type	Composite
Data Type	Folder
	A-STATE LIST
Name	**Referenced**
Synopsis	The potential benefit in defining a family has been recognized. Work can start on the set of artifacts used and produced by the FAST process. This may happen as a result of an organization realizing that it is developing a family and that it would benefit from applying FAST to its domain. The organization has been briefed on the FAST process and has committed resources to start domain engineering.
Condition	state-of(Economic_Model) = Referenced
Name	**Domain_Engineered**
Synopsis	The family has been defined, and the economics of producing an application engineering environment have been analyzed. If the economics are favorable, the application engineering environment has been designed, specified, and implemented; domain engineering has been completed.
Condition	state-of(Environment) = Implemented
Name	**Application_Engineered**
Synopsis	An application has been produced using the application engineering environment.
Condition	state-of(Application) = Application_Delivered_And_Supported
Name	**Application_Referenced**
Synopsis	Applications can be produced using the application engineering environment.
Condition	(state-of(Environment) = Implemented) and (state-of(Application_Model) = Customer_Requirements_Identified)

continued

Name	**Domain_Rejected**
Synopsis	The Economic_Model for the domain has been constructed and evaluated. The evaluation shows that it is not worth investing in the domain.
Condition	
Name	**Domain_Qualified**
Synopsis	An Economic_Model for the domain has been constructed and evaluated. The evaluation shows that it is worth investing in this domain.
Condition	
Name	**Domain_Evaluated**
Synopsis	An Economic_Model has been created and evaluated for the domain.
Condition	

SUBARTIFACT LIST

Name	**Environment**
Synopsis	Application engineering environment used to create and analyze application models and to generate code and documentation for application.
Name	**Application**
Synopsis	All artifacts delivered as part of an Application and all supporting artifacts needed to produce the deliverable artifacts.
Name	**Change_Report**
Synopsis	The form that is filed whenever a change is required.

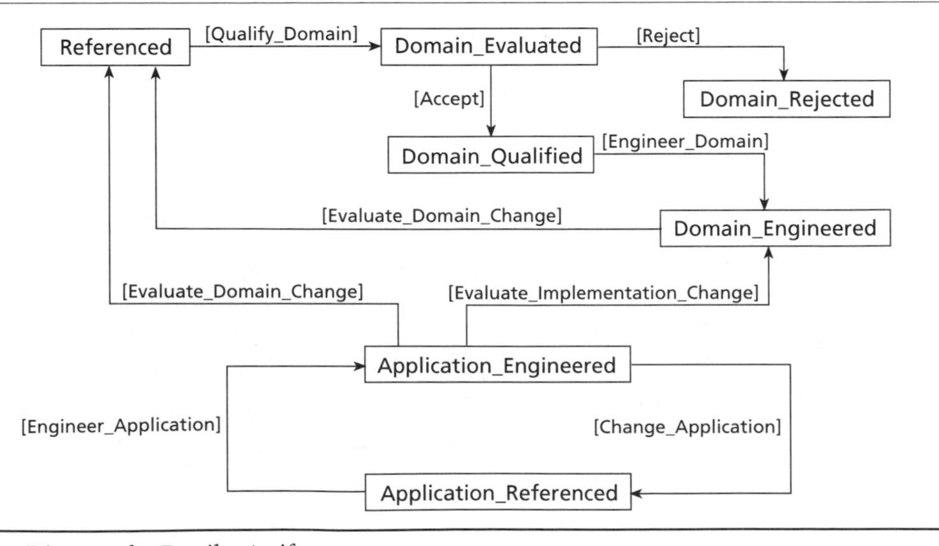

A-State Diagram for Family_Artifact

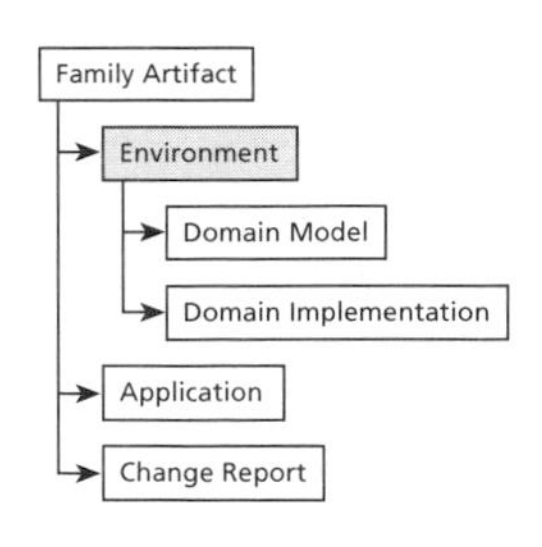

9.1 Environment

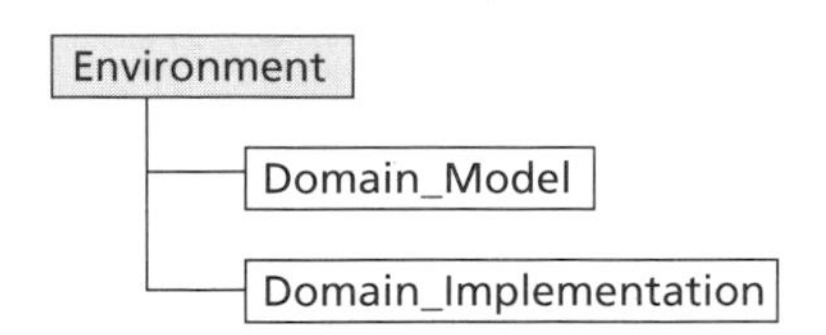

Artifact Definition Form

Name	**Environment**
Synopsis	Application engineering environment used to create and analyze application models and to generate code and documentation for applications.
Complexity Type	Composite
Data Type	Folder
	A-STATE LIST
Name	**Referenced**
Synopsis	In response to the creation of a domain (or changes in an existing domain model) the need to produce (or refine) an application engineering environment has been identified. Initially, this is usually the result of performing an economic analysis and a commonality analysis. Refinements are the result of feedback from application engineers concerning their difficulties in creating applications with existing application engineering environment, or changes in the business area that result in changes to the Domain_Model.
Condition	state-of(Domain_Model) = Referenced
Name	**Analyzed**
Synopsis	The domain for which the application engineering environment will be used has been analyzed or reanalyzed, resulting in a new Domain_Model or a refined Domain_Model.
Condition	((state-of(Domain_Model) = Decision_Model_Defined) and (state-of(Library) = Referenced) and (state-of(Generation_Tools) = Tool_Identified) and (state-of(Analysis_Tools) = Tool_Identified) and (state-of(Documentation) = Referenced))
Name	**Implemented**
Synopsis	The application engineering environment has been implemented or an existing implementation has been modified, resulting in a set of tools that can be used to generate members of the domain.
Condition	state-of(Domain_Implementation) = Domain_Implemented

continued

Family Artifact
- Environment
  - Domain Model
  - Domain Implementation
- Application
- Change Report

SUBARTIFACT LIST	
Name	**Domain_Model**
Synopsis	A specification for the application engineering environment and the artifacts needed to support analysis of the domain for the purpose of producing such a specification.
Name	**Domain_Implementation**
Synopsis	Documentation and code used in and resulting from development of the enviroment.

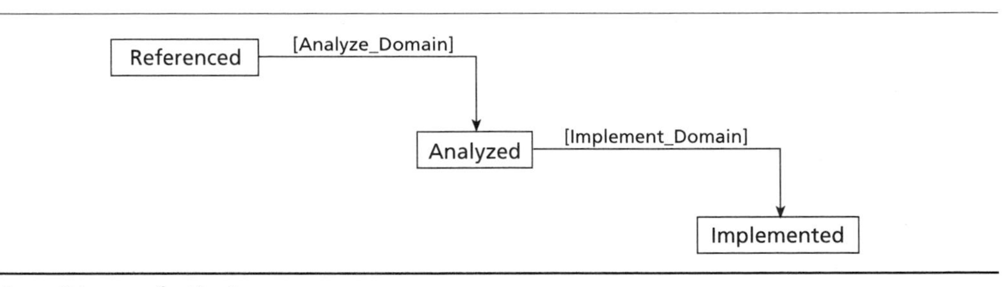

A-State Diagram for Environment

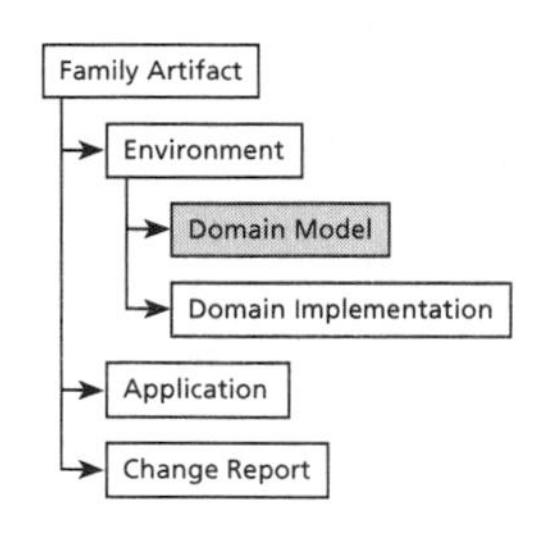

9.1.1 Domain_Model

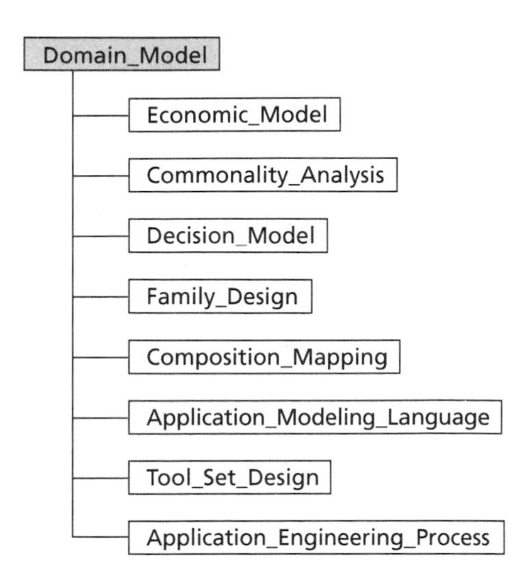

Artifact Definition Form

Name	**Domain_Model**
Synopsis	A specification for the application engineering environment and the artifacts needed to support analysis of the domain for the purpose of producing such a specification.
Complexity Type	Composite
Data Type	Group
	A-STATE LIST
Name	**Referenced**
Synopsis	The potential existence of a family and the potential economic benefits from investing in a domain model that will support generation of family members have been recognized, or the need to refine an existing Domain_Model has been recognized. The recognition may come from an organization's analysis of potential new markets or expanding existing markets.
Condition	((state-of(Family_Artifact) = Domain_Qualified) and (state-of(Commonality_Analysis) = Referenced) and (state-of(Decision_Model) = Referenced))
Name	**Domain_Qualified**
Synopsis	An Economic_Model of the domain has been created or refined, showing the potential benefit of investing in creating a new domain model or refining an existing one.
Condition	state-of(Economic_Model) = Reviewed

continued

Family Artifact
- Environment
  - Domain Model
  - Domain Implementation
- Application
- Change Report

Name	Commonality_Analyzed
Synopsis	The family that comprises the domain has been analyzed, or an existing Commonality_Analysis has been refined. The analysis includes identifying family commonalities and variabilities and defining terminology for the domain.
Condition	state-of(Commonality_Analysis) = Reviewed
Name	**Decision_Model_Defined**
Synopsis	A model describing the decisions that need to be made to distinguish among family members has been defined, or an existing decision model has been refined. Ordering among the decisions is included in the model. The model forms the basis for defining the application engineering process.
Condition	((state-of(Decision_Model) = Reviewed) and (state-of(Composition_Mapping) = Referenced) and (state-of(Commonality_Analysis) = Reviewed) and (state-of(Tool_Set_Design) = Language_Specified))
Name	**Composition_Mapping_Designed**
Synopsis	The Composition_Mapping has been designed, or an existing mapping has been refined in response to a refinement in the Application_Modeling_Language or Family_Design. The mapping identifies the modules in the Family_Design that are needed to implement each decision specified in an Application_Model. This mapping also identifies the parameters that will be used to adapt the module to the needs of the particular family member described by the Application_Model.
Condition	((state-of(Composition_Mapping) = Reviewed) and (state-of(Family_Design) = Commonality_Analysis_Reviewed))
Name	**Family_Designed**
Synopsis	The design for the family has been completed or refined in response to a change in the family members that will need to be produced. The design is a modular design in which each module is implemented as a template that can be adapted to the different family members.
Condition	((state-of(Family_Design) = Reviewed) and (state-of(Application_Modeling_Language) = Commonality_Analysis_Reviewed))
Name	**Application_Modeling_Language_Designed**
Synopsis	The syntax and semantics for the Application_Modeling_Language have been designed and defined, and the language has been reviewed.
Condition	state-of(Application_Modeling_Language) = Language_Specified

continued

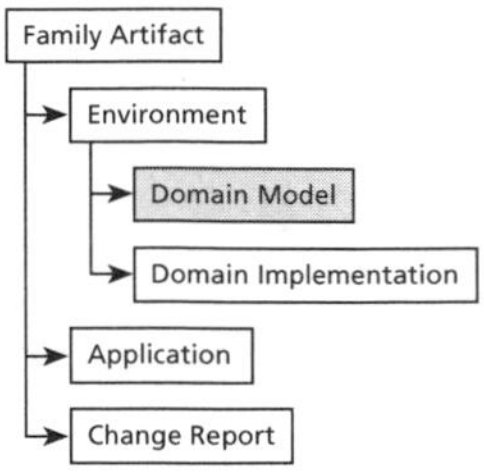

Family Artifact
- Environment
  - Domain Model
  - Domain Implementation
- Application
- Change Report

Name	Tool_Set_Designed
Synopsis	The tools needed to translate the Application_ Modeling_Language and to provide any other support needed by the application engineers in generating and validating family members have been identified and designed.
Condition	state-of(Tool_Set_Design) = Family_Designed

SUBARTIFACT LIST

Name	Economic_Model
Synopsis	An analysis of economic viability for the domain over its life cycle. The analysis includes an estimate of the number of family members in the domain, the cost of producing the application engineering environment, the cost of producing applications using the environment, and the cost of producing them without the environment.
Name	**Commonality_Analysis**
Synopsis	Definition of the family, containing both informal and formal descriptions. Primary elements are a set of terms that define a vocabulary for the family; a set of commonalities, in the form of assumptions, that are true for all family members; a set of variabilities, in the form of assumptions, that define how family members differ; and a set of parameters of variation that specify the range and binding time for each variability.
Name	**Decision_Model**
Synopsis	The Decision_Model describes the decisions that must be made and the order in which they are made to produce an application. The decision model defines the primary concerns of the Application_Engineering_Process.
Name	**Family_Design**
Synopsis	When the compositional approach is used, the family design is a design common to all family members. The family design specifies each abstract module in the design and the parameters used in generating each concrete module from the corresponding abstract module. When the SCR approach is used for the design, the design consists of the information hiding structure among the abstract modules, the process structure, and the uses structure. The templates used to generate code during application engineering are implementations of the abstract modules.
Name	**Composition_Mapping**
Synopsis	The composition mapping is used in the compositional approach to specify the abstract modules needed for each decision expressible in the Application_Modeling_Language. It specifies how decisions captured in an Application_Model are used to provide values to the parameters used to instantiate abstract modules.

continued

Family Artifact
- Environment
  - Domain Model
  - Domain Implementation
- Application
- Change Report

Name	**Application_Modeling_Language**
Synopsis	The Application_Modeling_Language is a specification language used to describe applications. The decisions that are identified by Variabilities and their corresponding Parameters_Of_Variation in the Commonality_Analysis must be expressible in the Application_Modeling_Language. A specification in the Application_Modeling_Language is an Application_Model and is used for generating the code and documentation for the application. It is also used as the basis for analyzing the characteristics of the application.

Name	**Tool_Set_Design**
Synopsis	The toolset comprises the tools that are part of the application engineering environment. They include tools for analyzing application models and generating applications from them. The toolset also includes supporting tools, such as editors. The Tool_Set_Design consists of the design for the set of tools, including at least a description of tools that are or will be included in the application engineering environment.

Name	**Application_Engineering_Process**
Synopsis	The Application_Engineering_Process for a domain is the process whereby an Application_Engineer uses the application engineering environment to make the decisions identified in the Decision_Model according to the order specified in the Decision_Model. Because the decisions and the tools are different for different domains, the application engineering process varies from domain to domain. In some domains there may be no tools and the process may be manual. A manual process may be used after the first iteration of domain engineering, when little investment has yet been made in domain engineering.

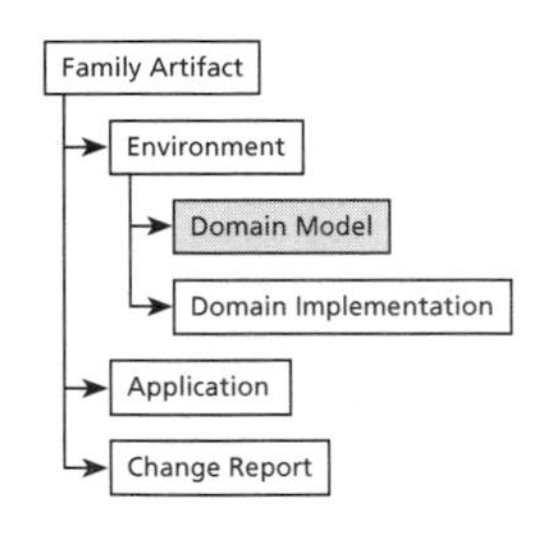

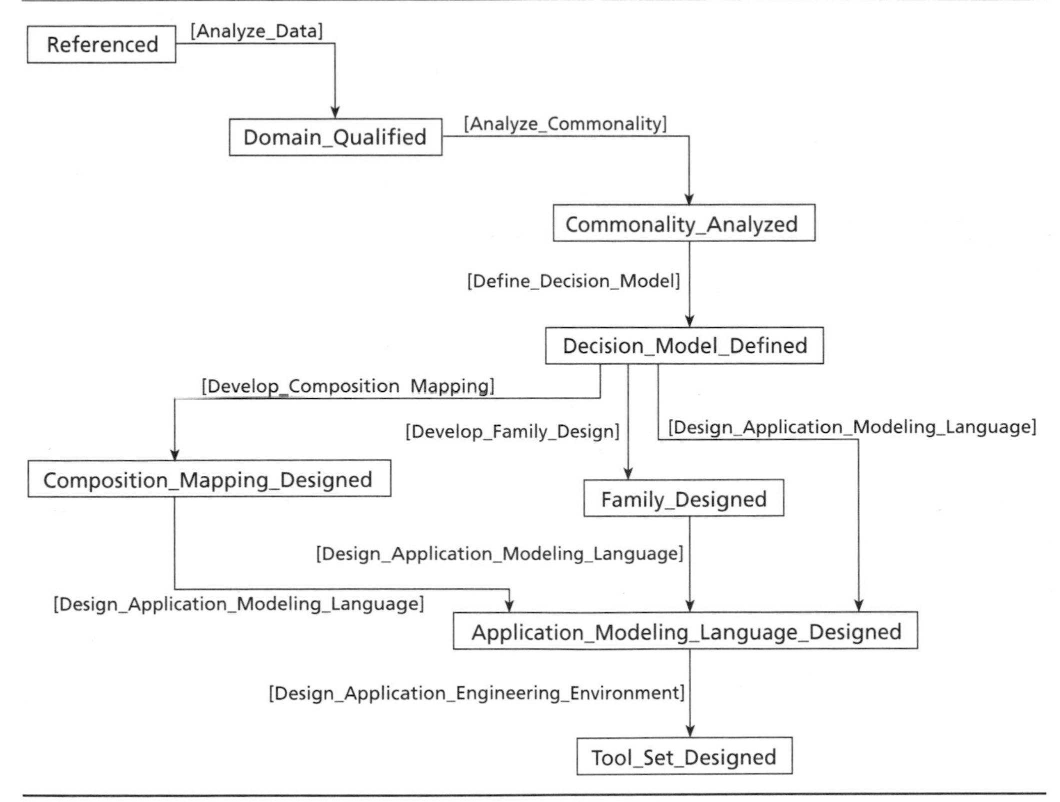

A-State Diagram for Domain_Model

Family Artifact
- Environment
  - Domain Model
  - Domain Implementation
- Application
- Change Report

9.1.1.1 Economic_Model

Artifact Definition Form

Name	**Economic_Model**
Synopsis	An analysis of economic viability for the domain over its life cycle. The analysis includes an estimate of the number of family members in the domain, the cost of producing the application engineering environment, the cost of producing applications using the environment, and the cost of producing them without the environment.
Complexity Type	Elementary
Data Type	Grid
	A-STATE LIST
Name	**Referenced**
Synopsis	An organization recognizes that it may gain an economic advantage by applying FAST to a domain, but the advantage has not been quantified; or changes in the market or the domain are sufficient to warrant refining the existing Economic_Model.
Condition	
Name	**Started**
Synopsis	The analysis needed to quantify the economics of applying FAST to a domain has been started, or the process of refining an existing model has started. The analysis includes gathering data on the cost of producing existing systems within the domain, the cost of producing the application engineering environment, and the cost of producing systems using the application engineering environment.
Condition	
Name	**Defined_And_Specified**
Synopsis	The Economic_Model has been created or refined using the data collected in the Started state.
Condition	
Name	**Reviewed**
Synopsis	The Economic_Model has been reviewed and its predictions verified.
Condition	

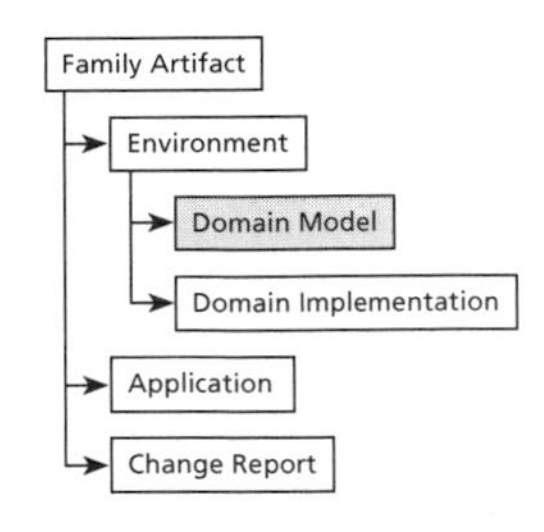

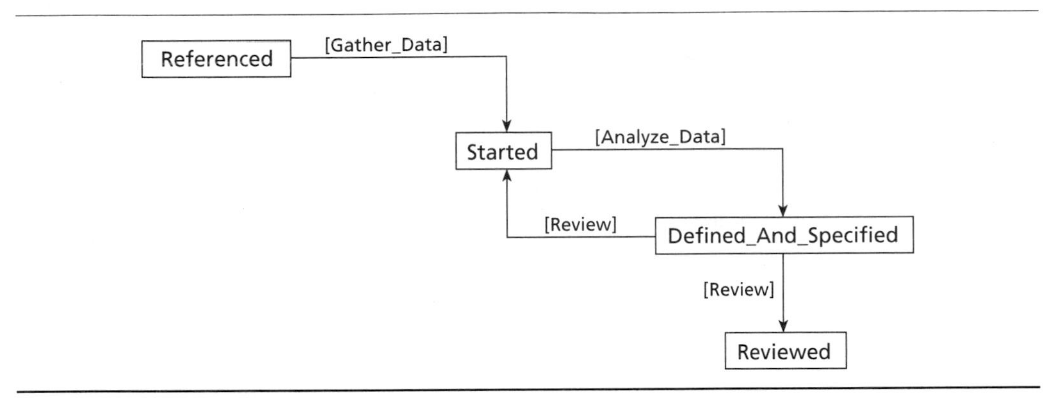

A-State Diagram for Economic_Model

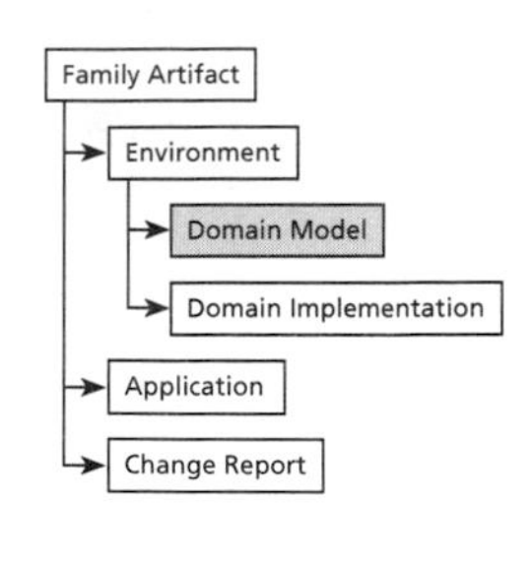

9.1.1.2 Commonality_Analysis

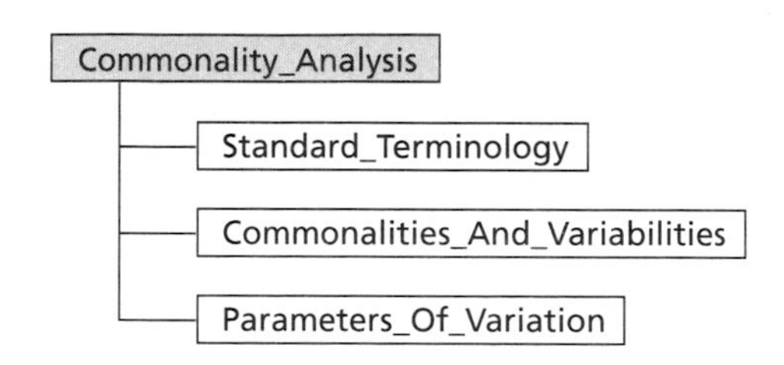

Artifact Definition Form

Name	**Commonality_Analysis**
Synopsis	Definition of the family, containing both informal and formal descriptions. Primary elements are a set of terms that define a vocabulary for the family; a set of commonalities, in the form of assumptions, that are true for all family members; a set of variabilities, in the form of assumptions, that define how family members differ; and a set of parameters of variation that specify the range and binding time for each variability.
Complexity Type	Composite
Data Type	Group
	A-STATE LIST
Name	**Referenced**
Synopsis	The potential for economic gain by treating a domain as a family and applying the FAST process or by refining an existing family has been recognized. As a result, the need for defining or redefining the family is evident.
Condition	state-of(Economic_Model) = Defined_And_Specified
Name	**Standard_Terminology_Established**
Synopsis	A set of standard terminology for the domain has been defined or refined; a dictionary of terms for the domain now exists or has been revised.
Condition	state-of(Standard_Terminology) = Established
Name	**Commonalities_And_Variabilities_Established**
Synopsis	Commonalities, which define what's common to all family members, and variabilities, which define how family members may differ, have been established or refined.
Condition	state-of(Commonalities_And_Variabilities) = Established
Name	**Variabilities_Parameterized**
Synopsis	The variabilities have been mapped to Parameters_Of_Variation, which quantify each variability.
Condition	state-of(Parameters_Of_Variation) = Established

continued

Family Artifact
Environment
Domain Model
Domain Implementation
Application
Change Report

Name	Reviewed
Synopsis	The Commonality_Analysis has been completed and reviewed for consistency, completeness, use of terminology, accuracy of prediction of potential family members, and other factors intended to improve confidence in how well the family is defined.
Condition	state-of(Parameters_Of_Variation) = Established

SUBARTIFACT LIST

Name	Standard_Terminology
Synopsis	Definition of significant terminology used by experts in discussing requirements and applications in the domain.
Name	**Commonalities_And_Variabilities**
Synopsis	A description of what is common to all systems in the domain and what varies among applications in the domain. Commonalities and variabilities are stated as assumptions.
Name	**Parameters_Of_Variation**
Synopsis	Each parameter of variation is a formalization of a decision that can vary to produce various family members. Parameters_Of_Variation are derived from Variabilities so that each variability is specified by at least one parameter of variation. It may require several parameters of variation to specify adequately some variabilities.

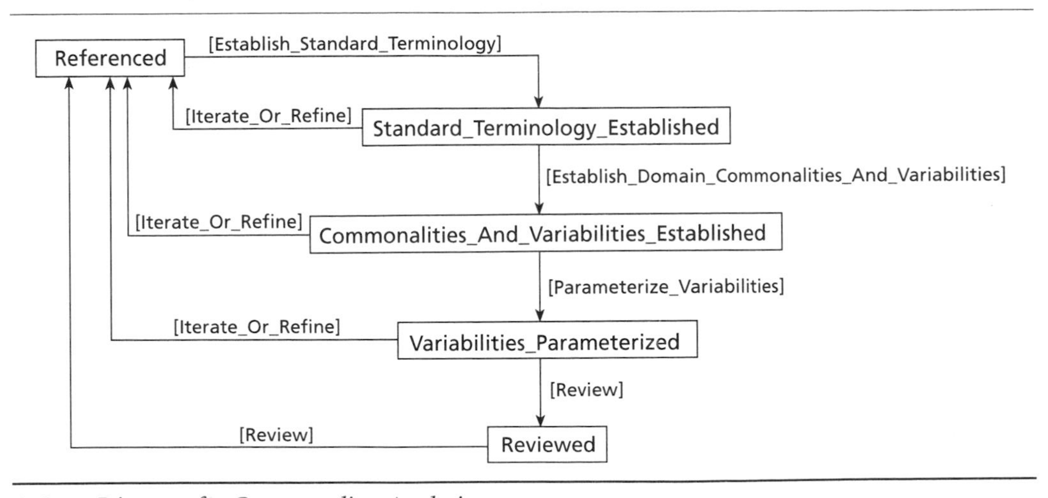

A-State Diagram for Commonality_Analysis

9.1.1.3 Decision_Model

Artifact Definition Form

Name	**Decision_Model**	
Synopsis	The Decision_Model describes the decisions that must be made and the order in which they are made to produce an application. The decision model defines the primary concerns of the Application_Engineering_Process.	
Complexity Type	Elementary	
Data Type	Group	
	A-STATE LIST	
Name	**Referenced**	
Synopsis	A set of variabilities for the domain has been established as part of performing a commonality analysis.	
Condition		
Name	**Defined_And_Specified**	
Synopsis	The set of decisions for the domain has been identified. These decisions are used to specify family members. Making a complete set of decisions completely identifies a family member. The order in which decisions must be made to specify family members has been defined.	
Condition		
Name	**Reviewed**	
Synopsis	The set of decisions has been reviewed to ensure that it captures all the variabilities defined in the Commonality_Analysis, that any ordering among decisions is necessary, and that every family member can be specified using the set of decisions.	
Condition		
	RELATION LIST	
Decision_Tool	Tool_Set_Design	From, To
Parameter_Decision	Parameters_Of_Variations	From, To
Decision_Process	Application_Engineering_Process	From, To

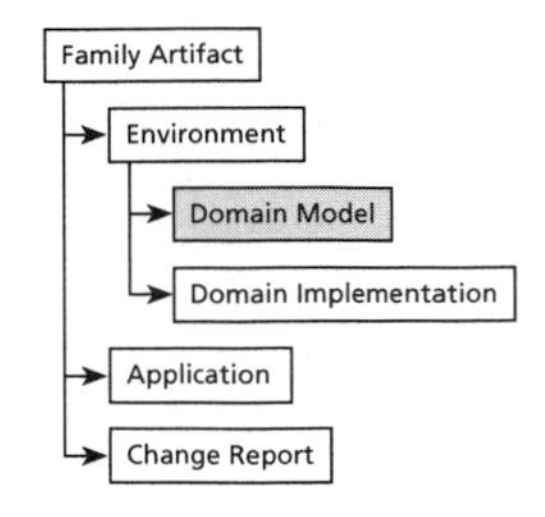

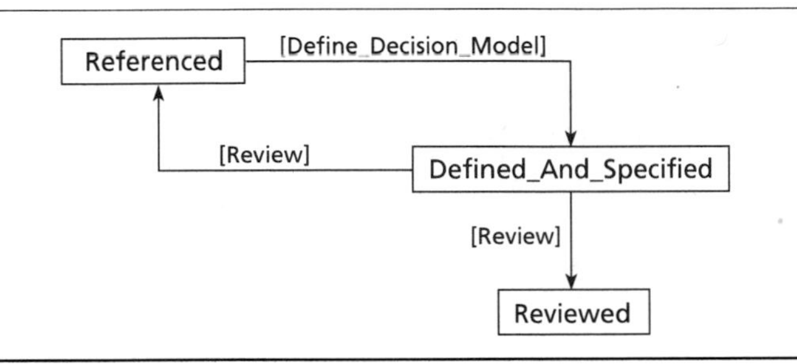

A-State Diagram for Decision_Model

Family Artifact
Environment
Domain Model
Domain Implementation
Application
Change Report

9.1.1.4 Family_Design

Artifact Definition Form

Name	**Family_Design**	
Synopsis	When the compositional approach is used, the family design is a design common to all family members. The family design specifies each abstract module in the design and the parameters used in generating each concrete module from the corresponding abstract module. When the SCR approach is used for the design, the design consists of the information hiding structure among the abstract modules, the process structure, and the uses structure. The templates used to generate code during application engineering are implementations of the abstract modules.	
Complexity Type	Elementary	
Data Type	Grid	
	A-STATE LIST	
Name	**Defined_And_Specified**	
Synopsis	An abstract interface specification has been developed for each leaf module in the information hiding structure, and the specifications have been reviewed using the standard review process for abstract interface specifications.	
Condition		
Name	**Reviewed**	
Synopsis	The abstract interface specifications have been reviewed using the standard process for reviewing abstract interface specifications.	
Condition		
Name	**Referenced**	
Synopsis	The decision to create a Family_Design has been made.	
Condition	state-of(Commonality_Analysis) = Reviewed and state-of(Decision_Model) = Reviewed	
	RELATION LIST	
Commonality_ Module	Commonalities	From, To
Module_Document	Documentation_Template	From, To
	Code_Template	From, To
Module_Implement	Code_Template	From, To
Parameter_Module	Parameters_Of_Variations	From, To

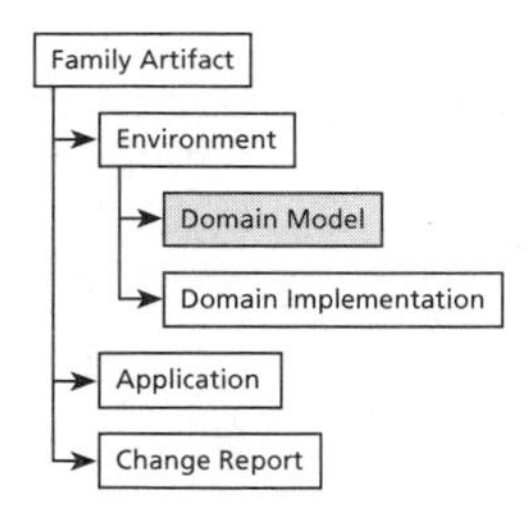

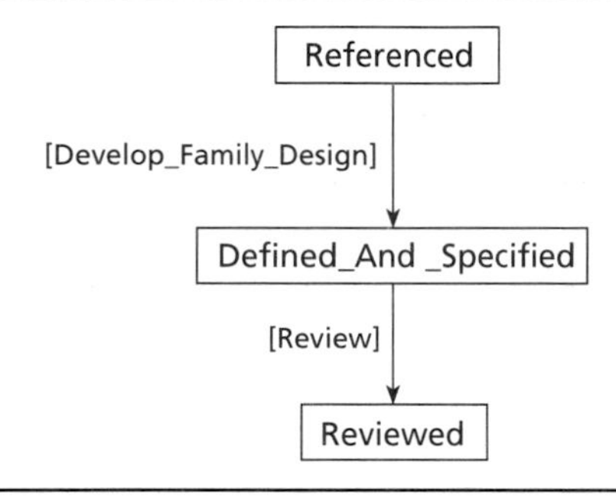

A-State Diagram for Family_Design

Family Artifact
- Environment
  - Domain Model
  - Domain Implementation
- Application
- Change Report

9.1.1.5 Composition_Mapping

Artifact Definition Form

Name	**Composition_Mapping**
Synopsis	The composition mapping is used in the compositional approach to specify the abstract modules needed for each decision expressible in the Application_Modeling_Language. It specifies how decisions captured in an Application_Model are used to provide values to the parameters used to instantiate abstract modules.
Complexity Type	Elementary
Data Type	Grid
	A-STATE LIST
Name	**Referenced**
Synopsis	A set of variabilities for the domain has been established as part of performing a commonality analysis, and a decision has been made to create a Composition_Mapping.
Condition	state-of(Commonality_Analysis) = Reviewed and state-of(Decision_Model) = Reviewed
Name	**Defined_And_Specified**
Synopsis	The Application_Modeling_Language has been defined and specified—that is, it is in the Specified state—the Family_Design has been defined and specified (is in the Defined_And_Specified state), and the Composition_Mapping has been defined and reviewed so that the following hold: 1. For every variability that is expressible in the Application_Modeling_Language, the set of modules from the Family_Design needed to provide the capabilities defined by the variability have been identified. 2. A mechanism for expressing the mapping from each variability to the set of modules has been developed.
Condition	
Name	**Reviewed**
Synopsis	The mapping has been reviewed for the following attributes. 1. Each variability represented in the language is mapped to the correct module. 2. Each module in the family design that hides a variability is included in the mapping.
Condition	
	RELATION LIST
Composition_Mapping_AML	Application_Modeling_Language — From, To

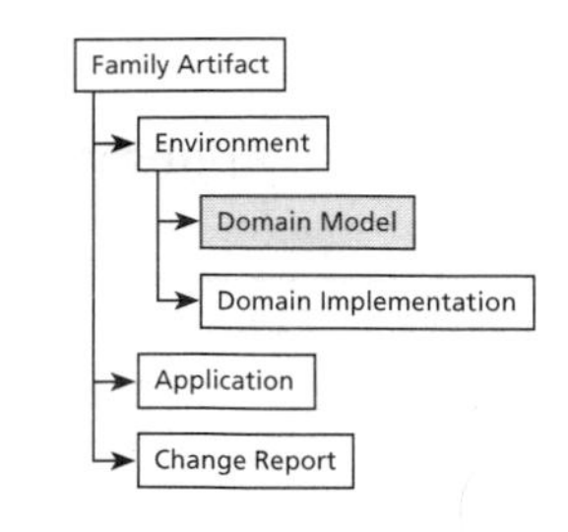

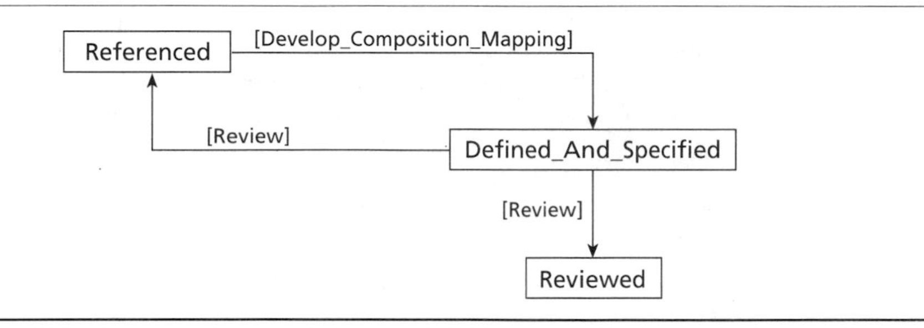

A-State Diagram for Composition_Mapping

- Family Artifact
  - Environment
    - Domain Model
    - Domain Implementation
  - Application
  - Change Report

9.1.1.6 Application_Modeling_Language

Artifact Definition Form

Name	**Application_Modeling_Language**	
Synopsis	The Application_Modeling_Language is a specification language used to describe applications. The decisions that are identified by Variabilities and their corresponding Parameters_Of_Variation in the Commonality_Analysis must be expressible in the Application_Modeling_Language. A specification in the Application_Modeling_Language is an Application_Model and is used for generating the code and documentation for the application. The specification is also used as the basis for analyzing the characteristics of the application.	
Complexity Type	Elementary	
Data Type	Text	
	A-STATE LIST	
Name	**Language_Type_Identified**	
Synopsis	The type of language that is needed for the domain has been identified—for example, whether it is a declarative language, an imperative language, or an applicative language.	
Condition		
Name	**Language_Specified**	
Synopsis	The syntax and semantics for the language have been designed and defined, and the language has been reviewed.	
Condition		
Name	**Referenced**	
Synopsis	The decision to create an application modeling language for the domain has been made.	
Condition	state-of(Commonality_Analysis) = Reviewed and state-of(Decision_Model) = Reviewed	
	RELATION LIST	
Composition_ Mapping_AML	Composition_Mapping	From, To

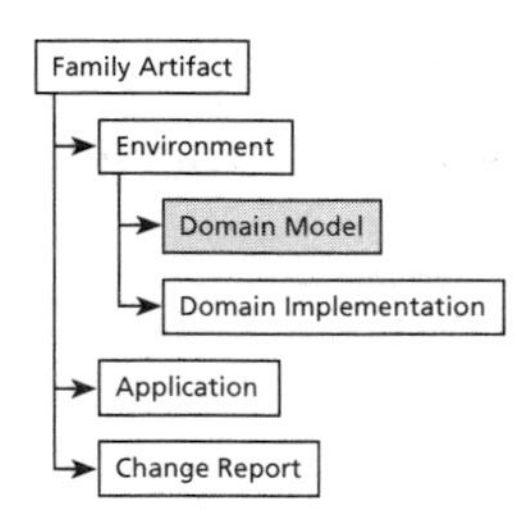

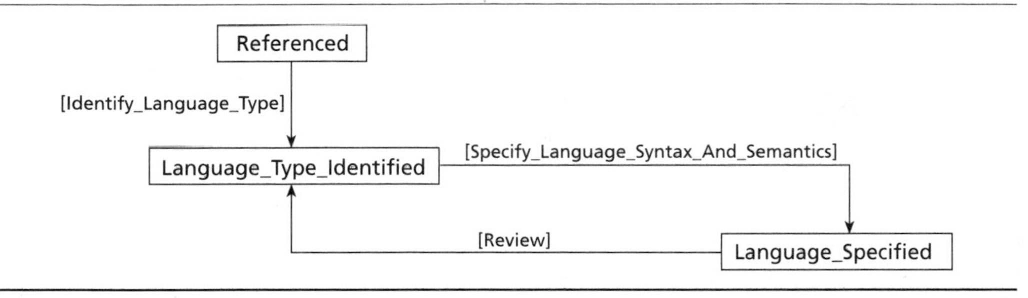

A-State Diagram for Application_Modeling_Language

Family Artifact
Environment
Domain Model
Domain Implementation
Application
Change Report

9.1.1.7 Tool_Set_Design

Artifact Definition Form

Name	**Tool_Set_Design**	
Synopsis	The toolset comprises the tools that are part of the application engineering environment. They include tools for analyzing application models and generating applications from them. The toolset also includes supporting tools, such as editors. The Tool_Set_Design consists of the design for the set of tools, including at least a description of tools that are or will be included in the application engineering environment.	
Complexity Type	Elementary	
Data Type	Text	
	A-STATE LIST	
Name	**Language_Specified**	
Synopsis	The Application_Modeling_Language is in the Language_Specified state; the syntax and semantics for the language have been designed and defined, and the language has been reviewed.	
Condition		
Name	**Tool_Family_Specified**	
Synopsis	The tools needed to translate the Application_Modeling_Language and to provide any other support needed by the application engineers in generating and validating family members have been identified, defined, and specified.	
Condition		
Name	**Tool_Set_Designed**	
Synopsis	The tools needed to translate the Application_Modeling_Language and to provide any other support needed by the application engineers in generating family members are designed.	
Condition		
	RELATION LIST	
Decision_Tool	Decision_Model	From, To
Tool_Implement	Analysis_Tools	From, To
Tool_Implement	Generation_Tools	From, To
Tool_Document	Documentation	From, To

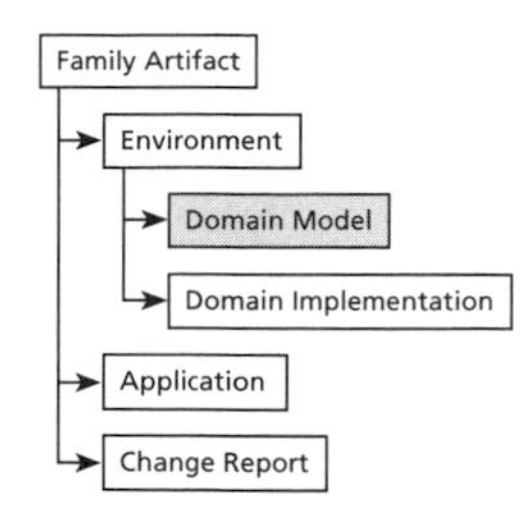

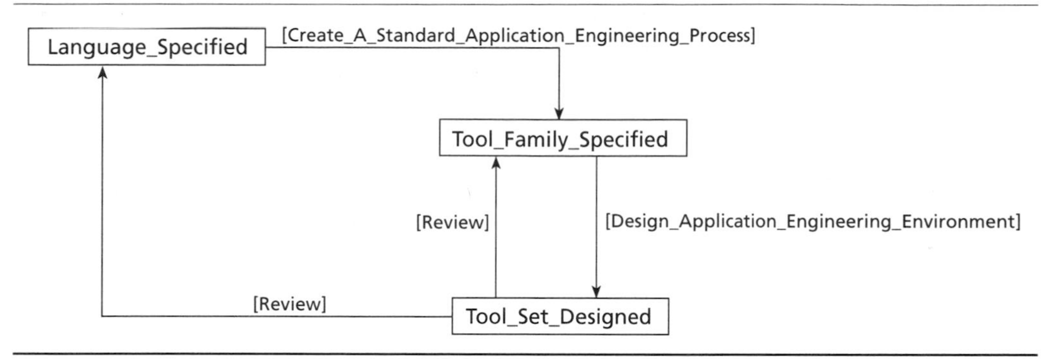

A-State Diagram for Tool_Set_Design

Family Artifact
Environment
Domain Model
Domain Implementation
Application
Change Report

9.1.1.8 Application_Engineering_Process

Artifact Definition Form

Name	**Application_Engineering_Process**	
Synopsis	The Application_Engineering_Process for a domain is the process whereby an Application_Engineer uses the application engineering environment to make the decisions identified in the Decision_Model according to the order specified in the Decision_Model. Because the decisions and the tools are different for different domains, the application engineering process varies from domain to domain. In some domains there may be no tools, and the process may be manual. A manual process may be used after the first iteration of domain engineering, when little investment has yet been made in domain engineering.	
Complexity Type	Elementary	
Data Type	Text	
	A-STATE LIST	
Name	**Reviewed**	
Synopsis	The Application_Engineering_Process has been reviewed.	
Condition		
Name	**Defined_And_Specified**	
Synopsis	The steps in the process, the ordering of the steps, and the tools used in each step have been specified.	
Condition		
Name	**Referenced**	
Synopsis	The Decision_Model has been completed.	
Condition		
	RELATION LIST	
Decision_Process	Decision_Model	From, To

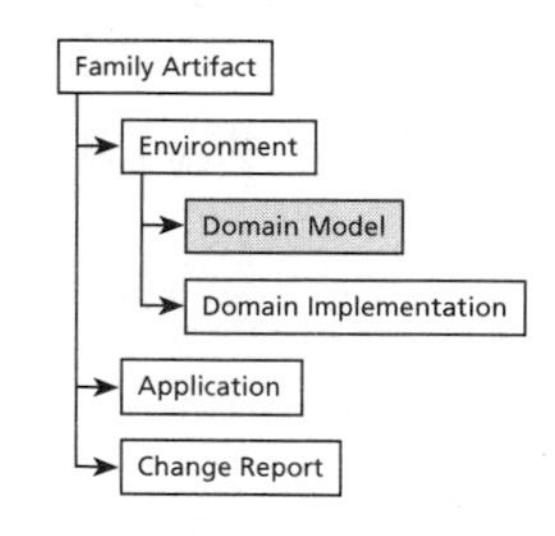

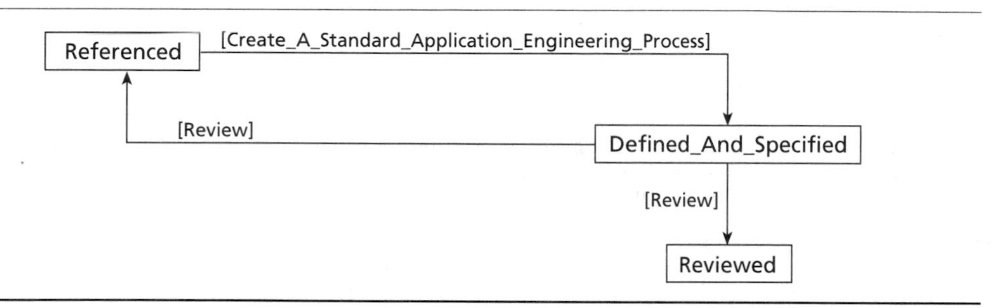

A-State Diagram for Application_Engineering_Process

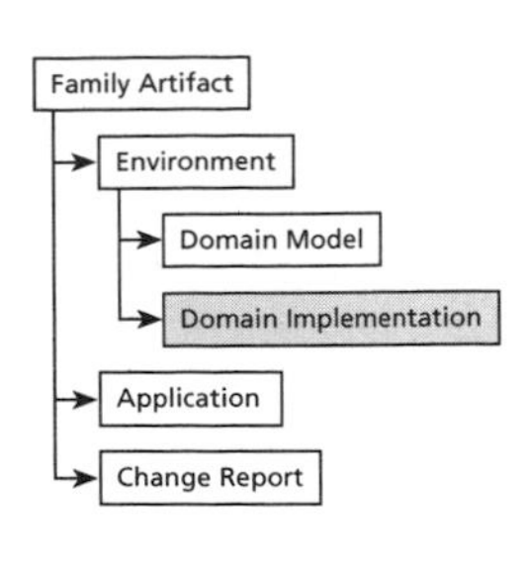

9.1.2 Domain_Implementation

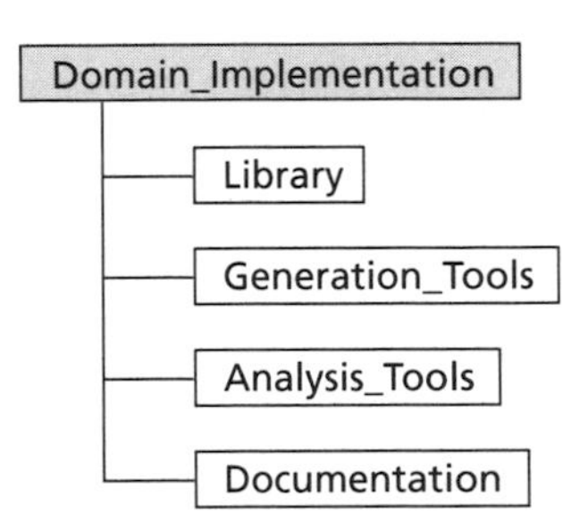

Artifact Definition Form

Name	**Domain_Implementation**
Synopsis	Documentation and code used in and resulting from development of the Environment.
Complexity Type	Composite
Data Type	Group
A-STATE LIST	
Name	**Tool_Set_Designed**
Synopsis	Tools needed to translate the AML and to provide any support needed by the application engineers in generating and validating family members have been designed.
Condition	state-of(Tool_Set_Design) = Tool_Set_Designed
Name	**Domain_Implemented**
Synopsis	An Application Engineering environment has been implemented or an existing implementation has been modified, resulting in a set of tools that can be used to generate members of the domain.
Condition	(state-of(Library) = Library_Implemented) and (state-of(Generation_Tools) = Tool_Produced) and (state-of(Analysis_Tools) = Tool_Produced) and (state-of(Documentation) = Reviewed))
SUBARTIFACT LIST	
Name	**Library**
Synopsis	Library of component templates used to create code and documentation for applications. Such a library is usually needed in the compositional approach in which applications are created by generating and integrating instances of templates stored in the library.

continued

Family Artifact
Environment
Domain Model
Domain Implementation
Application
Change Report

Name	**Generation_Tools**
Synopsis	Tools used to generate code and documentation for applications.
Name	**Analysis_Tools**
Synopsis	Tools used to analyze application models to help application engineer validate the models.
Name	**Documentation**
Synopsis	The documentation needed to understand how to use and maintain the application engineering environment.

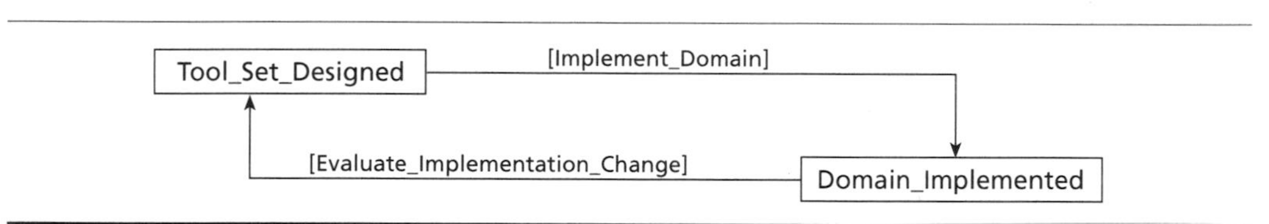

A-State Diagram for Domain_Implementation

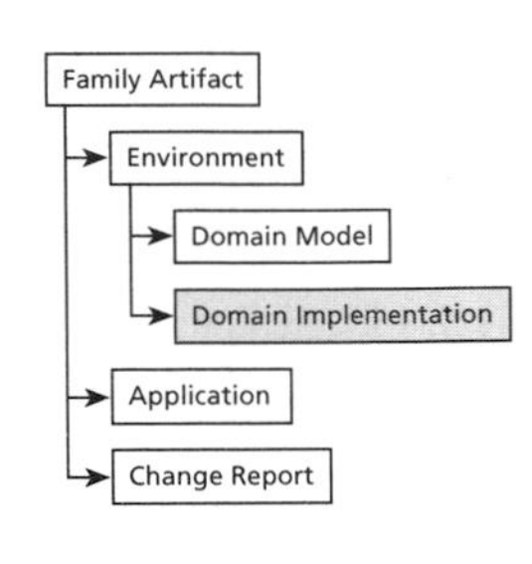

9.1.2.1 Library

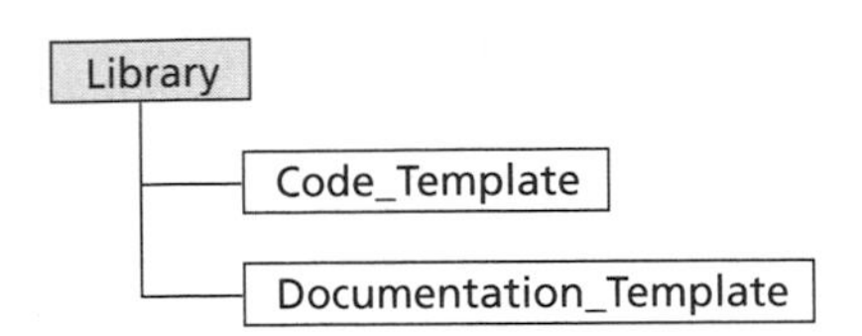

Artifact Definition Form

Name	**Library**
Synopsis	Library of component templates used to create code and documentation for applications. Such a library is usually needed in the compositional approach in which applications are created by generating and integrating instances of templates stored in the library.
Complexity Type	Composite
Data Type	Form
A-STATE LIST	
Name	**Referenced**
Synopsis	The need for creating or refining an environment library has been identified.
Condition	(state-of(Documentation_Template) = Reviewed) and (state-of(Code_Template) = Reviewed)
Name	**Library_Implemented**
Synopsis	The Library, including the templates used to generate the code and documentation for applications, has been implemented.
Condition	(state-of(Documentation_Template) = Implemented) and (state-of(Code_Template) = Implemented)
Name	**Verified**
Synopsis	The Library has been reviewed.
Condition	(state-of(Code_Template) = Reviewed) and (state-of(Documentation_Template) = Reviewed)
SUBARTIFACT LIST	
Name	**Code_Template**
Synopsis	Template used to generate code for applications.
Name	**Documentation_Template**
Synopsis	Template used to generate documentation for applications.

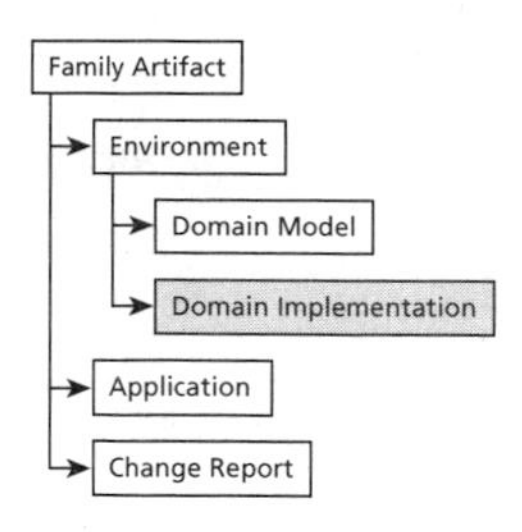

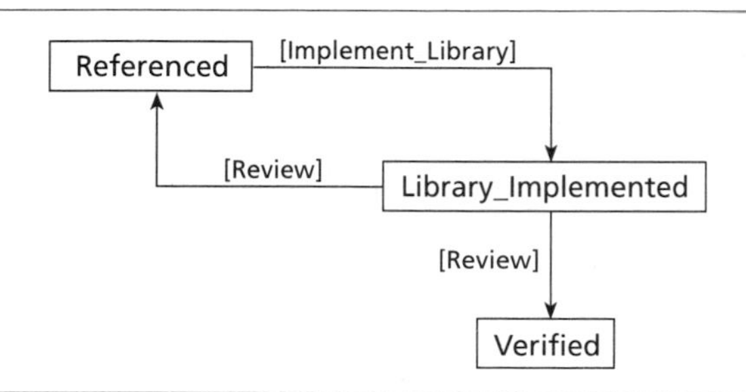

A-State Diagram for Library

9.1.2.2 Generation_Tools

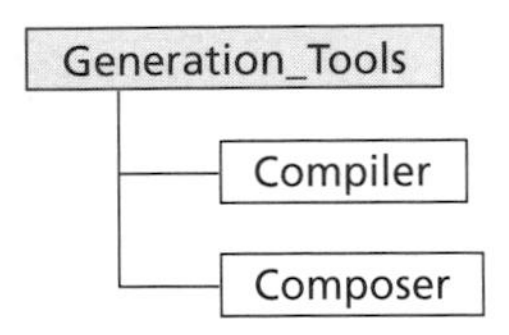

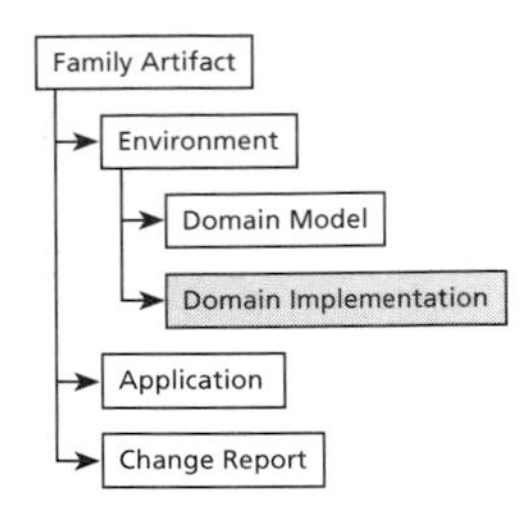

Artifact Definition Form

Name	**Generation_Tools**
Synopsis	Tools used to generate code and documentation for applications.
Complexity Type	Composite
Data Type	Group
	A-STATE LIST
Name	**Tools_Identified**
Synopsis	The generation tools needed as part of the application engineering environment have been identified. The type and number of the generation tools depend on the characteristics of the Application_Modeling_Language and the capabilities to be built into the application engineering environment.
Condition	state-of(Domain_Model) = Tool_Set_Designed
Name	**Reviewed**
Synopsis	Generation_Tools have been reviewed.
Condition	(state-of(Compiler) = Reviewed) or (state-of(Composer) = Reviewed)
Name	**Tools_Produced**
Synopsis	Generation_Tools have been produced.
Condition	(state-of(Compiler) = Tool_Produced) or (state-of(Composer) = Tool_Produced)
	SUBARTIFACT LIST
Name	**Compiler**
Synopsis	Tool used to compile application models into code and documentation for applications when the compiler approach is used.

continued

Family Artifact
Environment
Domain Model
Domain Implementation
Application
Change Report

Name	**Composer**	
Synopsis	Tool used to compose code and documentation into applications from application models when the compositional approach is used.	
	RELATION LIST	
Tool_Implement	Tool_Set_Design	From, To

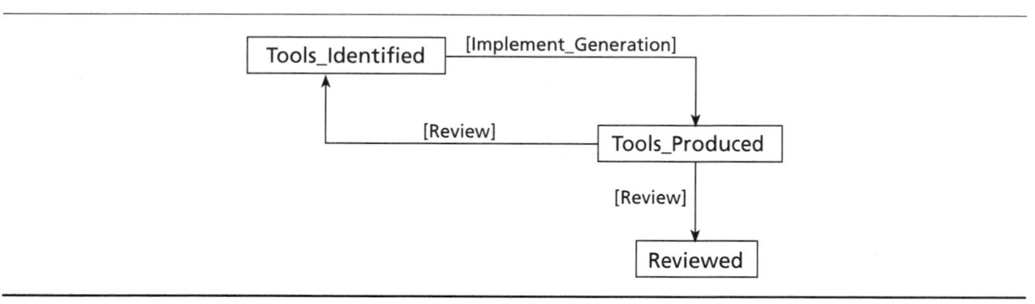

A-State Diagram for Generation_Tools

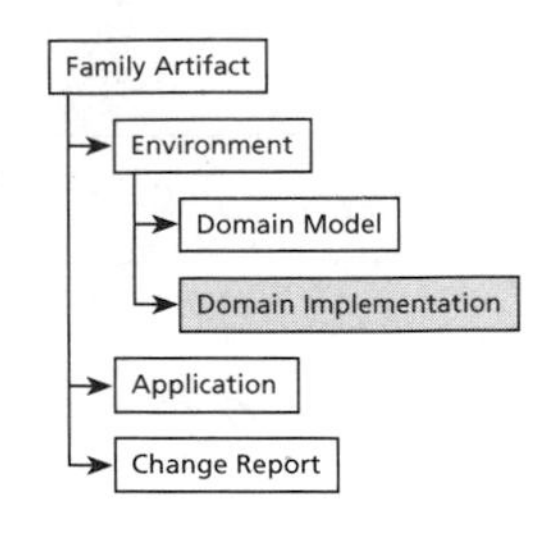

9.1.2.3 Analysis_Tools

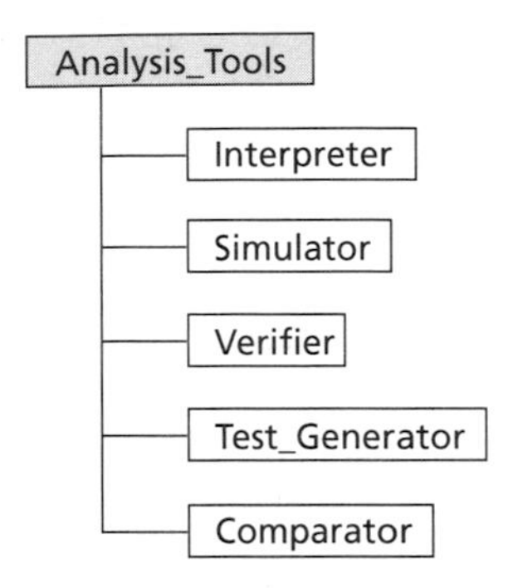

Artifact Definition Form

Name	**Analysis_Tools**
Synopsis	Tools used to analyze application models to help application engineer validate the models.
Complexity Type	Composite
Data Type	Group
	A-STATE LIST
Name	**Tools_Produced**
Synopsis	Analysis_Tools have been produced.
Condition	(state-of(Interpreter) = Tool_Produced) and (state-of(Simulator) = Tool_Produced) and (state-of(Verifier) = Tool_Produced) and (state-of(Comparator) = Tool_Produced) and (state-of(Test_Generator) = Tool_Produced)
Name	**Reviewed**
Synopsis	Analysis_Tools reviewed.
Condition	(state-of(Interpreter) = Reviewed) and (state-of(Simulator) = Reviewed) and (state-of(Verifier) = Reviewed) and (state-of(Test_Generator) = Reviewed) and (state-of(Comparator) = Reviewed)

continued

Family Artifact
Environment
Domain Model
Domain Implementation
Application
Change Report

Name	**Tools_Identified**	
Synopsis	Need for Analysis_Tools as part of the application engineering environment has been identified, or need to refine existing Analysis_Tools has been identified.	
Condition	state-of(Domain_Model) = Tool_Set_Designed	
	SUBARTIFACT LIST	
Name	**Interpreter**	
Synopsis	Tool used to interpret application models.	
Name	**Simulator**	
Synopsis	Tool used to simulate the operation of an application from an Application_Model.	
Name	**Verifier**	
Synopsis	Tool used to verify an Application_Model to help ensure consistency and completeness of the model.	
Name	**Test_Generator**	
Synopsis	Tool used to generate test cases from an Application_Model to test the generated application.	
Name	**Comparator**	
Synopsis	Tool used to compare application models to identify similarities and differences between them.	
	RELATION LIST	
Tool_Implement	Tool_Set_Design	From, To

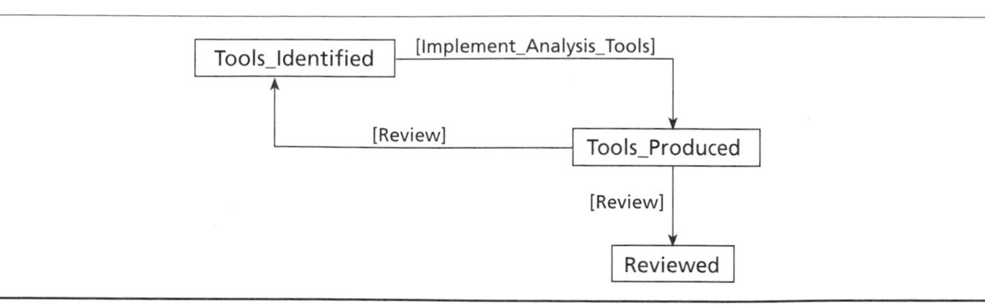

A-State Diagram for Analysis_Tools

9.1.2.4 Documentation

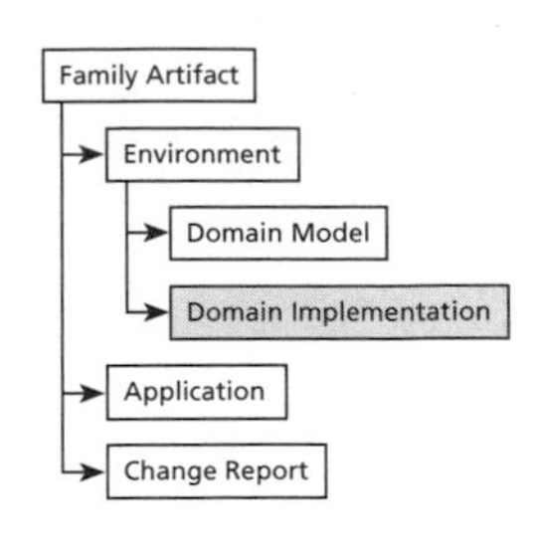

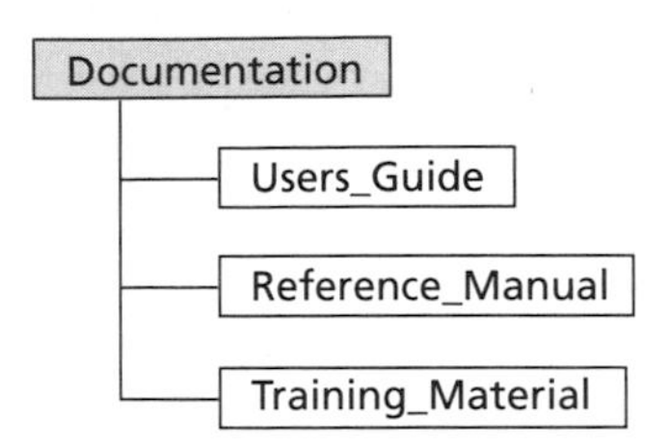

Artifact Definition Form

Name	**Documentation**
Synopsis	The documentation needed to understand how to use and maintain the application engineering environment.
Complexity Type	Composite
Data Type	Group
	A-STATE LIST
Name	**Referenced**
Synopsis	The following artifacts have been started and are in their initial states: 1. The Decision_Model 2. The Application_Engineering_Environment Also, the Application_Engineering_Process has been specified.
Condition	state-of(Domain_Model) = Tool_Set_Designed
Name	**Defined_And_Specified**
Synopsis	User documentation for each tool in the application engineering environment has been written; the Application_Engineering_Process has been documented; the Family_Design has been documented; a specification and design for each tool has been written; a description of how the tools work together has been written.
Condition	(state-of(Users_Guide) = Defined_And_Specified) and (state-of(Reference_Manual) = Defined_And_Specified) and (state-of(Training_Manual) = Defined_And_Specified)
Name	**Reviewed**
Synopsis	The user and maintenance documentation has been reviewed and baselined.
Condition	(state-of(Users_Guide) = Reviewed) and (state-of(Reference_Manual) = Reviewed) and (state-of(Training_Material) = Reviewed)

continued

Family Artifact
Environment
Domain Model
Domain Implementation
Application
Change Report

SUBARTIFACT LIST		
Name	**Users_Guide**	
Synopsis	Guide for the users of the application engineering environment.	
Name	**Reference_Manual**	
Synopsis	Reference manual for the application engineering environment.	
Name	**Training_Material**	
Synopsis	Training documents used to train application engineers in the use of the application engineering environment.	
RELATION LIST		
Tool_Document	Tool_Set_Design	From, To

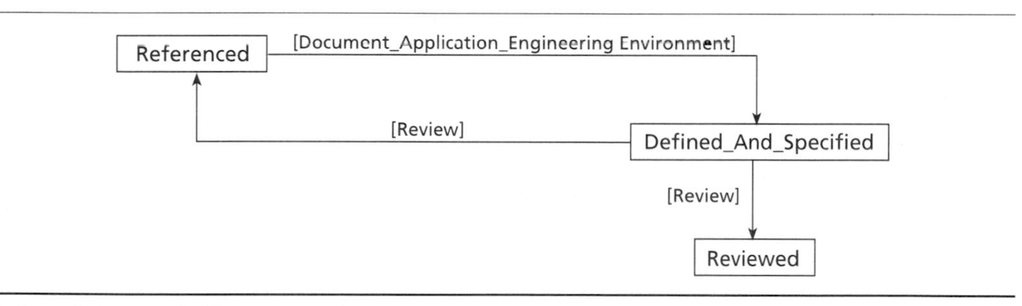

A-State Diagram for Documentation

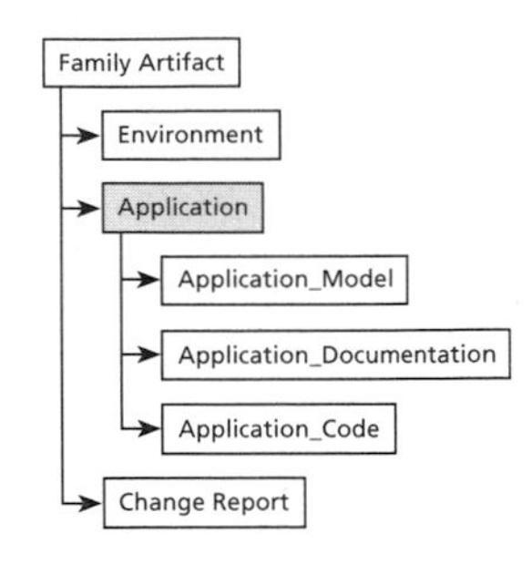

9.2 Application

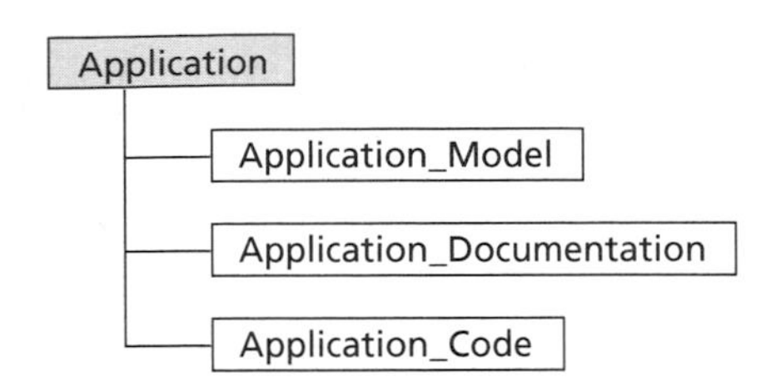

Artifact Definition Form

Name	**Application**
Synopsis	All artifacts delivered as part of an Application and all supporting artifacts needed to produce the deliverable artifacts.
Complexity Type	Composite
Data Type	Folder
	A-STATE LIST
Name	**Application_Referenced**
Synopsis	The need to produce an Application has been identified, and work is ready to begin.
Condition	state-of(Application_Model) = Customer_Requirements_Identified
Name	**Modeled**
Synopsis	A model of the application has been constructed in the Application_Modeling_Language. The model of the application has been analyzed and verified; such analysis can include consistency and completeness checking, simulation, comparison to other models, and other operations intended to ensure the correctness and validity of the model. The application engineer has conducted reviews of the model to validate it and ensure that it satisfies the customer's requirements.
Condition	state-of(Application_Model) = Established
Name	**Application_Produced**
Synopsis	The code and documentation for the application have been produced.
Condition	(state-of(Application_Code) = Defined_And_Specified) and (state-of(Application_Documentation) = Defined_And_Specified)
Name	**Application_Delivered_And_Supported**
Synopsis	The application has been delivered to the customer.
Condition	(state-of(Application_Documentation) = Reviewed) and (state of(Application_Code) = Reviewed)

continued

- Family Artifact
  - Environment
  - **Application**
    - Application_Model
    - Application_Documentation
    - Application_Code
  - Change Report

SUBARTIFACT LIST

Name	**Application_Model**
Synopsis	Model of the application from which deliverable code and documentation for the application is generated. The Application_Model is created by Application_Engineer; he or she analyzes it to ensure that the customer's requirements are properly met.
Name	**Application_Documentation**
Synopsis	Customer documentation for the Application. The decisions needed to generate the documentation are included in the Application_Model and the Application_Modeling_Language supports the specification of documentation. It may not be possible to generate all documentation for every application. Documentation parts that cannot be generated transition through the same states as the documentation that is generated from the Application_Model.
Name	**Application_Code**
Synopsis	Deliverable code for the application. The decisions needed to generate the code are included in the Application_Model. It may not be possible to generate all code for every application. Code parts that cannot be generated transition through the same states as the code that is generated from the Application_Model. These states generally correspond to typical manual code development processes.

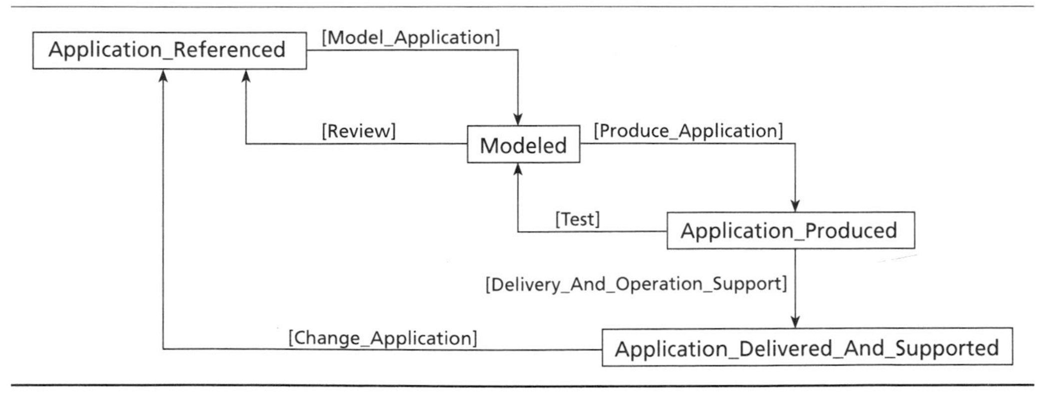

A-State Diagram for Application

9.2.1 Application_Model

- Family Artifact
  - Environment
  - Application
    - Application_Model
    - Application_Documentation
    - Application_Code
  - Change Report

Artifact Definition Form

Name	**Application_Model**	
Synopsis	Model of the application from which deliverable code and documentation for the application are generated. The Application_Model is created by Application_Engineer; he or she analyzes it to ensure that the customer's requirements are properly met.	
Complexity Type	Elementary	
Data Type	Text	
	A-STATE LIST	
Name	**Customer_Requirements_Identified**	
Synopsis	The need to produce an application has been identified. This may be the result of a contract with a customer or a perceived need for the application in the marketplace.	
Condition		
Name	**Defined_And_Specified**	
Synopsis	A model of the application has been constructed in the Application_Modeling_Language. The model of the application has been analyzed, and the Application_Engineer believes that the model is valid and satisfies the customer's requirements.	
Condition		
Name	**Established**	
Synopsis	The Application_Model has been reviewed to validate it.	
Condition		
	RELATION LIST	
Application_Model_Module	Application_Code	From, To
Product_Document	Application_Documentation	From, To

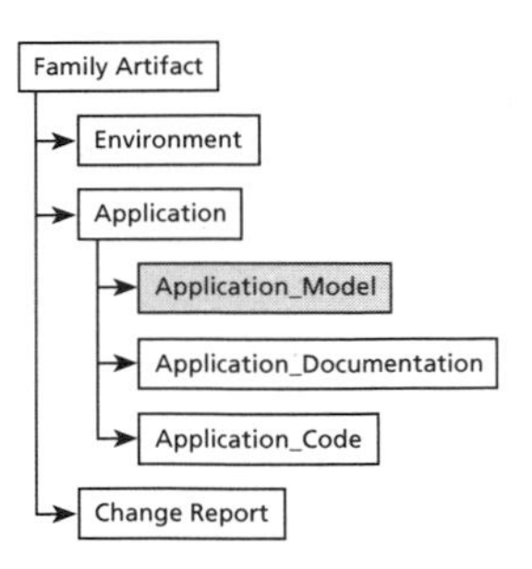

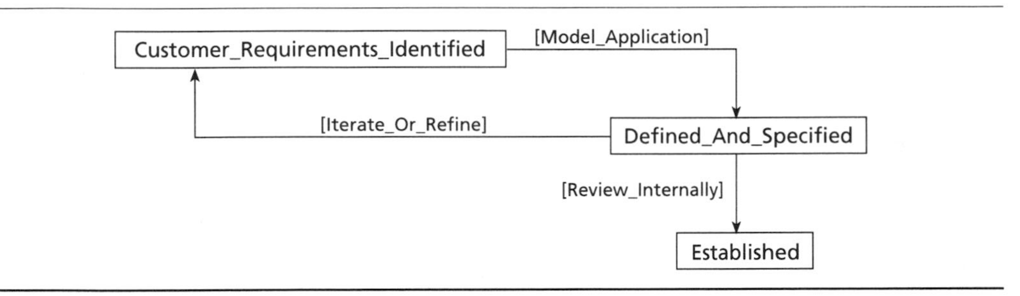

A-State Diagram for Application_Model

9.2.2 Application_Documentation

Family Artifact
Environment
Application
Application_Model
Application_Documentation
Application_Code
Change Report

Artifact Definition Form

Name	**Application_Documentation**	
Synopsis	Customer documentation for the Application. The decisions needed to generate the documentation are included in the Application_Model and the Application_Modeling_Language supports the specification of documentation. It may not be possible to generate all documentation for every application. Documentation parts that cannot be generated transition through the same states as the documentation that is generated from the Application_Model.	
Complexity Type	Elementary	
Data Type	Text	
	A-STATE LIST	
Name	**Referenced**	
Synopsis	The need to produce an application, and consequently the documentation for it, has been identified. This may be the result of a contract with a customer or a perceived need for the application in the marketplace.	
Condition		
Name	**Defined_And_Specified**	
Synopsis	A model of the application has been constructed in the Application_Modeling_Language, including the parts from which documentation will be generated. Those parts of the model have been analyzed, and the Application_Engineer believes that the model is valid and satisfies the customer's requirements.	
Condition		
Name	**Reviewed**	
Synopsis	The parts of the Application_Model from which documentation will be generated have been reviewed to validate them.	
Condition		
	RELATION LIST	
Product_Document	Application_Model	From, To

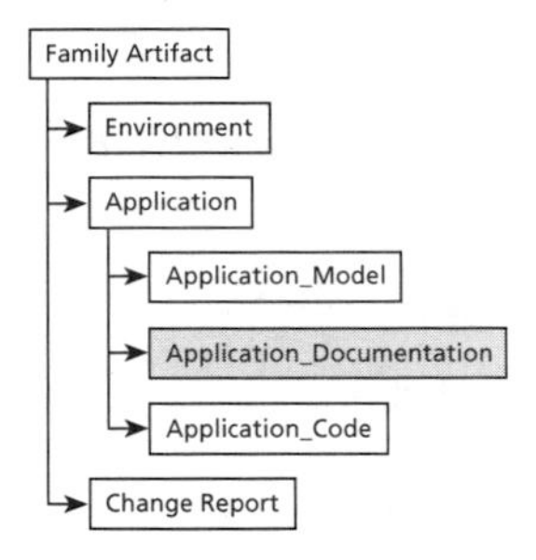

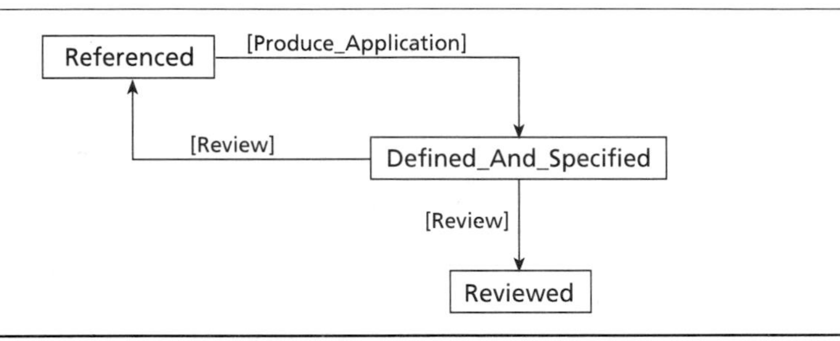

A-State Diagram for Application_Documentation

- Family Artifact
  - Environment
  - Application
    - Application_Model
    - Application_Documentation
    - Application_Code
  - Change Report

9.2.3 Application_Code

Artifact Definition Form

Name	**Application_Code**	
Synopsis	Deliverable code for the application. The decisions needed to generate the code are included in the Application_Model. It may not be possible to generate all code for every application. Code parts that cannot be generated transition through the same states as the code that is generated from the Application_Model. These states generally correspond to typical manual code development processes.	
Complexity Type	Elementary	
Data Type	Text	
	A-STATE LIST	
Name	**Referenced**	
Synopsis	The need to produce an application, and consequently the code for it, has been identified. This may be the result of a contract with a customer or a perceived need for the application in the marketplace.	
Condition		
Name	**Defined_And_Specified**	
Synopsis	A model of the application has been constructed in the Application_Modeling_Language, including the parts of the model from which code will be generated. Those parts of the model have been analyzed, and the Application_Engineer believes that the model is valid and satisfies the customer's requirements.	
Condition		
Name	**Reviewed**	
Synopsis	The parts of the Application_Model from which code will be generated have been reviewed to validate them, and the code has been generated and tested.	
Condition		
	RELATION LIST	
Application_Model_Module	Application_Model	From, To

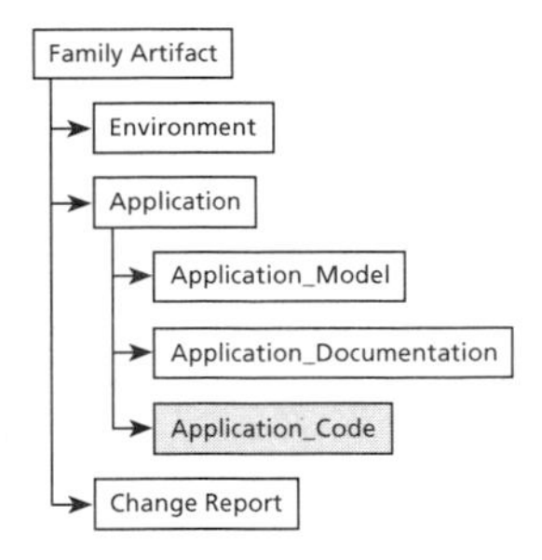

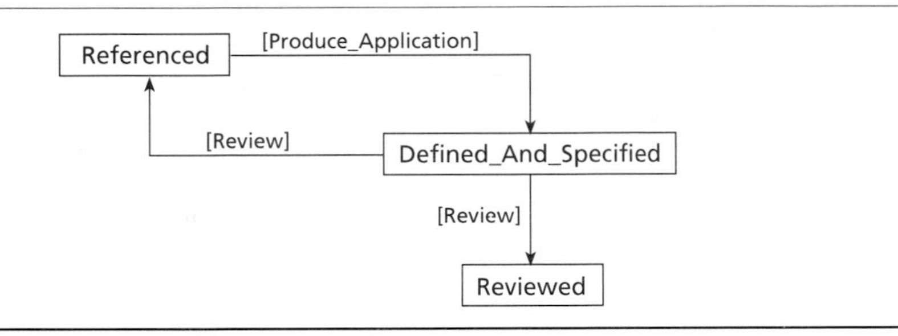

A-State Diagram for Application_Code

Family Artifact
- Environment
- Application
- Change Report

9.3 Change_Report

Artifact Definition Form

Name	**Change_Report**
Synopsis	The form that is filed when a change is required.
Complexity Type	Elementary
Data Type	Report

A-STATE LIST

Name	**Change_Identified**
Synopsis	The need to make a change to the domain or its implementation has been identified. This could be to correct an error, to respond to a change in the marketplace causing the need for new family members that were previously unanticipated, or to respond to requests to enhance the application engineering environment.
Condition	
Name	**Domain_Change_Requested**
Synopsis	The Change_Report has been filed to request a domain change.
Condition	
Name	**Implementation_Change_Requested**
Synopsis	The Change_Report has been filed to request an implementation change.
Condition	
Name	**Implementation_Change_Authorized**
Synopsis	A Change_Report proposing a change to the domain implementation has been accepted.
Condition	state-of(Change_Report)=Change_Accepted and (state-of(Decision_Model)=Referenced or state-of(Family_Design)=Referenced or state-of(Composition_Mapping)=Referenced or state-of(Application_Modeling_Language)=Commonality_Analysis_Reviewed or state-of(Tool_Set_Design)=Language_Specified or state-of(Application_Engineering_Process)=Referenced)
Name	**Change_Rejected**
Synopsis	The change requested has not been authorized, and the Change_Report has been filed.
Condition	

continued

Family Artifact
Environment
Application
Change Report

Name	**Domain_Change_Authorized**
Synopsis	A Change_Report proposing a change to the family has been accepted.
Condition	state-of(Change_Report)=Change_Accepted and state-of(Economic_Model)=Referenced

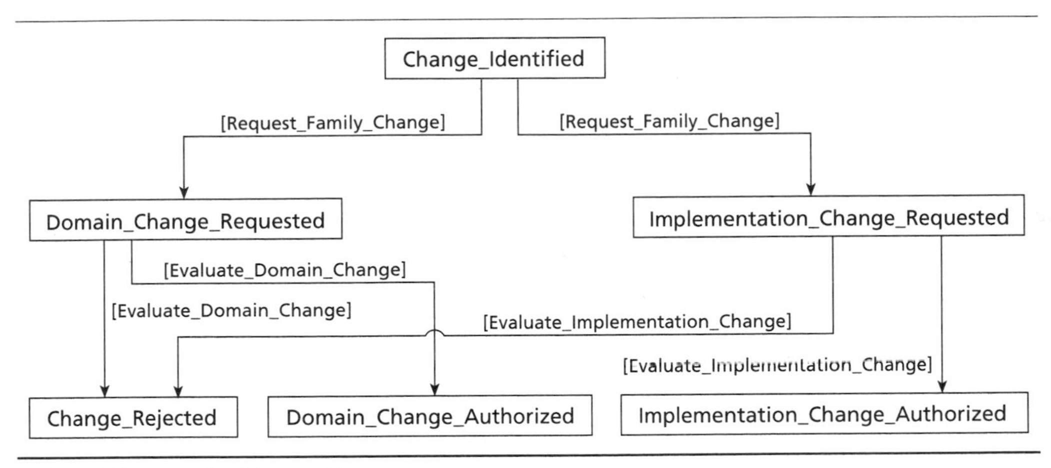

A-State Diagram for Change_Report

10 Activity Definitions

THIS CHAPTER CONTAINS THE DEFINITIONS OF THE ACTIVITIES IN the FAST PASTA model, including P-states and operations. There is a section in the chapter for each P-state and for some of the operations. For some operations, the operation definition form is omitted because the operation is adequately defined in its parent P-state definition form. Sections in the chapter contain the following elements.

- A tree diagram showing the P-state's substates, if any
- A definition form for the activity
- A P-state transition diagram for P-states

Figure 10-1 shows the FAST activity tree to four levels. P-states in the tree that have substates that are not shown in the figure are outlined in double lines. The nodes in the trees are labeled with the numbers of the sections in this chapter that define the P-state. For example, Qualify_Domain is defined in Section 10.1.

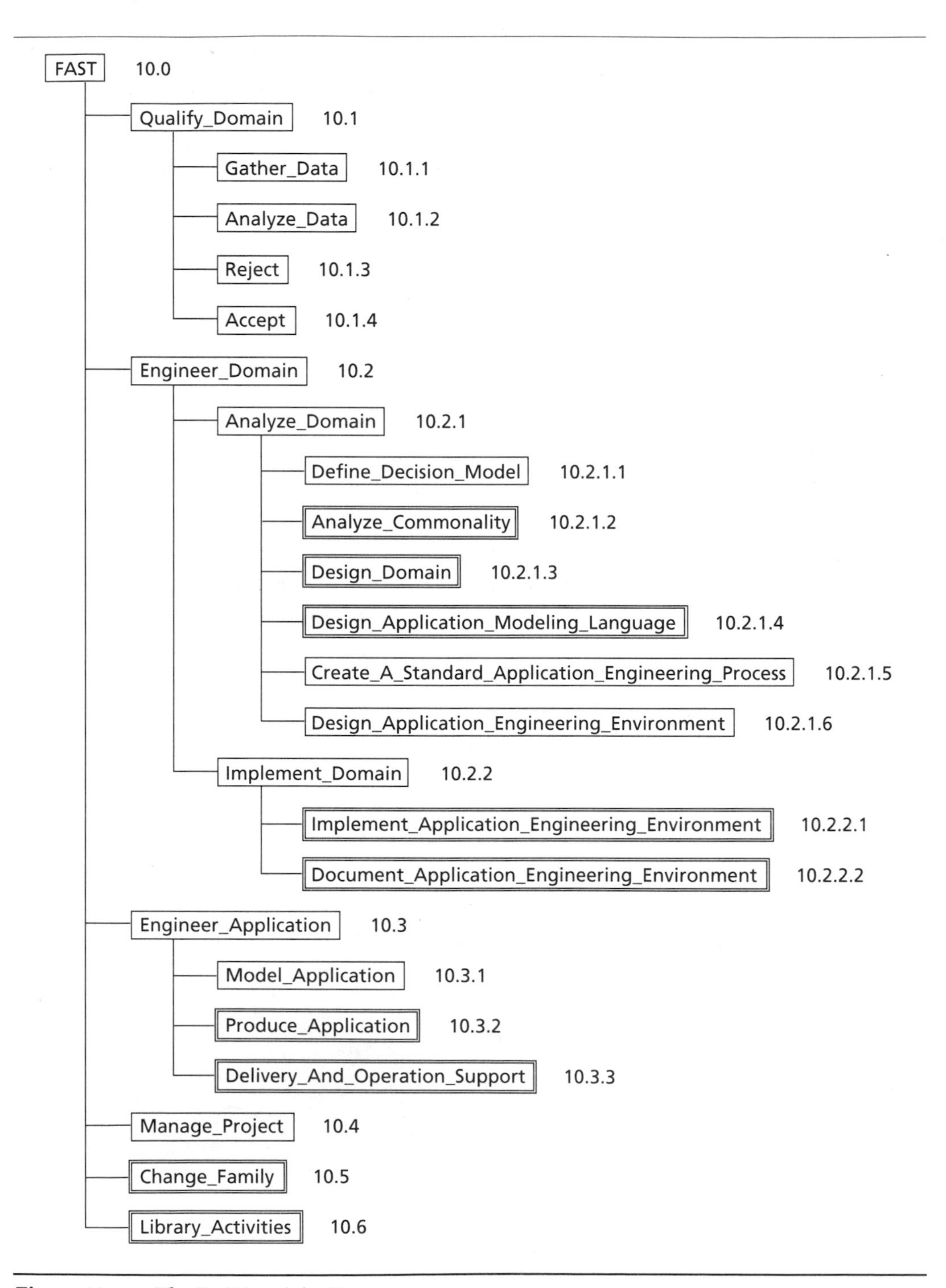

Figure 10-1. *The FAST Activity Tree*

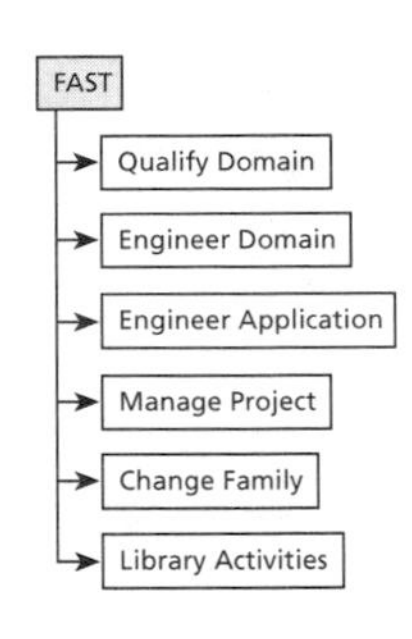

10.0 FAST

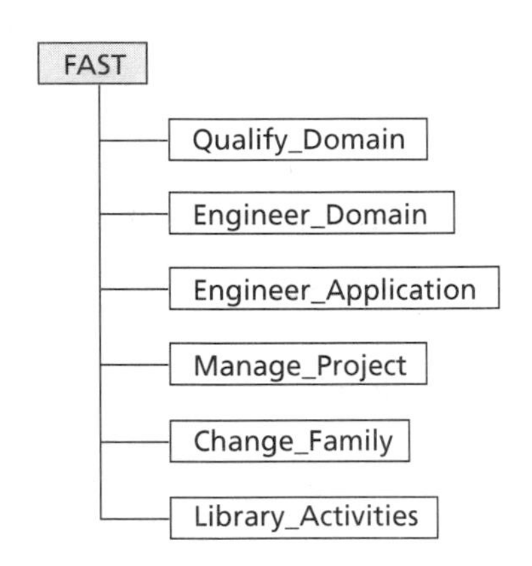

Process State Definition Form

Name	**FAST**
Synopsis	A process for creating application software systems as members of a family.
Main Role	Project_Manager
Entrance Condition	state-of(Family_Artifact) = Referenced
Artifacts List	Family_Artifact, Application, Environment
Information Artifacts	
	SUB-P-STATE LIST
Name	**Qualify_Domain**
Synopsis	Domain qualification is the process by which economic viability is determined for a domain. A domain is economically viable when the investment in domain engineering is more than repaid by the value obtained from domain engineering. The process consists of predicting the number of family members in the domain, the value of those family members, the cost of investing in domain engineering, and the cost of not investing in domain engineering. The result is an Economic_Model for the domain.
Name	**Engineer_Domain**
Synopsis	The activity that creates and supports a standardized application engineering process and an application engineering environment that supports the process.
Name	**Engineer_Application**
Synopsis	An iterative process for constructing application systems to meet customer requirements. Each application system is considered a member of a family and is defined by an Application_Model. An application engineering environment for the family is used to analyze application models and generate software from them.

continued

Name	**Change_Family**
Synopsis	Make a change to the family that results either in a different set of family members or in different ways of generating family members. The change requires that the domain be reanalyzed or reimplemented in part or in whole.
Name	**Library_Activities**
Synopsis	These activities are common to a number of FAST P-states and are gathered into a library for simplicity and convenience.
	OPERATION LIST
Name	**Manage_Project**
Synopsis	Managing the project consists of managing the job of identifying and satisfying customer requirements using an application engineering environment. It includes the traditional tasks of management, such as scheduling, allocating, and monitoring resources.
	ANALYSIS LIST
Name	**Progress_Analysis**
Synopsis	This analysis generates a report on the progress of the project. The report describes what is next in the process and what is the current state of the active artifacts.
Name	**Risk_Analysis**
Synopsis	This analysis generates a list of risky events after comparing progress on various P-states and A-states of active artifacts.
Name	**Defect_Analysis**
Synopsis	This analysis generates statistics on various types of defects by P-state, operation, and artifact to show the distribution of defects.
Name	**Resource_Analysis**
Synopsis	This analysis generates a report on resource usage, resource balancing, resource estimation, and resource allocation. The information resulting from the analysis helps the Project_Manager, Domain_Manager, and Application_Manager make decisions on the management of a project using FAST.
Exit Condition	state-of(Application) = Application_Delivered_And_Supported

continued

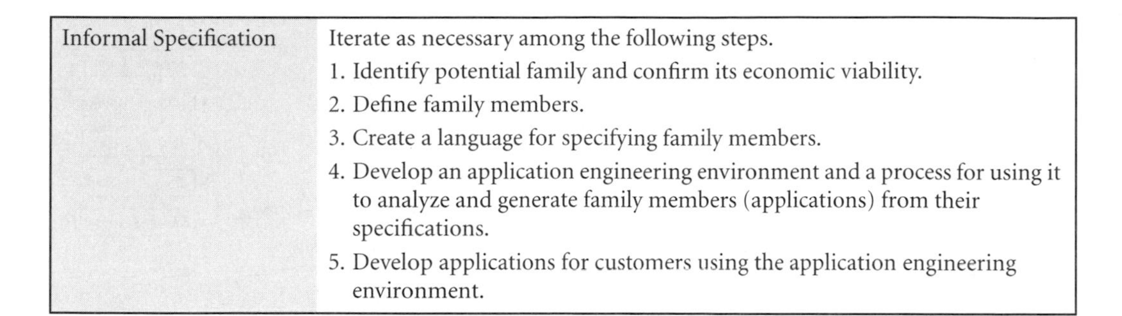

Informal Specification	Iterate as necessary among the following steps. 1. Identify potential family and confirm its economic viability. 2. Define family members. 3. Create a language for specifying family members. 4. Develop an application engineering environment and a process for using it to analyze and generate family members (applications) from their specifications. 5. Develop applications for customers using the application engineering environment.

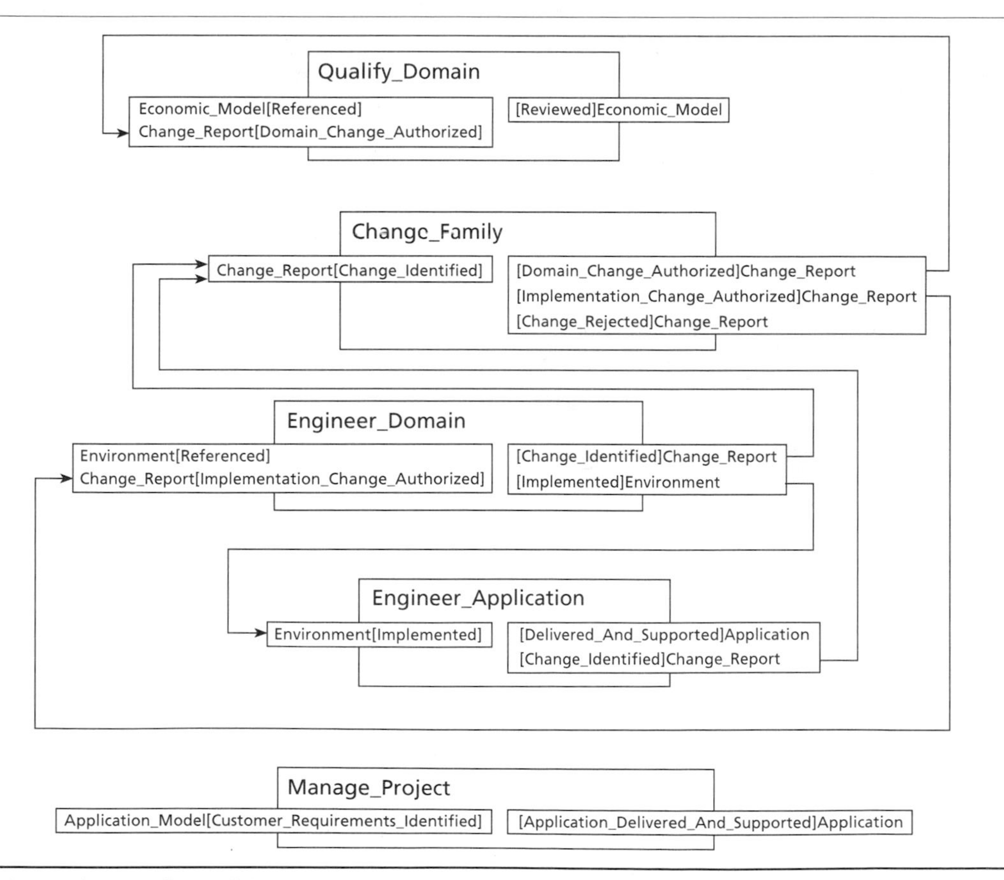

P-State Diagram for FAST

10.1 Qualify_Domain

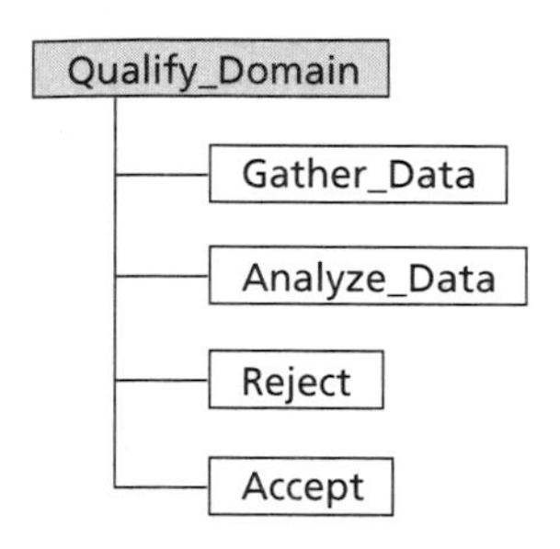

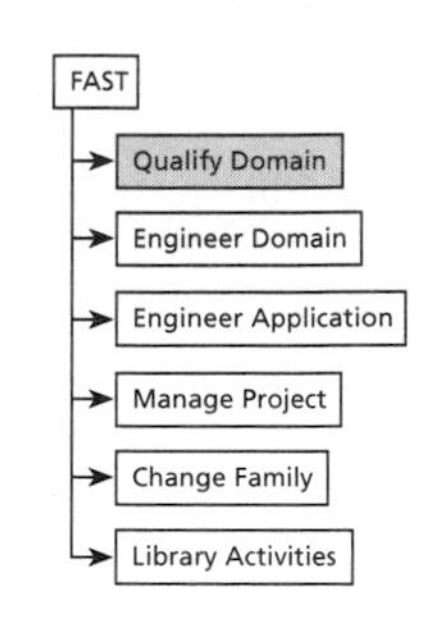

Process State Definition Form

Name	**Qualify_Domain**
Synopsis	Domain qualification is the process by which economic viability is determined for a domain. A domain is economically viable when the investment in domain engineering is more than repaid by the value obtained from domain engineering. The process consists of predicting the number of family members in the domain, the value of those family members, the cost of investing in domain engineering, and the cost of not investing in domain engineering. The result is an Economic_Model for the domain.
Main Role	Domain_Engineer, Domain_Manager
Entrance Condition	state-of(Economic_Model)=Referenced or state-of(Change_Report)=Domain_Change_Authorized
Artifacts List	Economic_Model
Information Artifacts	Environment
	OPERATION LIST
Name	**Gather_Data**
Synopsis	Gather the data needed to decide whether a domain exists and is worth engineering.
Name	**Analyze_Data**
Synopsis	Create an Economic_Model for the domain that can be used to evaluate the cost and time savings from applying domain engineering.
Name	**Reject**
Synopsis	The Economic_Model has been created and evaluated for the domain. It is not worth investing in the domain.

continued

FAST
Qualify Domain
Engineer Domain
Engineer Application
Manage Project
Change Family
Library Activities

Name	**Accept**
Synopsis	Based on the evaluation of the Economic_Model for the domain, it is worth investing in the domain.
Exit Condition	state-of(Economic_Model)=Reviewed
Informal Specification	1. Gather data on the number of expected family members, current cost, and time to develop family members. 2. Characterize process currently used to develop family members and identify potential savings in time and cost from automation. 3. Create an economic model that shows the difference in cost and time to develop family members using the current process and using domain engineering; include the cost of domain engineering in the model. 4. Use the model to decide whether the investment in domain engineering is worth the savings in cost and time for the domain.

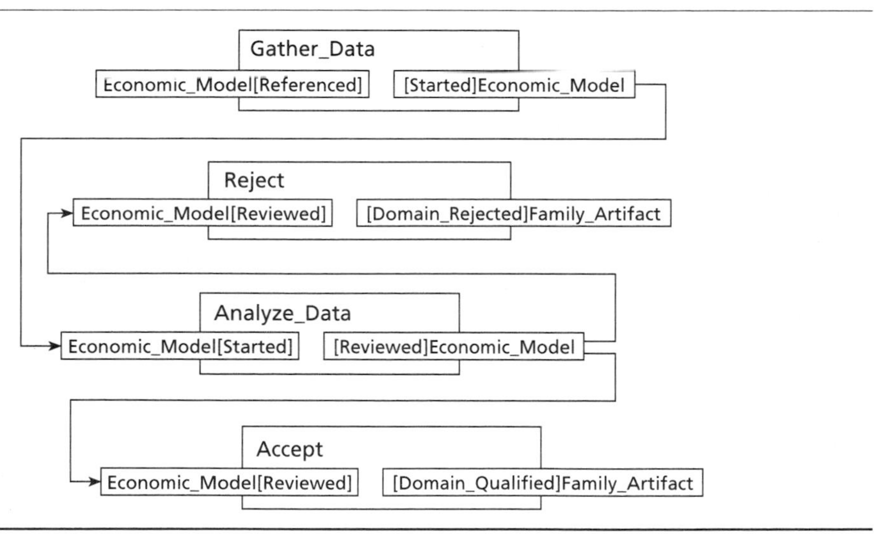

P-State Diagram for Qualify_Domain

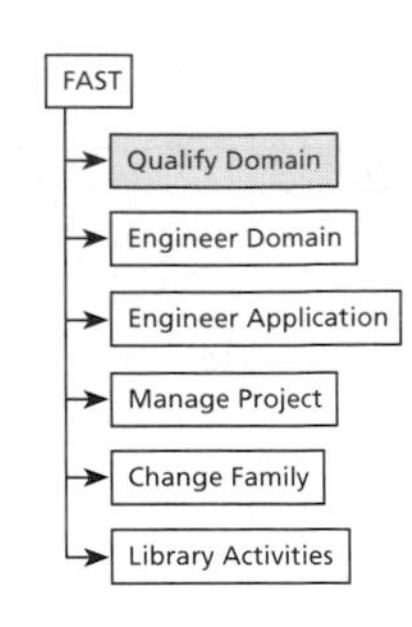

10.1.1 Gather_Data

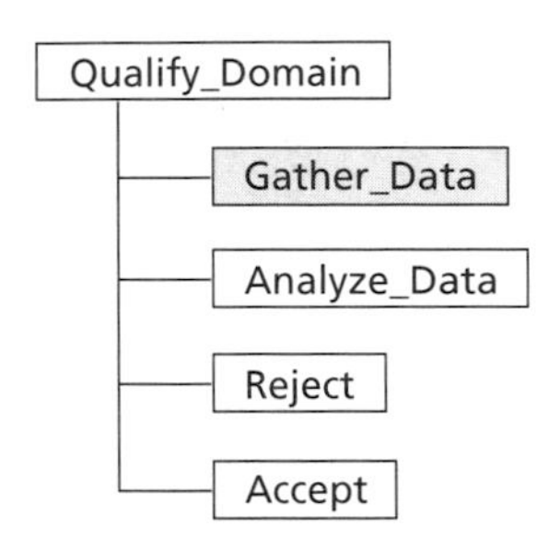

Operation Definition Form

Name	**Gather_Data**
Synopsis	Gather the data needed to decide whether a domain exists and is worth engineering.
Role List	Domain_Engineer
Entrance Condition	state-of(Economic_Model) = Referenced
Operation Type	Manual
Artifacts List	Economic_Model
Information Artifacts	
Exit Condition	state-of(Economic_Model) = Started
Informal Specification	Gather the data needed to do an analysis of economic viability for the domain. Data consists of expected number of domain members, current cost and time to develop domain members, and description of current process used to develop domain members. Sources of data are as follows. 1. Analysis of marketplace conditions 2. Logs of customer requests 3. History of existing applications and the changes made to them 4. Cost accounting records 5. Developers of domain members

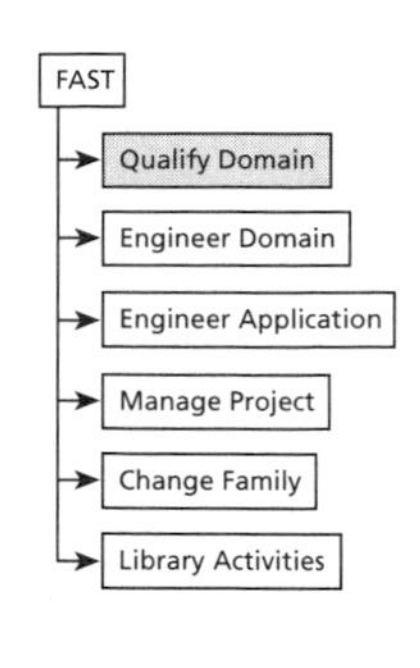

10.1.2 Analyze_Data

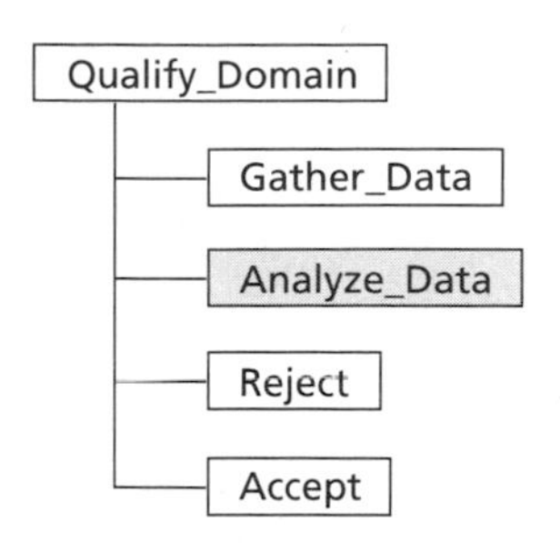

Operation Definition Form

Name	**Analyze_Data**
Synopsis	Create an Economic_Model for the domain that can be used to evaluate the cost and time savings from applying domain engineering.
Role List	Domain_Manager
Entrance Condition	state-of(Economic_Model) = Started
Operation Type	Manual
Artifacts List	Economic_Model
Information Artifacts	Environment
Exit Condition	state-of(Economic_Model) = Reviewed
Name	**Analyze_Data**
Informal Specification	Calculate the cost difference between 1. Developing and using an application engineering environment to generate family members 2. Continuing to develop family members without using FAST Cost difference is calculated as a function of the number of family members. Assume unit cost of family member and cost of domain engineering can be reliably estimated. The cost difference = (unit cost of family member development) * (average number of units per family member) * (number of family members) – (unit cost for family member generation using the application engineering environment) * (number of family members) – (cost of developing the application engineering environment). If the cost difference becomes positive for some family member N, the use of FAST has a payback when the number of family member reaches N. The break-even point is reached when the cost difference in the preceding equation is zero. As a result, the break-even number of family members is the cost of domain engineering divided by (the unit cost for family development without FAST – cost for family member generation with FAST).

continued

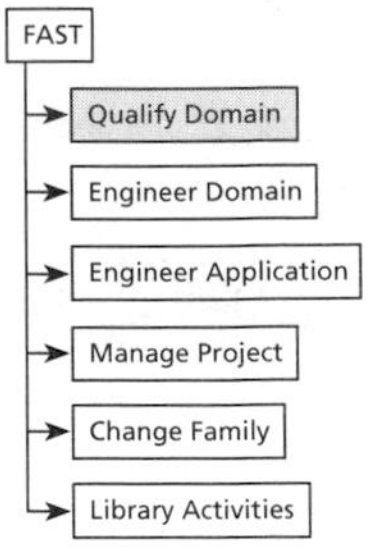

FAST
Qualify Domain
Engineer Domain
Engineer Application
Manage Project
Change Family
Library Activities

Informal Specification *continued*	For example, consider the domain of database screens, in which each screen provides a way to read, update, delete, or insert data. Each screen is a member of a family. Assume the following. 1. The cost of encoding a line on a screen manually is 0.001 staff years, and there are 20 lines per screen on the average. 2. The cost of performing domain engineering to produce an environment that can be used to generate screens from an application modeling language is 2 staff years. 3. The cost of producing a specification from which a screen can be generated is 0.0001 staff years. The cost of generating a line on a screen on the average is then 0.0001/20 = 0.00005. Then the number of screens on the average that would have to be generated using the environment to pay back the cost of producing and using it is [2/(0.001 – 0.00005)] / 20, or approximately 100 screens. Accordingly, the domain is viable if more than 100 screens will need to be generated.
Formal Specification	Cost Difference = Number_Of_Units * Units_Cost – Number_Of_Units * Unit_Cost_FAST – Environment_Cost Break_Even_Number_Of_Units = Environment_Cost / (Unit_Cost – Unit_Cost_FAST)

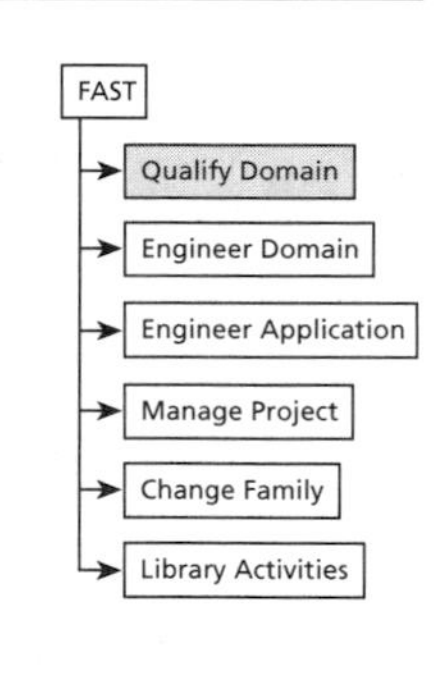

10.1.3 Reject

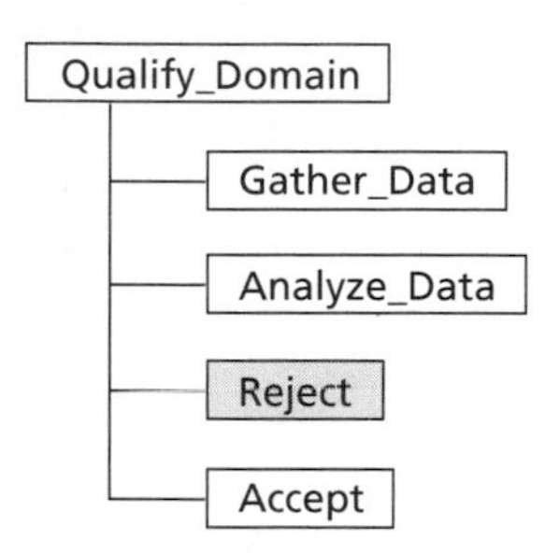

Operation Definition Form

Name	**Reject**
Synopsis	The Economic_Model has been created and evaluated for the domain. It is not worth investing in the domain.
Role List	Domain_Manager
Entrance Condition	state-of(Economic_Model) = Reviewed
Operation Type	Manual
Artifacts List	Family_Artifact
Information Artifacts	Economic_Model
Exit Condition	state-of(Family_Artifact) = Domain_Rejected
Informal Specification	The predicted number of family members is less than the number needed to offset the cost of domain engineering.
Formal Specification	Predicted-Number_Of_Family_Member_Units <= Break_Even_Number_Of_Units (see specifications for Analyze_Domain)

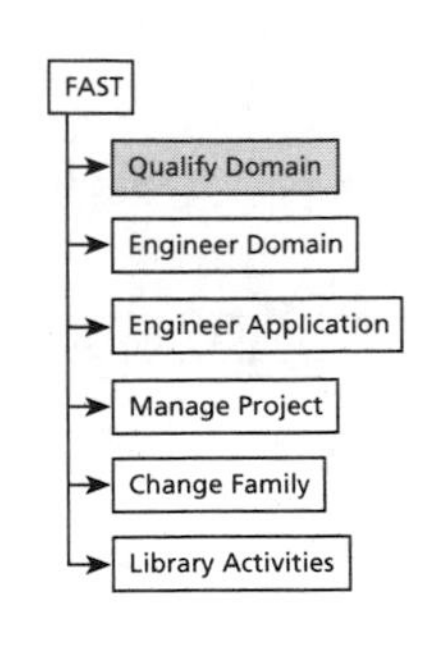

10.1.4 Accept

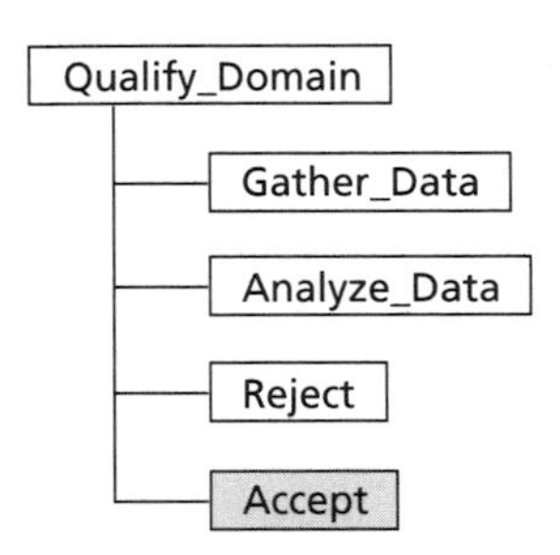

Operation Definition Form

Name	**Accept**
Synopsis	Based on the evaluation of the Economic_Model for the domain, it is worth investing in the domain.
Role List	Domain_Manager
Entrance Condition	state-of(Economic_Model) = Reviewed
Operation Type	Manual
Artifacts List	Family_Artifact
Information Artifacts	Economic_Model
Exit Condition	state-of(Family_Artifact) = Domain_Qualified
Informal Specification	The predicted number of family members is greater than the number needed to offset the cost of domain engineering.
Formal Specification	Predicted_Number_Of_Family_Member_Units >= Break_Even_Number_Of_Units (see Analyze_Data specification)

FAST
- Qualify Domain
- Engineer Domain
  - Analyze Domain
  - Implement Domain
- Engineer Application
- Manage Project
- Change Family
- Library Activities

10.2 Engineer_Domain

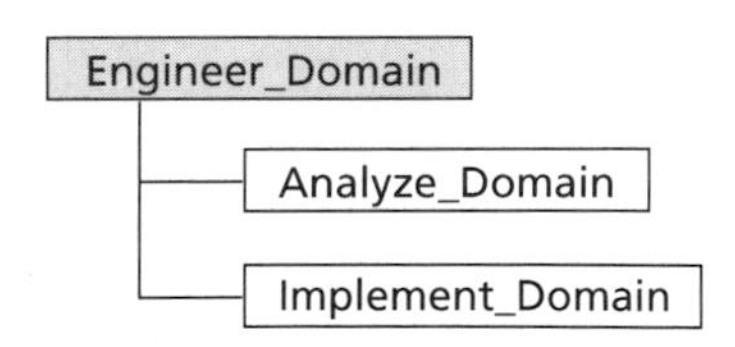

Process State Definition Form

Name	**Engineer_Domain**
Synopsis	The activity that creates and supports a standardized application engineering process and an application engineering environment that supports the process.
Main Role	Domain_Manager
Entrance Condition	state-of(Environment)=Referenced or state-of(Change_Report)=Implementation_Change_Authorized
Artifacts List	Environment
Information Artifacts	
	SUB-P-STATE LIST
Name	**Analyze_Domain**
Synopsis	The activities for creating and refining the specifications for an Application_Engineering_Environment. Key activities include defining the family that makes up the domain, designing an Application_Modeling_Language in which to describe members of the family, and specifying the tools needed to analyze Application_Models and to generate family members from Application_Models.
Name	**Implement_Domain**
Synopsis	Implementing a domain consists of constructing the application engineering environment for it. The environment is built to the specifications determined during domain engineering—that is, the Domain_Model.
	ANALYSIS LIST
Name	**Resource_Analysis**
Synopsis	This analysis generates a report on resource usage, resource balancing, resource estimation, and resource allocation. The information resulting from the analysis helps the Project_Manager, Domain_Manager, and Application_Manager make decisions on the management of a project using FAST.

continued

Name	**Progress_Analysis**
Synopsis	This analysis generates a report on the progress of the project. The report describes what is next in the process and what is the current state of the active artifacts.
Name	**Risk_Analysis**
Synopsis	This analysis generates a list of risky events after comparing progress on various P-states and A-states of active artifacts.
Name	**Defect_Analysis**
Synopsis	This analysis generates statistics on various types of defects by P-state, operation, and artifact to show the distribution of defects.
Name	**Terminology_Analysis**
Synopsis	This analysis generates a report on the usage of terminology, including the percentage of technical terms defined in Engineer_Domain that are used, and the definitions that are not used. This analysis checks all artifacts produced during Engineer_Domain for terminology usage.
Exit Condition	state-of(Environment)=Implemented or state-of(Change_Report)=Change_Identified
Informal Specification	Iterate as necessary among the following steps. 1. Define family members. 2. Create a language for specifying family members. 3. Develop an application engineering environment and a process for using it to analyze and generate family members from their specifications.

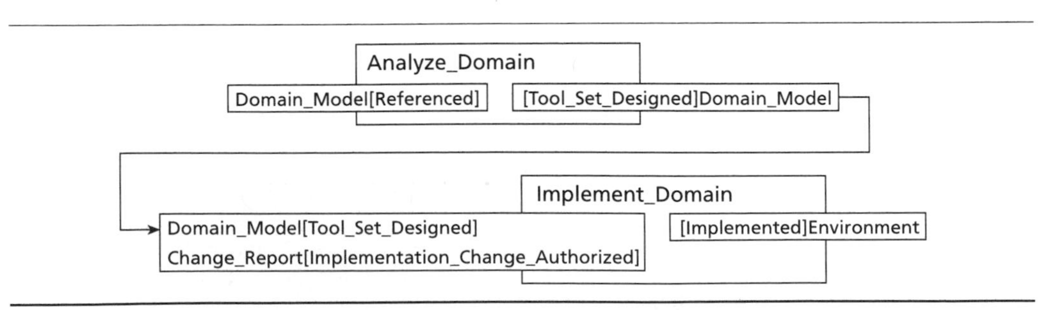

P-State Diagram for Engineer_Domain

10.2.1 Analyze_Domain

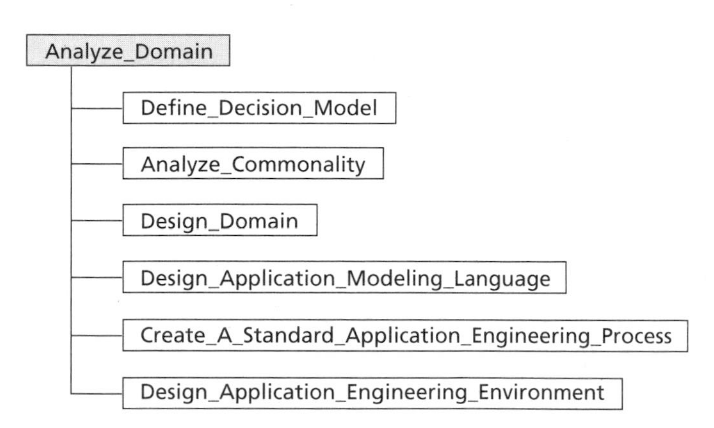

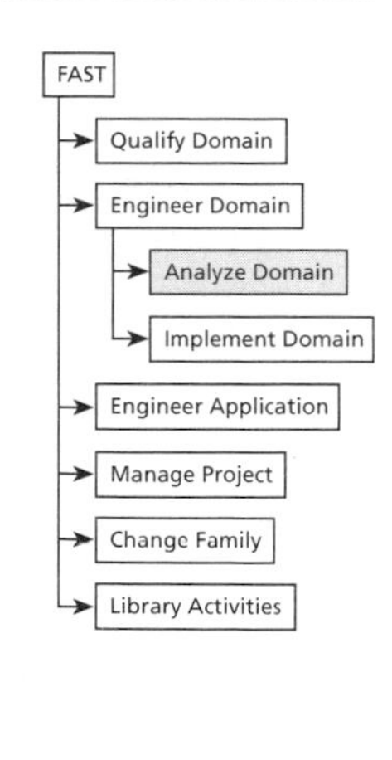

Process State Definition Form

Name	**Analyze_Domain**
Synopsis	The activities for creating and refining the specifications for an Application_ Engineering_Environment. Key activities include defining the family that makes up the domain, designing an Application_Modeling_Language in which to describe members of the family, and specifying the tools needed to analyze Application_Models and to generate family members from Application_Models.
Main Role	Domain_Engineer
Entrance Condition	state-of(Domain_Model)=Referenced
Artifacts List	Domain_Model
Information Artifacts	
	SUB-P-STATE LIST
Name	**Analyze_Commonality**
Synopsis	The commonality analysis defines and bounds the family. Analyzing commonality includes identifying assumptions that are common to all family members (commonalities), assumptions that distinguish family members from one another (variabilities), and parameters of variation that quantify variabilities, as well as establishing a dictionary of technical terms for the family.
Name	**Design_Domain**
Synopsis	Designing a domain consists of creating a design common to all family members, known as a Family_Design, and creating a mapping between the application modeling language for the domain and the components specified in the design, known as the Composition_Mapping.

continued

FAST
- Qualify Domain
- Engineer Domain
  - Analyze Domain
  - Implement Domain
- Engineer Application
- Manage Project
- Change Family
- Library Activities

Name	Design_Application_Modeling_Language
Synopsis	The application modeling language for a family is a language used for specifying family members. The language must provide a syntax for expressing the parameters of variation identified in the Commonality_Analysis and a semantics that embodies the Commonality_Analysis. The language design includes the syntax and semantics of the language and the internal representation of the language.

OPERATION LIST

Name	Define_Decision_Model
Synopsis	This operation creates a Decision_Model, which defines the set of requirements and engineering decisions that an Application_Engineer must resolve in order to describe and construct a product. It is a precursor of the Application_Engineering_Process for the domain. It is also an elaboration of a domain's variability assumptions and hence an abstract form of an Application_Modeling_Language.
Name	**Create_A_Standard_Application_Engineering_Process**
Synopsis	Creating an application engineering process for a domain consists of mapping the Decision_Model for the domain into operations performed using the application engineering environment for the domain. The Decision_Model embodies all the decisions that the Application_Engineer must make in creating an Application_Model for an application.
Name	**Design_Application_Engineering_Environment**
Synopsis	Designing the Application_Engineering_Environment consists of identifying the tools that compose the environment and describing how they will be used.

ANALYSIS LIST

Name	Application_Engineering_Process_To_Tool_Trace_Analysis
Synopsis	Check that each step in the application engineering process is supported by a tool in the toolset.
Name	**Parameter_Of_Variation_To_Module_Trace_Analysis**
Synopsis	Check that every Parameter_Of_Variation is mapped by the Composition_Mapping to a module in the Family_Design. Note that this analysis cannot be performed until the Family_Design is reviewed.
Name	**Parameter_Of_Variation_To_Decision_Trace_Analysis**
Synopsis	Check every Parameter_Of_Variation to see whether there exists a corresponding decision in the Decision_Model.

continued

FAST
Qualify Domain
Engineer Domain
Analyze Domain
Implement Domain
Engineer Application
Manage Project
Change Family
Library Activities

Name	**Composition_Mapping_To_Module_Trace_Analysis**
Synopsis	Check that each construct in the AML is mapped by the Composition_Mapping into at least one module in the Family_Design.
Name	**Commonality_To_Module_Trace_Analysis**
Synopsis	Check that every commonality is maintained by the Family_Design.
Name	**Parameters_Of_Variation_To_Application_Modeling_Language_Constructs_Trace_Analysis**
Synopsis	Check that each Parameter_Of_Variation with an AML binding time is represented by a construct in the AML and that its value can be expressed in the AML.
Exit Condition	state-of(Domain_Model)=Tool_Set_Designed
Informal Specification	Iterate as necessary among the following steps. 1. Define family members and the decisions that distinguish among them. 2. Design an application modeling language. 3. Design an application engineering environment. 4. Create an application engineering process for using the environment.

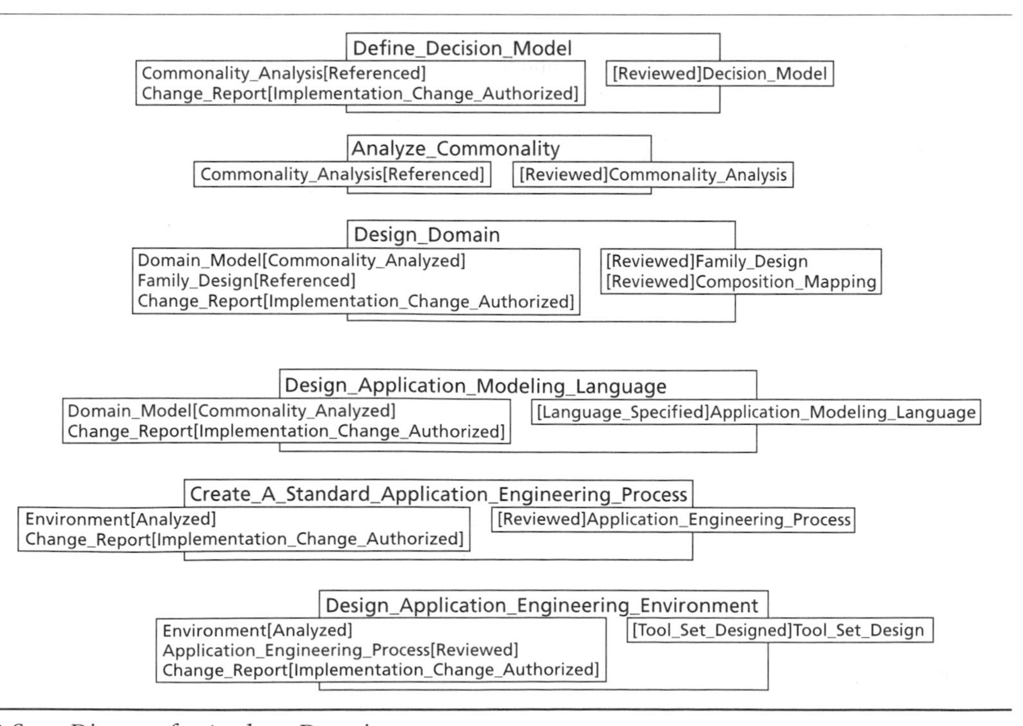

P-State Diagram for Analyze_Domain

- FAST
  - Qualify Domain
  - Engineer Domain
    - Analyze Domain
    - Implement Domain
  - Engineer Application
  - Manage Project
  - Change Family
  - Library Activities

10.2.1.1 Define_Decision_Model

Operation Definition Form

Name	**Define_Decision_Model**
Synopsis	This operation creates a Decision_Model, which defines the set of requirements and engineering decisions that an Application_Engineer must resolve in order to describe and construct a product. It is a precursor of the Application_Engineering_Process for the domain. It is also an elaboration of a domain's variability assumptions and hence an abstract form of an Application_Modeling_Language.
Role List	Domain_Engineer
Entrance Condition	state-of(Commonality_Analysis)=Referenced or state-of(Change_Report)=Implementation_Change_Authorized
Operation Type	Manual
Artifacts List	Decision_Model
Information Artifacts	Commonality_Analysis
Exit Condition	state-of(Decision_Model)=Reviewed
Informal Specification	The decision model for a domain identifies the decisions that need to be made by an Application_Engineer to define a member of the family in a domain and identifies any sequencing required of those decisions. Define the Decision_Model using the following process. 1. List the Parameters_Of_Variation according to their binding times: the time at which the value of the parameter must be supplied, as defined in the table of Parameters_Of_Variation (usually Section 6) of the Commonality_Analysis. 2. For each binding time that precedes runtime, perform the following procedure. 2a. Identify the order in which values must be supplied for the Parameters_Of_Variation. Note that this may be a total order or a partial order, or there may be no required order. 2b. List the decisions corresponding to the Parameters_Of_Variation (obtained from the meaning column of the table of Parameters_Of_Variation in the Commonality_Analysis) in the order in which they must be made, as specified by the order identified in step 2a. The list of decisions that results from this procedure is the Decision_Model.

10.2.1.2 Analyze_Commonality

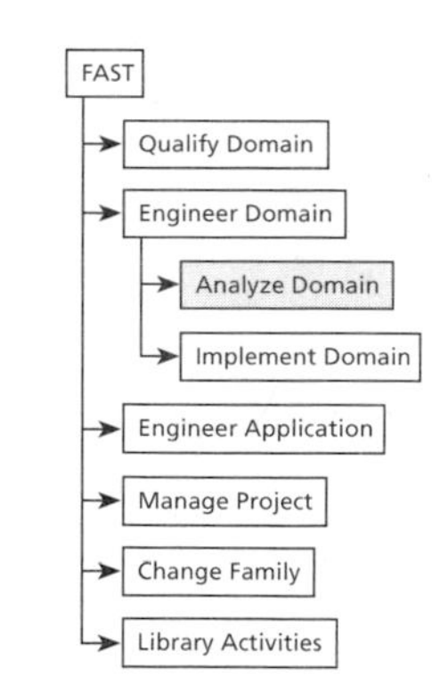

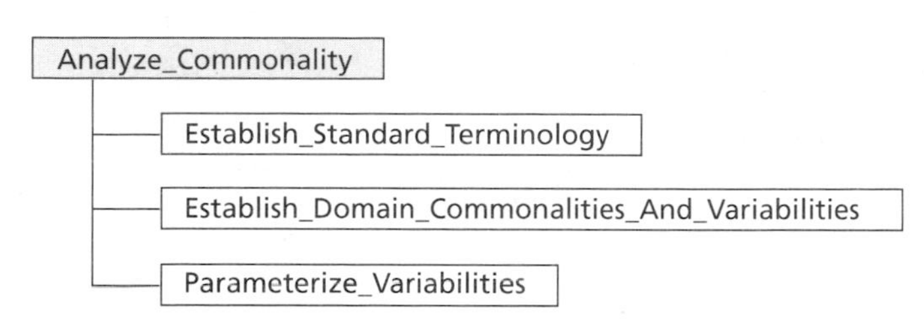

Process State Definition Form

Name	**Analyze_Commonality**
Synopsis	The commonality analysis defines and bounds the family. Analyzing commonality includes identifying assumptions that are common to all family members (commonalities), assumptions that distinguish family members from one another (variabilities), and parameters of variation that quantify variabilities, as well as establishing a dictionary of technical terms for the family.
Main Role	Moderator, Recorder, Domain_Engineer
Entrance Condition	state-of(Commonality_Analysis) = Referenced
Artifacts List	Commonality_Analysis
Information Artifacts	Domain_Model
	SUB-P-STATE LIST
Name	**Establish_Standard_Terminology**
Synopsis	Define all significant technical terms used by domain experts in discussing the requirements or engineering of systems in the domain.
Name	**Establish_Domain_Commonalities_And_Variabilities**
Synopsis	Create a list of the assumptions that define what's true of all family members (commonalities) and the assumptions that distinguish among family members (variabilities).
Name	**Parameterize_Variabilities**
Synopsis	Parameters_Of_Variation quantify the variabilities of the domain. Each parameter is defined by a name, a domain, a binding time, and a default value.
	ANALYSIS LIST
Name	**Variation_Parameter_To_Variability_Trace_Analysis**
Synopsis	Are there any parameters of variation that cannot be traced to variabilities?
Name	**Variability_To_Variation_Parameter_Trace_Analysis**
Synopsis	Check that each variability has a corresponding Parameter_Of_Variation.

continued

FAST
- Qualify Domain
- Engineer Domain
  - Analyze Domain
  - Implement Domain
- Engineer Application
- Manage Project
- Change Family
- Library Activities

Name	**Parameter_Of_Variation_To_Module_Trace_Analysis**
Synopsis	Check that every Parameter_Of_Variation is mapped by the Composition_Mapping to a module in the Family_Design. Note that this analysis cannot be performed until the Family_Design is reviewed.
Exit Condition	state-of(Commonality_Analysis) = Reviewed
Informal Specification	The commonality analysis process is organized into the following stages. 1. Prepare. Select a moderator, who ensures that all resources needed for the initial sessions are in place. The moderator directs and guides all sessions that are part of the analysis. 2. Plan. The moderator and domain engineers meet to agree on the purpose and scope of the analysis and to review briefly the expected activities and results of the commonality analysis process. 3. Analyze. The moderator and domain engineers meet to analyze the family and characterize its members by • Establishing standard terminology for the family (identifying and defining key technical terms for the family) • Establishing domain commonalities and variabilities by identifying commonalities (assumptions that are true for all family members), and by identifying variabilities (assumptions about how family members may vary). 4. Quantify. The moderator and domain experts meet to define the parameters of variation for the family. For each variability, its Parameter_Of_Variation includes the set of possible values for the variability, the time at which a value for the variability must be selected when defining a family member, and the default value used when defining family members. 5. Review. Reviewers outside the team that produced the analysis conduct a review of it. During the analyze, quantify, and review stages, important issues that arise are recorded, including, for each issue, what the issue is, the alternatives to its resolution, the selected alternative, and the rationale for selecting that alternative.

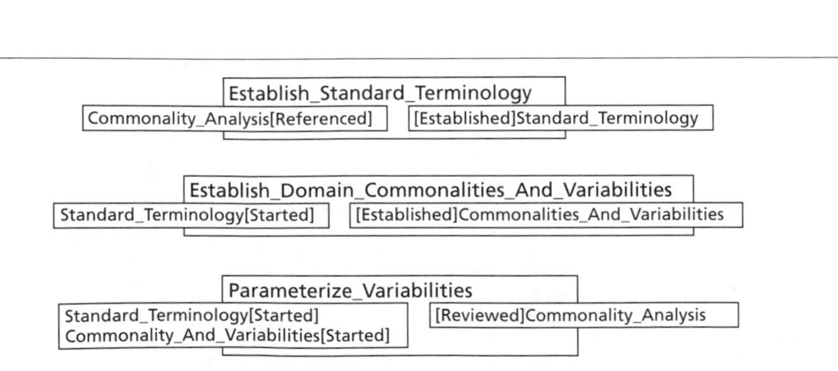

P-State Diagram for Analyze_Commonality

FAST
Qualify Domain
Engineer Domain
Analyze Domain
Implement Domain
Engineer Application
Manage Project
Change Family
Library Activities

10.2.1.2.1 Establish_Standard_Terminology

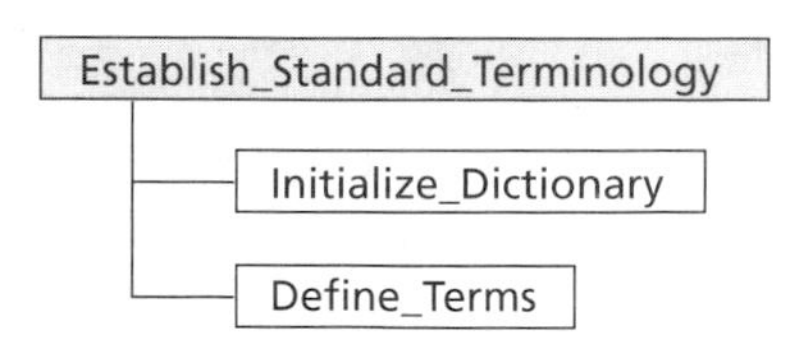

Process State Definition Form

Name	**Establish_Standard_Terminology**
Synopsis	Define all significant technical terms used by domain experts in discussing the requirements or engineering of systems in the domain.
Main Role	Moderator, Recorder, Domain_Engineer
Entrance Condition	state-of(Commonality_Analysis) = Referenced
Artifacts List	Standard_Terminology
Information Artifacts	Domain_Model
	OPERATION LIST
Name	**Initialize_Dictionary**
Synopsis	Create a template for the dictionary of terms for the domain.
Name	**Define_Terms**
Synopsis	Definition of terms used in describing the domain.
Exit Condition	state-of(Standard_Terminology) = Established
Informal Specification	Standard terminology for the domain consists of words and phrases that represent key ideas or abstractions in the domain. Such terminology is commonly used in discussing the domain. During the analysis of commonality for the domain, a dictionary of standard terminology is constructed as follows: 1. While creating a Commonality_Analysis, domain experts frequently use a term, consisting of a word or a short phrase, to describe a key idea or abstraction in the domain, or a participant in the analysis identifies the need for a term to express some idea or abstraction. 2. Domain experts participating in the analysis identify possible definitions of the term. 3. Domain experts attempt to achieve consensus quickly on the definition of the term that best defines the key idea or abstraction. 4. If consensus is quickly achieved, the definition is entered into the dictionary section of the Commonality_Analysis, and all uses of the term are italicized or otherwise typographically distinguished. 5. If consensus is not quickly achieved, defining the term is made into an issue and assigned to a domain expert.

continued

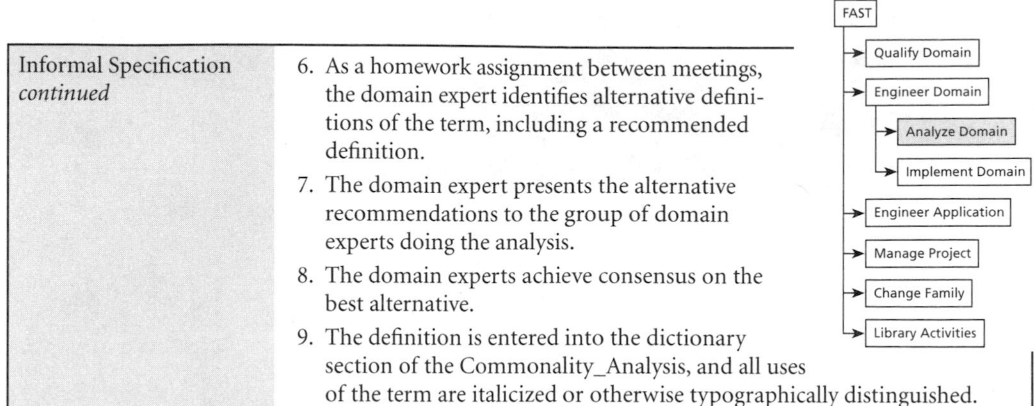

Informal Specification *continued*	6. As a homework assignment between meetings, the domain expert identifies alternative definitions of the term, including a recommended definition. 7. The domain expert presents the alternative recommendations to the group of domain experts doing the analysis. 8. The domain experts achieve consensus on the best alternative. 9. The definition is entered into the dictionary section of the Commonality_Analysis, and all uses of the term are italicized or otherwise typographically distinguished. 10. Uses of the term in the body of the commonality analysis may be linked to the definition.

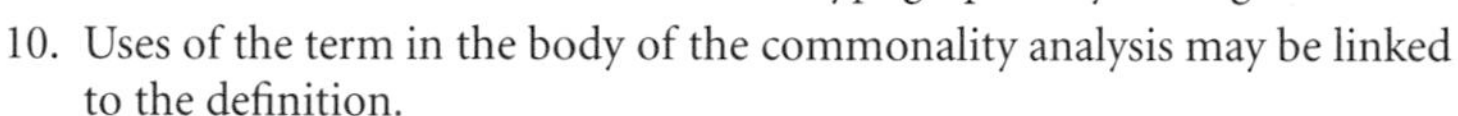

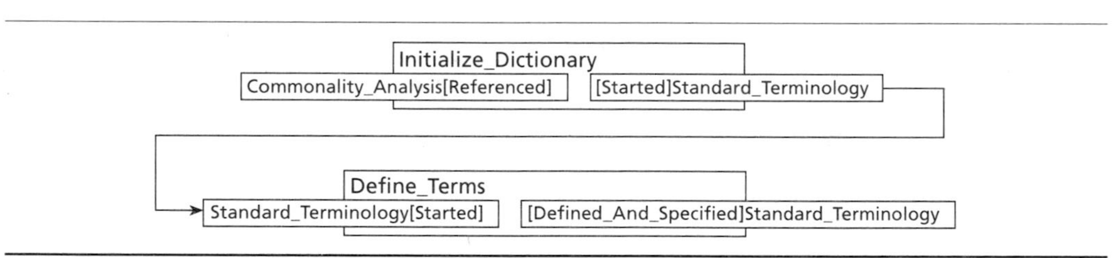

P-State Diagram for Establish_Standard_Terminology

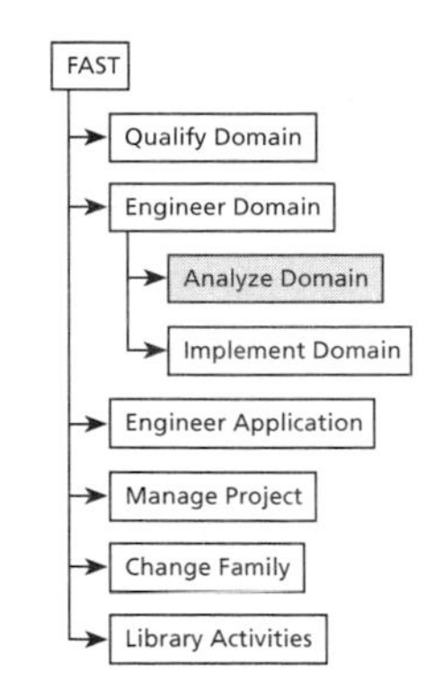

10.2.1.2.2 Establish_Domain_Commonalities_And_Variabilities

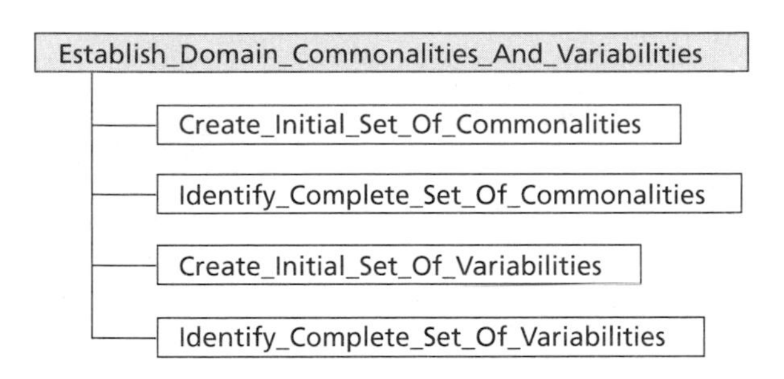

Process State Definition Form

Name	**Establish_Domain_Commonalities_And_Variabilities**
Synopsis	Create a list of the assumptions that define what's true of all family members (commonalities) and the assumptions that distinguish among family members (variabilities).
Main Role	Domain_Engineer, Moderator, Recorder
Entrance Condition	state-of(Standard_Terminology) = Started
Artifacts List	Commonalities_And_Variabilities, Standard_Terminology
Information Artifacts	Domain_Model
OPERATION LIST	
Name	**Create_Initial_Set_Of_Commonalities**
Synopsis	Create a template for the domain commonalities and include a few initial proposed commonalities.
Name	**Identify_Complete_Set_Of_Commonalities**
Synopsis	Complete the identification of commonalities, the assumptions that are true for all the family members.
Name	**Create_Initial_Set_Of_Variabilities**
Synopsis	Create a template for the domain variabilities and include a few initial proposed variabilities.
Name	**Identify_Complete_Set_Of_Variabilities**
Synopsis	Complete the identification of variabilities, the assumptions that distinguish the family members.
Exit Condition	state-of(Commonalities_And_Variabilities) = Established

continued

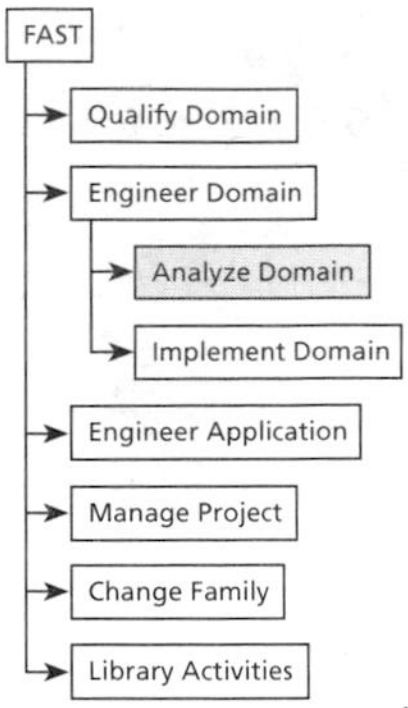

FAST
- Qualify Domain
- Engineer Domain
  - Analyze Domain
  - Implement Domain
- Engineer Application
- Manage Project
- Change Family
- Library Activities

Informal Specification	Establishing the commonalities and variabilities for the domain defines the members of the domain. Each commonality is an assumption that is true for all members of the domain. Each variability is an assumption about how members of the domain can differ. Domain experts meet in a moderated group to determine the commonalities and variabilities, which are recorded in a Commonality_Analysis. The commonality analysis contains the following sections. 1. Introduction to the analysis and its objectives 2. Overview of the domain 3. Dictionary of terms (see Family_Artifact. Environment. Domain_Model. Commonality_Analysis. Standard_Terminology) 4. A list of commonalities (Family_Artifact.Environment. Domain_Model. Commonality_Analysis.Commonalities_And_Variabilities) 5. A list of variabilities (Family_Artifact.Environment. Domain_Model. Commonalities_And_Variabilities) 6. A table of parameters of variation (Family_Artifact. Environment. Domain_Model. Commonality_Analysis. Parameters_Of_Variation) 7. A list of issues that arose during the discussion and, for each issue, an explanation of its resolution 8. Appendices as needed A moderator directs the discussions and establishes the agenda. A recorder modifies the commonality analysis based on the results of the discussion. Commonalities and variabilities are established by repeating the following process until no more commonalities and variabilities are identified and no issues are left. The process is organized into tasks, which can be executed repeatedly in any order. The steps within each task are executed in order. Task I: Identify commonalities. 1. The domain experts propose assumptions that are true for all members of the domain. 2. When the group reaches consensus that an assumption is true for all members of the domain, the recorder enters it as a commonality in the appropriate subsection of the commonality section of the Commonality_Analysis, and assigns an index. 3. When the group reaches consensus that a proposed assumption is not true for all members of the domain, the assumption is discarded. 4. When the group cannot reach consensus on whether or not a proposed assumption is true for all members of the domain, the question of its truth is made an issue, and the issue is assigned to a domain expert. The responsibility of the domain expert is to identify alternatives for resolution of the issues, including alternative assumptions, and to recommend a resolution. 5. Each commonality is analyzed to see whether there are corresponding variabilities, and the variabilities are treated as proposed variabilities in Task II.

continued

FAST
Qualify Domain
Engineer Domain
Analyze Domain
Implement Domain
Engineer Application
Manage Project
Change Family
Library Activities

Informal Specification *continued*

Task II: Identify variabilities.

6. The domain experts propose assumptions that define how members of the domain can vary.
7. When the group reaches consensus that an assumption correctly specifies a way in which domain members can vary, the recorder enters it as a variability in the appropriate subsection of the Variability section of the Commonality_Analysis, assigns an index, and, when appropriate, cross-references to a related commonality.
8. When the group reaches consensus that a proposed assumption does not correctly specify how domain members can vary and cannot specify such variation by restating it, the assumption is discarded. When the group feels that it is valuable to record the reason that the assumption is not a variability, they can create an issue explaining why.
9. When the group cannot reach consensus on whether a proposed assumption specifies a variability for the domain, the question of the appropriate assumption is made an issue, the recorder enters it in the issue section of the analysis, and the issue is assigned to a domain expert. The responsibility of the expert is to identify alternative assumptions and to present a recommended choice among those assumptions to the group of domain experts during one of the commonality analysis sessions. The domain experts then make a choice, either accepting the recommendation or selecting another assumption. The alternatives considered and the choice made are recorded as part of the issue.

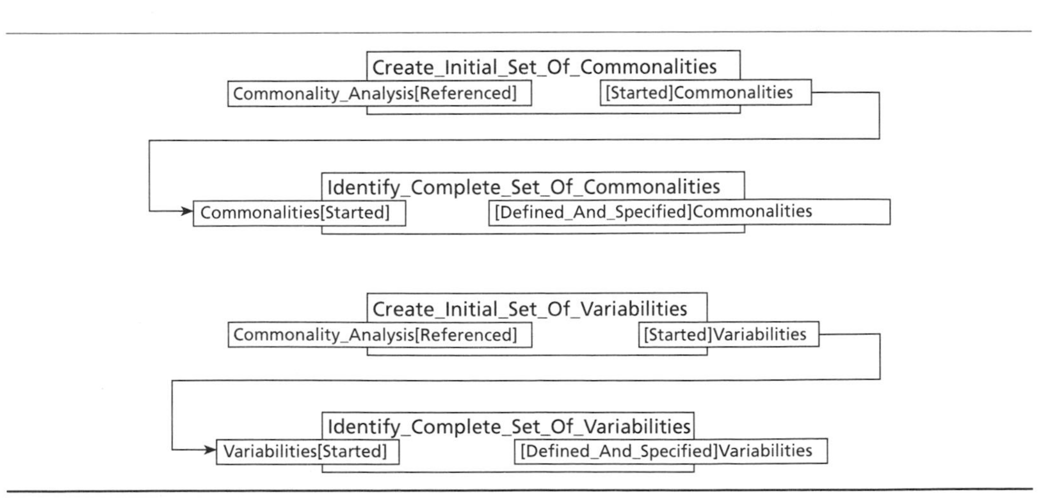

P-State Diagram for Establish_Domain Commonality_And_Variability

10.2.1.2.3 Parameterize_Variabilities

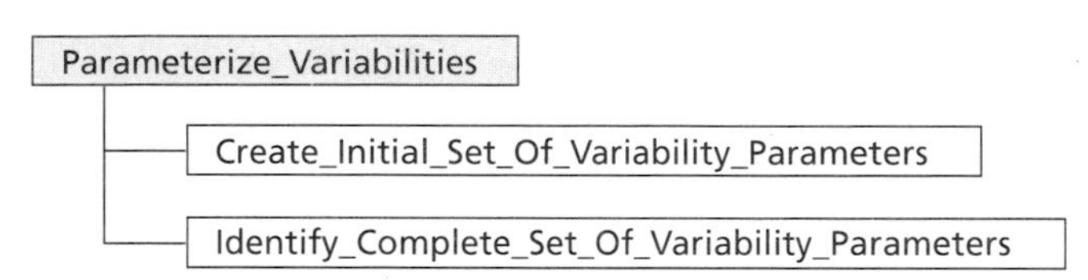

FAST
Qualify Domain
Engineer Domain
Analyze Domain
Implement Domain
Engineer Application
Manage Project
Change Family
Library Activities

Process State Definition Form

Name	**Parameterize_Variabilities**
Synopsis	Parameters_Of_Variation quantify the variabilities of the domain. Each parameter is defined by a name, a domain, a binding time, and a default value.
Main Role	Domain_Engineer, Moderator, Recorder
Entrance Condition	(state-of(Standard_Terminology) = Started) and (state-of(Commonalities_And_Variabilities) = Started)
Artifacts List	Parameters_Of_Variations
Information Artifacts	Domain_Model

OPERATION LIST

Name	**Create_Initial_Set_Of_Variability_Parameters**
Synopsis	Create a template for the parameters of variation and include a few initial parameters of variation for the proposed variabilities.
Name	**Identify_Complete_Set_Of_Variability_Parameters**
Synopsis	Complete the identification of Parameters_Of_Variation.
Exit Condition	state-of(Commonality_Analysis) = Reviewed
Informal Specification	Parameterizing variabilities means defining a parameter of variation for each variability. The parameter represents the range of values for the variability, the time at which the value of the variability is determined, and the default value of the variability. Parameters of variation are established by Domain_Engineers as part of the process of creating a commonality analysis. The Parameters_Of_Variation are defined after the commonalities and variabilities have been identified. Domain engineers use the following procedure to define the parameters of variation, which are specified in a table that forms Section 6 of the Commonality_Analysis, with one column of the table for each of the following attributes of the parameters: name, meaning, range of values, binding time, default value.

continued

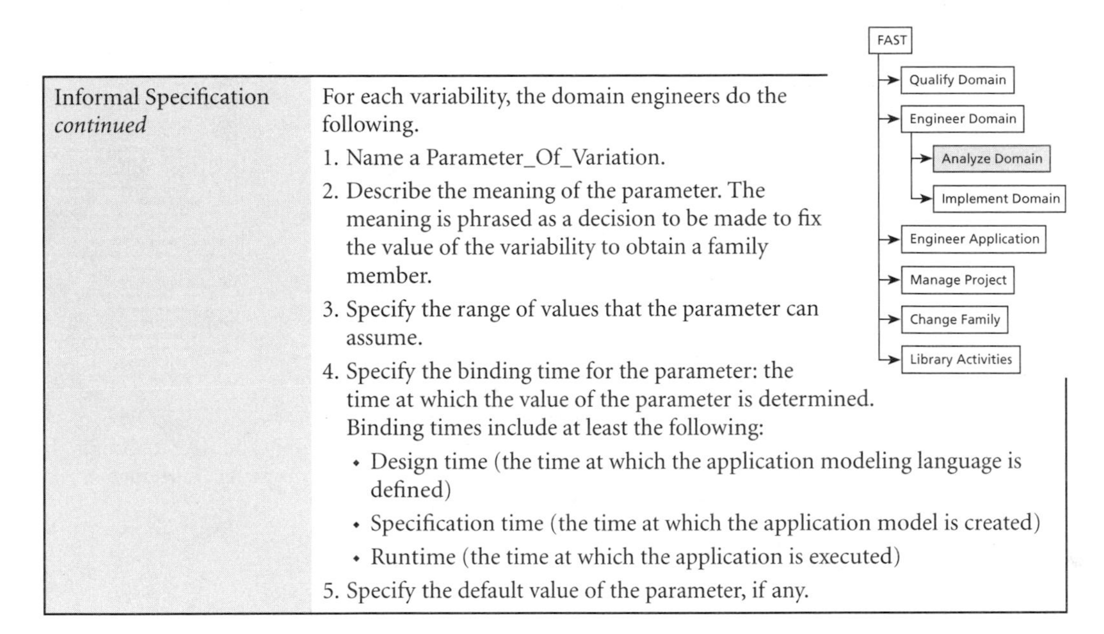

Informal Specification *continued*	For each variability, the domain engineers do the following. 1. Name a Parameter_Of_Variation. 2. Describe the meaning of the parameter. The meaning is phrased as a decision to be made to fix the value of the variability to obtain a family member. 3. Specify the range of values that the parameter can assume. 4. Specify the binding time for the parameter: the time at which the value of the parameter is determined. Binding times include at least the following: • Design time (the time at which the application modeling language is defined) • Specification time (the time at which the application model is created) • Runtime (the time at which the application is executed) 5. Specify the default value of the parameter, if any.

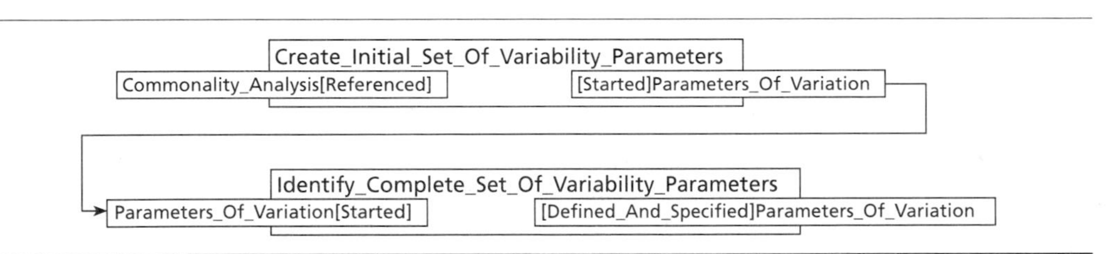

P-State Diagram for Parameterize_Variabilities

10.2.1.3 Design_Domain

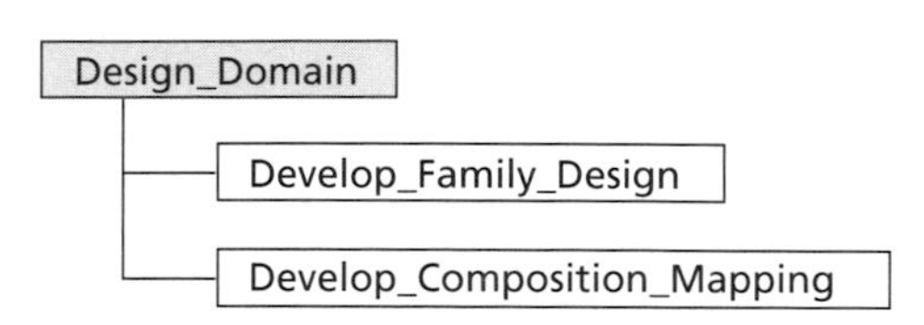

FAST
Qualify Domain
Engineer Domain
Analyze Domain
Implement Domain
Engineer Application
Manage Project
Change Family
Library Activities

Process State Definition Form

Name	**Design_Domain**
Synopsis	Designing a domain consists of creating a design common to all family members, known as a Family_Design, and creating a mapping between the application modeling language for the domain and the components specified in the design, known as the Composition_Mapping.
Main Role	Domain_Engineer, Environment_Engineer
Entrance Condition	state-of(Domain_Model)=Commonality_Analyzed and state-of(Family_Design)=Referenced or state-of(Change_Report)=Implementation_Change_Authorized
Artifacts List	Family_Design
Information Artifacts	
	OPERATION LIST
Name	**Develop_Family_Design**
Synopsis	Creating a Family_Design consists of creating a design that can be used for generating members of the family. Such a design can be created by organizing the software into modules; each module's secret is how to implement a parameter of variation. One way to implement such a design is to make a template for each module that is parameterized according to possible values of the corresponding parameter of variation.
Name	**Develop_Composition_Mapping**
Synopsis	The Composition_Mapping provides automated traceability between specifications in the Application_Modeling_Language and templates specified by the Family_Design. The mapping is used to generate applications by mapping the values of Parameters_Of_Variation expressed in the Application_Modeling_Language into values of parameters to the templates specified in the Family_Design, and then instantiating and integrating those templates.

continued

FAST
- Qualify Domain
- Engineer Domain
  - Analyze Domain
  - Implement Domain
- Engineer Application
- Manage Project
- Change Family
- Library Activities

ANALYSIS LIST	
Name	**Application_Modeling_Language_To_Family_Design_Trace_Analysis**
Synopsis	Check each language construct to see whether there exists a corresponding module in the Family_Design.
Name	**Composition_Mapping_To_Language_Construct_Mapping_Analysis**
Synopsis	Check that each construct in the Application_Modeling_Language that is used to express a variability whose binding time is specification time or later is mapped by the Composition_Mapping.
Name	**Composition_Mapping_To_Family_Design**
Synopsis	Check that each module in the Family_Design is in the range of the Composition_Mapping either by a direct mapping from a language construct in the AML or by the transitive closure of the uses relation for (programs in) a module mapped directly from a language construct.
Exit Condition	(state-of(Family_Design)=Reviewed) and (state-of(Composition Mapping)=Reviewed)

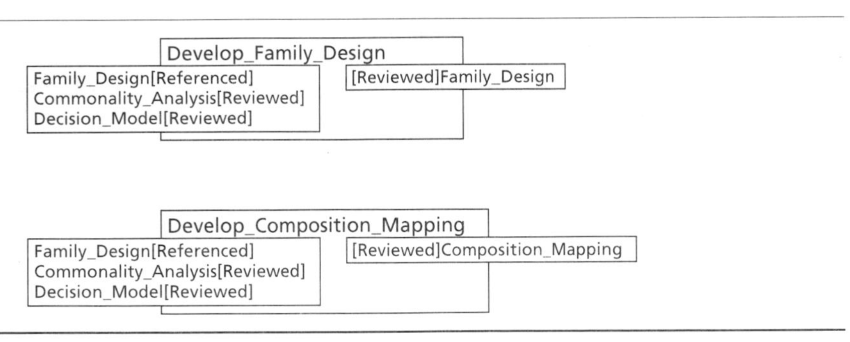

P-State Diagram for Design_Domain

FAST
- Qualify Domain
- Engineer Domain
  - Analyze Domain
  - Implement Domain
- Engineer Application
- Manage Project
- Change Family
- Library Activities

10.2.1.3.1 Develop_Family_Design

Operation Definition Form

Name	**Develop_Family_Design**
Synopsis	Creating a Family_Design consists of creating a design that can be used for generating members of the family. Such a design can be created by organizing the software into modules; each module's secret is how to implement a parameter of variation. One way to implement such a design is to make a template for each module that is parameterized according to possible values of the corresponding parameter of variation.
Role List	Domain_Engineer
Entrance Condition	state-of(Family_Design) = Referenced and state-of(Commonality_Analysis) = Reviewed and state-of(Decision_Model) = Reviewed
Operation Type	Manual
Artifacts List	Family_Design
Information Artifacts	Domain_Model
Exit Condition	state-of(Family_Design) = Reviewed
Informal Specification	One alternative for creating a Family_Design is to create an information-hiding design for the family by applying the SCR design process. For each variability or related set of variabilities there is a module in the design whose secret is how to implement the variability or related set of variabilities. See the design of the Floating Weather Station in Chapter 5 for an example.

FAST
- Qualify Domain
- Engineer Domain
  - Analyze Domain
  - Implement Domain
- Engineer Application
- Manage Project
- Change Family
- Library Activities

10.2.1.3.2 Develop_Composition_Mapping

Operation Definition Form

Name	**Develop_Composition_Mapping**
Synopsis	The Composition_Mapping provides automated traceability between specifications in the Application_Modeling_Language and templates specified by the reuse architecture. The mapping is used to generate applications by mapping the values of Parameters_Of_Variation expressed in the Application_Modeling_Language into values of parameters to the templates specified in the Family_Design, and then instantiating and integrating those templates.
Role List	Domain_Engineer
Entrance Condition	state-of(Family_Design) = Referenced and state-of(Commonality_Analysis) = Reviewed and state-of(Decision_Model) = Reviewed
Operation Type	Manual
Artifacts List	Composition_Mapping
Information Artifacts	Domain_Model, Commonality_Analysis, Family_Design
Exit Condition	state-of(Composition_Mapping) = Reviewed
Informal Specification	When an SCR design is used, for each Parameter_Of_Variation, identify the module in the SCR design that encapsulates the decision embodied by the parameter. For each program in the identified module, apply the uses relation from the SCR design to find other modules that must be included in the family member when the identified module is included. Continue this process until the transitive closure of the branch of the uses relation starting at the identified module has been formed. Call the set of modules formed by this process the target set of the Parameter_Of_Variation. The Composition_Mapping maps the Parameters_Of_Variation into their corresponding target sets.

FAST
Qualify Domain
Engineer Domain
Analyze Domain
Implement Domain
Engineer Application
Manage Project
Change Family
Library Activities

10.2.1.4 Design_Application_Modeling_Language

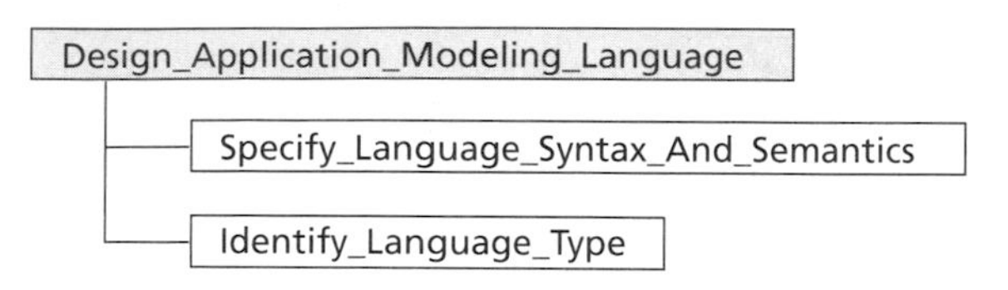

Process State Definition Form

Name	**Design_Application_Modeling_Language**
Synopsis	The application modeling language for a family is a language used for specifying family members. The language must provide a syntax for expressing the parameters of variation identified in the Commonality_Analysis and a semantics that embodies the Commonality_Analysis. The language design includes the syntax and semantics of the language and the internal representation of the language.
Main Role	Domain_Engineer
Entrance Condition	state-of(Domain_Model)=Commonality_Analyzed or state-of(Change_Report)=Implementation_Change_Authorized
Artifacts List	Application_Modeling_Language
Information Artifacts	Domain_Model
	OPERATION LIST
Name	**Specify_Language_Syntax_And_Semantics**
Synopsis	Define the Backus Normal Form (BNF) production rules, or the equivalent, including semantics, for each construct in the language.
Name	**Identify_Language_Type**
Synopsis	Application modeling languages tend to be one of several different types; they form families of languages. Examples are languages that describe state machines, languages that describe properties of objects, and languages that describe concurrent threads of events. Identifying the language type is a key step in designing the constructs of the language.
	ANALYSIS LIST
Name	**Application_Modeling_Language_To_Family_Design_Trace_Analysis**
Synopsis	Check each language construct to see whether there exists a corresponding module in the Family_Design.
Exit Condition	state-of(Application_Modeling_Language)=Language_Specified
Informal Specification	

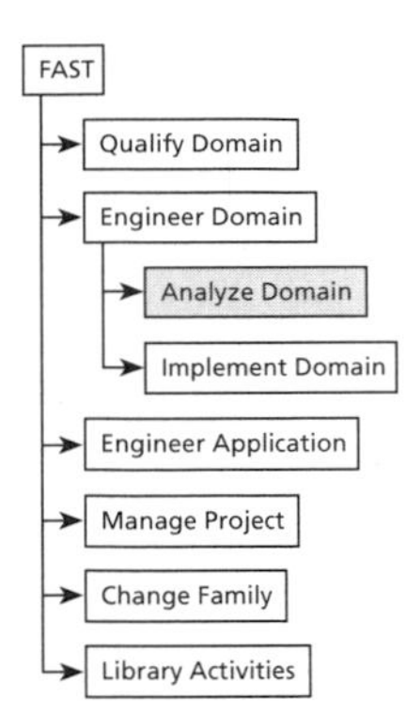

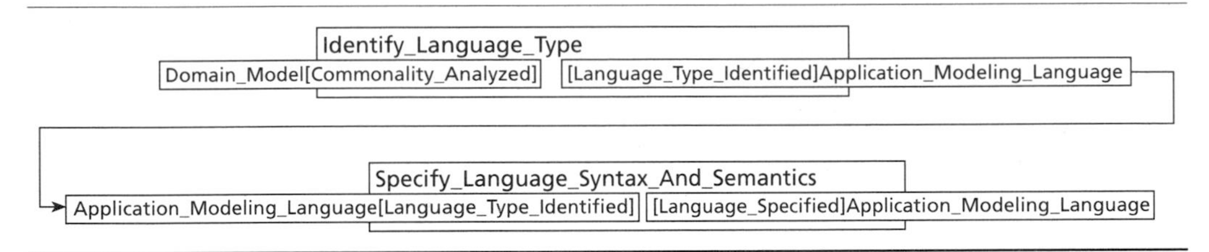

P-State Diagram for Design_Application_Modeling_Language

FAST
- Qualify Domain
- Engineer Domain
  - Analyze Domain
  - Implement Domain
- Engineer Application
- Manage Project
- Change Family
- Library Activities

10.2.1.4.1 *Specify_Language_Syntax_And_Semantics*

Operation Definition Form

Name	**Specify_Language_Syntax_And_Semantics**
Synopsis	Define the BNF production rules, or the equivalent, including semantics, for each construct in the language.
Role List	Domain_Engineer
Entrance Condition	state-of(Application_Modeling_Language) = Language_Type_Identified
Operation Type	Manual
Artifacts List	Application_Modeling_Language
Information Artifacts	Environment
Exit Condition	state-of(Application_Modeling_Language) = Language_Specified
Informal Specification	Build on the analysis performed to identify the language type to create the syntax and semantics for the language. The basis for the semantics is the commonality analysis. Each parameter of variation must be expressible in the language. The table of parameters of variation can be considered a primitive form of an application modeling language. The abstractions that are used in the language should be derived from the commonality analysis, particularly from the terms defined in the dictionary and from the commonalities. Data types in the language often embody variabilities that are derived from or associated with commonalities. For example, in the SPEC language (see Chapter 3), a command definition can be considered a data type, with attributes such as action name, object name, and parameter names. Think of this as a data type built into the language. The command abstraction is established in both the definitions and the commonalities that define a command and its structure. The variable aspects of a command, and hence the components of the command data type used in the language, are defined as variabilities, and their value spaces are specified in the parameters of variation. Extend the set of sample family members to cover a wide variation of real family members. Keep the language as simple as possible, but include sufficient capability to make it useful; create the minimal language needed. Allow a few users to experiment with the language to obtain feedback on how well it does its job. Create documentation, including training materials and a reference manual, for the language. Introduce it slowly to a progressively larger set of users, garnering feedback and remembering that at each release, more users are affected by changes to the language.

FAST
- Qualify Domain
- Engineer Domain
  - Analyze Domain
  - Implement Domain
- Engineer Application
- Manage Project
- Change Family
- Library Activities

10.2.1.4.2 *Identify_Language_Type*

Operation Definition Form

Name	**Identify_Language_Type**
Synopsis	Application modeling languages tend to be one of several different types; they form families of languages. Examples are languages that describe state machines, languages that describe properties of objects, and languages that describe concurrent threads of events. Identifying the language type is a key step in designing the constructs of the language.
Role List	Domain_Engineer
Entrance Condition	state-of(Domain_Model) = Commonality_Analyzed
Operation Type	Manual
Artifacts List	Application_Modeling_Language
Information Artifacts	Environment
Exit Condition	state-of(Application_Modeling_Language) = Language_Type_Identified
Informal Specification	Choice of language type is based on the results of the commonality analysis and the background and experience of the domain engineers who design the language. It may not be worthwhile to create a language for the domain on the first iteration of domain engineering. When it is deemed worthwhile, a simple table, similar in form to the table of parameters of variation from the commonality analysis, may be a good first approximation of a language. The fundamental semantics of the language—the abstractions that it must specify—should be derivable from the commonality analysis for the family. Study the dictionary of terms and, in particular, the variabilities, to try to identify data types and control constructs needed in the language. Using the commonality analysis, create a set of sample family members that must be specifiable in the language.

FAST
Qualify Domain
Engineer Domain
Analyze Domain
Implement Domain
Engineer Application
Manage Project
Change Family
Library Activities

10.2.1.5 Create_A_Standard_Application_Engineering_Process

Operation Definition Form

Name	**Create_A_Standard_Application_Engineering_Process**
Synopsis	Creating an application engineering process for a domain consists of mapping the Decision_Model for the domain into operations performed using the application engineering environment for the domain. The Decision_Model embodies all the decisions that the Application_Engineer must make in creating an Application_Model for an application.
Role List	Domain_Engineer, Environment_Engineer
Entrance Condition	state-of(Environment)=Analyzed or state-of(Change_Report)=Implementation_Change_Authorized
Operation Type	Manual
Artifacts List	Application_Engineering_Process
Information Artifacts	Domain_Model
Exit Condition	state-of(Application_Engineering_Process)=Reviewed
Informal Specification	The standard application engineering process for a domain is the process whereby an Application_Engineer uses the application engineering environment to make the decisions identified in the Decision_Model according to the order specified in the Decision_Model. Because the decisions and the tools vary among domains, the application engineering process varies from domain to domain. In some domains there may be no tools, and the process may be manual. A manual process can be used after the first iteration of domain engineering, when little investment has yet been made in domain engineering. Creating the Application_Engineering_Process consists of the following steps, which are performed together and iteratively. The procedure terminates when all decisions in the Decision_Model have been incorporated into the Application_Engineering_Process and it is clear how each tool in the application engineering environment is used as part of the Application_Engineering_Process. 1. For each step in the Decision_Model, identify the tools from the application engineering environment needed to perform the step. 1a. For each tool used in the step, show how it is directly used to make or contributes to making the decision(s) made in the step. If there is no tool for the step, explain how the step is performed manually, including the input to the step, the output from the step, and how the inputs are transformed into the outputs. 1b. For each tool in the step, show how the results of making the decision(s) are represented and captured. 2. For each sequence of decisions in the Decision_Model, map the sequence into a scenario that shows how the tools and manual procedures identified in step 1 will be used to accomplish the sequence.

FAST
- Qualify Domain
- Engineer Domain
  - Analyze Domain
  - Implement Domain
- Engineer Application
- Manage Project
- Change Family
- Library Activities

10.2.1.6 Design_Application_Engineering_Environment

Operation Definition Form

Name	Design_Application_Engineering_Environment
Synopsis	Designing the Application_Engineering_Environment consists of identifying the tools that compose the environment and describing how they will be used.
Role List	Environment_Engineer
Entrance Condition	(state-of(Environment)=Analyzed) and (state-of(Application_Engineering_Process)=Reviewed) or (state-of(Change_Report)=Implementation_Change_Authorized)
Operation Type	Manual
Artifacts List	Environment
Information Artifacts	
Exit Condition	state-of(Tool_Set_Design)=Tool_Set_Designed
Informal Specification	The application engineering environment consists of a set of tools and methods that are used to produce domain members using the standard Application_Engineering_Process. Some tools may be used directly by the Application_Engineer; others may provide support for him or her without being directly visible. The Environment includes mechanisms (and methods when no tools are available to implement the mechanisms), such as shared files and message passing, for connecting the inputs and outputs of tools and methods, for creating sequences of tools and methods, for using tools and methods concurrently, and for using tools and methods cooperatively, as needed. Designing the Environment consists of the following. 1. For each decision in the Decision_Model, identify and specify a tool or method to support making the decision, or identify an existing tool or method that will support making the decision. Following are examples of some tools that may need to be created or used. • Compiler for the Application_Modeling_Language that generates code for the domain members (may not be needed when composer is used); supports making all the decisions embedded in the AML. • Composer for the AML that composes domain members from templates (may not be needed when compiler is used); supports making all the decisions embedded in the AML. • Simulator that simulates the behavior of a domain member that is described in the AML; supports all the decisions made in the AML that can be simulated. • Validator for the AML that checks the behavior of a domain member described in the AML against a set of required constraints, such as freedom from deadlock; supports all the decisions made in the AML that are relevant to the constraints checked.

continued

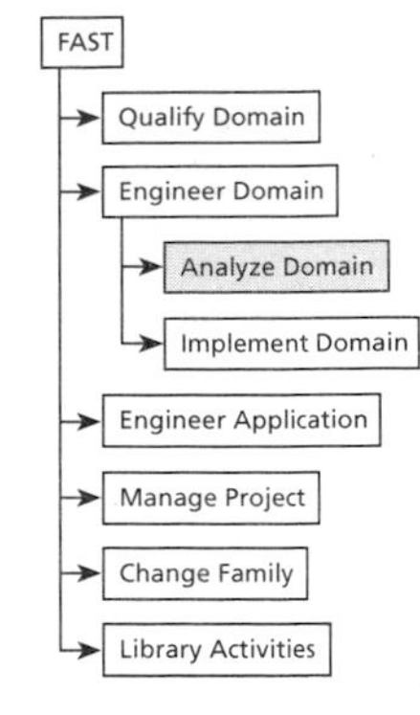

Informal Specification *continued*

2. Identify a minimal useful subset of tools from the toolset identified in step 1. The minimal useful subset is the smallest subset of tools that can be used to generate domain members and that provides a significant advantage over producing domain members manually or by an existing process.
3. Identify a collection of supersets of the minimal useful subset. (Note that some supersets can be arranged in sequences; each superset in a sequence provides significantly more capability than its predecessor, and the supersets can be built in the identified sequence.)
4. For each tool in the minimal useful subset, and in any supersets to be built in the next Implement_Domain state, identify the following:
   - The source of its inputs
   - The destination of its outputs
   - How it is invoked
   - How it is used
5. Ensure that the tool can obtain its inputs and that its outputs are useful (although they may not be immediately used). Specify where it will store its intermediate results.
6. When a composer is used to produce code or documentation from templates, specify each template and the system composition mapping, as follows.

   6a. Templates
   - For each module in the Family_Design that represents a variability that is expressible in the Application_Modeling_Language, define a template that, when completed, implements the decision represented by the variability. The completed template can be a set of code or a set of documentation or both. The template definition should include a specification of the parameters needed to produce an instance of the template and should represent an implementation of the abstract interface for the module.
   - Specify the method of invocation and completion of the template—for example, macro call, function call, or parse tree traversal.

   6b. System Composition Mapping
   - For each decision expressible in the Application_Modeling_Language, identify the template that implements the decision. Apply the uses relation among the modules of the family design to find all other templates and modules that are needed when the template is included in the domain member.
   - Remove redundancies among the sets of templates and modules identified in the preceding step.
   - The system composition mapping is the set of correspondences between decisions expressible in the Application_Modeling_Language and the sets of templates and modules identified in the preceding step.

FAST
Qualify Domain
Engineer Domain
Analyze Domain
Implement Domain
Engineer Application
Manage Project
Change Family
Library Activities

10.2.2 Implement_Domain

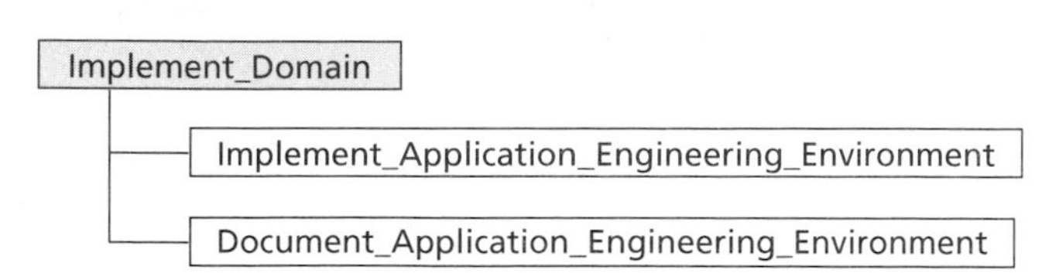

Process State Definition Form

Name	**Implement_Domain**
Synopsis	Implementing a domain consists of constructing the application engineering environment for it. The environment is built to the specifications determined during domain engineering—that is, the Domain_Model.
Main Role	Domain_Engineer, Environment_Engineer, Domain_Manager
Entrance Condition	state-of(Domain_Model)=Tool_Set_Designed or state-of(Change_Report)=Implementation_Change_Authorized
Artifacts List	Environment
Information Artifacts	Domain_Model
	SUB-P-STATE LIST
Name	**Implement_Application_Engineering_Environment**
Synopsis	Implementing the application engineering environment consists of implementing the design for the environment. It includes building or finding the tools that are part of the environment and the data on which those tools operate—for example, the code and documentation templates that are used by the tools to generate applications.
Name	**Document_Application_Engineering_Environment**
Synopsis	Produce the documentation needed by the application engineers who use an application engineering environment, including users guide, reference manuals, training manuals, and any other necessary documentation.
	ANALYSIS LIST
Name	**Application_Engineering_Process_To_Decision_Trace_Analysis**
Synopsis	Check that each decision of the Decision_Model has a corresponding step in the standard application engineering process.
Name	**Resource_Analysis**
Synopsis	This analysis generates a report on resource usage, resource balancing, resource estimation, and resource allocation. The information resulting from the analysis helps the Project_Manager, Domain_Manager, and Application_Manager make decisions on the management of a project using FAST.

continued

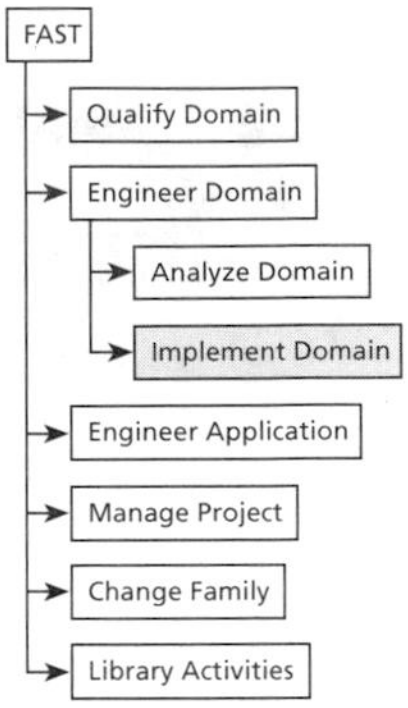

FAST
- Qualify Domain
- Engineer Domain
  - Analyze Domain
  - Implement Domain
- Engineer Application
- Manage Project
- Change Family
- Library Activities

Name	**Progress_Analysis**
Synopsis	This analysis generates a report on the progress of the project. The report describes what is next in the process and what is the current state of the active artifacts.
Name	**Risk_Analysis**
Synopsis	This analysis generates a list of risky events after comparing progress on various P-states and A-states of active artifacts.
Name	**Defect_Analysis**
Synopsis	This analysis generates statistics on various types of defects by P-state, operation, and artifact to show the distribution of defects.
Name	**Decision_To_Tool_Trace_Analysis**
Synopsis	Check that the decisions supported by the tools used in the application engineering process correspond to decisions to be made in the application engineering process.
Name	**Application_Engineering_Support_Analysis**
Synopsis	Check that for each step in the application engineering process there is sufficient information and facilities available for the Application_Engineer to make decisions corresponding to parameters of variation for the step.
Name	**Application_Modeling_Language_Parser_Assurance_Analysis**
Synopsis	Check that the parser for the Application_Modeling_Language parses every construct of the language correctly.
Name	**Application_Modeling_Language_Editor_Assurance_Analysis**
Synopsis	Check that there is an editor implemented for the Application_Modeling_Language.
Name	**Tool_Implementation_Assurance_Analysis**
Synopsis	Check that every tool defined in the Application_Engineering_Environment has been implemented.
Name	**Artifact_Implementation_Assurance_Analysis**
Synopsis	Check that every artifact defined in the application engineering environment has been implemented.
Name	**Tool_Documentation_Assurance_Analysis**
Synopsis	Check that every tool defined in the application engineering environment has been documented.
Exit Condition	state-of(Environment)=Implemented
Informal Specification	Implement each tool in the toolset design, integrate them as specified in the toolset design, and test them both as individual tools and as an integrated toolset that supports the application engineering process.

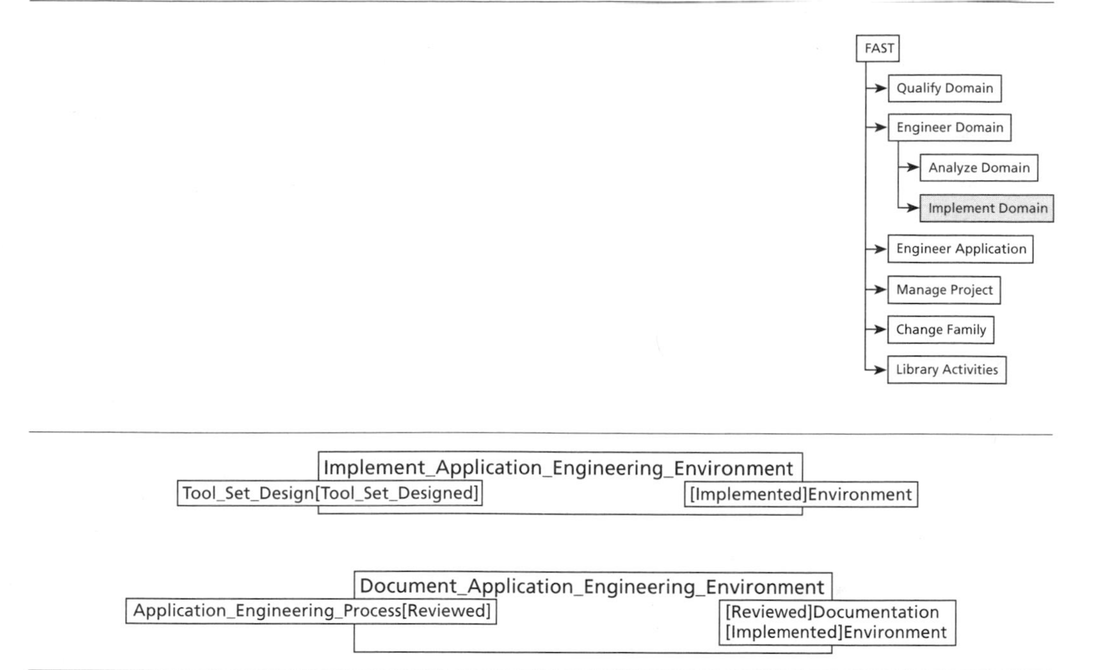

P-State Diagram for Implement_Domain

10.2.2.1 Implement_Application_Engineering_Environment

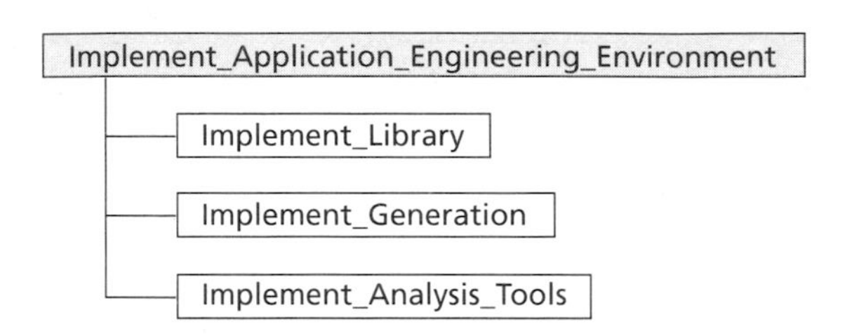

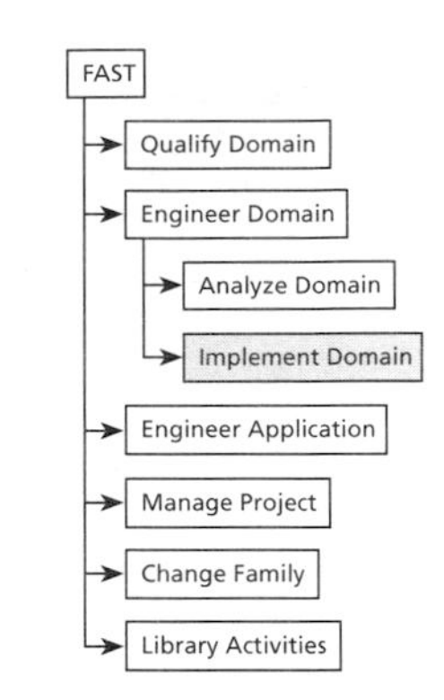

Process State Definition Form

Name	**Implement_Application_Engineering_Environment**
Synopsis	Implementing the application engineering environment consists of implementing the design for the environment. It includes building or finding the tools that are part of the environment and the data on which those tools operate—for example, the code and documentation templates that are used by the tools to generate applications.
Main Role	Environment_Engineer
Entrance Condition	state-of(Tool_Set_Design) = Tool_Set_Designed
Artifacts List	Environment
Information Artifacts	
	SUB-P-STATE LIST
Name	**Implement_Library**
Synopsis	The library contains the templates and components for code and documentation that are used to generate applications. Implementing the library means finding or developing those templates and components.
Name	**Implement_Generation**
Synopsis	FAST uses two primary generation techniques: compilation and composition. In the compilation approach, FAST users write a compiler for each application modeling language. In the compositional approach, FAST users implement the system composition mapping that composes applications from templates in the library.
Name	**Implement_Analysis_Tools**
Synopsis	Analysis tools perform consistency and completeness checks, simulations, performance estimates, and other forms of analysis. For example, one kind provides the Application_Engineer with information about his or her Application_Model to help to validate the model. Another kind gauges the progress of application engineering and domain engineering, calculating resources used, estimating resources needed, reporting defect distributions, and providing other measures of interest. This activity implements Analysis_Tools.

continued

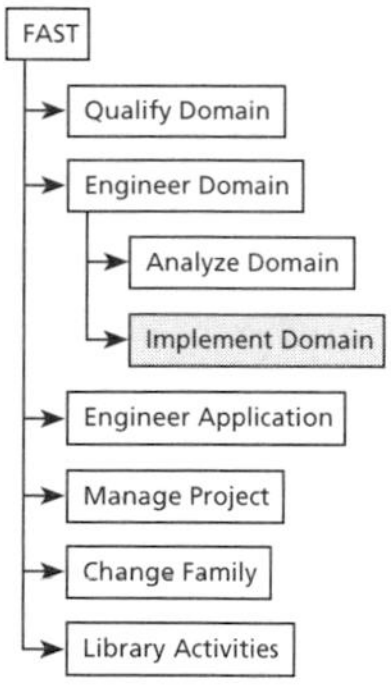

ANALYSIS LIST	
Name	**Resource_Analysis**
Synopsis	This analysis generates a report on resource usage, resource balancing, resource estimation, and resource allocation. The information resulting from the analysis helps the Project_Manager, Domain_Manager, and Application_Manager make decisions on the management of a project using FAST.
Name	**Progress_Analysis**
Synopsis	This analysis generates a report on the progress of the project. The report describes what is next in the process and what is the current state of the active artifacts.
Name	**Risk_Analysis**
Synopsis	This analysis generates a list of risky events after comparing progress on various P-states and A-states of active artifacts.
Name	**Defect_Analysis**
Synopsis	This analysis generates statistics on various types of defects by P-state, operation, and artifact to show the distribution of defects.
Name	**Application_Modeling_Language_Parser_Assurance_Analysis**
Synopsis	Check that the parser for the Application_Modeling_Language parses every construct of the language correctly.
Name	**Application_Modeling_Language_Editor_Assurance_Analysis**
Synopsis	Check that there is an editor implemented for the Application_Modeling_Language.
Name	**Tool_Implementation_Assurance_Analysis**
Synopsis	Check that every tool defined in the Application_Engineering_Environment has been implemented.
Name	**Tool_Documentation_Assurance_Analysis**
Synopsis	Check that every tool defined in the application engineering environment has been documented.
Name	**Module_Implementation_Assurance_Analysis**
Synopsis	Check that every module defined in the Family_Design has been implemented.
Name	**Module_Documentation_Assurance_Analysis**
Synopsis	Check that every module defined in the application engineering environment has been documented.
Exit Condition	state-of(Environment) = Implemented

continued

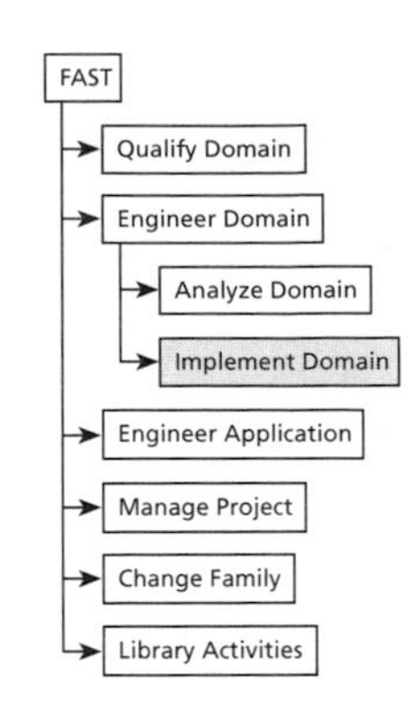

Informal Specification	Implement each tool in the toolset design and integrate them based on the toolset specified in the toolset design. Test the tools to ensure that they properly support the application engineering process. Generally, the toolset that composes the application engineering environment will at least include a generation tool, also known as a translator, a library of adaptable, reusable components used in translation (especially if the translator is a composer), and a set of analysis tools, some of which may be packaged as part of the translator.

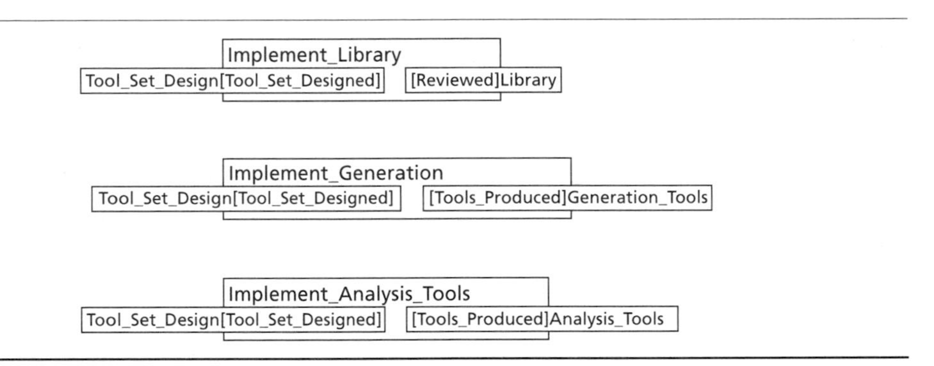

P-State Diagram for Implement_Application_Engineering_Environment

FAST
- Qualify Domain
- Engineer Domain
  - Analyze Domain
  - Implement Domain
- Engineer Application
- Manage Project
- Change Family
- Library Activities

10.2.2.1.1 *Implement_Library*

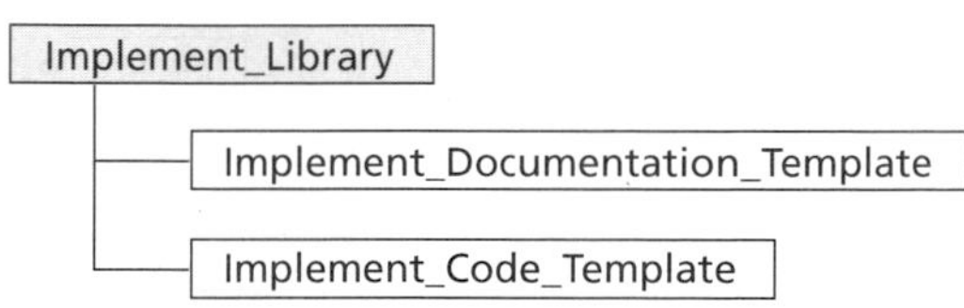

Process State Definition Form

Name	**Implement_Library**
Synopsis	The library contains the templates and components for code and documentation that are used to generate applications. Implementing the library means finding or developing those templates and components.
Main Role	Environment_Engineer
Entrance Condition	state-of(Tool_Set_Design) = Tool_Set_Designed
Artifacts List	Library
Information Artifacts	Domain_Model
	OPERATION LIST
Name	**Implement_Documentation_Template**
Synopsis	Documentation can be generated by instantiating documentation templates that are contained in the Library and then integrating the instantiated templates to form the documentation that is part of the application. Implementing the templates consists of writing the templates in a suitable language to meet the specifications produced as part of creating the Family_Design.
Name	**Implement_Code_Template**
Synopsis	Code can be generated by instantiating code templates that are contained in the library and then integrating the instantiated templates to form the code that is part of the application. Implementing the templates consists of writing the templates in a suitable language to meet the specifications produced as part of creating the Family_Design.
	ANALYSIS LIST
Name	**Resource_Analysis**
Synopsis	This analysis generates a report on resource usage, resource balancing, resource estimation, and resource allocation. The information resulting from the analysis helps the Project_Manager, Domain_Manager, and Application_Manager make decisions on the management of a project using FAST.

continued

- FAST
  - Qualify Domain
  - Engineer Domain
    - Analyze Domain
    - Implement Domain
  - Engineer Application
  - Manage Project
  - Change Family
  - Library Activities

Name	**Progress_Analysis**
Synopsis	This analysis generates a report on the progress of the project. The report describes what is next in the process and what is the current state of the active artifacts.

Name	**Risk_Analysis**
Synopsis	This analysis generates a list of risky events after comparing progress on various P-states and A-states of active artifacts.

Name	**Defect_Analysis**
Synopsis	This analysis generates statistics on various types of defects by P-state, operation, and artifact to show the distribution of defects.

Name	**Module_Documentation_Assurance_Analysis**
Synopsis	Check that every module defined in the application engineering environment has been documented.

Name	**Module_Implementation_Assurance_Analysis**
Synopsis	Check that every module defined in the Family_Design has been implemented.
Exit Condition	state-of(Library) = Reviewed
Informal Specification	When a composer is used to generate family members from the application modeling language, templates in the library correspond to modules or components specified in the family design. For each component specified in the family design, either implement the component or find an existing component that meets the specification. When the component is an adaptable component, implementing it may consist of either creating several versions of it, creating a partial component with placeholders for code to be inserted later, creating a parameterized component, or using other means to form a template. See the code templates for the Floating Weather Station in Chapter 5 for examples.

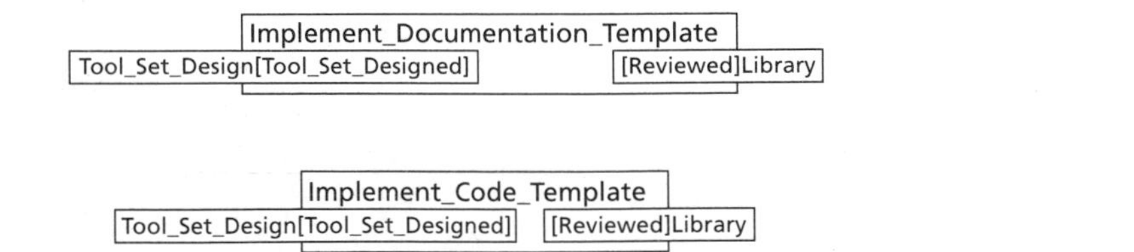

P-State Diagram for Implement_Library

FAST
Qualify Domain
Engineer Domain
Analyze Domain
Implement Domain
Engineer Application
Manage Project
Change Family
Library Activities

10.2.2.1.2 *Implement_Generation*

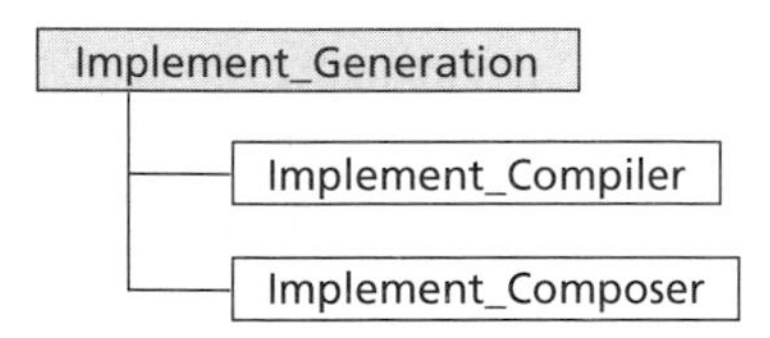

Process State Definition Form

Name	**Implement_Generation**
Synopsis	FAST uses two primary generation techniques: compilation and composition. In the compilation approach, FAST users write a compiler for each application modeling language. In the compositional approach, FAST users implement a system composition mapping that composes applications from templates in the library.
Main Role	Environment_Engineer
Entrance Condition	state-of(Tool_Set_Design) = Tool_Set_Designed
Artifacts List	Generation_Tools
Information Artifacts	Domain_Model
	OPERATION LIST
Name	**Implement_Compiler**
Synopsis	Implementing the compiler consists of writing a compiler for the Application_Modeling_Language. The compiler is used to generate applications from the specifications written in the AML. The compiler for the Application_Modeling_Language can be implemented using standard compiler development techniques. One technique is to use a parser generator such as YACC. Another is to use a tool such as METATOOL to produce parse tree manipulation tools and then use those tools to implement the compiler. Another approach is to use a language production system such as InfoWiz.
Name	**Implement_Composer**
Synopsis	Implementing the composer consists of implementing the Composition_Mapping between the Application_Modeling_Language and the templates in the Library. For each decision embodied in the AML, the mapping identifies the templates in the Library needed when the decision is made. The composer implements the mapping by parsing the program to get the values of the decisions, retrieving the corresponding templates from the library, instantiating the templates with the values supplied for the decisions, and integrating the instantiated templates.

continued

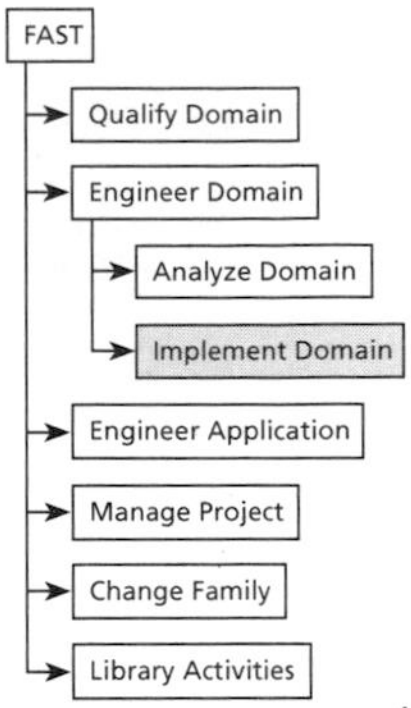

Synopsis *continued*	One possible implementation uses a table and a set of code (and documentation) templates. Each row of the table corresponds to a decision expressible in the Application_Modeling_Language. The templates are exactly those needed to implement the decisions. Each row can have an entry that contains a value for the parameter of a template. As a specification in the AML is parsed, the Composition_Mapping looks up in the table the templates corresponding to the decisions made. The values of the parameters are obtained from the parse and are substituted in the templates to obtain the necessary template instances. For code templates, the resulting source code is collected into a file or files and compiled and linked to obtain the implementation of the domain member. A similar process is followed for documentation templates. See the generator for the Floating Weather Station in Chapter 5 for an example.
	ANALYSIS LIST
Name	**Resource_Analysis**
Synopsis	This analysis generates a report on resource usage, resource balancing, resource estimation, and resource allocation. The information resulting from the analysis helps the Project_Manager, Domain_Manager, and Application_Manager make decisions on the management of a project using FAST.
Name	**Progress_Analysis**
Synopsis	This analysis generates a report on the progress of the project. The report describes what is next in the process and what is the current state of the active artifacts.
Name	**Risk_Analysis**
Synopsis	This analysis generates a list of risky events after comparing progress on various P-states and A-states of active artifacts.
Name	**Defect_Analysis**
Synopsis	This analysis generates statistics on various types of defects by P-state, operation, and artifact to show the distribution of defects.
Name	**Application_Modeling_Language_Editor_Assurance_Analysis**
Synopsis	Check that there is an editor implemented for the Application_Modeling_Language.
Name	**Tool_Implementation_Assurance_Analysis**
Synopsis	Check that every tool defined in the Application_Engineering_Environment has been implemented.

continued

FAST
Qualify Domain
Engineer Domain
Analyze Domain
Implement Domain
Engineer Application
Manage Project
Change Family
Library Activities

Name	**Tool_Documentation_Assurance_Analysis**
Synopsis	Check that every tool defined in the application engineering environment has been documented.
Exit Condition	state-of(Generation_Tools) = Tools_Produced
Informal Specification	When the family design uses the compositional approach, implement the composer. When it uses a compiler approach, implement the compiler.

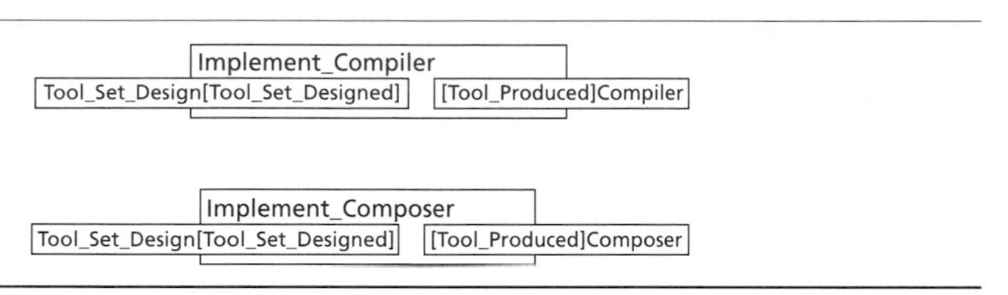

P-State Diagram for Implement–Generation

10.2.2.1.3 Implement_Analysis_Tools

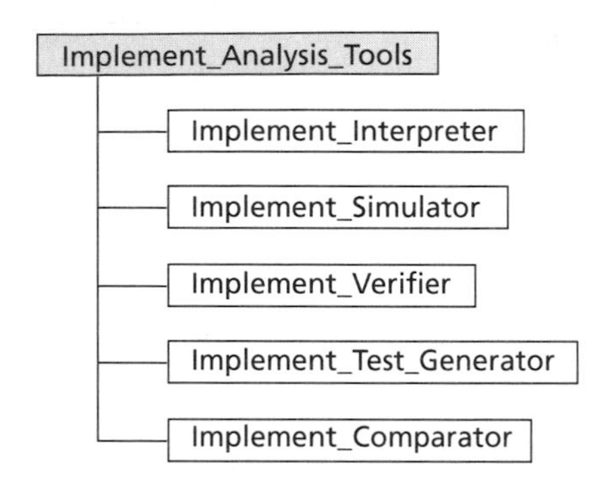

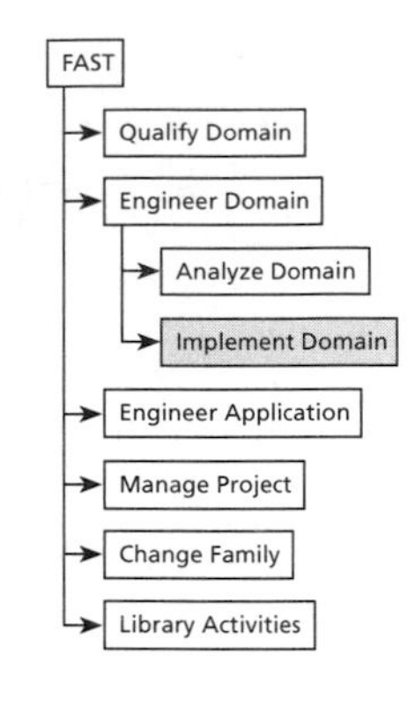

Process State Definition Form

Name	**Implement_Analysis_Tools**
Synopsis	Analysis tools perform consistency and completeness checks, simulations, performance estimates, and other forms of analysis. For example, one kind provides the Application_Engineer with information about his or her Application_Model to help to validate the model. Another kind gauges the progress of application engineering and domain engineering, calculating resources used, estimating resources needed, reporting defect distributions, and providing other measures of interest. This activity implements Analysis_Tools.
Main Role	Environment_Engineer
Entrance Condition	state-of(Tool_Set_Design) = Tool_Set_Designed
Artifacts List	Analysis_Tools
Information Artifacts	Domain_Model
	OPERATION LIST
Name	**Implement_Interpreter**
Synopsis	An Interpreter is an analysis tool that interprets the Application_Modeling_Language. This operation implements such an Interpreter.
Name	**Implement_Simulator**
Synopsis	This operation implements a Simulator for application models specified in the Application_Modeling_Language for the domain.
Name	**Implement_Verifier**
Synopsis	This operation implements a Verifier for application models specified in the Application_Modeling_Language for a domain. The Verifier performs tasks such as verifying the completeness and consistency of an Application_Model when possible.

continued

FAST
- Qualify Domain
- Engineer Domain
  - Analyze Domain
  - Implement Domain
- Engineer Application
- Manage Project
- Change Family
- Library Activities

Name	**Implement_Test_Generator**
Synopsis	A Test_Generator generates test cases from an Application_Model written in the Application_ Modeling_Language for a domain. This operation implements a Test_Case_Generator.
Name	**Implement_Comparator**
Synopsis	A comparator compares two or more specifications written in an Application_Modeling_Language and identifies their differences and similarities. This operation implements such a comparator.

ANALYSIS LIST

Name	**Resource_Analysis**
Synopsis	This analysis generates a report on resource usage, resource balancing, resource estimation, and resource allocation. The information resulting from the analysis helps the Project_Manager, Domain_Manager, and Application_Manager make decisions on the management of a project using FAST.
Name	**Progress_Analysis**
Synopsis	This analysis generates a report on the progress of the project. The report describes what is next in the process and what is the current state of the active artifacts.
Name	**Risk_Analysis**
Synopsis	This analysis generates a list of risky events after comparing progress on various P-states and A-states of active artifacts.
Name	**Defect_Analysis**
Synopsis	This analysis generates statistics on various types of defects by P-state, operation, and artifact to show the distribution of defects.
Name	**Tool_Implementation_Assurance_Analysis**
Synopsis	Check that every tool defined in the Application_Engineering_Environment has been implemented.
Name	**Tool_Documentation_Assurance_Analysis**
Synopsis	Check that every tool defined in the application engineering environment has been documented.
Exit Condition	state-of(Analysis_Tools) = Tools_Produced

continued

FAST
Qualify Domain
Engineer Domain
Analyze Domain
Implement Domain
Engineer Application
Manage Project
Change Family
Library Activities

Informal Specification	Implement the analysis tools specified in the toolset design. The set may contain some or all of the following tools. • An interpreter, which interprets programs in the AML • A simulator, which simulates the operation of family members specified in the AML • A verifier, which assists in verifying specifications in the AML • A test generator, which generates test programs for family members • A comparator, which compares various specifications in the AML and identifies differences between them In addition, there may be other analysis tools appropriate for the domain that must be implemented.

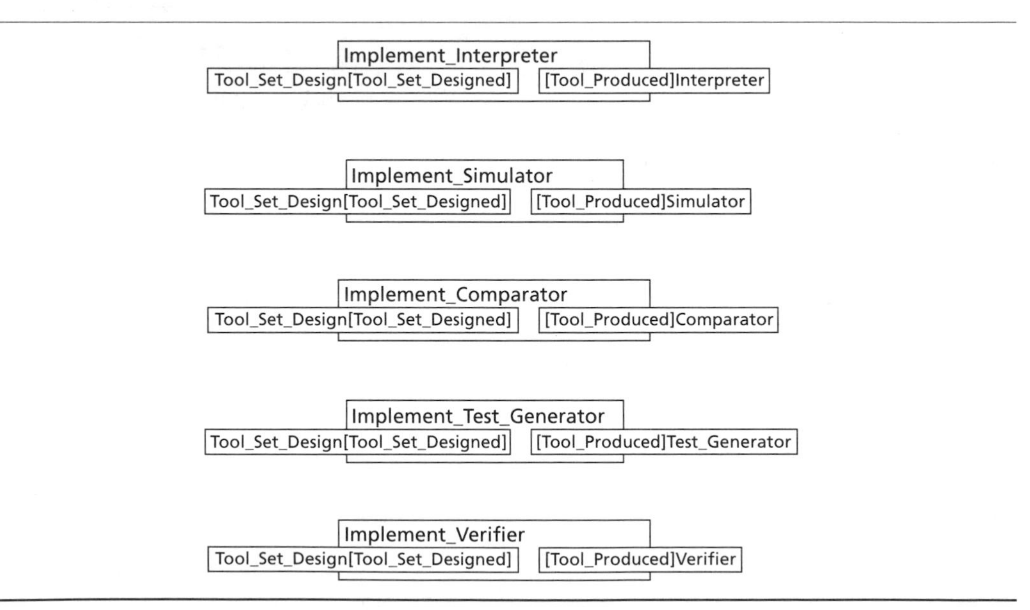

P-State Diagram for Implement_Analysis_Tools

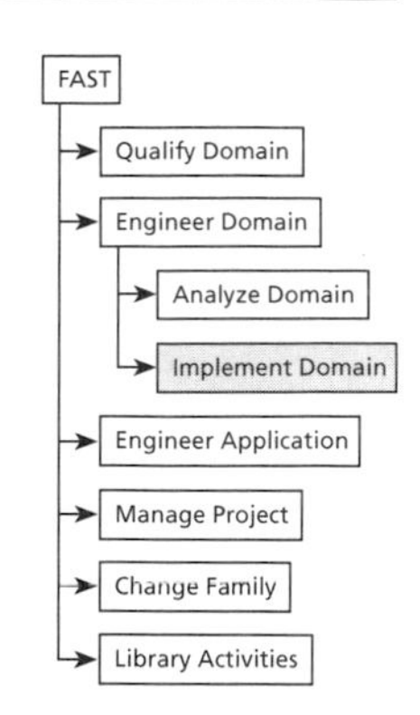

10.2.2.2 Document_Application_Engineering_Environment

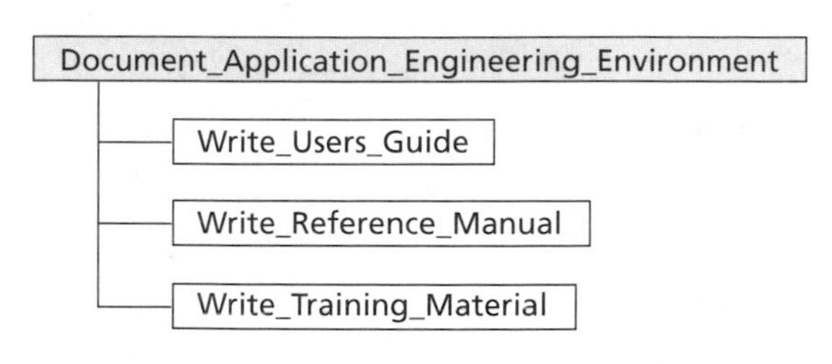

Process State Definition Form

Name	Document_Application_Engineering_Environment
Synopsis	Produce the documentation needed by the application engineers who use an application engineering environment, including users guide, reference manuals, training manuals, and any other necessary documentation.
Main Role	Environment_Engineer
Entrance Condition	state-of(Application_Engineering_Process)=Reviewed
Artifacts List	Documentation
Information Artifacts	Environment
	OPERATION LIST
Name	**Write_Users_Guide**
Synopsis	Users Guide is written for the users of the application engineering environment. It should contain a description of every tool in the environment along with instructions on how to use them. This operation consists of the following steps. 1. Create a tutorial that shows by example how to use the environment. 2. Describe the application engineering process in user-oriented terms. 3. Create a description of the operations that are part of the application engineering process.
Name	**Write_Reference_Manual**
Synopsis	Create the Reference_Manual for the environment.
Name	**Write_Training_Material**
Synopsis	Create Training_Material for the application engineers.
Exit Condition	state-of(Documentation)=Reviewed and state-of(Environment)=Implemented

continued

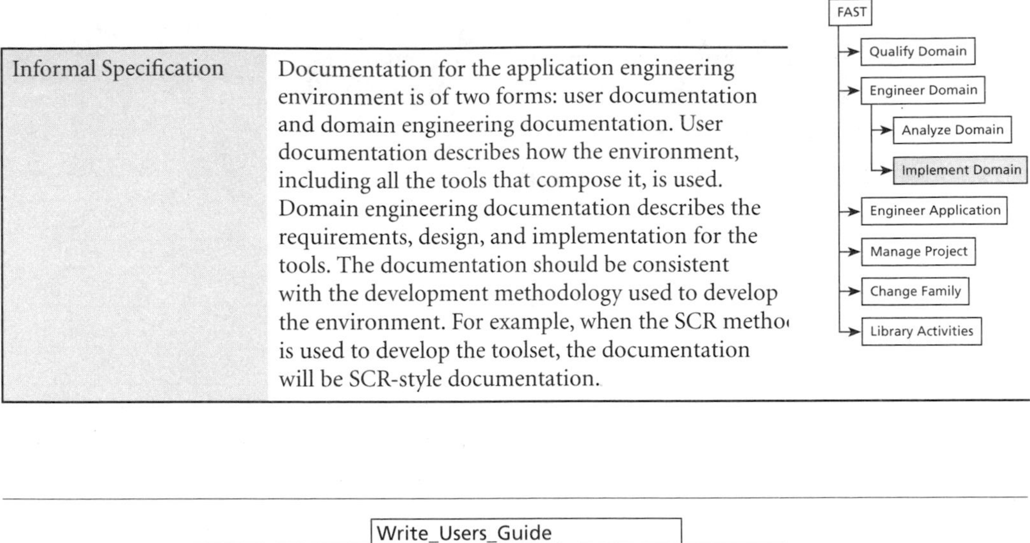

Informal Specification	Documentation for the application engineering environment is of two forms: user documentation and domain engineering documentation. User documentation describes how the environment, including all the tools that compose it, is used. Domain engineering documentation describes the requirements, design, and implementation for the tools. The documentation should be consistent with the development methodology used to develop the environment. For example, when the SCR metho is used to develop the toolset, the documentation will be SCR-style documentation.

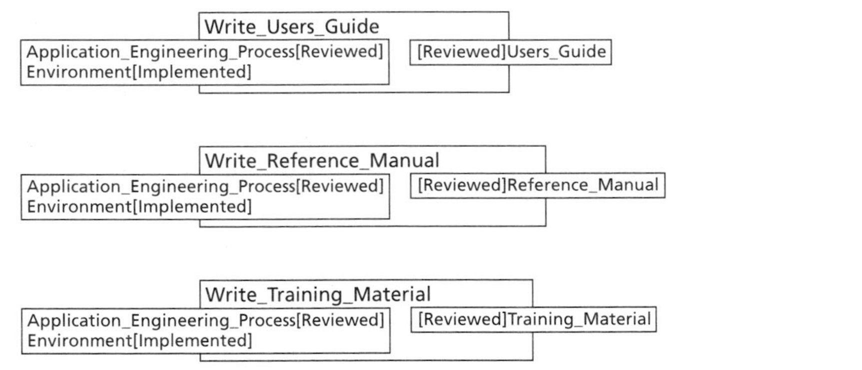

P-State Diagram for Document_Application_Engineering_Environment

10.3 Engineer_Application

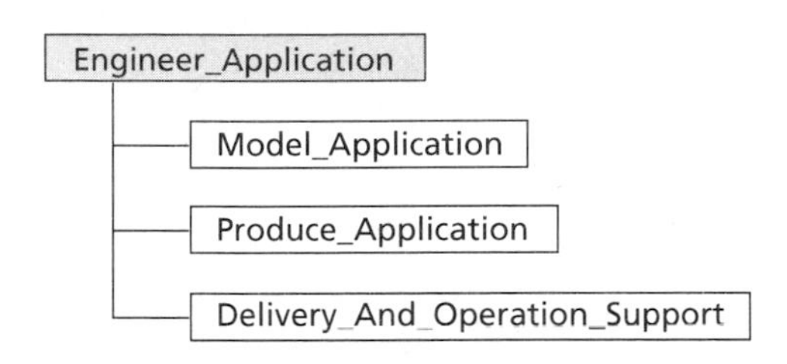

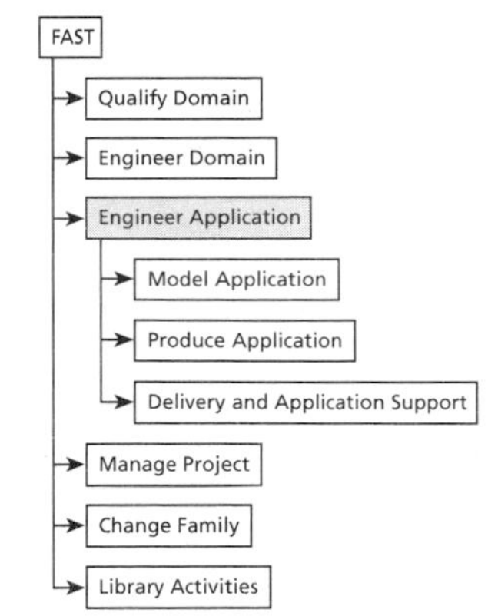

Process State Definition Form

Name	**Engineer_Application**
Synopsis	An iterative process for constructing application systems to meet customer requirements. Each application system is considered a member of a family and is defined by an Application_Model. An application engineering environment for the family is used to analyze application models and generate software from them.
Main Role	Application_Manager
Entrance Condition	state-of(Environment)=Implemented
Artifacts List	Application
Information Artifacts	Environment
	SUB-P-STATE LIST
Name	**Produce_Application**
Synopsis	Producing the application consists of using the generation tools in the application engineering environment to generate the application. When not all of the application can be generated, some parts of the application will be produced in traditional manual ways. Such parts will then be integrated with the generated parts.
Name	**Delivery_And_Operation_Support**
Synopsis	This operation consists of delivering the application to the customer and providing operational support as contracted.
	OPERATION LIST
Name	**Model_Application**
Synopsis	Modeling the application is a key activity in application engineering. It consists of modeling the customer's requirements for the application as a specification in the Application_Modeling_Language. After such a model has been constructed, it can be analyzed using tools in the application engineering environment, and the code and documentation for the application can be generated from it.

continued

FAST
- Qualify Domain
- Engineer Domain
- Engineer Application
  - Model Application
  - Produce Application
  - Delivery and Application Support
- Manage Project
- Change Family
- Library Activities

ANALYSIS LIST	
Name	**Final_Product_Validation_Analysis**
Synopsis	Check whether all the decisions made in the application model exist in the final product.
Name	**Resource_Analysis**
Synopsis	This analysis generates a report on resource usage, resource balancing, resource estimation, and resource allocation. The information resulting from the analysis helps the Project_Manager, Domain_Manager, and Application_Manager make decisions on the management of a project using FAST.
Name	**Progress_Analysis**
Synopsis	This analysis generates a report on the progress of the project. The report describes what is next in the process and what is the current state of the active artifacts.
Name	**Risk_Analysis**
Synopsis	This analysis generates a list of risky events after comparing progress on various P-states and A-states of active artifacts.
Name	**Defect_Analysis**
Synopsis	This analysis generates statistics on various types of defects by P-state, operation, and artifact to show the distribution of defects.
Name	**Final_Product_Documentation_Assurance_Analysis**
Synopsis	Check that all decisions made in the application model exist in the product documentation.
Name	**Customer_Satisfaction**
Synopsis	Check that the customer is satisfied.
Exit Condition	state-of(Application)=Delivered_And_Supported or state-of(Change_Report)=Change_Identified

continued

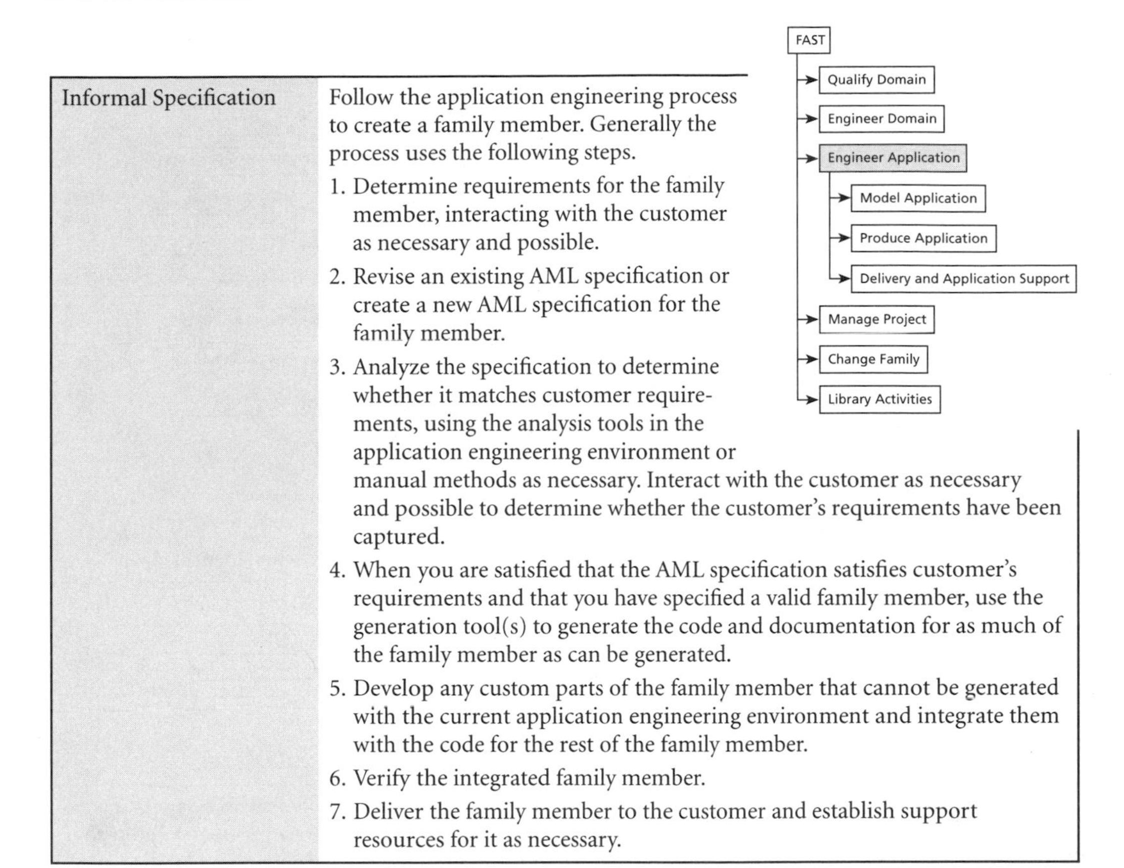

Informal Specification	Follow the application engineering process to create a family member. Generally the process uses the following steps. 1. Determine requirements for the family member, interacting with the customer as necessary and possible. 2. Revise an existing AML specification or create a new AML specification for the family member. 3. Analyze the specification to determine whether it matches customer requirements, using the analysis tools in the application engineering environment or manual methods as necessary. Interact with the customer as necessary and possible to determine whether the customer's requirements have been captured. 4. When you are satisfied that the AML specification satisfies customer's requirements and that you have specified a valid family member, use the generation tool(s) to generate the code and documentation for as much of the family member as can be generated. 5. Develop any custom parts of the family member that cannot be generated with the current application engineering environment and integrate them with the code for the rest of the family member. 6. Verify the integrated family member. 7. Deliver the family member to the customer and establish support resources for it as necessary.

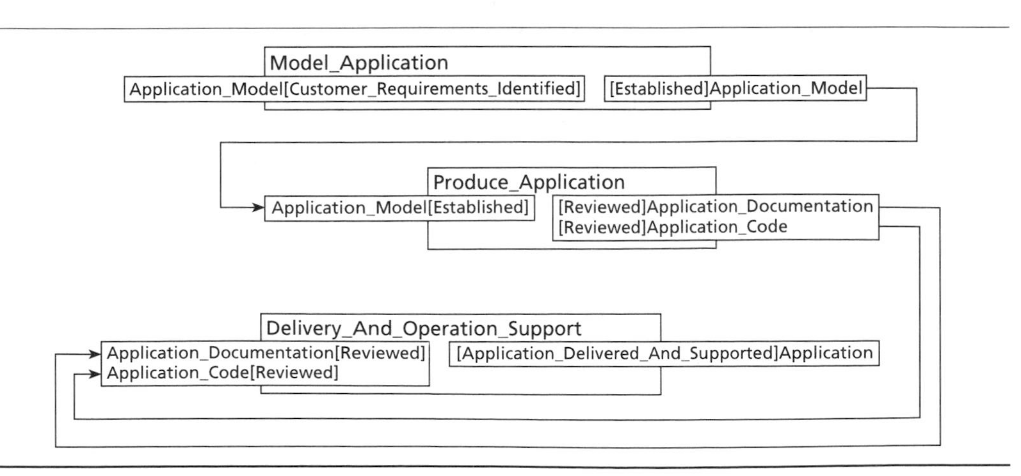

P-State Diagram for Engineer_Application

- FAST
  - Qualify Domain
  - Engineer Domain
  - Engineer Application
    - Model Application
    - Produce Application
    - Delivery and Application Support
  - Manage Project
  - Change Family
  - Library Activities

10.3.1 Model Application

Operation Definition Form

Name	**Model_Application**
Synopsis	Modeling the application is a key activity in application engineering. It consists of modeling the customer's requirements for the application as a specification in the Application_Modeling_Language. After such a model has been constructed, it can be analyzed using tools in the application engineering environment, and the code and documentation for the application can be generated from it.
Role List	Application_Engineer, Application_Producer
Entrance Condition	state-of(Application_Model) = Customer_Requirements_Identified
Operation Type	Manual
Artifacts List	Application_Model
Information Artifacts	Application_Modeling_Language, Analysis_Tools, Generation_Tools, Documentation
Exit Condition	state-of(Application_Model) = Established
Informal Specification	Interact with the customer for the new family member as necessary and possible to determine the requirements for the new family member. Express the requirements in the AML. If the customer has special requirements, it may not be possible to express all requirements in the AML. If an existing family member has requirements that are close to the new requirements, it may be best to start with the AML specification for the existing family member and revise them. Use the analysis tools provided with the application engineering environment to validate and verify the AML specification. As necessary, possible, and desirable, show the customer the behavior of the family member to validate that it meets the customer's requirements. It may happen that the customer decides to change requirements after seeing the real or simulated behavior of the new family member.

- FAST
  - Qualify Domain
  - Engineer Domain
  - Engineer Application
    - Model Application
    - Produce Application
    - Delivery and Application Support
  - Manage Project
  - Change Family
  - Library Activities

10.3.2 Produce_Application

Process State Definition Form

Name	**Produce_Application**
Synopsis	Producing the application consists of using the generation tools in the application engineering environment to generate the application. When not all of the application can be generated, some parts of the application will be produced in traditional manual ways. Such parts will then be integrated with the generated parts.
Main Role	Application_Engineer, Application_Producer
Entrance Condition	state-of(Application_Model) = Established
Artifacts List	Application_Code, Application_Documentation
Information Artifacts	Application_Model, Library, Generation_Tools, Analysis_Tools, Documentation

OPERATION LIST

Name	**Test**
Synopsis	The application should be tested to ensure that it meets the customer's requirements.
Exit Condition	(state-of(Application_Code) = Reviewed) and (state-of(Application_Documentation) = Reviewed)
Informal Specification	When the application model has been validated, use the generation tools to generate as much of the application as possible. If the customer has special requirements, it may not be possible to express all the requirements in the AML, or the AML may not have the capability to generate all of the application. Develop by other methods any parts of the application that have not been generated, and integrate them with the generated part. Test the integrated application.

10.3.3 Delivery_And_Operation_Support

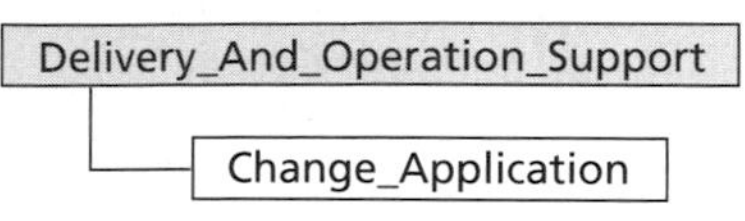

- FAST
  - Qualify Domain
  - Engineer Domain
  - Engineer Application
    - Model Application
    - Produce Application
    - Delivery and Application Support
  - Manage Project
  - Change Family
  - Library Activities

Process State Definition Form

Name	**Delivery_And_Operation_Support**
Synopsis	This operation consists of delivering the application to the customer and providing operational support as contracted.
Main Role	System_Maintainer_Or_Supporter
Entrance Condition	(state-of(Application_Code) = Reviewed) and (state-of(Application_Documentation) = Reviewed)
Artifacts List	Application
Information Artifacts	Application, Library, Generation_Tools, Analysis_Tools, Documentation

OPERATION LIST

Name	**Change_Application**
Synopsis	Revise the model of the application in the AML to correspond better to customer requirements.
Exit Condition	state-of(Application) = Application_Delivered_And_Supported
Informal Specification	Provide maintenance to the customer for the application as specified in the agreement with the customer—for example, in the customer's contract.

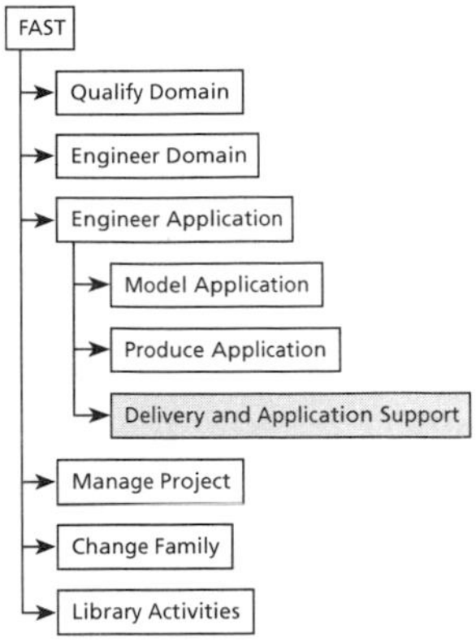

10.3.3.1 Change_Application

Operation Definition Form

Name	**Change_Application**
Synopsis	Revise the model of the application in the AML to correspond better to customer requirements.
Role List	Application_Engineer
Entrance Condition	(state-of(Application) = Application_Produced) or (state-of(Application) = Application_Delivered_And_Supported)
Operation Type	Manual
Artifacts List	Application
Information Artifacts	Environment
Exit Condition	state-of(Application) = Application_Referenced
Informal Specification	The need to make a change in the application has been recognized. This operation embodies everything needed to initiate the process of changing the Application_Model and regenerating the code and the documentation: the process of putting the application back into the Referenced state.

FAST
Qualify Domain
Engineer Domain
Engineer Application
Manage Project
Change Family
Library Activities

10.4 Manage_Project

Operation Definition Form

Name	**Manage_Project**
Synopsis	Managing the project consists of managing the job of identifying and satisfying customer requirements using an application engineering environment. It includes the traditional tasks of management, such as scheduling, allocating, and monitoring resources.
Role List	Application_Manager
Entrance Condition	state-of(Application_Model) = Customer_Requirements_Identified
Operation Type	Manual
Artifacts List	Application
Information Artifacts	
Exit Condition	state-of(Application) = Application_Delivered_And_Supported
Informal Specification	Manage the job of creating an application for a customer. Managing includes the traditional tasks of scheduling, allocating, and monitoring the use of resources. The tasks and roles managed and the artifacts to be produced are those defined in the Engineer_Application P-state and its substates and operations.

10.5 Change_Family

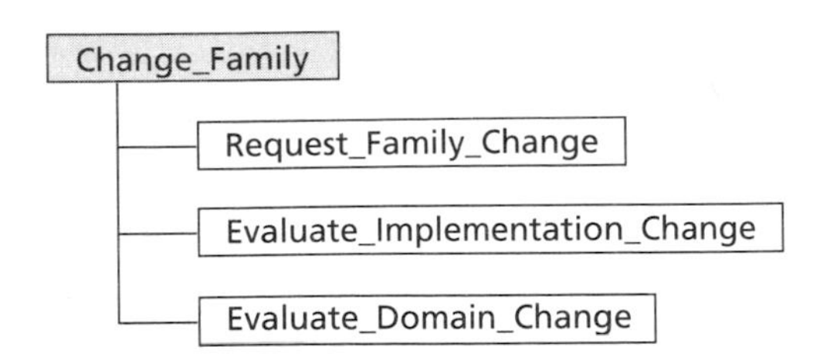

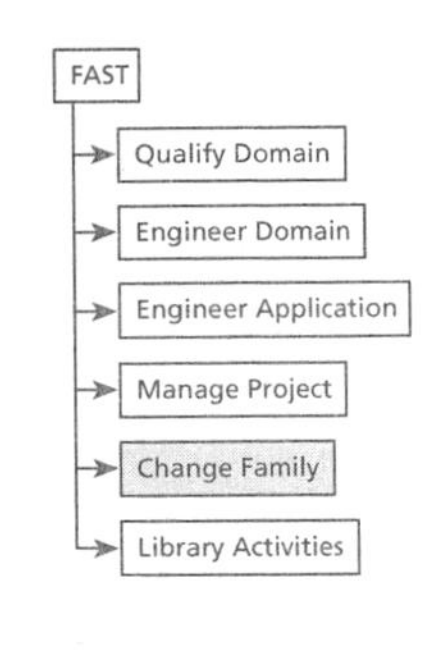

Process State Definition Form

Name	**Change_Family**
Synopsis	Make a change to the family that results either in a different set of members for the family or in different ways of generating family members. The change requires that the domain be reanalyzed or reimplemented in part or in whole.
Main Role	Domain_Engineer, Domain_Manager, Environment_Engineer
Entrance Condition	state-of(Change_Report)=Change_Identified
Artifacts List	Family_Artifact
Information Artifacts	Family_Artifact
OPERATION LIST	
Name	**Request_Family_Change**
Synopsis	Decide whether a proposed change is a domain change (a change that will result in a change in the set of family members for the domain) or an implementation change (a change that will affect the implementation of the Application_Engineering_Environment but will not affect the set of family members for the domain). A domain change is usually made in response to new, unforeseen customer requirements, and an implementation change is usually made in response to an application engineer's request to make the Application_Engineering_Environment easier or better to use.
Name	**Evaluate_Implementation_Change**
Synopsis	Evaluate a proposed implementation change to the family to determine whether it is worth making.
Name	**Evaluate_Domain_Change**
Synopsis	Evaluate a proposed domain change to the family to determine whether it is worth making.
Exit Condition	state-of(Change_Report)=Domain_Change_Authorized or state-of(Change_Report)=Implementation_Change_Authorized or state-of(Change_Report)=Change_Rejected

continued

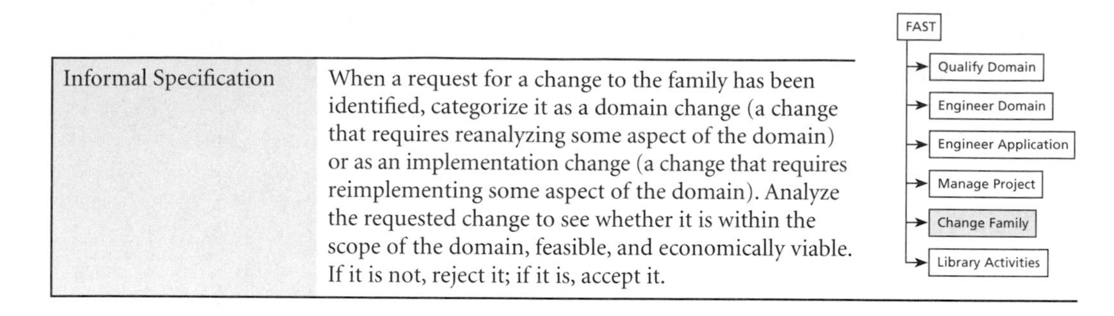

Informal Specification	When a request for a change to the family has been identified, categorize it as a domain change (a change that requires reanalyzing some aspect of the domain) or as an implementation change (a change that requires reimplementing some aspect of the domain). Analyze the requested change to see whether it is within the scope of the domain, feasible, and economically viable. If it is not, reject it; if it is, accept it.

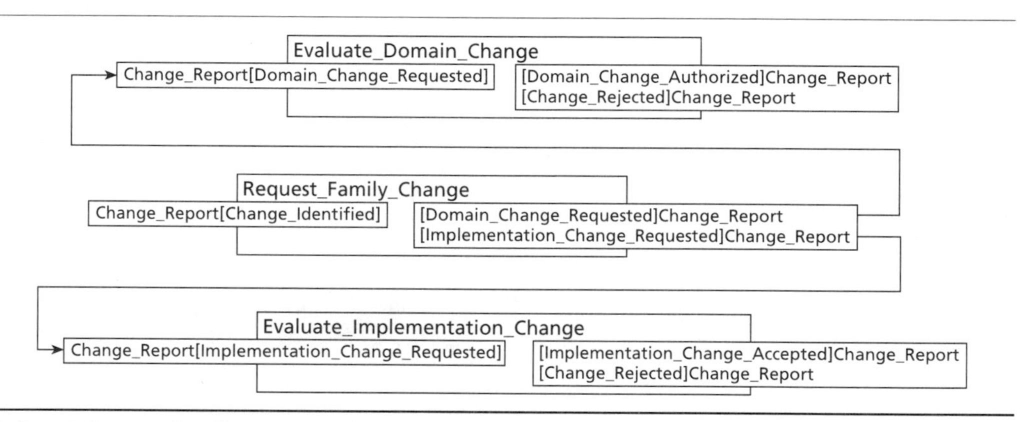

P-State Diagram for Change_Family

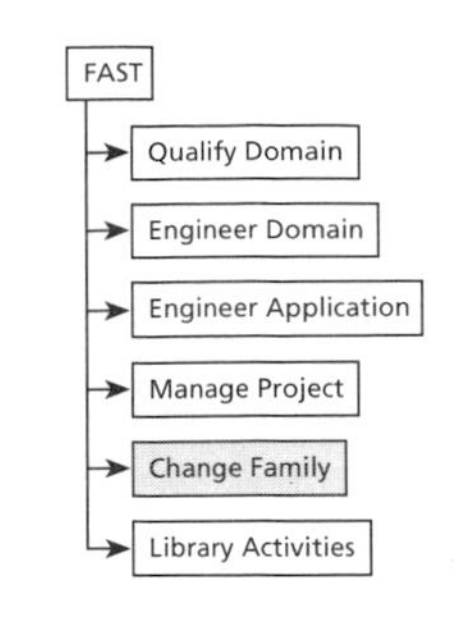

10.5.1 Request_Family_Change

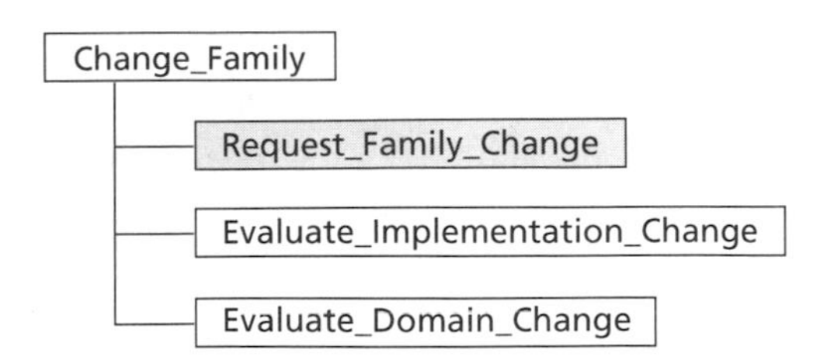

Operation Definition Form

Name	**Request_Family_Change**
Synopsis	Decide whether a proposed change is a domain change (a change that will result in a change in the set of family members for the domain) or an implementation change (a change that will affect the implementation of the Application_Engineering_Environment but will not affect the set of family members for the domain). A domain change is usually made in response to new, unforeseen customer requirements, and an implementation change is usually made in response to an application engineer's request to make the Application_Engineering_Environment easier or better to use.
Role List	Domain_Engineer, Domain_Manager
Entrance Condition	state-of(Change_Report) = Change_Identified
Operation Type	Manual
Artifacts List	Change_Report
Information Artifacts	Domain_Model, Environment
Exit Condition	state-of(Change_Report) = Domain_Change_Requested or state-of(Change_Report) = Implementation_Change_Requested
Informal Specification	Determine whether the proposed change violates any existing variabilities or commonalities, resulting in a new set of family members for the domain, or whether it involves only a change to the implementation, including user interface(s), of the set of tools that compose the Application_Engineering_Environment.

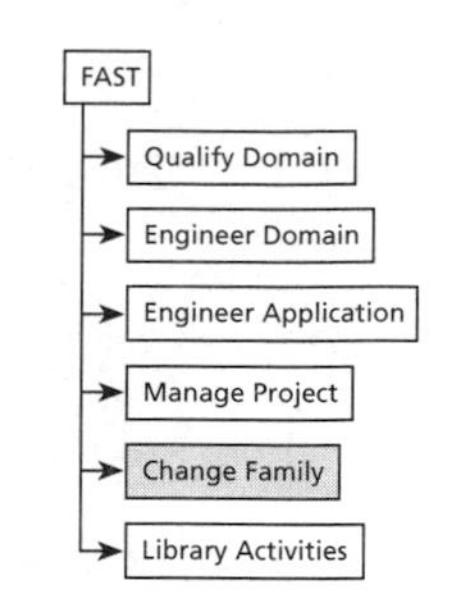

10.5.2 Evaluate_Implementation_Change

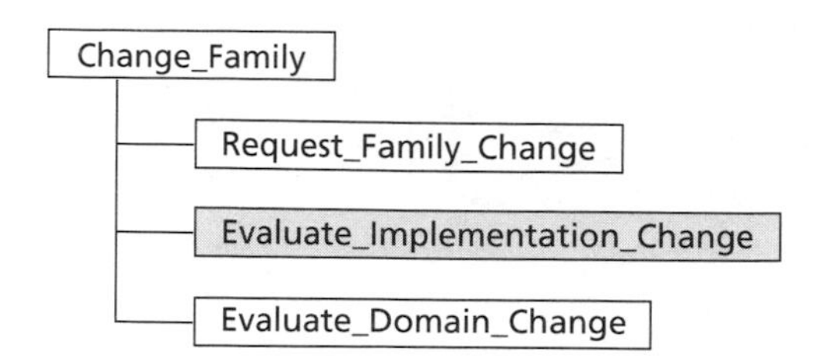

Operation Definition Form

Name	**Evaluate_Implementation_Change**
Synopsis	Evaluate a proposed implementation change to the family to determine whether it is worth making.
Role List	Domain_Engineer, Environment_Engineer, Domain_Manager
Entrance Condition	state-of(Change_Report)=Implementation_Change_Requested
Operation Type	Manual
Artifacts List	Change_Report
Information Artifacts	Environment, Economic_Model
Exit Condition	state-of(Change_Report)=Implementation_Change_Accepted or state-of(Change_Report)=Change_Rejected
Informal Specification	Evaluate the proposed change by identifying what parts of the environment must be modified to make the change. Use the economic model to help determine whether the change is cost-effective.

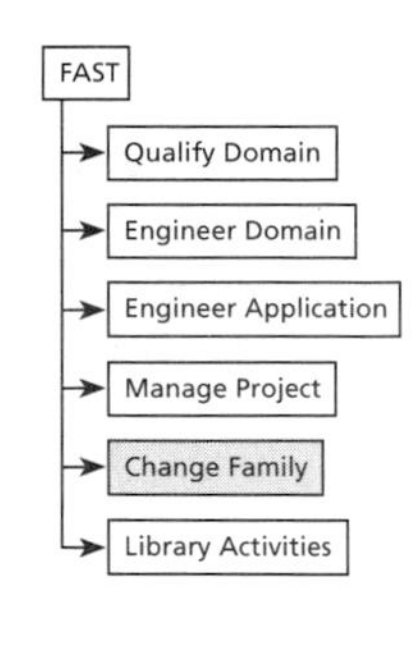

10.5.3 Evaluate_Domain_Change

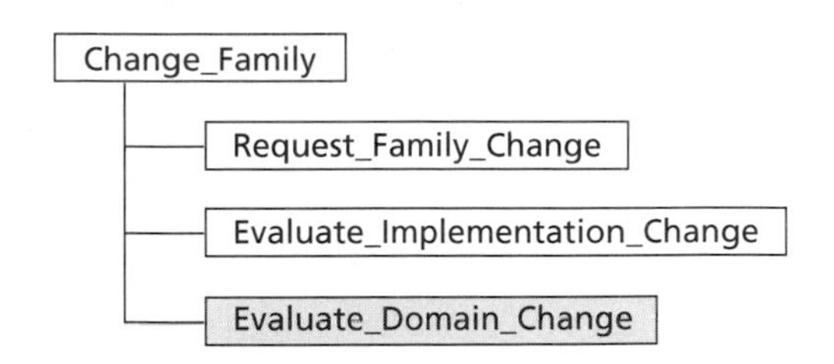

Operation Definition Form

Name	**Evaluate_Domain_Change**
Synopsis	Evaluate a proposed domain change to the family to determine whether it is worth making.
Role List	Domain_Engineer, Domain_Manager, Environment_Engineer
Entrance Condition	state-of(Change_Report)=Domain_Change_Requested
Operation Type	Manual
Artifacts List	Change_Report
Information Artifacts	Domain_Model, Economic_Model
Exit Condition	state-of(Change_Report)=Domain_Change_Authorized or state-of(Change_Report)=Change_Rejected
Informal Specification	Evaluate the proposed change by identifying the commonalities and variabilities that are affected by it, and the changes to the Application_Engineering_Environment that will be needed. Use the Economic_Model to determine whether the change is viable.

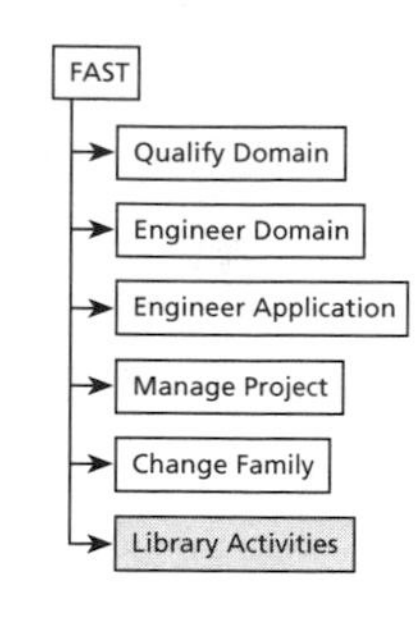

10.6 Library_Activities

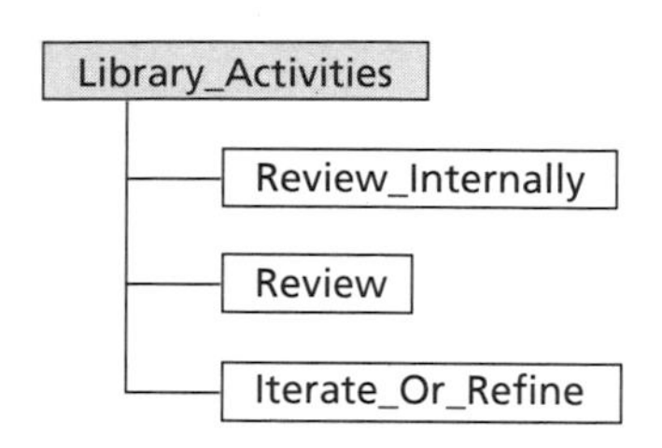

Process State Definition Form

Name	**Library_Activities**
Synopsis	These activities are common to a number of FAST P-states and are gathered into a library for simplicity and convenience.
Main Role	
Entrance Condition	TRUE
Artifacts List	
Information Artifacts	
OPERATION LIST	
Name	**Review_Internally**
Synopsis	Conduct an informal review of an ARTIFACT by its creators.
Name	**Review**
Synopsis	Review an artifact.
Name	**Iterate_Or_Refine**
Synopsis	Revise the artifact based on 1. Resolution of outstanding issues 2. New insights 3. New information becoming available 4. Change to a related artifact
Exit Condition	TRUE

10.6.1 Review_Internally

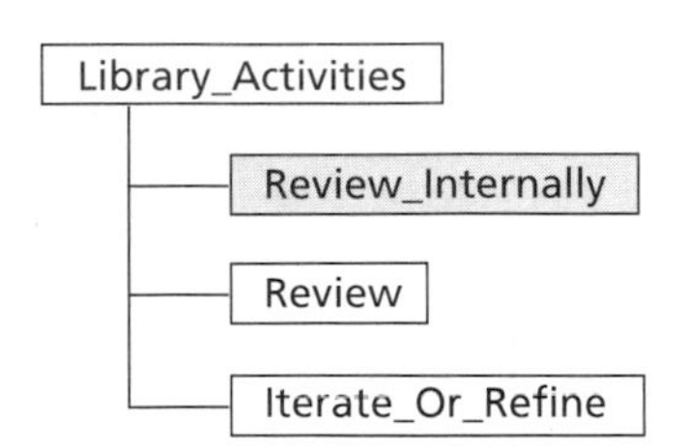

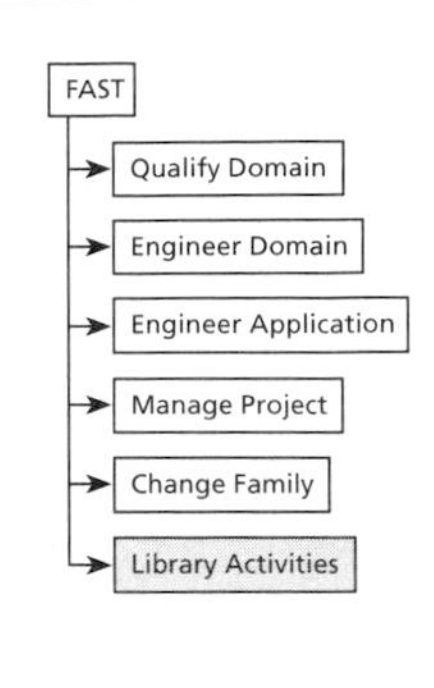

Operation Definition Form

Name	**Review_Internally**
Synopsis	Conduct an informal review of an ARTIFACT by its creators.
Role List	Domain_Engineer, Application_Engineer
Entrance Condition	state-of(ARTIFACT)=Defined_And_Specified
Operation Type	Manual
Artifacts List	Application_Model, Commonalities, Commonalities_And_Variabilities, Parameters_Of_Variation, Standard_Terminology, Variabilities
Information Artifacts	
Exit Condition	state-of(ARTIFACT)=Established
Informal Specification	ARTIFACT refers to any artifact in the FAST artifact tree that may be subject to review. The same review process as that used in a formal review of the artifact can be used to conduct an informal review. The difference is that an informal review is conducted by the creators of the artifact, and the review results and the process for resolving issues that arise during the review are determined by the authors and not formally defined. See the P-state Review for some alternative review methods.

10.6.2 Review

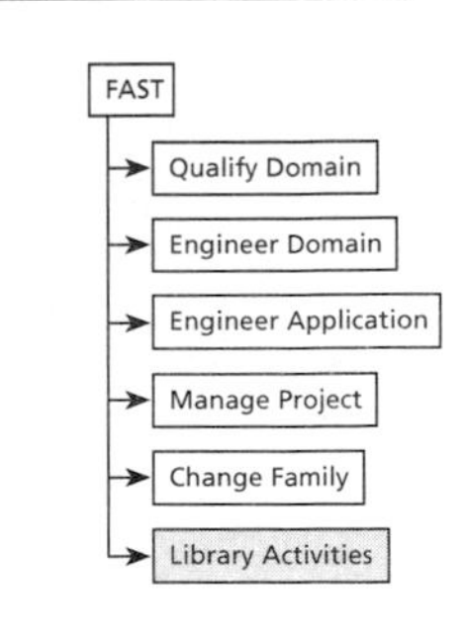

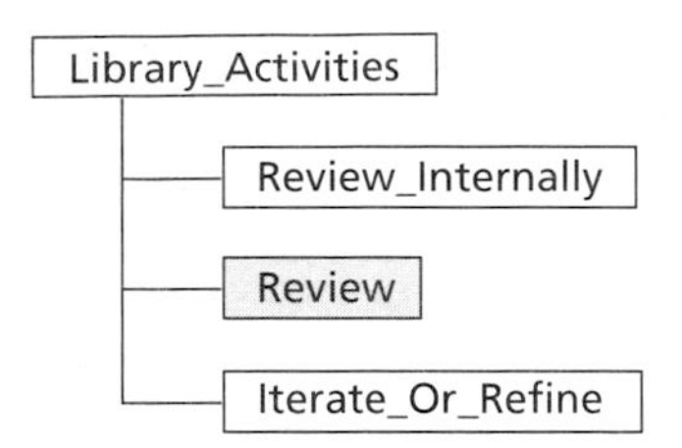

Operation Definition Form

Name	**Review**
Synopsis	Review an artifact.
Role List	Application_Engineer, Application_Manager, Application_Producer, Domain_Engineer, Domain_Manager, Environment_Engineer, Project_Manager, System_Maintainer_Or_Supporter
Entrance Condition	(state-of(ARTIFACT)=Defined_And_Specified) or (state-of(TOOL)=Tool_Produced) or (state-of(Application)=Modeled) or (state-of(Application_Modeling_Language)=Language_Specified) or (state-of(Code_Template)=Implemented) or (state-of(Commonality_Analysis)=Reviewed) or (state-of(Commonality_Analysis)=Variabilities_Parameterized) or (state-of(Documentation_Template)=Implemented) or (state-of(Library)=Library_Implemented) or (state-of(Tool_Set_Design)=Tool_Set_Designed)
Operation Type	Manual
Name	**Review**
Artifacts List	Family_Artifact
Information Artifacts	
Exit Condition	(state-of(ARTIFACT)=Reviewed) or (state-of(ARTIFACT)=Referenced) or (state-of(TOOL)=Tool_Identified) or (state-of(Application_Modeling_Language)= Commonality_Analysis_Reviewed) or (state-of(Application_Modeling_Language)=Language_Type_Identified) or (state-of(Code_Template)=Specified) or (state-of(Commonality_Analysis)=Reviewed) or (state-of(Documentation_Template)=Specified) or (state-of(Economic_Model)=Started) or (state-of(Family_Design)=Commonality_Analysis_Reviewed) or (state-of(Tool_Set_Design)=Tool_Family_Specified) or (state-of(Tool_Set_Design)=Language_Specified)

continued

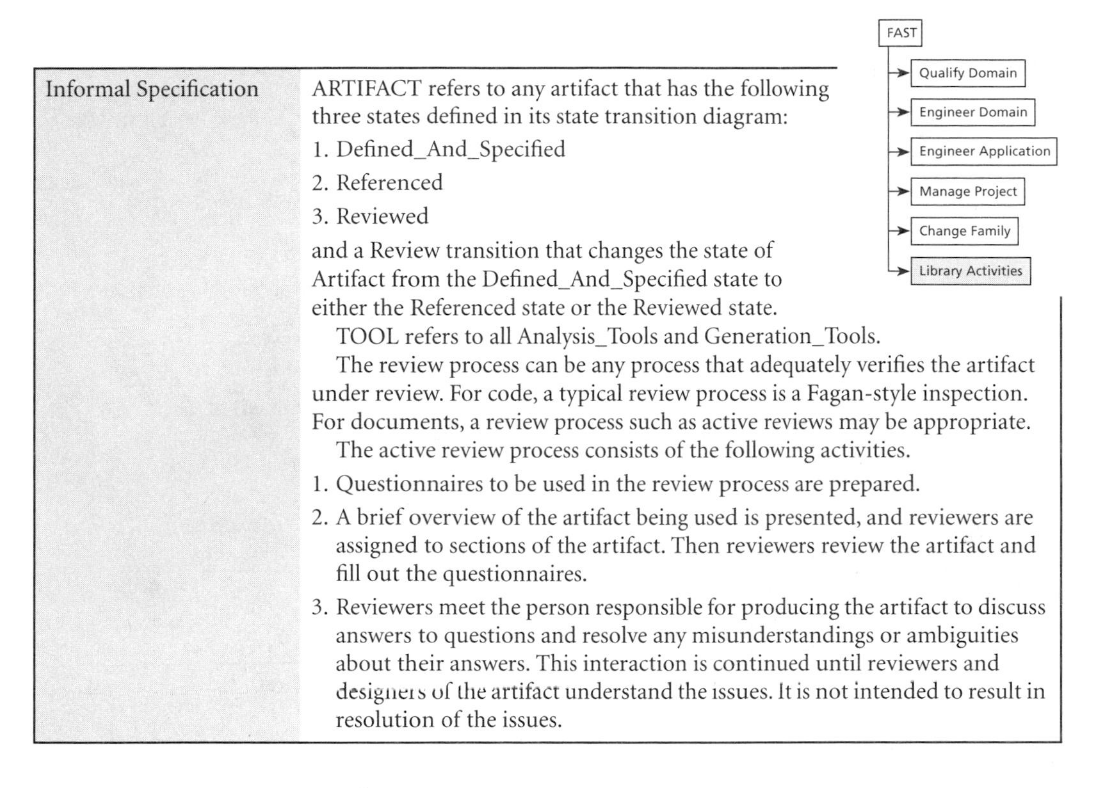

Informal Specification	ARTIFACT refers to any artifact that has the following three states defined in its state transition diagram: 1. Defined_And_Specified 2. Referenced 3. Reviewed and a Review transition that changes the state of Artifact from the Defined_And_Specified state to either the Referenced state or the Reviewed state. TOOL refers to all Analysis_Tools and Generation_Tools. The review process can be any process that adequately verifies the artifact under review. For code, a typical review process is a Fagan-style inspection. For documents, a review process such as active reviews may be appropriate. The active review process consists of the following activities. 1. Questionnaires to be used in the review process are prepared. 2. A brief overview of the artifact being used is presented, and reviewers are assigned to sections of the artifact. Then reviewers review the artifact and fill out the questionnaires. 3. Reviewers meet the person responsible for producing the artifact to discuss answers to questions and resolve any misunderstandings or ambiguities about their answers. This interaction is continued until reviewers and designers of the artifact understand the issues. It is not intended to result in resolution of the issues.

10.6.3 Iterate_Or_Refine

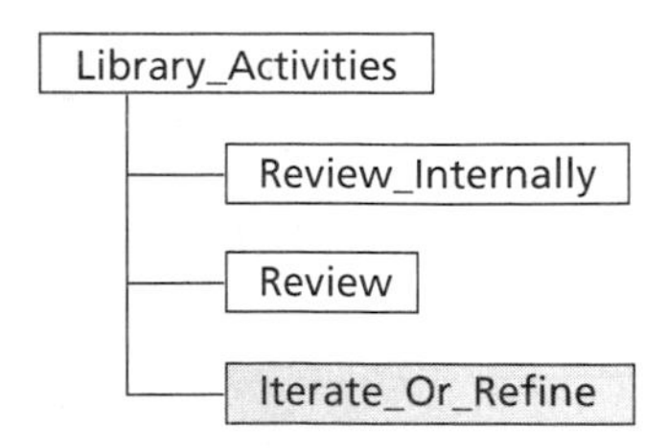

Operation Definition Form

Name	**Iterate_Or_Refine**
Synopsis	Revise the artifact based on 1. Resolution of outstanding issues 2. New insights 3. Availability of new information 4. Change to a related artifact
Role List	Domain_Engineer, Application_Engineer

continued

Entrance Condition	(state-of(ARTIFACT)=Defined_And_Specified) or (state-of(Commonality_Analysis)=Standard_Terminology_Established) or (state-of(Commonality_Analysis)= Commonalities_And_Variabilities_Established) or (state-of(Commonality_Analysis)=Variabilities_Parameterized)
Operation Type	Manual
Artifacts List	Application_Model, Commonalities, Commonalities_And_Variabilities, Parameters_Of_Variation, Standard_Terminology, Variabilities
Information Artifacts	
Exit Condition	(state-of(Application_Model)=Requirements_Identified) or (state-of(Commonalities)=Started) or (state-of(Commonalities_And_Variabilities)=Referenced) or (state-of(Commonality_Analysis)=Referenced) or (state-of(Standard_Terminology)=Started) or (state-of(Variabilities)=Started)
Informal Specification	Change the artifact based on 1. Resolution of outstanding issues 2. New insights 3. Availability of new information 4. Change to a related artifact

10.7 Reading for Chapter 10

[1] Parnas, D.L., and Weiss, D.M. "Active Design Reviews: Principles and Practices." *Proc. 8th Int. Conf. Soft. Eng.*, London (August 1985): 132–136.

A description of a review process wherein authors of a design identify questions about the design for the reviewers to answer. Each reviewer is focused on a particular area of expertise. Rather than hold a large meeting to discuss the design, reviewers' answers to the questions are discussed by a small group, usually the reviewer and an author.

11 Role Definitions

THIS CHAPTER CONTAINS THE DEFINITIONS OF THE ROLES IN THE FAST PASTA model. For each role in the model there is a section in the chapter that contains its role definition form. Figure 11-1 shows the FAST role tree. The nodes in the trees are labeled with the numbers of the sections in this chapter that contain their role definition forms. For example, Project_Manager is defined in Section 11.1.

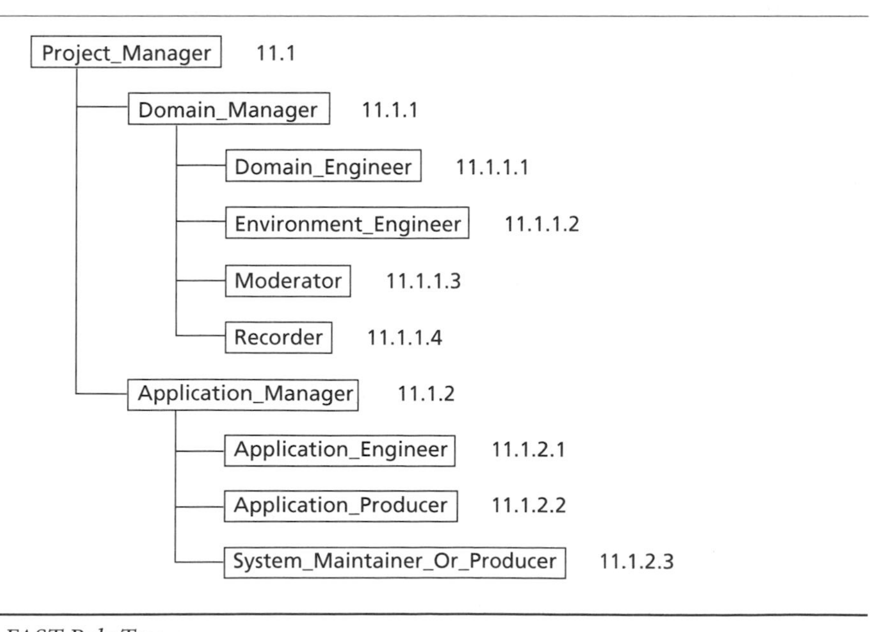

Figure 11-1. *FAST Role Tree*

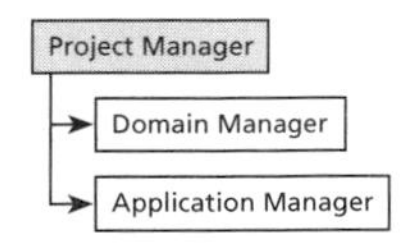

11.1 Project_Manager

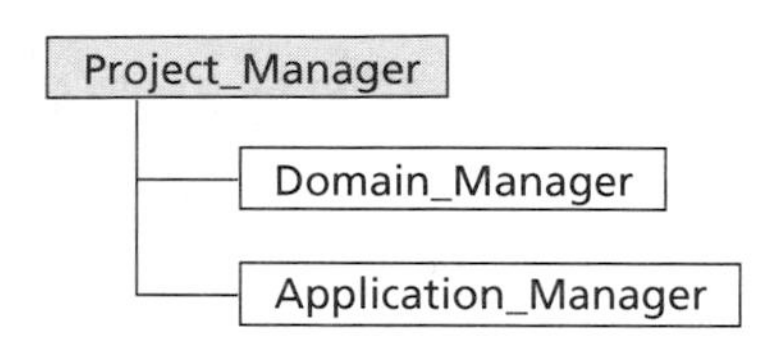

Role Definition Form

Name	**Project_Manager**
Synopsis	Project managers manage the engineering and evolution of the domain and the engineering of the applications in the domain.
Member List	Domain_Manager, Application_Manager
	P-OPERATION LIST
Name	**Review**
Synopsis	Review an artifact.
Name	**FAST**
Synopsis	A process for creating application software systems as members of a family.
	ANALYSIS LIST
Name	**Artifact_Implementation_Assurance_Analysis**
Synopsis	Check that every artifact defined in the application engineering environment has been implemented.
Name	**Customer_Satisfaction**
Synopsis	Check that the customer is satisfied.
Name	**Defect_Analysis**
Synopsis	This analysis generates statistics on various types of defects by P-state, operation, and artifact to show the distribution of defects.
Name	**Risk_Analysis**
Synopsis	This analysis generates a list of risky events after comparing progress on various P-states and A-states of active artifacts.
Name	**Progress_Analysis**
Synopsis	This analysis generates a report on the progress of the project. The report describes what is next in the process and what is the current state of the active artifacts.
Name	**Resource_Analysis**
Synopsis	This analysis generates a report on resource usage, resource balancing, resource estimation, and resource allocation. The information resulting from the analysis helps the Project_Manager, Domain_Manager, and Application_Manager make decisions on the management of a project using FAST.

11.1.1 Domain_Manager

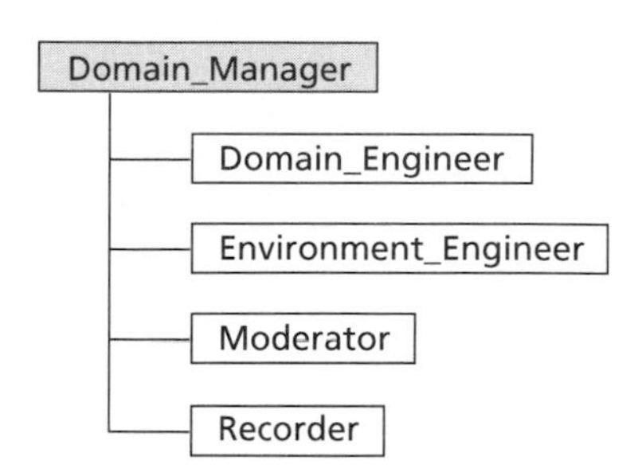

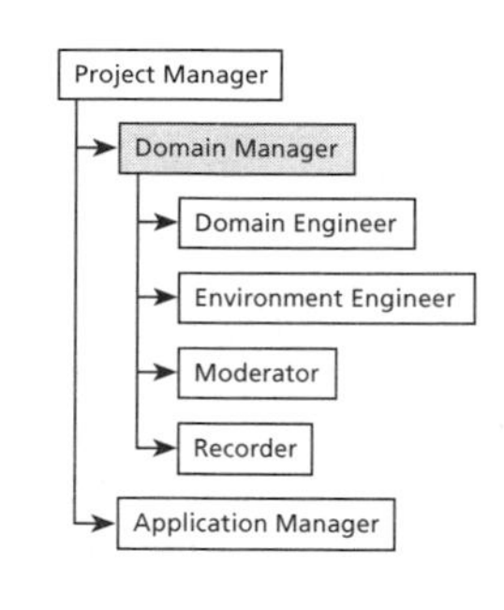

Role Definition Form

Name	**Domain_Manager**
Synopsis	The domain manager manages the engineering of the domain, monitoring progress, setting priorities, and allocating resources to the domain engineering tasks.
Member List	Domain_Engineer, Environment_Engineer, Moderator, Recorder
	P-OPERATION LIST
Name	**Request_Family_Change**
Synopsis	Decide whether a proposed change is a domain change (a change that will result in a change in the set of family members for the domain) or an implementation change (a change that will affect the implementation of the Application_Engineering_Environment but will not affect the set of family members for the domain). A domain change is usually made in response to new, unforeseen customer requirements, and an implementation change is usually made in response to an application engineer's request to make the Application_Engineering_Environment easier to use.
Name	**Evaluate_Implementation_Change**
Synopsis	Evaluate a proposed implementation change to the family to determine whether it is worth making.
Name	**Evaluate_Domain_Change**
Synopsis	Evaluate a proposed domain change to the family to determine whether it is worth making.
Name	**Change_Family**
Synopsis	Make a change to the family that results either in a different set of family members or in different ways of generating family members. The change requires that the domain be reanalyzed or reimplemented in part or in whole.

continued

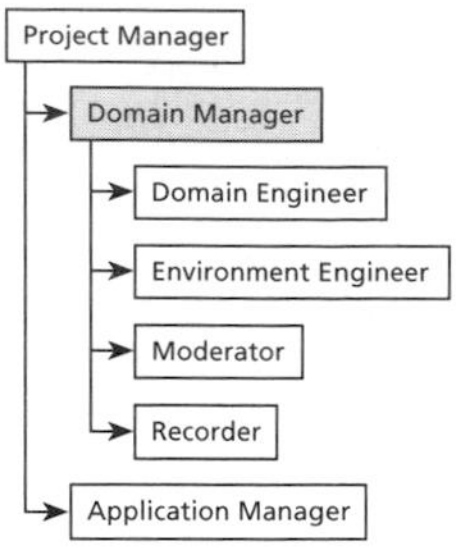

Project Manager
- Domain Manager
  - Domain Engineer
  - Environment Engineer
  - Moderator
  - Recorder
- Application Manager

Name	Reject
Synopsis	The Economic_Model has been created and evaluated for the domain. It is not worth investing in the domain.
Name	**Accept**
Synopsis	Based on the evaluation of the Economic_Model for the domain, it is worth investing in the domain.
Name	**Implement_Domain**
Synopsis	Implementing a domain consists of constructing the application engineering environment for it. The environment is built to the specifications determined during domain engineering—that is, the Domain_Model.
Name	**Qualify_Domain**
Synopsis	Domain qualification is the process by which economic viability is determined for a domain. A domain is economically viable when the investment in domain engineering is more than repaid by the value obtained from domain engineering. The process consists of predicting the number of family members in the domain, the value of those family members, the cost of investing in domain engineering, and the cost of not investing in domain engineering. The result is an Economic_Model for the domain.
Name	**Review**
Synopsis	Review an artifact.
Name	**Analyze_Data**
Synopsis	Create an Economic_Model for the domain that can be used to evaluate the cost and time savings from applying domain engineering.
Name	**Engineer_Domain**
Synopsis	The activity that creates and supports a standardized application engineering process and an application engineering environment that supports the process.

ANALYSIS LIST

Name	Artifact_Implementation_Assurance_Analysis
Synopsis	Check that every artifact defined in the application engineering environment has been implemented.
Name	**Parameter_Of_Variation_To_Decision_Trace_Analysis**
Synopsis	Check every Parameter_Of_Variation to see whether there exists a corresponding decision in the Decision_Model.

continued

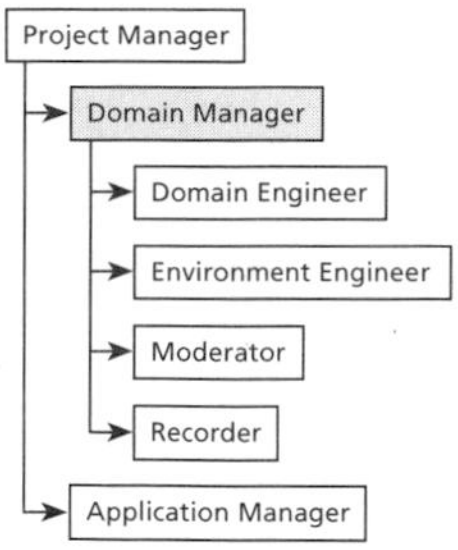

Project Manager
- Domain Manager
  - Domain Engineer
  - Environment Engineer
  - Moderator
  - Recorder
- Application Manager

Name	Parameter_Of_Variation_To_Language_Trace_Analysis
Synopsis	Check that every parameter of variation can be expressed in the language or determines what is expressible in the language.
Name	**Parameter_Of_Variation_To_Module_Trace_Analysis**
Synopsis	Check that every Parameter_Of_Variation is mapped by the Composition_Mapping to a module in the Family_Design. Note that this analysis cannot be performed until the Family_Design is reviewed.
Name	**Variation_Parameter_To_Variability_Trace_Analysis**
Synopsis	Are there any parameters of variation that cannot be traced to variabilities?
Name	**Variability_To_Variation_Parameter_Trace_Analysis**
Synopsis	Check that each variability has a corresponding Parameter_Of_Variation.
Name	**Defect_Analysis**
Synopsis	This analysis generates statistics on various types of defects by P-state, operation, and artifact to show the distribution of defects.
Name	**Risk_Analysis**
Synopsis	This analysis generates a list of risky events after comparing progress on various P-states and A-states of active artifacts.
Name	**Progress_Analysis**
Synopsis	This analysis generates a report on the progress of the project. The report describes what is next in the process and what is the current state of the active artifacts.
Name	**Resource_Analysis**
Synopsis	This analysis generates a report on resource usage, resource balancing, resource estimation, and resource allocation. The information resulting from the analysis helps the Project_Manager, Domain_Manager, and Application_Manager make decisions on the management of a project using FAST.

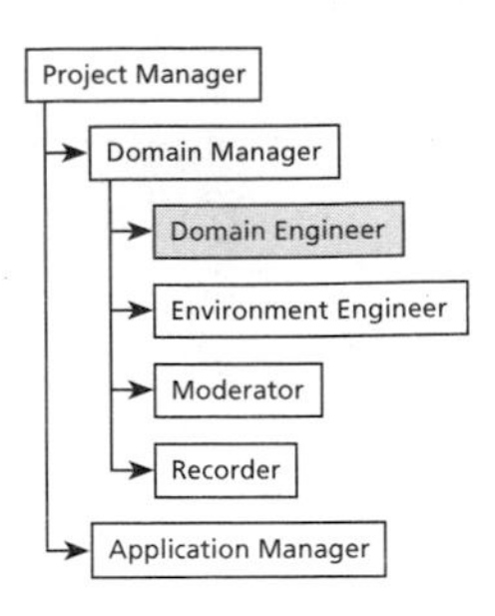

11.1.1.1 Domain_Engineer

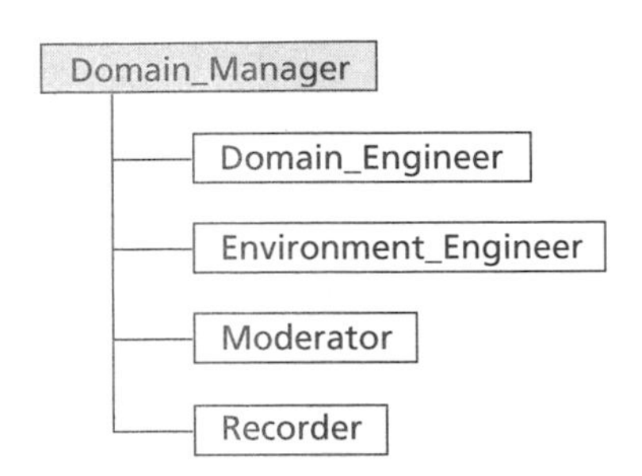

Role Definition Form

Name	**Domain_Engineer**
Synopsis	The domain engineer is responsible for carrying out all activities needed to produce the domain model, to create a standard application engineering process, and to design the application engineering environment. He or she performs the latter two duties in cooperation with the environment engineer.
Member List	
	P-OPERATION LIST
Name	**Request_Family_Change**
Synopsis	Decide whether a proposed change is a domain change (a change that will result in a change in the set of family members for the domain) or an implementation change (a change that will affect the implementation of the Application_Engineering_Environment, but will not affect the set of family members for the domain). A domain change is usually made in response to new, unforeseen customer requirements, and an implementation change is usually made in response to an application engineer's request to make the Application_Engineering_Environment easier or better to use.
Name	**Evaluate_Implementation_Change**
Synopsis	Evaluate a proposed implementation change to the family to determine whether it is worth making.
Name	**Evaluate_Domain_Change**
Synopsis	Evaluate a proposed domain change to the family to determine whether it is worth making.
Name	**Change_Family**
Synopsis	Make a change to the family that results either in a different set of family members or in different ways of generating family members. The change requires that the domain be reanalyzed or reimplemented in part or in whole.

continued

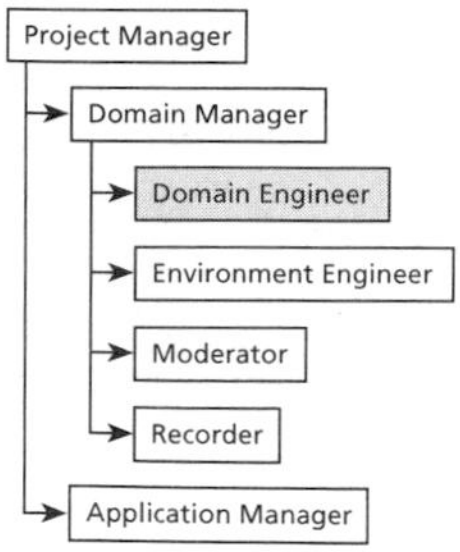

Project Manager
- Domain Manager
  - Domain Engineer
  - Environment Engineer
  - Moderator
  - Recorder
- Application Manager

Name	Design_Domain
Synopsis	Designing a domain consists of creating a design common to all family members, known as a Family_Design, and creating a mapping between the Application_Modeling_Language for the domain and the components specified in the design, known as the Composition_Mapping.
Name	**Establish_Domain_Commonalities_And_Variabilities**
Synopsis	Create a list of assumptions that define what's true of all family members (commonalities) and assumptions that distinguish among family members (variabilities).
Name	**Parameterize_Variabilities**
Synopsis	Parameters_Of_Variation quantify the variabilities of the domain. Each parameter is defined by a name, a domain, a binding time, and a default value.
Name	**Establish_Standard_Terminology**
Synopsis	Define all significant technical terms used by domain experts in discussing the requirements or engineering of systems in the domain.
Name	**Define_Decision_Model**
Synopsis	This operation creates a Decision_Model, which defines the set of requirements and engineering decisions that an Application_Engineer must resolve in order to describe and construct a product. It is a precursor of the Application_Engineering_Process for the domain. It is also an elaboration of a domain's variability assumptions and hence an abstract form of an Application_Modeling_Language.
Name	**Analyze_Commonality**
Synopsis	The commonality analysis defines and bounds the family. Analyzing commonality includes identifying assumptions that are common to all family members (commonalities), assumptions that distinguish family members from one another (variabilities), and parameters of variation that quantify variabilities, as well as establishing a dictionary of technical terms for the family.
Name	**Analyze_Domain**
Synopsis	The activities for creating and refining the specifications for an Application_Engineering_Environment. Key activities include defining the family that composes the domain, designing an Application_Modeling_Language in which to describe members of the family, and specifying the tools needed to analyze Application_Models and to generate family members from Application_Models.
Name	**Implement_Domain**
Synopsis	Implementing a domain consists of constructing the application engineering environment for it. The environment is built to the specifications determined during domain engineering—that is, the Domain_Model.

continued

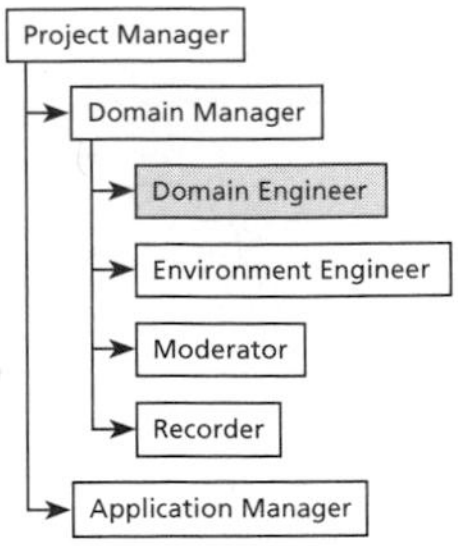

Project Manager
- Domain Manager
  - Domain Engineer
  - Environment Engineer
  - Moderator
  - Recorder
- Application Manager

Name	Develop_Family_Design
Synopsis	Creating a Family_Design consists of creating a design that can be used for generating members of the family. Such a design can be created by organizing the software into modules; each module's secret is how to implement a parameter of variation. One way to implement such a design is to make a template for each module that is parameterized according to possible values of the corresponding parameter of variation.
Name	**Identify_Complete_Set_Of_Variability_Parameters**
Synopsis	Complete the identification of Parameters_Of_Variation.
Name	**Identify_Complete_Set_Of_Variabilities**
Synopsis	Complete the identification of variabilities, the assumptions that distinguish among the family members.
Name	**Create_Initial_Set_Of_Variability_Parameters**
Synopsis	Create a template for the parameters of variation and include a few initial parameters of variation for the proposed variabilities.
Name	**Create_Initial_Set_Of_Variabilities**
Synopsis	Create a template for the domain variabilities and include a few initial proposed variabilities.
Name	**Identify_Complete_Set_Of_Commonalities**
Synopsis	Complete the identification of commonalities, the assumptions that are true for all the family members.
Name	**Create_Initial_Set_Of_Commonalities**
Synopsis	Create a template for the domain commonalities and include a few initial proposed commonalities.
Name	**Review_Internally**
Synopsis	Conduct an informal review of an ARTIFACT by its creators.
Name	**Define_Terms**
Synopsis	Define terms used in describing the domain.
Name	**Initialize_Dictionary**
Synopsis	Create a template for the dictionary of terms for the domain.

continued

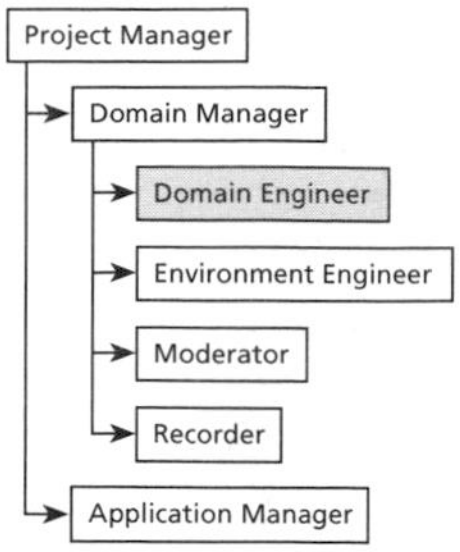

Project Manager
Domain Manager
Domain Engineer
Environment Engineer
Moderator
Recorder
Application Manager

Name	Iterate_Or_Refine
Synopsis	Revise the artifact based on 1. Resolution of outstanding issues 2. New insights 3. Availability of new information 4. Change to a related artifact
Name	**Qualify_Domain**
Synopsis	Domain qualification is the process by which economic viability is determined for a domain. A domain is economically viable when the investment in domain engineering is more than repaid by the value obtained from domain engineering. The process consists of predicting the number of family members in the domain, the value of those family members, the cost of investing in domain engineering, and the cost of not investing in domain engineering. The result is an Economic_Model for the domain.
Name	**Review**
Synopsis	Review an artifact.
Name	**Identify_Language_Type**
Synopsis	Application modeling languages tend to be one of several different types; they form families of languages. Examples are languages that describe state machines, languages that describe properties of objects, and languages that describe concurrent threads of events. Identifying the language type is a key step in designing the constructs of the language.
Name	**Specify_Language_Syntax_And_Semantics**
Synopsis	Define the BNF production rules, or the equivalent, including semantics, for each construct in the language.
Name	**Gather_Data**
Synopsis	Gather the data needed to decide whether a domain exists and is worth engineering.

ANALYSIS LIST

Name	Decision_To_Tool_Trace_Analysis
Synopsis	Check that the decisions supported by the tools used in the application engineering process correspond to decisions to be made in the application engineering process.
Name	**Application_Engineering_Support_Analysis**
Synopsis	Check that for each step in the application engineering process there is sufficient information and facilities available for the Application_Engineer to make decisions corresponding to parameters of variation for the step.

continued

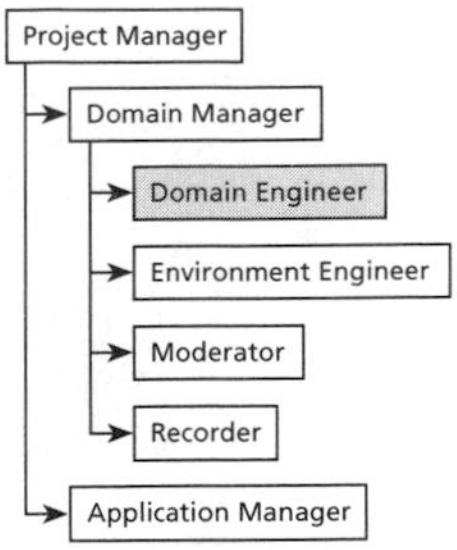

Project Manager
- Domain Manager
  - Domain Engineer
  - Environment Engineer
  - Moderator
  - Recorder
- Application Manager

Name	Composition_Mapping_To_Family_Design
Synopsis	Check that each module in the Family_Design is in the range of the Composition_Mapping either by a direct mapping from a language construct in the AML or by the transitive closure of the uses relation for (programs in) a module mapped directly from a language construct.
Name	**Commonality_To_Module_Trace_Analysis**
Synopsis	Check that every Commonality is maintained by the Family_Design.
Name	**Module_Documentation_Assurance_Analysis**
Synopsis	Check that every module defined in the application engineering environment has been documented.
Name	**Application_Engineering_Process_To_Tool_Trace_Analysis**
Synopsis	Check that each step in the application engineering process is supported by a tool in the toolset.
Name	**Application_Engineering_Process_To_Decision_Trace_Analysis**
Synopsis	Check that each decision of the Decision_Model has a corresponding step in the standard application engineering process.
Name	**Application_Modeling_Language_To_Family_Design_Trace_Analysis**
Synopsis	Check each language construct to see whether there exists a corresponding module in the Family_Design.
Name	**Parameter_Of_Variation_To_Decision_Trace_Analysis**
Synopsis	Check every Parameter_Of_Variation to see whether there exists a corresponding decision in the Decision_Model.
Name	**Composition_Mapping_To_Language_Construct_Mapping_Analysis**
Synopsis	Check that each construct in the Application_Modeling_Language that is used to express a variability whose binding time is specification time or later is mapped by the Composition_Mapping.
Name	**Parameter_Of_Variation_To_Language_Trace_Analysis**
Synopsis	Check that every parameter of variation can be expressed in the language or determines what is expressible in the language.
Name	**Terminology_Analysis**
Synopsis	This analysis generates a report on the usage of terminology, including the percentage of technical terms defined in Engineer_Domain that are used, and the definitions that are not used. This analysis checks all artifacts produced during Engineer_Domain for terminology usage.

continued

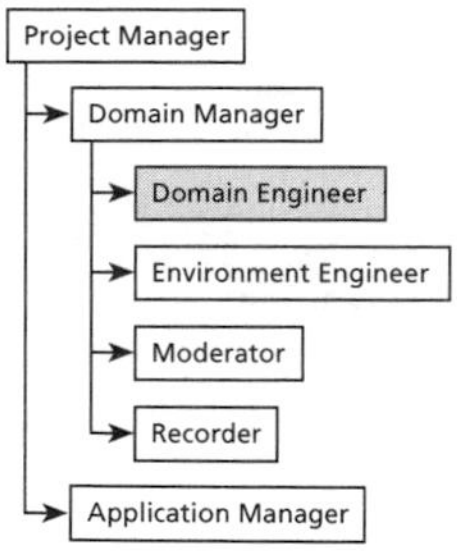

Project Manager
- Domain Manager
  - Domain Engineer
  - Environment Engineer
  - Moderator
  - Recorder
- Application Manager

Name	Parameter_Of_Variation_To_Module_Trace_Analysis
Synopsis	Check that every Parameter_Of_Variation is mapped by the Composition_Mapping to a module in the Family_Design. Note that this analysis cannot be performed until the Family_Design is reviewed.
Name	**Variation_Parameter_To_Variability_Trace_Analysis**
Synopsis	Are there any parameters of variation that cannot be traced to variabilities?
Name	**Variability_To_Variation_Parameter_Trace_Analysis**
Synopsis	Check that each variability has a corresponding Parameter_Of_Variation.

11.1.1.2 Environment_Engineer

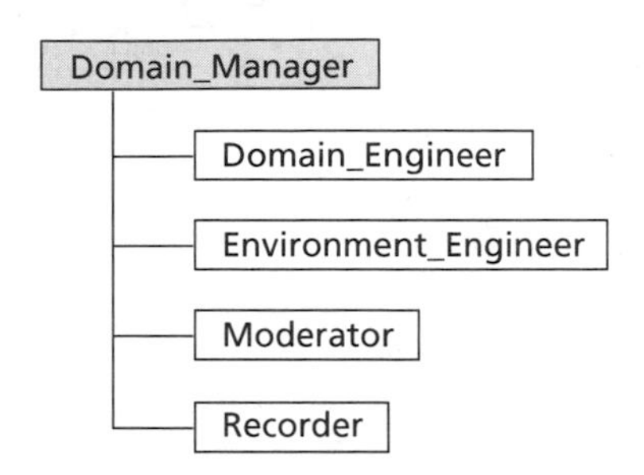

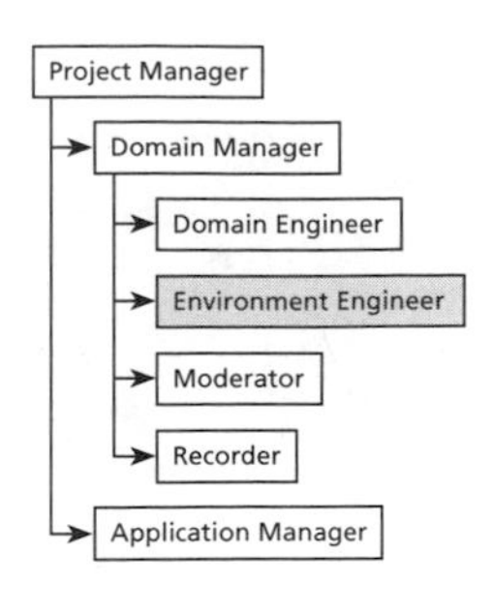

Role Definition Form

Name	**Environment_Engineer**
Synopsis	The environment engineer is responsible for carrying out all activities needed to implement the domain model.
Member List	
	P-OPERATION LIST
Name	**Evaluate_Implementation_Change**
Synopsis	Evaluate a proposed implementation change to the family to determine whether it is worth making.
Name	**Evaluate_Domain_Change**
Synopsis	Evaluate a proposed domain change to the family to determine whether it is worth making.
Name	**Change_Family**
Synopsis	Make a change to the family that results either in a different set of family members for the family or in different ways of generating family members. The change requires that the domain be reanalyzed or reimplemented in part or in whole.
Name	**Implement_Domain**
Synopsis	Implementing a domain consists of constructing the application engineering environment for it. The environment is built to the specifications determined during domain engineering—that is, the Domain_Model.
Name	**Review**
Synopsis	Review an artifact.
Name	**Write_Users_Guide**
Synopsis	Create Users_Guide for the users of the Application_Engineering_Environment.

continued

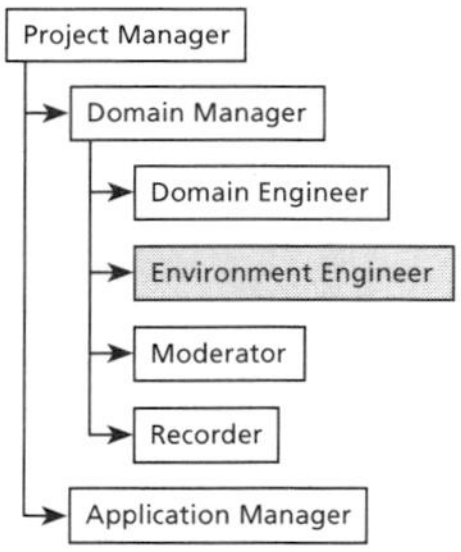

Project Manager
- Domain Manager
  - Domain Engineer
  - Environment Engineer
  - Moderator
  - Recorder
- Application Manager

Name	Write_Training_Material
Synopsis	Create Training_Material for the application engineers.
Name	**Write_Reference_Manual**
Synopsis	Create the Reference_Manual for the environment.
Name	**Design_Domain**
Synopsis	Designing a domain consists of creating a design common to all family members, known as a Family_Design, and creating a mapping between the application modeling language for the domain and the components specified in the design, known as the Composition_Mapping.
Name	**Document_Application_Engineering_Environment**
Synopsis	Produce the documentation needed by the application engineers who use an application engineering environment, including users guide, reference manuals, training manuals, and any other necessary documentation.
Name	**Implement_Comparator**
Synopsis	A comparator compares two or more specifications written in an Application_Modeling_Language and identifies their differences and similarities. This operation implements such a comparator.
Name	**Implement_Test_Generator**
Synopsis	A Test_Generator generates test cases from an Application_Model written in the Application_Modeling_Language for a domain. This operation implements a Test_Case_Generator.
Name	**Implement_Verifier**
Synopsis	This operation implements a Verifier for application models specified in the Application_Modeling_Language for a domain. The Verifier performs tasks such as verifying the completeness and consistency of an Application_Model when possible.
Name	**Implement_Interpreter**
Synopsis	An Interpreter is an analysis tool that interprets the Application_Modeling_Language. This operation implements such an Interpreter.
Name	**Implement_Simulator**
Synopsis	This operation implements a Simulator for application models specified in the Application_Modeling_Language for the domain.

continued

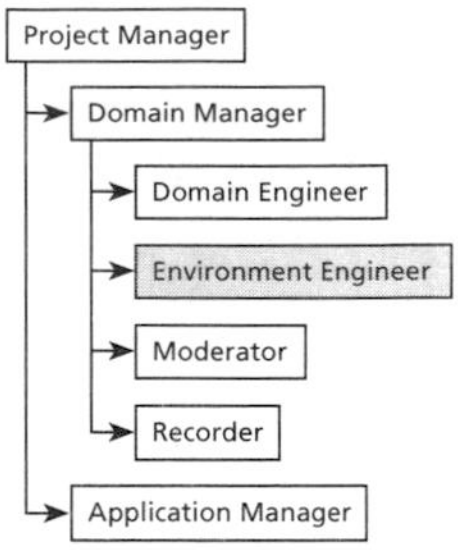

Project Manager
Domain Manager
Domain Engineer
Environment Engineer
Moderator
Recorder
Application Manager

Name	**Implement_Analysis_Tools**
Synopsis	Analysis tools perform consistency and completeness checks, simulations, performance estimates, and other form of analysis. For example, one kind provides the Application_Engineer with information about his or her Application_Model to help validate the model. Another kind gauges the progress of application engineering and domain engineering, calculating resources used, estimating resources needed, reporting defect distributions, and providing other measures of interest. This activity implements Analysis_Tools.
Name	**Implement_Composer**
Synopsis	Implementing the composer consists of implementing the Composition_Mapping between the Application_Modeling_Language and the templates in the Library. For each decision embodied in the AML, the mapping identifies the templates in the Library needed when the decision is made. The composer implements the mapping by parsing the program to get the values of the decisions, retrieving the corresponding templates from the library, instantiating the templates with the values supplied for the decisions, and integrating the instantiated templates.
Name	**Implement_Compiler**
Synopsis	Implementing the compiler consists of writing a compiler for the Application_Modeling_Language. The compiler is used to generate applications from the specifications written in the AML.
Name	**Implement_Generation**
Synopsis	FAST uses two primary generation techniques: compilation and composition. In the compilation approach, FAST users write a compiler for each application modeling language. In the compositional approach, FAST users implement the system composition mapping, which composes applications from templates in the library.
Name	**Implement_Code_Template**
Synopsis	Code can be generated by instantiating code templates that are contained in the library and then integrating the instantiated templates to form the code that is part of the application. Implementing the templates consists of writing the templates in a suitable language to meet the specifications produced as part of creating the Family_Design.
Name	**Implement_Documentation_Template**
Synopsis	Documentation can be generated by instantiating documentation templates that are contained in the Library and then integrating the instantiated templates to form the documentation that is part of the application. Implementing the templates consists of writing the templates in a suitable language to meet the specifications produced as part of creating the Family_Design.

continued

Project Manager
- Domain Manager
  - Domain Engineer
  - Environment Engineer
  - Moderator
  - Recorder
- Application Manager

Name	Implement_Library
Synopsis	The library contains the templates and components for code and documentation that are used to generate applications. Implementing the library means finding or developing those templates and components.
Name	**Implement_Application_Engineering_Environment**
Synopsis	Implementing the application engineering environment consists of implementing the design for the environment. It includes building or finding the tools that are part of the environment and the data on which those tools operate—for example, the code and documentation templates that are used by the tools to generate applications.
Name	**Design_Application_Engineering_Environment**
Synopsis	Designing the Application_Engineering_Environment consists of identifying the tools that compose the environment and describing how they will be used.
	ANALYSIS LIST
Name	**Module_Documentation_Assurance_Analysis**
Synopsis	Check that every module defined in the application engineering environment has been documented.
Name	**Tool_Documentation_Assurance_Analysis**
Synopsis	Check that every tool defined in the application engineering environment has been documented.
Name	**Application_Modeling_Language_Editor_Assurance_Analysis**
Synopsis	Check that there is an editor implemented for the Application_Modeling_Language.
Name	**Application_Modeling_Language_Parser_Assurance_Analysis**
Synopsis	Check that the parser for the Application_Modeling_Language parses every construct of the language correctly.
Name	**Application_Engineering_Process_To_Tool_Trace_Analysis**
Synopsis	Check that each step in the application engineering process is supported by a tool in the toolset.
Name	**Application_Engineering_Process_To_Decision_Trace_Analysis**
Synopsis	Check that each decision of the Decision_Model has a corresponding step in the standard application engineering process.
Name	**Application_Modeling_Language_To_Family_Design_Trace_Analysis**
Synopsis	Check each language construct to see whether there exists a corresponding module in the Family_Design.

continued

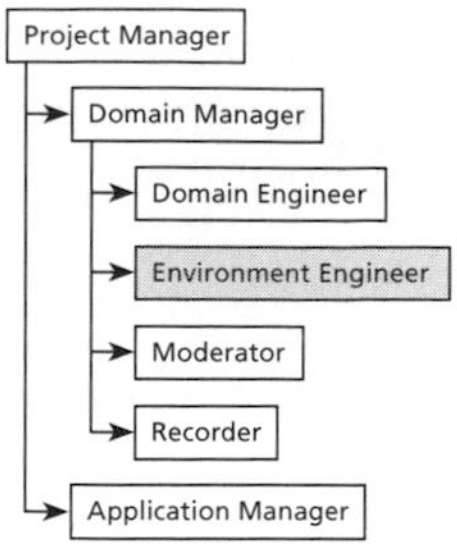

Project Manager
Domain Manager
Domain Engineer
Environment Engineer
Moderator
Recorder
Application Manager

Name	**Composition_Mapping_To_Language_Construct_Mapping_Analysis**
Synopsis	Check that each construct in the Application_Modeling_Language that is used to express a variability whose binding time is specification time or later is mapped by the Composition_Mapping.
Name	**Parameter_Of_Variation_To_Language_Trace_Analysis**
Synopsis	Check that every parameter of variation can be expressed in the language or determines what is expressible in the language.
Name	**Terminology_Analysis**
Synopsis	This analysis generates a report on the usage of terminology, including the percentage of technical terms defined in Engineer_Domain that are used and the definitions that are not used. This analysis checks all artifacts produced during Engineer_Domain for terminology usage.
Name	**Parameter_Of_Variation_To_Module_Trace_Analysis**
Synopsis	Check that every Parameter_Of_Variation is mapped by the Composition_Mapping to a module in the Family_Design. Note that this analysis cannot be performed until the Family_Design is reviewed.

11.1.1.3 Moderator

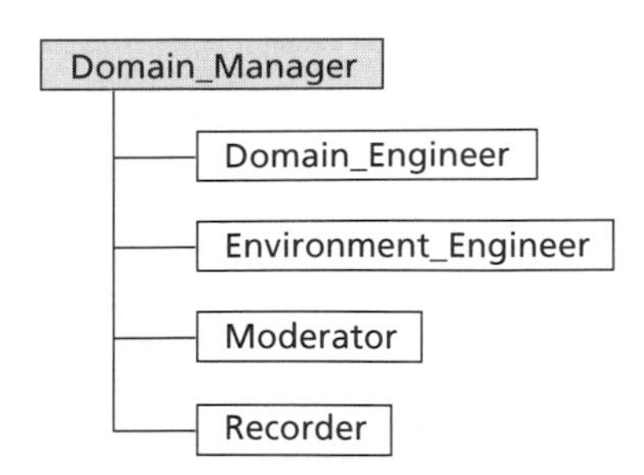

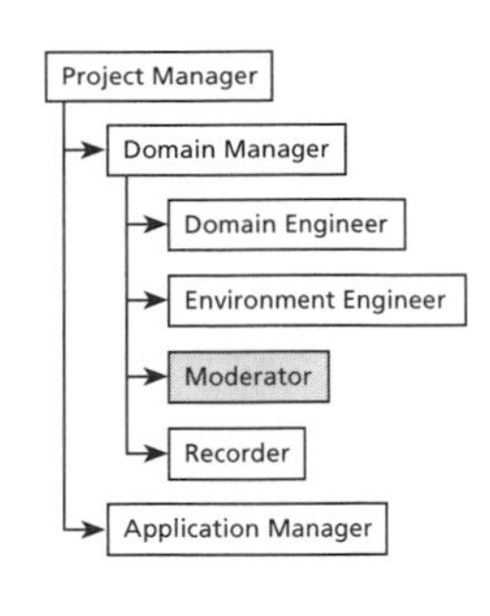

Role Definition Form

Name	**Moderator**
Synopsis	Moderates the commonality analysis process, guiding and directing all group discussions.
Member List	
	P-OPERATION LIST
Name	**Identify_Complete_Set_Of_Variabilities**
Synopsis	Complete the identification of variabilities, the assumptions that distinguish the family members.
Name	**Identify_Complete_Set_Of_Commonalities**
Synopsis	Complete the identification of commonalities, the assumptions that are true for all family members.
Name	**Initialize_Dictionary**
Synopsis	Create a template for the dictionary of terms for the domain.
Name	**Establish_Domain_Commonalities_And_Variabilities**
Synopsis	Create a list of the assumptions that define what's true of all family members (commonalities) and the assumptions that distinguish among family members (variabilities).
Name	**Parameterize_Variabilities**
Synopsis	Parameters_Of_Variation quantify the variabilities of the domain. Each parameter is defined by a name, a domain, a binding time, and a default value.
Name	**Create_Initial_Set_Of_Variability_Parameters**
Synopsis	Create a template for the parameters of variation and include a few initial parameters of variation for the proposed variabilities.
Name	**Identify_Complete_Set_Of_Variability_Parameters**
Synopsis	Complete the identification of Parameters_Of_Variation.

continued

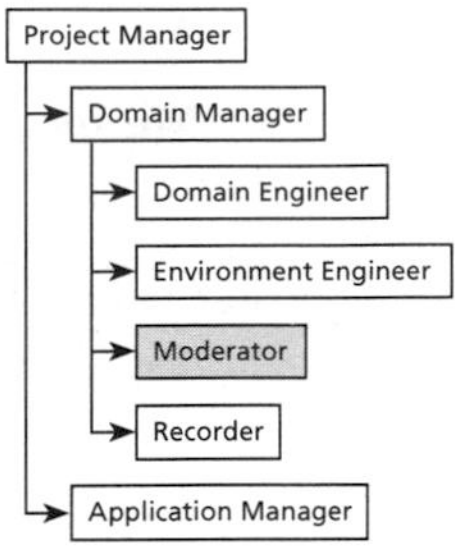

Project Manager
- Domain Manager
  - Domain Engineer
  - Environment Engineer
  - Moderator
  - Recorder
- Application Manager

Name	Create_Initial_Set_Of_Variabilities
Synopsis	Create a template for the domain variabilities and include a few initial proposed variabilities.
Name	**Create_Initial_Set_Of_Commonalities**
Synopsis	Create a template for the domain commonalities and include a few initial proposed commonalities.
Name	**Define_Terms**
Synopsis	Define terms used in describing the domain.
Name	**Establish_Standard_Terminology**
Synopsis	Define all significant technical terms used by domain experts in discussing the requirements or engineering of systems in the domain.
Name	**Analyze_Commonality**
Synopsis	The commonality analysis defines and bounds the family. Analyzing commonality includes identifying assumptions that are common to all family members (commonalities), assumptions that distinguish family members from one another (variabilities), and parameters of variation that quantify variabilities, as well as establishing a dictionary of technical terms for the family.

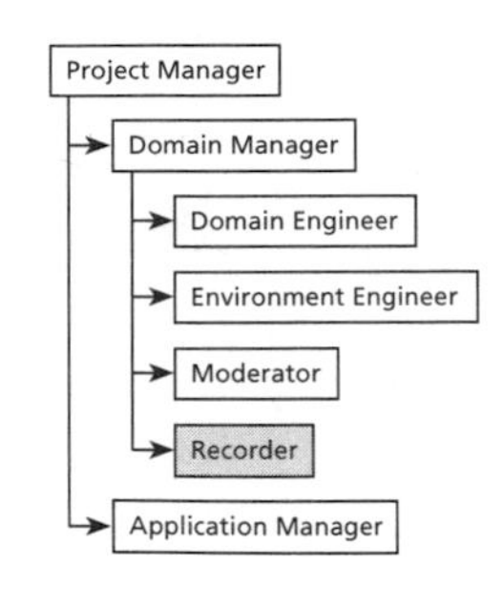

11.1.1.4 Recorder

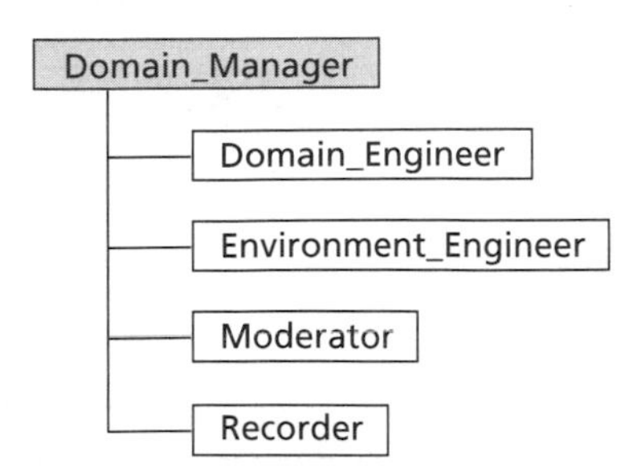

Role Definition Form

Name	**Recorder**
Synopsis	Records the results of the commonality analysis process in the form of the Commonality_Analysis artifact.
Member List	
	P-OPERATION LIST
Name	**Identify_Complete_Set_Of_Variabilities**
Synopsis	Complete the identification of variabilities, the assumptions that distinguish the family members.
Name	**Identify_Complete_Set_Of_Commonalities**
Synopsis	Complete the identification of commonalities, the assumptions that are true for all the family members.
Name	**Initialize_Dictionary**
Synopsis	Create a template for the dictionary of terms for the domain.
Name	**Establish_Domain_Commonalities_And_Variabilities**
Synopsis	Create a list of the assumptions that define what's true of all family members (commonalities) and the assumptions that distinguish among family members (variabilities).
Name	**Parameterize_Variabilities**
Synopsis	Parameters_Of_Variation quantify the variabilities of the domain. Each parameter is defined by a name, a domain, a binding time, and a default value.
Name	**Create_Initial_Set_Of_Variability_Parameters**
Synopsis	Create a template for the parameters of variation and include a few initial parameters of variation for the proposed variabilities.
Name	**Identify_Complete_Set_Of_Variability_Parameters**
Synopsis	Complete the identification of Parameters_Of_Variation.

continued

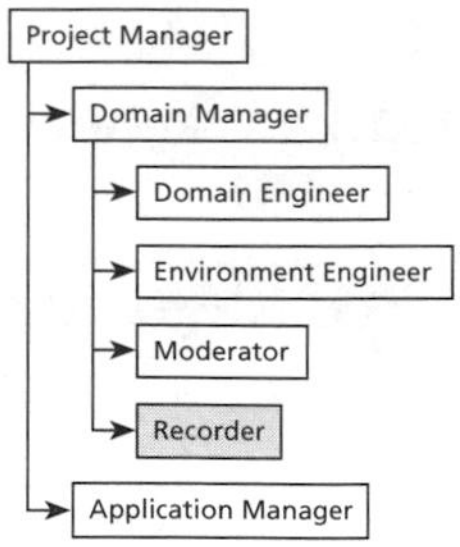

Project Manager
- Domain Manager
  - Domain Engineer
  - Environment Engineer
  - Moderator
  - Recorder
- Application Manager

Name	**Create_Initial_Set_Of_Variabilities**
Synopsis	Create a template for the domain variabilities and include a few initial proposed variabilities.
Name	**Create_Initial_Set_Of_Commonalities**
Synopsis	Create a template for the domain commonalities and include a few initial proposed commonalities.
Name	**Define_Terms**
Synopsis	Define terms used in describing the domain.
Name	**Establish_Standard_Terminology**
Synopsis	Define all significant technical terms used by domain experts in discussing the requirements or engineering of systems in the domain.
Name	**Analyze_Commonality**
Synopsis	The commonality analysis defines and bounds the family. Analyzing commonality includes identifying assumptions that are common to all family members (commonalities), assumptions that distinguish family members from one another (variabilities), and parameters of variation that quantify variabilities, as well as establishing a dictionary of technical terms for the family.

11.1.2 Application_Manager

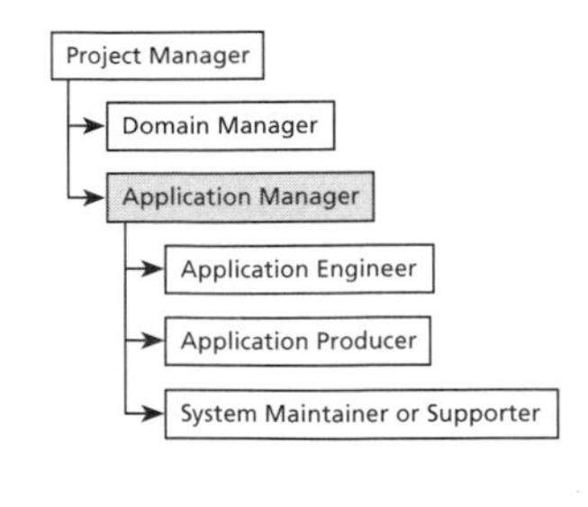

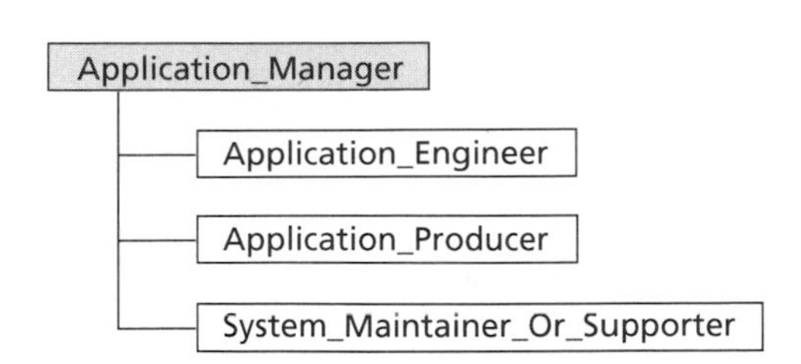

Role Definition Form

Name	**Application_Manager**
Synopsis	The application manager is responsible for managing the production of applications, including monitoring the process, setting priorities, and allocating resources to the application engineering tasks.
Member List	Application_Engineer, Application_Producer, System_Maintainer_Or_Supporter
	P-OPERATION LIST
Name	**Review**
Synopsis	Review an artifact.
Name	**Manage_Project**
Synopsis	Managing the project consists of managing the job of identifying and satisfying customer requirements using an application engineering environment. It includes the traditional tasks of management, such as scheduling, allocating, and monitoring resources.
Name	**Engineer_Application**
Synopsis	An iterative process for constructing application systems to meet customer requirements. Each application system is considered a member of a family and is defined by an Application_Model. An application engineering environment for the family is used to analyze application models and generate software from them.
	ANALYSIS LIST
Name	**Customer_Satisfaction**
Synopsis	Check that the customer is satisfied.
Name	**Final_Product_Documentation_Assurance_Analysis**
Synopsis	Check that all decisions made in the application model exist in the product documentation.

continued

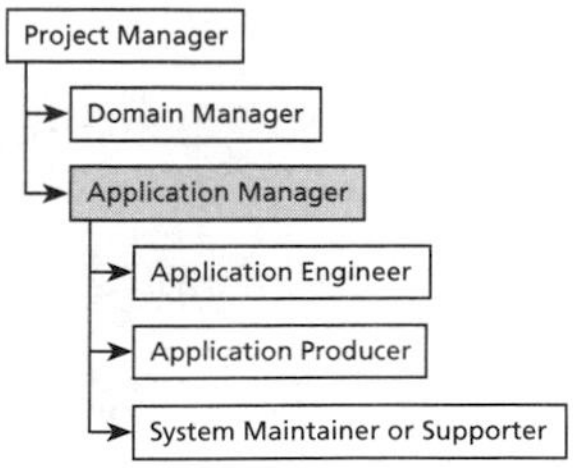

Name	Final_Product_Validation_Analysis
Synopsis	Check whether all the decisions made in the application model exist in the final product.
Name	**Defect_Analysis**
Synopsis	This analysis generates statistics on various types of defects by P-State, operation, and artifact to show the distribution of defects.
Name	**Risk_Analysis**
Synopsis	This analysis generates a list of risky events after comparing progress on various P-states and A-states of active artifacts.
Name	**Progress_Analysis**
Synopsis	This analysis generates a report on the progress of the project. The report describes what is next in the process and what is the current state of the active artifacts.
Name	**Resource_Analysis**
Synopsis	This analysis generates a report on resource usage, resource balancing, resource estimation, and resource allocation. The information resulting from the analysis helps the Project_Manager, Domain_Manager, and Application_Manager make decisions on the management of a project using FAST.

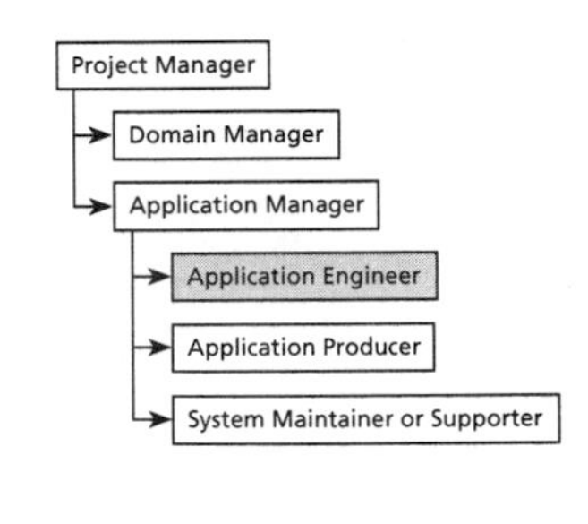

11.1.2.1 Application_Engineer

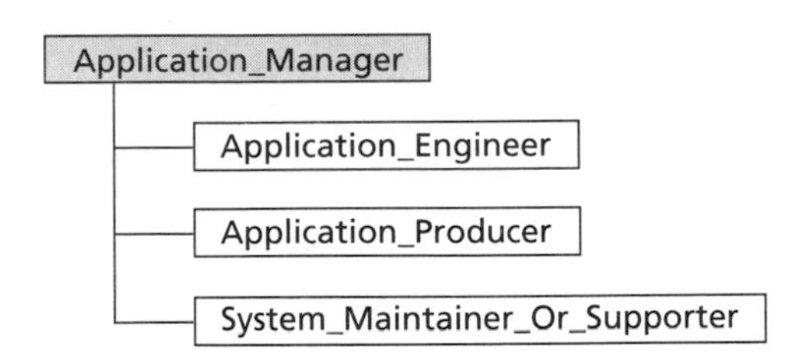

Role Definition Form

Name	**Application_Engineer**
Synopsis	The application engineer is responsible for performing all the activities of application engineering, including determining and validating customer requirements and generating applications using the application engineering environment.
Member List	
	P-OPERATION LIST
Name	**Review_Internally**
Synopsis	Conduct an informal review of an ARTIFACT by its creators.
Name	**Iterate_Or_Refine**
Synopsis	Revise the artifact based on 1. Resolution of outstanding issues 2. New insights 3. Availability of new information 4. Change to a related artifact
Name	**Review**
Synopsis	Review an artifact.
Name	**Test**
Synopsis	The application should be tested to ensure that it meets the customer's requirements.
Name	**Change_Application**
Synopsis	Revise the model of the application in the AML to correspond better to customer requirements.

continued

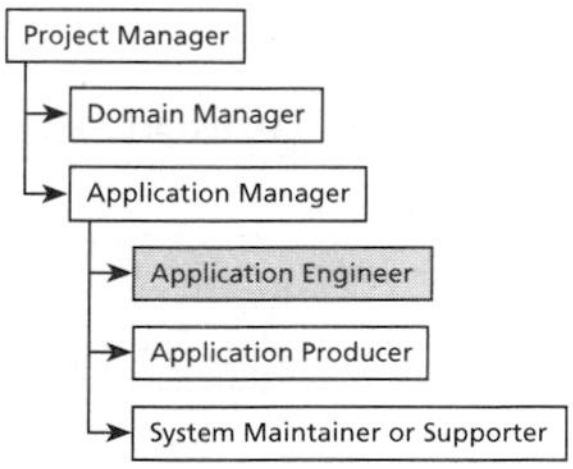

Project Manager
- Domain Manager
- Application Manager
  - Application Engineer
  - Application Producer
  - System Maintainer or Supporter

Name	**Model_Application**
Synopsis	Modeling the application is a key activity. It consists of modeling the customer's requirements for the application as a specification in the Application_Modeling_Language. After such a model has been constructed, it can be analyzed using tools in the application engineering environment, and the code and documentation for the application can be generated from it.
Name	**Produce_Application**
Synopsis	Producing the application consists of using the generation tools in the application engineering environment to generate the application. When not all of the application can be generated, some parts of the application will be produced in traditional manual ways. Such parts will then be integrated with the generated parts.
	ANALYSIS LIST
Name	**Decision_To_Tool_Trace_Analysis**
Synopsis	Check that the decisions supported by the tools used in the application engineering process correspond to decisions to be made in the application engineering process.
Name	**Final_Product_Documentation_Assurance_Analysis**
Synopsis	Check that all decisions made in the application model exist in the product documentation.
Name	**Final_Product_Validation_Analysis**
Synopsis	Check whether all the decisions made in the application model exist in the final product.

11.1.2.2 Application_Producer

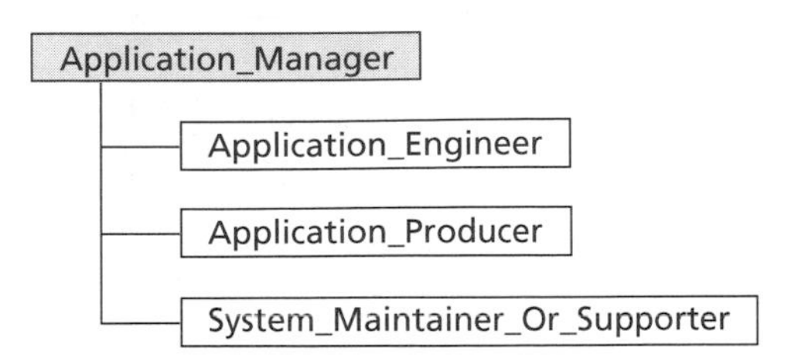

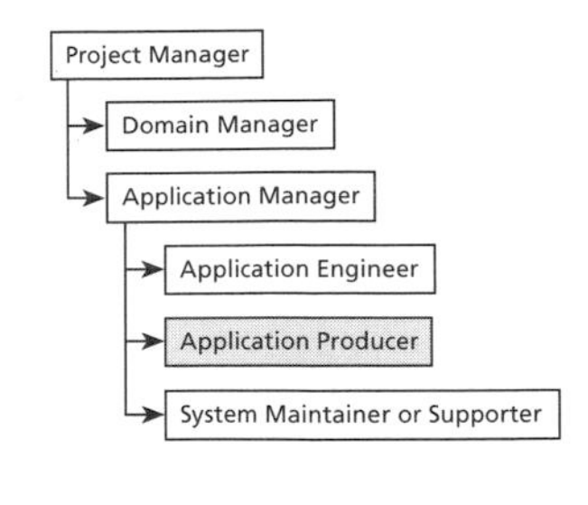

Role Definition Form

Name	**Application_Producer**
Synopsis	The application producer is responsible for integrating the system produced by the application engineer(s) with any software that is not produced using the application engineering environment. Such software includes preexisting software that is being reused and that is not included in the environment's generational capabilities, and software that is produced by a process other than application engineering. The application producer also assists the application engineer to model the application.
Member List	
P-OPERATION LIST	
Name	**Review**
Synopsis	Review an artifact.
Name	**Test**
Synopsis	The application should be tested to ensure that it meets the customer's requirements.
Name	**Produce_Application**
Synopsis	Producing the application consists of using the generation tools in the application engineering environment to generate the application. When not all of the application can be generated, some parts of the application will be produced in traditional manual ways. Such parts will then be integrated with the generated parts.
Name	**Model_Application**
Synopsis	Modeling the application is a key activity in application engineering. It consists of modeling the customer's requirements for the application as a specification in the Application_Modeling_Language. After such a model has been constructed, it can be analyzed using tools in the application engineering environment, and the code and documentation for the application can be generated from it.

11.1.2.3 System_Maintainer_Or_Supporter

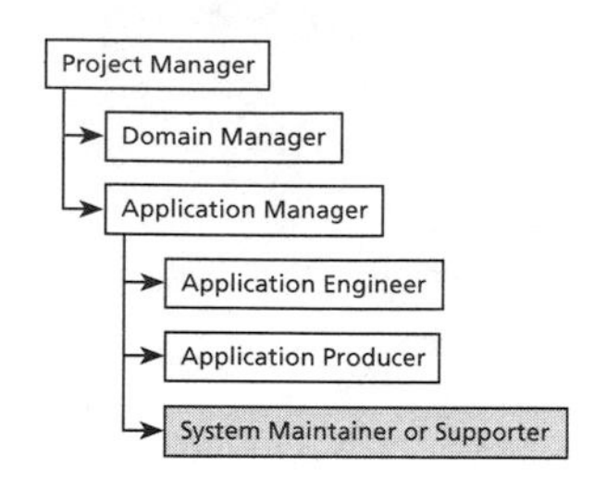

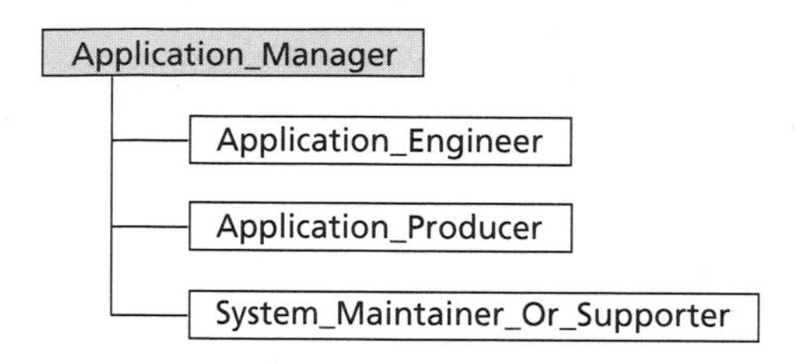

Role Definition Form

Name	**System_Maintainer_Or_Supporter**
Synopsis	The system maintainer or supporter is responsible for delivering the application to the customer and maintaining it after it is delivered. His or her activities may be no different from those performed by an application engineer or may include both an application engineer's and an application producer's activities.
Member List	
	P-OPERATION LIST
Name	**Review**
Synopsis	Review an artifact.
Name	**Delivery_And_Operation_Support**
Synopsis	This operation consists of delivering the application to the customer and providing operational support as contracted.

12 FAST Analyses

THIS CHAPTER CONTAINS THE DEFINITIONS OF THE ANALYSES IN the FAST PASTA model. Each analysis is defined in a section of the chapter. Many of them are defined using the relations shown in Chapter 13. Figure 12-1 shows all the analyses and the section where each is defined. Note that these are suggested analyses, how and when they are implemented depends on how and where you use FAST.

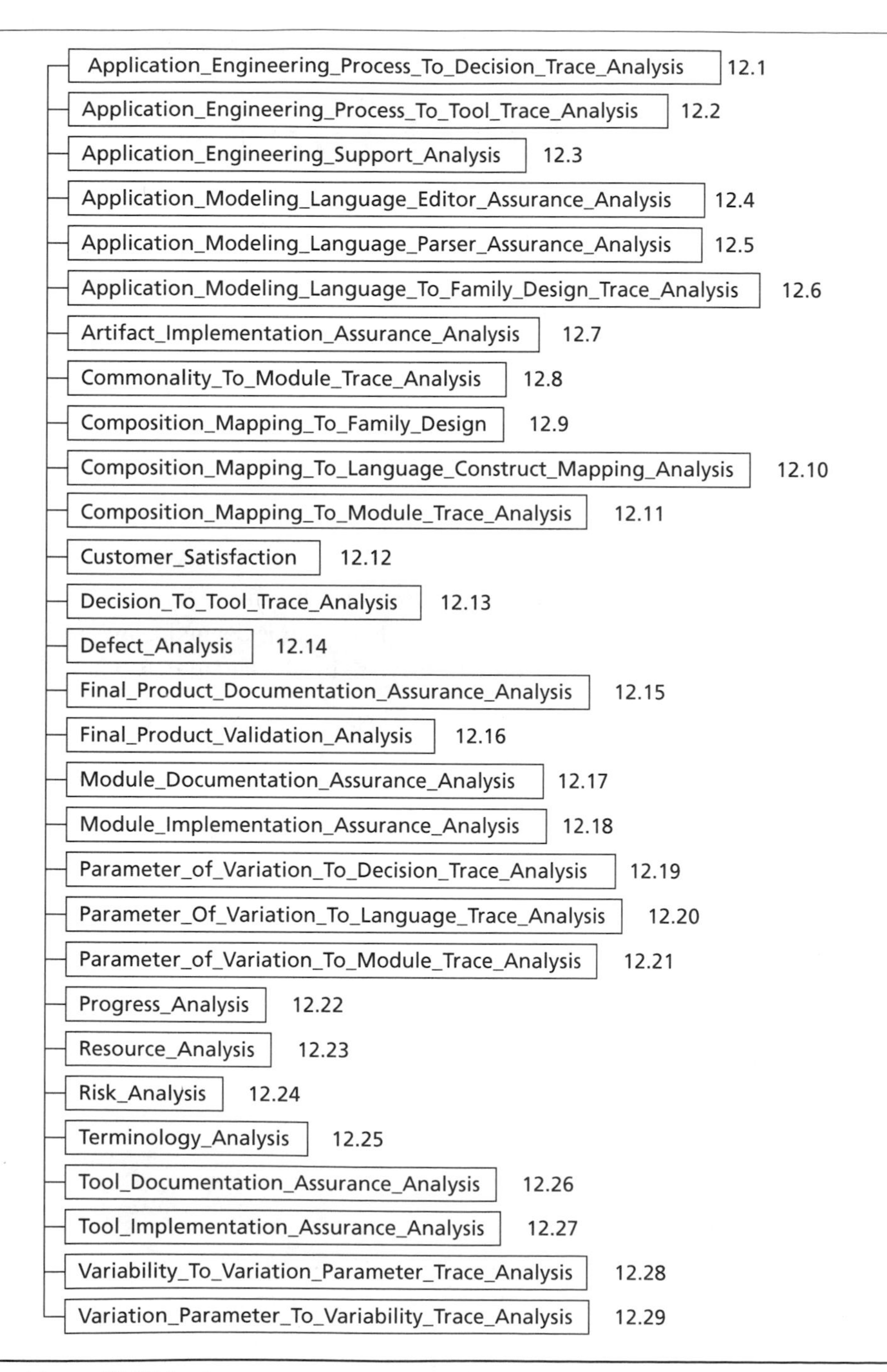

Figure 12-1. *FAST Analyses*

12.1 Application_Engineering_Process_To_Decision_Trace_Analysis

Analysis Definition Form

Name	**Application_Engineering_Process_To_Decision_Trace_Analysis**
Synopsis	Check that each decision of the Decision_Model has a corresponding step in the standard application engineering process.
Information Artifacts	Decision_Model, Application_Engineering_Process
Analysis Function	
Analysis Type	Consistency
Artifacts	
Informal Action	Note: The table produced is known as Disp_Table. Check that each decision of the decision model has a corresponding step in the standard application engineering process.
Formal Action	For all X where X = Sub_artifact(Decision_Model) if there exists no Y where ((Y = Sub_artifact(Application_Engineering_Process) and (Y = Decision_Process(X)) Disp_Table ← X
Role List	Domain_Engineer, Environment_Engineer
Trigger Type	User
Result Type	File
Action Type	Save To File

12.2 Application_Engineering_Process_To_Tool_Trace_Analysis

Analysis Definition Form

Name	**Application_Engineering_Process_To_Tool_Trace_Analysis**
Synopsis	Check that each step in the application engineering process is supported by a tool in the toolset.
Information Artifacts	Decision_Model, Tool_Set_Design
Analysis Function	Decision_tool_analysis
Analysis Type	Consistency
Artifacts	
Informal Action	Note: The table produced is called Disp_Table. Check whether each decision in the decision model is supported by a tool.
Formal Action	For all X where X = Sub_artifact(Decision_Model) if there exists no Y where ((Y = Sub_artifact(Tool_Set_Design) and (Y = Decision_Tool(X)) Disp_Table ← X
Role List	Domain_Engineer, Environment_Engineer
Trigger Type	User
Result Type	File
Action Type	Save To File

12.3 Application_Engineering_Support_Analysis

Analysis Definition Form

Name	**Application_Engineering_Support_Analysis**
Synopsis	Check that for each step in the application engineering process there is sufficient information and facilities available for the Application_Engineer to make decisions corresponding to parameters of variation for the step.
Information Artifacts	Application_Engineering_Process, Commonality_Analysis
Analysis Function	Service
Analysis Type	Management
Artifacts	
Informal Action	For each step in the application engineering process, identify the information needed to complete the step and the tools available during the step. Identify any missing information or tools.
Formal Action	
Role List	Domain_Engineer
Trigger Type	Uscr
Result Type	File
Action Type	Prompt Message

12.4 Application_Modeling_Language_Editor_Assurance_Analysis

Analysis Definition Form

Name	**Application_Modeling_Language_Editor_Assurance_Analysis**
Synopsis	Check that there is an editor implemented for the Application_Modeling_Language.
Information Artifacts	Application_Modeling_Language
Analysis Function	AML_edit-analysis
Analysis Type	Consistency
Artifacts	
Informal Action	Check that there exists a tool for editing application models.
Formal Action	
Role List	Environment_Engineer
Trigger Type	User
Result Type	Data_Structure
Action Type	Prompt Message

12.5 Application_Modeling_Language_Parser_Assurance_Analysis

Analysis Definition Form

Name	**Application_Modeling_Language_Parser_Assurance_Analysis**
Synopsis	Check that the parser for the Application_Modeling_Language parses every construct of the language correctly.
Information Artifacts	Application_Modeling_Language
Analysis Function	AML_editor_analysis
Analysis Type	Consistency
Artifacts	
Informal Action	Construct sample specifications in the AML that include all constructs in the AML. Input the set of sample specifications to the AML translator and other tools in the application engineering environment. Check that all the sample specifications are correctly parsed.
Formal Action	
Role List	Environment_Engineer
Trigger Type	User
Result Type	Data_Structure
Action Type	Prompt Message

12.6 Application_Modeling_Language_To_Family_Design_Trace_Analysis

Analysis Definition Form

Name	**Application_Modeling_Language_To_Family_Design_Trace_Analysis**
Synopsis	Check each language construct to see whether there exists a corresponding module in the Family_Design.
Information Artifacts	Family_Design, Application_Modeling_Language
Analysis Function	AML_family_design_analysis
Analysis Type	Consistency
Artifacts	
Informal Action	Note: The table is called Disp_Table. Check each language construct to see whether there exists a corresponding module in the family design.
Formal Action	For all X where X = Sub_artifact(Application_Modeling_Language) if there exists no Y where ((Y = Sub_artifact(Application_Modeling_Language) and (Y = AML_module(X)) Disp_Table ← X
Role List	Domain_Engineer, Environment_Engineer
Trigger Type	User
Result Type	Data_Structure
Action Type	Prompt Message

12.7 Artifact_Implementation_Assurance_Analysis

Analysis Definition Form

Name	Artifact_Implementation_Assurance_Analysis
Synopsis	Check that every artifact defined in the application engineering environment has been implemented.
Information Artifacts	Environment
Analysis Function	Artifact_imp_assurance_analysis
Analysis Type	Consistency
Artifacts	
Informal Action	
Formal Action	Disp_Table ← X such-that X = Sub_artifact(Family_Artifact) and state-of(X) ← Reviewed
Role List	Project_Manager, Domain_Manager
Trigger Type	User
Result Type	Data_Structure
Action Type	Prompt Message

12.8 Commonality_To_Module_Trace_Analysis

Analysis Definition Form

Name	**Commonality_To_Module_Trace_Analysis**
Synopsis	Check that every Commonality is maintained by the Family_Design.
Information Artifacts	Family_Design, Commonality_Analysis
Analysis Function	Commonality_to_module_analysis
Analysis Type	Quality
Artifacts	
Informal Action	
Formal Action	Table refers to Disp_Table For all X where X = Sub_artifact(Commonalities) if there exists no Y where ((Y = Sub_artifact(Family_Design)) and (Y = Commonality_module(X)) Disp_Table ← X
Role List	Domain_Engineer
Trigger Type	User
Result Type	File
Action Type	Save To File

12.9 Composition_Mapping_To_Family_Design

Analysis Definition Form

Name	**Composition_Mapping_To_Family_Design**
Synopsis	Check that each module in the Family_Design is in the range of the Composition_Mapping either by a direct mapping from a language construct in the AML or by the transitive closure of the uses relation for programs in a module mapped directly from a language construct.
Information Artifacts	Composition_Mapping, Family_Design
Analysis Function	Comp_map_to_family_design_analysis
Analysis Type	Quality
Artifacts	
Informal Action	
Formal Action	For all X where X = Sub_artifact(Family_Design) if there exists no Y where ((Y = Sub_artifact(Composition_Mapping)) and (Y = Comp_mapping_module(X)) Disp_Table ← X
Role List	Domain_Engineer
Trigger Type	User
Result Type	File
Action Type	Save To File

12.10 Composition_Mapping_To_Language_Construct_Mapping_Analysis

Analysis Definition Form

Name	**Composition_Mapping_To_Language_Construct_Mapping_Analysis**
Synopsis	Check that each construct in the Application_Modeling_Language that is used to express a variability whose binding time is specification time or later is mapped by the Composition_Mapping.
Information Artifacts	Composition_Mapping, Application_Modeling_Language
Analysis Function	Mapping_to_AML_analysis
Analysis Type	Quality, Consistency
Artifacts	
Informal Action	
Formal Action	Note: The table produced in this analysis is called Disp_Table. For all X where X = Sub_artifact(Variabilities) if there exists no Y where ((Y = Sub_artifact(Composition_Mapping) and (Y = Variability_construct(X)) and (Binding_time(X) ≥ Specification)) Disp_Table ← X
Role List	Domain_Engineer, Environment_Engineer
Trigger Type	User
Result Type	file: Disp_Table, table
Action Type	prompt_message: Disp_Table

12.11 Composition_Mapping_To_Module_Trace_Analysis

Analysis Definition Form

Name	**Composition_Mapping_To_Module_Trace_Analysis**
Synopsis	Check that each construct in the AML is mapped by the Composition_ Mapping into at least one module in the Family_Design.
Information Artifacts	Composition_Mapping, Family_Design
Analysis Function	Mapping_to_module_analysis
Analysis Type	Quality, Consistency
Artifacts	
Informal Action	For each construct in the AML identify the set of modules to which it is mapped by the composition mapping. Identify all constructs for which there are no modules.
Formal Action	Note: The table is called Disp_Table. For all X where X = Sub_artifact(Application_Modeling_Language) if there exists no Y where Y = Sub_artifact(Composition_Mapping) and Y = Comp_Mapping_AML Disp_Table ← X
Role List	Domain_Engineer
Trigger Type	(state-exit, user)
Result Type	(file: Report)
Action Type	(save-to-file: Report)

12.12 Customer_Satisfaction

Analysis Definition Form

Name	**Customer_Satisfaction**
Synopsis	Check that the customer is satisfied.
Information Artifacts	Application
Analysis Function	Cust_satisfy_analysis
Analysis Type	Quality
Artifacts	
Informal Action	Interview the customer to see whether he or she is satisfied.
Formal Action	
Role List	Application_Manager, Project_Manager
Trigger Type	(state-exit, user)
Result Type	(file: Report)
Action Type	(save-to-file: Report)

12.13 Decision_To_Tool_Trace_Analysis

Analysis Definition Form

Name	**Decision_To_Tool_Trace_Analysis**
Synopsis	Check that the decisions supported by the tools used in the application engineering process correspond to decisions to be made in the application engineering process.
Information Artifacts	Decision_Model, Tool_Set_Design, Application_Engineering_Process
Analysis Function	Dec_to_tool_analysis
Analysis Type	Consistency
Artifacts	
Informal Action	For each tool in the application engineering process there is at least one decision supported by that tool.
Formal Action	
Role List	Domain_Engineer, Application_Engineer
Trigger Type	(state-exit, user)
Result Type	(file: Report, table: Table)
Action Type	(save-to-file: Report, prompt-message: Table)

12.14 Defect_Analysis

Analysis Definition Form

Name	**Defect_Analysis**
Synopsis	This analysis generates statistics on various types of defects by P-state, operation, and artifact to show the distribution of defects.
Information Artifacts	Family_Artifact
Analysis Function	Defect_calculation
Analysis Type	Quality
Artifacts	
Informal Action	Retrieve from the defect database the defects detected in various iterations/versions of P-states. Calculate the defect distributions and prepare them for display.
Formal Action	Note: The table produced in this analysis is called Disp_Table. 1. Defect_Data_By_P-state ← Defect_calculation(defect_file) 2. Defect_Report ← Defect_report_generator(Defect_Data_By_P-State)
Role List	Project_Manager, Domain_Manager, Application_Manager
Trigger Type	(state_exit, periodic, operation)
Result Type	(file:defect_report_file, text_report:defect_report_format)
Action Type	(prompt, save_to_file)

12.15 Final_Product_Documentation_Assurance_Analysis

Analysis Definition Form

Name	**Final_Product_Documentation_Assurance_Analysis**
Synopsis	Check that all decisions made in the application model exist in the product documentation.
Information Artifacts	Application_Model, Application_Documentation
Analysis Function	Prod_doc_analysis
Analysis Type	Quality, Consistency
Artifacts	
Informal Action	Check whether all the decisions made in the application model exist in the product documentation.
Formal Action	
Role List	Application_Manager, Application_Engineer
Trigger Type	User
Result Type	(file: Disp_Table, table)
Action Type	(prompt_message: Disp_Table)

12.16 Final_Product_Validation_Analysis

Analysis Definition Form

Name	**Final_Product_Validation_Analysis**
Synopsis	Check that all the decisions made in the application model exist in the final product.
Information Artifacts	Application_Model, Application_Code
Analysis Function	Prod_vald_analysis
Analysis Type	Quality, Consistency
Artifacts	
Informal Action	Check that all the decisions made in the application model exist in the final product.
Formal Action	Note: The table produced in this analysis is called Disp_Table. For all X where X = Sub_artifact(Application_model) if there exists no Y where ((Y = Sub_artifact(Application_Code) and (Y = Application_model_module(X)) Disp_Table ← X
Role List	Application_Manager, Application_Engineer
Trigger Type	User
Result Type	(file: Disp_Table, table)
Action Type	(prompt_message: Disp_Table)

12.17 Module_Documentation_Assurance_Analysis

Analysis Definition Form

Name	**Module_Documentation_Assurance_Analysis**
Synopsis	Check that every module defined in the application engineering environment has been documented.
Information Artifacts	Family_Design, Documentation_Template
Analysis Function	Module_doc_analysis
Analysis Type	Quality, Consistency
Artifacts	
Informal Action	Check that every module defined in the application engineering environment has been documented.
Formal Action	Note: The table produced in this analysis is called Disp_Table. For all X where X = Sub_artifact(Family_Design) if there exists no Y where ((Y = Sub_artifact(Documentation_Template) and (Y = Module_document(X)) Disp_Table ← X
Role List	Domain_Engineer, Environment_Engineer
Trigger Type	User
Result Type	(file: Disp_Table, table)
Action Type	(prompt_message: Disp_Table)

12.18 Module_Implementation_Assurance_Analysis

Analysis Definition Form

Name	**Module_Implementation_Assurance_Analysis**
Synopsis	Check that every module defined in the Family_Design has been implemented.
Information Artifacts	Family_Design, Code_Template
Analysis Function	Module_imple_analysis
Analysis Type	Quality, Consistency
Artifacts	
Informal Action	Check that every module defined in the application engineering environment has been implemented.
Formal Action	Note: The table produced in this analysis is called Disp_Table. For all X where X = Sub_artifact(Family_Design) if there exists no Y where ((Y = Sub_artifact(Code_Template)) and (Y = Module_implement(X)) Disp_Table ← X
Role List	Domain_Engineer, Environment_Engineer
Trigger Type	User
Result Type	(file: Disp_Table, table)
Action Type	(prompt_message: Disp_Table)

12.19 Parameter_Of_Variation_To_Decision_Trace_Analysis

Analysis Definition Form

Name	**Parameter_Of_Variation_To_Decision_Trace_Analysis**
Synopsis	Check every Parameter_Of_Variation to see whether there exists a corresponding decision in the Decision_Model.
Information Artifacts	Parameters_Of_Variation, Decision_Model
Analysis Function	Variability_decision_analysis
Analysis Type	Quality, Consistency
Artifacts	
Informal Action	Check every parameter of variation to see whether there exists a decision in the decision model for it.
Formal Action	Note: The table produced in this analysis is called Disp_Table. For all X where X = Sub_artifact(Parameters_Of_Variation) if there exists no Y where (Y = Sub_artifact(Decision_Model)) and (Y = Parameter_decision(X)) Disp_Table ← X
Role List	Domain_Engineer, Domain_Manager
Trigger Type	User
Result Type	(file: Disp_Table, table)
Action Type	(prompt_message: Disp_Table)

12.20 Parameter_Of_Variation_To_Language_Trace_Analysis

Analysis Definition Form

Name	**Parameter_Of_Variation_To_Language_Trace_Analysis**
Synopsis	Check that every parameter of variation can be expressed in the language.
Information Artifacts	Application_Modeling_Language, Parameters_Of_Variation
Analysis Function	Parameter_language_analysis
Analysis Type	Quality, Consistency
Artifacts	
Informal Action	Parameters of variation either are embodied in the language constructs or are used to determine different versions of the language. As a result, every parameter of variation either should be expressible in the language or should constrain what's expressible in the language. Check to see that every parameter of variation has one of these two effects.
Formal Action	Note: The table produced in this analysis is called Disp_Table. For all X where X = Sub_artifact(Commonality_Analysis) if there exists no Y where (Y = Sub_artifact(Application_Modeling_Language)) and (Y = Variability_parameter(X)) Disp_Table ← X
Role List	Domain_Manager, Domain_Engineer, Environment_Engineer
Trigger Type	User
Result Type	(file:Disp_Table, table)
Action Type	(prompt_message: Disp_Table)

12.21 Parameter_Of_Variation_To_Module_Trace_Analysis

Analysis Definition Form

Name	**Parameter_Of_Variation_To_Module_Trace_Analysis**
Synopsis	Check that every Parameter_Of_Variation is mapped by the Composition_Mapping to a module in the Family_Design. Note that this analysis cannot be performed until the Family_Design is reviewed.
Information Artifacts	Family_Design, Parameters_Of_Variation
Analysis Function	Var_par_to_module_analysis
Analysis Type	Quality, Consistency
Artifacts	
Informal Action	For each parameter of variation check to see if there exists a corresponding module in the Family_Design.
Formal Action	Note: The table produced in this analysis is called Disp_Table. For all X where X = Sub_artifact(Parameters_Of_Variation) if there exists no Y where (Y = Sub_artifact(Family_Design)) and (Y = (Parameter_module(X)) Disp_Table ← X
Role List	Domain_Engineer, Domain_Manager, Environment_Engineer
Trigger Type	User
Result Type	(file: table, table)
Action Type	(prompt_message: Disp_Table)

12.22 Progress_Analysis

Analysis Definition Form

Name	**Progress_Analysis**
Synopsis	This analysis generates a report on the progress of the project. The report describes what is next in the process and what is the current state of the active artifacts.
Information Artifacts	Family_Artifact
Analysis Function	Progress_calculation
Analysis Type	Management, Process_status
Artifacts	
Informal Action	Note: The report is called Progress_Report. Progress is calculated based on the following information: • The set of active P-states • The set of active artifacts • The set of current and possible next A-states for each active artifact • The set of P-states that could become active based on the next possible A-states of the active artifacts and the entry conditions for all P-states A report on progress that identifies the existing P-states, the set of P-states that may become active next, the set of Artifacts, their existing A-states, and their next possible A-states is stored in Progress_Report in a form ready for presentation.
Formal Action	1. Progress_Report.Current_Active_Artifact ← Identify_current_active_artifact() 2. Progress_Report.Current_Active_P-State ← Collect_current_active_ P-State(Progress_Report.Current_Active_Artifact) 3. Progress_Report.Next_Possible_Active_P-State ← Collect_next_possible_active_P-State(Progress_Report.Current_Active_ Artifact)
Role List	Project_Manager, Domain_Manager, Application_Manager
Trigger Type	(state_entrance, state-exit, user)
Result Type	(file:progress_file, table:progress_table)
Action Type	(prompt_message, save_to_file)

12.23 Resource_Analysis

Analysis Definition Form

Name	**Resource_Analysis**
Synopsis	This analysis generates a report on resource usage, resource balancing, resource estimation, and resource allocation. The information resulting from the analysis helps the Project_Manager, Domain_Manager, and Application_Manager make decisions on the management of a project using FAST.
Information Artifacts	
Analysis Function	Resource_calculation(P_State, Resource_Database)
Analysis Type	Management
Artifacts	
Informal Action	Note: The report is called Resource_Report. Resource_Report contains the result of resource calculations recursively back to the first operation in the process. The results are precalculated and stored in a form ready for display.
Formal Action	1. initiate(Resource_Report) 2. Resource_Report ← Resource_calculation(P_State, Resource_Database)
Role List	Project_Manager, Domain_Manager, Application_Manager
Trigger Type	(state_exit, user)
Result Type	(file:resource_file, table:resource_table)
Action Type	(prompt_message, save_to_file)

12.24 Risk_Analysis

Analysis Definition Form

Name	**Risk_Analysis**
Synopsis	This analysis generates a list of risky events after comparing progress on various P-states and A-states of active artifacts.
Information Artifacts	Family_Artifact
Analysis Function	Risk_analysis_function
Analysis Type	Management
Artifacts	
Informal Action	Risk_Analysis identifies the current active artifact and its possible direct next A-State(s). If an active artifact has a next A-state that appears in three or more entrance conditions of a possible next P-state and if production of the artifact is late, then the current operation on the artifact is a risky event. The result of the analysis is sent to those working on the artifact, those working on the related artifacts, and the manager of the task.
Formal Action	Note: The table produced in this analysis is called Risk_Report. 1. Progress_Report.Current_Active_Artifact ← Identify_current_active_artifact() 2. Progress_Report.Current_Active_P-State ← Collect_current_active_ P-State(Progress_Report.Current_Active_Artifact) 3. Progress_Report.Next_Possible_Active_P-State ← Collect_next_possible_active_ P-State(Progress_Report.Current_Active_Artifact) 4. Late_Activity ← Collect_late_activity(Progress_Report.Current_Active.Artifact) 5. Risky_Events ← Collect_risky_event(Progress_Report.Current_Active_Artifact) 6. Risk_Report ← Risk_report_generator(Risky_Events)
Role List	Project_Manager, Domain_Manager, Application_Manager
Trigger Type	(state_entrance, state_exit, user, periodic)
Result Type	(file:risk_file, diagram:risk_chart)
Action Type	(prompt_message, save_to_file(risk_file), mail_to_role(risk_chart, FAST_Manager))

12.25 Terminology_Analysis

Analysis Definition Form

Name	**Terminology_Analysis**
Synopsis	This analysis generates a report on the usage of terminology, including the percentage of technical terms defined in Engineer_Domain that are used, the definitions that are not used, and unitalicized usage of terms. This analysis checks all artifacts produced during Engineer_Domain for terminology usage.
Information Artifacts	Standard_Terminology
Analysis Function	Terminology_usage
Analysis Type	Quality, Consistency
Artifacts	
Informal Action	Generate the list of words for analysis and form them into the set Set_Words. Create a set, Set_Standard, consisting of all the terms in the standard_ Terminology. Use set difference to calculate terminology usage.
Formal Action	Note: The report produced in this analysis is called Terminology_Usage_Report. 1. Set_Word_Used ← Set_intersect(Set_Words, Set_Standard) 2. Set_Word_Not_Used ← Set_difference(Set_Standard, Set_Words) 3. Terminology_Usage_Rate ← 100.0 * (Number_of_element(Set_Word_Used)) / (Number_of_element(Set_Standard)) 4. Terminology_Usage_Report ← Terminology_report_generate(Set_Word_Used, Set_Word_Not_Used, Terminology_Usage_Rate)
Role List	Domain_Engineer, Environment_Engineer
Trigger Type	Periodic
Result Type	(file: terminology_report, text_report: terminology_report)
Action Type	(prompt_message, save_to_file:terminology_report)

12.26 Tool_Documentation_Assurance_Analysis

Analysis Definition Form

Name	**Tool_Documentation_Assurance_Analysis**
Synopsis	Check that every tool defined in the application engineering environment has been documented.
Information Artifacts	Tool_Set_Design, Documentation
Analysis Function	Tool_docu_analysis
Analysis Type	Quality, Consistency
Artifacts	
Informal Action	Check that every tool defined in the application engineering environment has been documented.
Formal Action	Note: The table produced in this analysis is called Disp_Table. For all X where X = Sub_artifact(Tool_Set_Design) if there exists no Y where (Y = Sub_artifact(Documentation)) and (Y = Tool_document(X)) Disp_table ← X
Role List	Environment_Engineer
Trigger Type	User
Result Type	(file: Disp_Table, table)
Action Type	(prompt_message: Disp_Table)

12.27 Tool_Implementation_Assurance_Analysis

Analysis Definition Form

Name	**Tool_Implementation_Assurance_Analysis**
Synopsis	Check that every tool defined in the Application_Engineering_Environment has been implemented.
Information Artifacts	Tool_Set_Design, Analysis_Tools, Generation_Tools
Analysis Function	Tool_implement_analysis
Analysis Type	Quality, Consistency
Artifacts	
Informal Action	Check that every tool defined in the application engineering environment has been implemented.
Formal Action	Note: The table produced in this analysis is called Disp_Table. For all X where X = Sub_artifact(Tool_Set_Design) if there exists no Y where ((Y = Sub_artifact(Generation_Tools)) or (Y = Sub_artifact(Analysis_Tools))) and (Y = Tool_implement(X)) Disp_Table ← X
Role List	Environment_Engineer
Trigger Type	User
Result Type	(file: Disp_Table, table)
Action Type	(prompt_message: Disp_table)

12.28 Variability_To_Variation_Parameter_Trace_Analysis

Analysis Definition Form

Name	**Variability_To_Variation_Parameter_Trace_Analysis**
Synopsis	Check that each variability has a corresponding Parameter_Of_Variation.
Information Artifacts	Commonality_Analysis
Analysis Function	Variability_to_parameter_analysis
Analysis Type	Quality, Consistency
Artifacts	
Informal Action	For each variability, check to see whether there exists a parameter of variation to represent it.
Formal Action	Note: The table produced in this analysis is called Disp_Table. For all X where X = Sub_artifact(Variabilities) if there exists no Y where (Y = Sub_artifact(Parameters_Of_Variation)) and (Y = Variability_parameter(X)) Disp_Table ← X
Role List	Domain_Engineer, Domain_Manager
Trigger Type	User
Result Type	(file:table, table)
Action Type	(prompt_message:Disp_Table)

12.29 Variation_Parameter_To_Variability_Trace_Analysis

Analysis Definition Form

Name	**Variation_Parameter_To_Variability_Trace_Analysis**
Synopsis	Are there any parameters of variation that cannot be traced to variabilities?
Information Artifacts	Commonality_Analysis
Analysis Function	Parameter_to_variability_analysis
Analysis Type	Quality, Consistency
Artifacts	
Informal Action	For each parameter of variation, check to see whether there exists a corresponding variability.
Formal Action	Note: The table produced in this analysis is called Disp_Table. For all X where X = Sub_artifact(Parameters_Of_Variation) if there exists no Y where (Y = Sub_artifact(Variabilities)) and (Y= Variability_parameter(X)) Disp_Table ← X
Role List	Domain_Engineer, Domain_Manager
Trigger Type	User
Result Type	(file: table, table)
Action Type	(prompt_message: Disp_Table)

13 FAST Relations

THE FOLLOWING SECTIONS DEFINE THE RELATIONS USED IN THE FAST PASTA model. Each relation is defined in a relation definition form in a section of the chapter. Relations are defined on artifacts and usually indicate a dependency between artifacts. The dependencies help you to identify the effects of making a change to an artifact such as commonalities, i.e., they indicate the other artifacts that may have to be changed when you change commonalities. Many of the analyses defined in Chapter 12 operate by tracing relations. As a result, when support for using the model is automated, you may be automatically notified of the potential impact of making a change to an artifact.

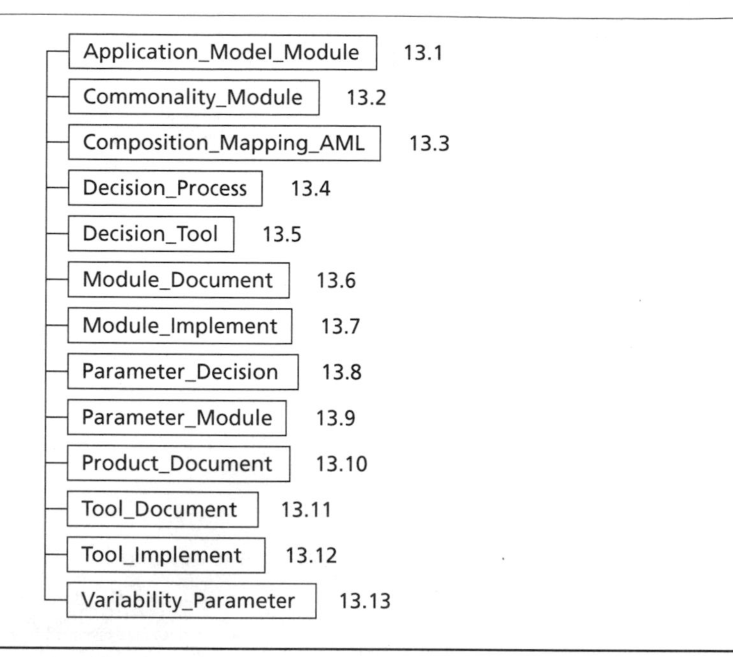

Figure 13.1 FAST Relations

13.1 Application_Model_Module

Relation Definition Form

Name	**Application_Model_Module**
Synopsis	The application code is generated from the application model. Code can be generated when the decisions represented in the application model are made.
Possible Artifact Pair List	
From:	Application_Code
To:	Application_Model
From:	Application_Model
To:	Application_Code

13.2 Commonality_Module

Relation Definition Form

Name	**Commonality_Module**
Synopsis	Some commonalities are represented by modules in the family design that are included in every application.
Possible Artifact Pair List	
From:	Commonalities
To:	Family_Design
From:	Family_Design
To:	Commonalities

13.3 Composition_Mapping_AML

Relation Definition Form

Name	**Composition_Mapping_AML**
Synopsis	For each construct in the application modeling language that binds a value for a parameter of variation, there is a part of the composition mapping that describes the module(s) needed in the family design to implement the binding.
Possible Artifact Pair List	
From:	Composition_Mapping
To:	Application_Modeling_Language
From:	Application_Modeling_Language
To:	Composition_Mapping

13.4 Decision_Process

Relation Definition Form

Name	**Decision_Process**
Synopsis	For each decision in the decision model, there is at least one step in the application engineering process that implements the decision. The application engineering process describes how the application engineer uses the facilities in the application engineering environment to carry out the decisions identified in the decision model.
Possible Artifact Pair List	
From:	Application_Engineering_Process
To:	Decision_Model
From:	Decision_Model
To:	Application_Engineering_Process

13.5 Decision_Tool

Relation Definition Form

Name	**Decision_Tool**
Synopsis	Each tool in the toolset supports the making of a decision in the decision model. Note that some tools may provide indirect support for a number of decisions or for the decision model as a whole—for example, tools that can be used to maintain the state of the application engineering process.
Possible Artifact Pair List	
From:	Tool_Set_Design
To:	Decision_Model
From:	Decision_Model
To:	Tool_Set_Design

13.6 Module_Document

Relation Definition Form

Name	**Module_Document**
Synopsis	For each parameter of variation that describes how documentation can vary, there is a corresponding documentation template in the environment library used to generate the documentation when the value of the parameter is bound.
Possible Artifact Pair List	
From:	Documentation_Template
To:	Family_Design
From:	Family_Design
To:	Documentation_Template

13.7 Module_Implement

Relation Definition Form

Name	**Module_Implement**
Synopsis	Each code template in the environment library is an implementation of a module in the family design, although not every module may be implemented as a template. Establishing the value of the parameter of variation encapsulated in such modules produces an instance of the template, which is an implementation of the module.
Possible Artifact Pair List	
From:	Code_Template
To:	Family_Design
From:	Family_Design
To:	Code_Template

13.8 Parameter_Decision

Relation Definition Form

Name	**Parameter_Decision**
Synopsis	For each parameter of variation that is bound at specification time or later, there is a decision in the decision model that corresponds to the decision represented by the parameter.
Possible Artifact Pair List	
From:	Decision_Model
To:	Parameters_Of_Variation
From:	Parameters_Of_Variation
To:	Decision_Model

13.9 Parameter_Module

Relation Definition Form

Name	**Parameter_Module**
Synopsis	When the composition approach is used to implement a domain model, each parameter of variation that is bound at specification time or later is encapsulated in a module in the family design. Depending on how the domain model is implemented, there may also be modules that encapsulate parameters of variation that are bound at tool generation time.
Possible Artifact Pair List	
From:	Parameters_Of_Variation
To:	Family_Design
From:	Family_Design
To:	Parameters_Of_Variation

13.10 Product_Document

Relation Definition Form

Name	**Product_Document**
Synopsis	The application documentation is generated from the application model. Documentation can be generated when the decisions represented in the application model are made.
Possible Artifact Pair List	
From:	Application_Documentation
To:	Application_Model
From:	Application_Model
To:	Application_Documentation

13.11 Tool_Document

Relation Definition Form

Name	**Tool_Document**
Synopsis	Each tool specified in the toolset design is documented in the user's manual(s) and reference documentation for the environment.
Possible Artifact Pair List	
From:	Documentation
To:	Tool_Set_Design
From:	Tool_Set_Design
To:	Documentation

13.12 Tool_Implement

Relation Definition Form

Name	**Tool_Implement**
Synopsis	Each tool in the toolset design is implemented as a tool in the application engineering environment. For example, all generation tools and analysis tools are described in the toolset design, and their implementations are included in the application engineering environment.
Possible Artifact Pair List	
From:	Generation_Tools
To:	Tool_Set_Design
From:	Tool_Set_Design
To:	Generation_Tools
From:	Analysis_Tools
To:	Tool_Set_Design
From:	Tool_Set_Design
To:	Analysis_Tools

13.13 Variability_Parameter

Relation Definition Form

Name	**Variability_Parameter**
Synopsis	Parameters of variation are derived from variabilities. Although not all variabilities have associated parameters of variation, most of them do. Every parameter of variation has at least one associated variability.
Possible Artifact Pair List	
From:	Variabilities
To:	Parameters_Of_Variation
From:	Parameters_Of_Variation
To:	Variabilities

14 Summary

THIS CHAPTER DESCRIBES THE SHIFT IN THOUGHT AND WORK patterns engendered by FAST and shows how FAST is compatible with such software development ideas as object orientation, reuse, and multiparadigm design. It also provides guidelines on where to apply FAST, how to make a gradual transition to a FAST process, and the role of PASTA models in such a transition.

14.1 Patterns of Thought and Work

A FAST process can be applied without the introduction of new tools or technologies as long as the software developers are willing to try new patterns of thought and work. A central concept of FAST is to encourage software developers to think of their task as family development. They should organize themselves so that some of them are concerned with future family needs and capabilities and others are concerned with producing family members for current customers. The developers are not relieved of any of the difficult burdens of requirements determination, design, implementation, and testing; indeed, FAST requires them to perform these activities while making explicit predictions for the future.

Furthermore, developers are asked to exploit their predictions to the maximum extent possible. Previously, such efficiency in software production has usually been attained in an ad hoc fashion. Tools and production facilities such as YACC, TEDIUM, and the Toshiba Software Factory were developed without a systematic process to guide their developers. Using the activities and artifacts described earlier, FAST attempts to systematize the development of resources—such as languages, tools, designs, classes, and libraries of components—that enable efficient software production based on the oracle hypothesis (see Chapter 2). As you understand your FAST process better, you will be able to find or create the tools and environment that best support it for you. PASTA gives you a way of thinking about, designing, and representing your process, and the tools associated with PASTA give you a way to generate the documentation and environment that you need.

Having a systematic process whose goal is rapid generation of family members significantly increases the probability of success in achieving software generation and significantly decreases the time needed to achieve it. Much of the systematization is concerned with guiding developers to think about planning for change in a standardized way and then capturing the resulting decisions in standardized artifacts. The developers' attention is then focused on one concern at a time. The FAST PASTA model serves to identify which concern they should focus on and helps them to understand what they should be trying to do and to produce at that time.

For example, an early activity in a FAST process is to analyze commonality among family members. Domain engineers are asked to identify requirements that are common to family members (commonalities) and requirements that can vary among family members (variabilities). They are asked to produce the commonality analysis artifact, which uses a standard structure for describing commonalities and variabilities. A later activity, designing the application modeling language, uses the result of the commonality analysis to help design a language that can be used to specify a family member by the way it varies from other family members. The language must be able to express the variabilities identified during the commonality analysis.

The concern of determining commonality and variability is quite different from the concern of designing the syntax and semantics of a language. Addressing each concern is, in itself, quite difficult; attempting to address both concerns at the same time is beyond the reach of most of us. Separating them and iterating several times between them while integrating the results improves the probability of success in achieving both goals. Using Frederick P. Brooks's terminology, the domain engineers have been freed to concentrate on the essence of each concern. They have been focused on the individual activities that require the most creativity without being required to accomplish several or all of those activities at once. Furthermore, they need not invent a way to express the result of each activity at the same time that they are performing it.

An additional benefit of having a standard, systematic process is that the decisions made by the engineers during each activity are captured in an artifact that can be used to review those decisions. The artifact is also used as input to other activities and serves as a record of the decisions made. In addition, it is used in later iterations of the activity and can be used to train new engineers. We intend all of the artifacts in FAST to be living artifacts—to be useful and to evolve over time—and not to be mere snapshots of decisions made at one time and never updated. Similarly, the PASTA artifacts that we use to represent the FAST process are intended to help the process itself evolve.

Explicit attention to making, capturing, reviewing, and using decisions in an integrated way is the essence of careful engineering. We cannot tell domain engineers which decisions are right for their domain, but we can tell them the kinds of decisions they need to make, when they should make them, and how they should represent them. This structure frees the engineers to be more creative, makes them more efficient, and allows them to explore more possibilities. The ideas underlying the process establish the patterns of thought; the type and ordering of activities and the type and structure of artifacts establish the patterns of work.

14.2 FAST and Reuse

The principal motivation for FAST is to make the software production process more efficient in the face of pressures to create carefully engineered software rapidly. Reuse is one of the mechanisms that FAST uses to achieve this goal. The FAST process encourages software engineers to reuse many kinds of artifacts, including requirements, specifications, design, code, tests, and documentation. Reuse in FAST is focused through the lens of family-oriented development. You identify reusable artifacts by considering what's common to family members. Restricting the domain of development to a family enables the software engineers to identify systematically reusable aspects of the family (the oracle hypothesis, Chapter 2). It also lets them take advantage of those reusable aspects in producing the software, including documentation, for family members (the organizational hypothesis).

In practice, you often realize reuse in the FAST process by creating a common architecture for all family members and generating code for family members based on that architecture. When we implement the architecture as a collection of components, we make them adaptable so as to accommodate the variabilities for the family. The Floating Weather Station architecture discussed in Chapter 5, Section 5.2.2.1, demonstrates several mechanisms for component adaptation.

Although effective code reuse for a family is often realized by the implementation of adaptable components, the entire FAST process can be viewed as creating standards for a family that promote reuse across the family. Examples include a standard vocabulary for the family (established in the commonality analysis) and a standard language for describing family members (created during the design of the application modeling language). The patterns of thought established by creating a family make reuse a pervasive mechanism in service to effective production of family members.

14.3 FAST as a Multiparadigm Process

Generating code and documentation for family members is a common element of all FAST processes. FAST allows considerable flexibility in how you achieve that goal. Different domains and different organizations require the use of different paradigms for achieving generation. Even when generation is not the objective, different domains require different design methods. As a result, FAST is sometimes characterized as a multi-paradigm approach to software production.[1]

14.4 FAST and Object Orientation

A common set of paradigms for software development is the set of object-oriented paradigms. Although all of them are based on the same fundamental principles, various object-oriented development methods use various analysis and design methods and various implementation languages. Because FAST emphasizes planning for change and design for change, object-oriented methods tend to fit well into FAST processes. For example, object-oriented frameworks may be a good basis for a family design, with classes playing the role of the adaptable components discussed in Section 14.2.

1. J. Coplien discusses the multi-paradigm approach to software development in more detail. See Chapter 1, reading [3].

14.5 Applicability of FAST

The fundamental law of family production (Chapter 4, Section 4.1.3) shows that the FAST process is worth applying when the cost of domain engineering is repaid by the decrease in cost and development time for future family members—that is, when the domain engineering cost can be amortized over the family members that are produced with the results of domain engineering. Such repayment occurs in the following situations:

- When a system will exist in many variations over a long period of time
- When considerable time and effort are being devoted to making continual changes to a system
- When there are many customers for a system, each of whom wants the system customized for his or her purposes
- When it is important to produce variations on a system quickly

Much of our experience in applying FAST has been in legacy systems that are still in demand, where there is a reservoir of knowledge about the system, and where change to the system has become slow and costly compared with marketplace demands. Users of FAST often view it as a way to gain a competitive advantage in speed and cost. This advantage is available whether you are applying FAST to a legacy system or to a new system development; it requires only that you can make reasonably good predictions about the directions in which your family will evolve. Even when you have only modest confidence in your predictions, making them will pay dividends in understanding your family and in finding standardized ways to talk and think about your family.

Predicting the types of changes that will need to be accommodated by a software system always happens, whether implicitly or explicitly. FAST explicitly provides time and structure for making such predictions and for taking advantage of them. It focuses attention on the need for later change and on the speed with which such changes can be made. Allowing only implicit predictions of changes usually leads to software that is difficult and costly to change.

Software development organizations turn to processes such as FAST because they must do so to remain in business, not just because they want to produce software that is more easily changeable than their current processes allow. The need to expand into competitive new markets and accommodate a greater variety of customer requirements forces them into a search for new processes that have the characteristics of FAST. They cannot continue to do business in the same way as in the past.

14.5.1 Finding Domains Where FAST Is Worth Applying

We usually apply FAST within a legacy system by seeking a domain in which there is frequent change occurring at relatively high cost. Such a domain is often an isolatable section of the system where the changes can be encapsulated and where a single group of software developers is responsible for making the changes.

The economic analysis suggested in Chapter 4, Section 4.1, is a worthwhile exercise and is incorporated into an early step of the FAST process. However, you often don't need a formal economic analysis to decide whether domain engineering is worth attempting, particularly when you are dealing with existing or legacy systems. The best strategy may be to identify within the system a few domains at a time where reengineering gives you a clear advantage. Our rule of thumb is to look for areas in a system where there is continual change and where we can make informed predictions about family requirements. If the cost of making changes and the time needed to make them is constant or increasing and if the number of new family members expected per year is constant or increasing, then FAST is worth applying.

Note that for a new system this rule applies equally well except that here you have a better chance to organize the system into a set of clearly defined domains, each of whose members can be generated independently of the others. (Some people might refer to such domains as highly cohesive and loosely coupled.) You also may have a less conclusive basis for estimating cost and frequency of change, making it less clear where greater investments in domain engineering should be made.

For any domain, the amount of investment is closely related to the number of domain members and the variability across the domain—that is, the nature of the differences among domain members. Some variability is easy to accommodate. For example, for a domain that stores information about items of a particular type, it may be relatively easy to generate various domain members that handle various numbers of items of the type. We sometimes call this *positive variability* because it is easy to create a generator or an architecture for the domain that handles such variability. The result is that it takes little additional investment to broaden the domain.

On the other hand, some forms of variability are difficult to accommodate. We call this *negative variability* because creating the generator or architecture to handle these forms requires considerable effort and may mean only a slight broadening of the domain for large additional investment.[2]

2. The ideas and terms *positive* and *negative variability* were suggested by Jim Coplien.

The market scope of the domain is often the most important factor in determining how much investment in domain engineering is required for a given return. One way to think about the investment and payback is in terms of the number of customers and lifetime of the product family in which the domain will be used. We can discern several situations here, discussed next.

14.5.2 The Single-Customer, Single-Product-Family Situation

You can have one customer with one product over a long period of time, with continual change as the customer's needs evolve. In this case, all the domains are used within one system and may become specialized to the application. Specialty systems created for the U.S. Department of Defense often have this characteristic. Figure 14-1 illustrates this situation. Note that there may be several main branches of the family as it evolves. We say that the family distributes over time.

14.5.3 The Many-Customers, Single-Product-Family Situation

You can have many customers wanting variations on the same product, each for different lengths of time, as markets change. This also leads to domains that become tuned to one application. Telecommunications switches are a good example of this situation. Figure 14-2 illustrates this situation. In the figure, we start with two family members: one for customer 1 and a second one for customers 2 and 3. As in the single-customer, single-product situation, the family may grow several distinct major branches. We say that the family distributes over time and space. It may become worthwhile to treat the branches as separate families over time, with shared subfamilies.

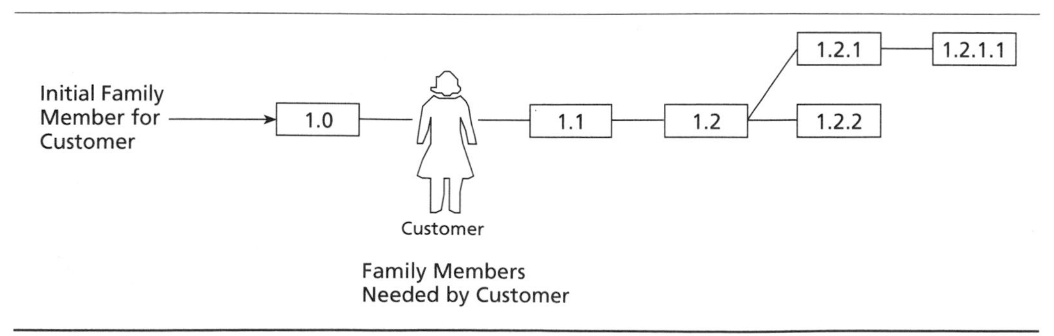

Figure 14-1. Single Customer, Single Application

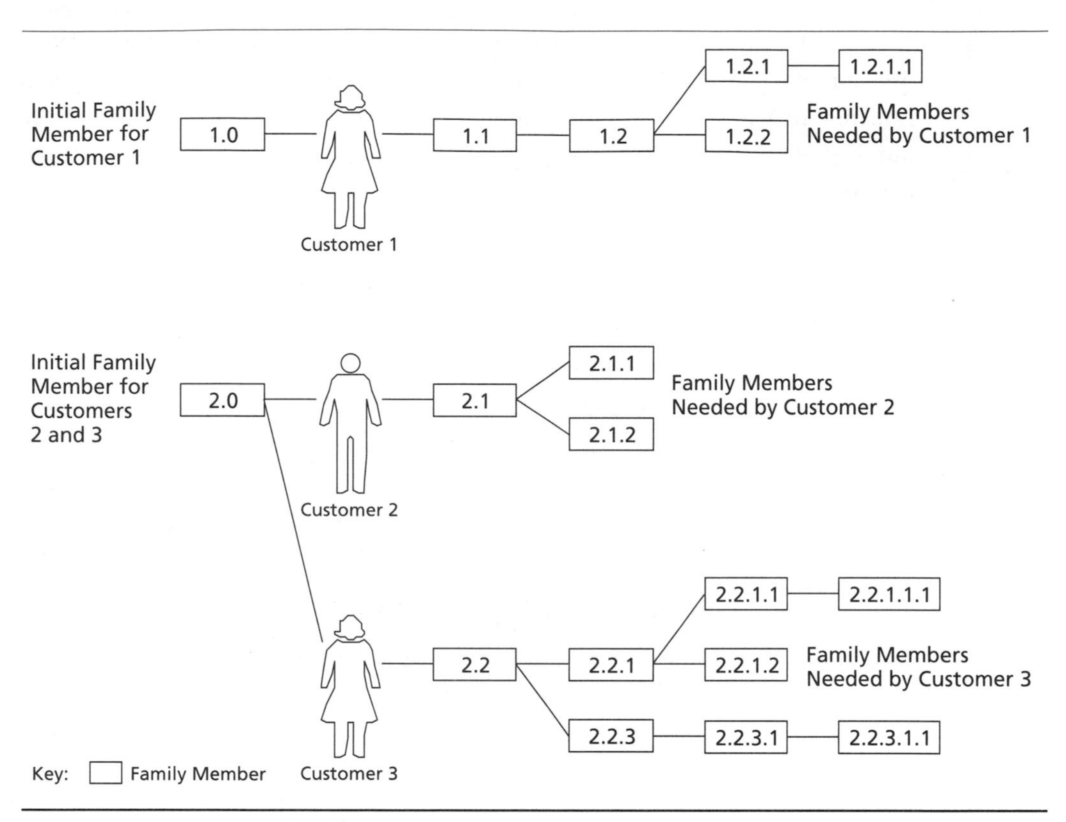

Figure 14-2. *Many Customers, Single Product Family*

14.5.4 The Many-Customers, Many-Product-Families Situation

You can have many customers for a variety of products, with a number of domains shared among products. Investment in each domain is then amortized over many products, and you are likely to see greater savings in total development costs. This situation may also require a change in organizational structure to make domain ownership clear and to ensure feedback to the domain owner (who employs the domain engineers) from the domain users (who employ the application engineers). Systems that process financial transactions in different industries have this characteristic; all of them must process transactions but use the transaction data in very different ways. Transaction processing can be considered a common domain among them. This situation is similar to that in Figure 14-2, except that instead of having one family distributed in time and space, we have several families that have common domains distributed in time and space, as shown in Figure 14-3.

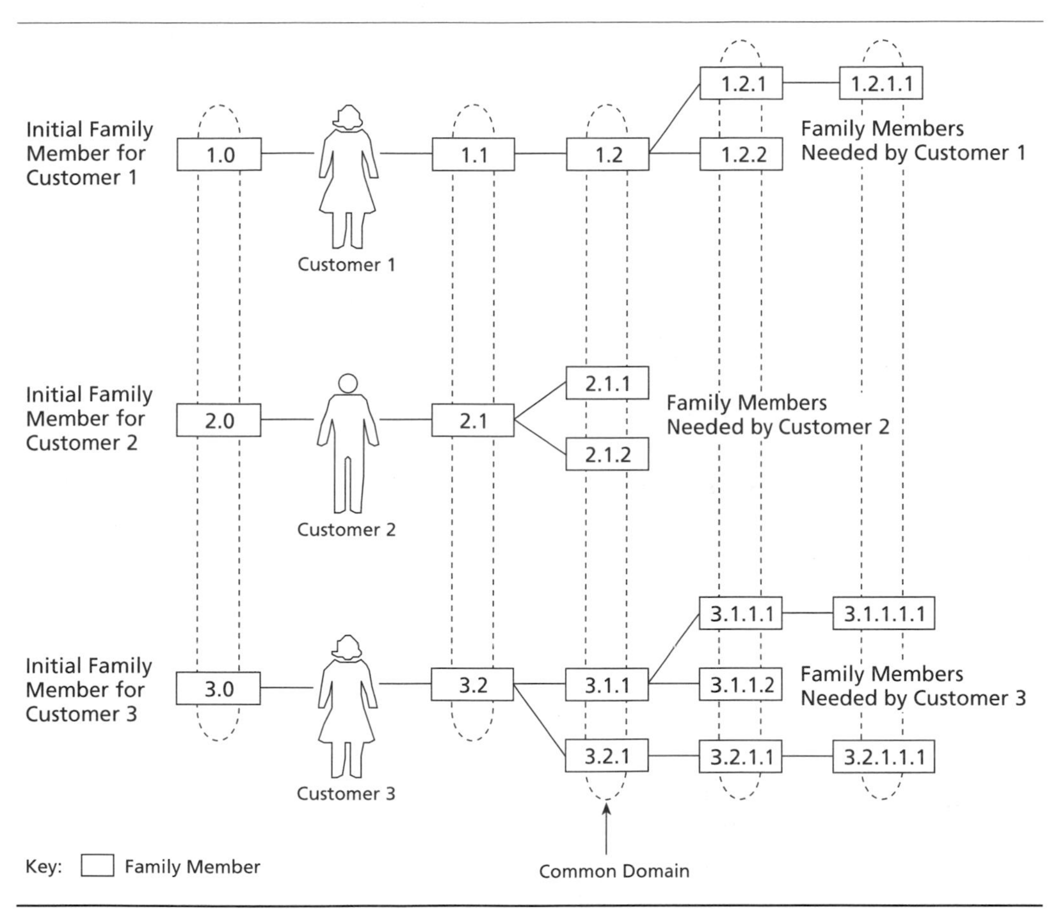

Figure 14-3. *Many Customers, Many Product Families*

14.6 Applying FAST Incrementally

The FAST process is designed so that its users gain immediate benefit from its application and so that it can be applied iteratively, with increasing investment and benefit at each iteration. The incremental nature of FAST is manifest in the following ways.

- In the early activities of FAST its users gain better understanding of their market, customers, and requirements, and they define a standard terminology for describing their domain. Such understanding and terminology facilitate their communication with one another, facilitate training of new team members, and provide information crucial to the design of members of the domain. The commonality analysis is a particularly good example of an activity that helps FAST users gain a deep understanding of their domain at modest cost.

- Later activities of FAST are designed to make effective use of the information and understanding gained in early activities, helping FAST users to create improved designs and mechanisms for generating code and documentation. In particular, early activities supply understanding and documented information about changes that must be accommodated by architectures. They also suggest stable abstractions for the domain.
- The FAST process is designed to be applied iteratively, with each cycle improving on the results of previous cycles. For example, in the first cycle team members might decide only to perform a commonality analysis and use the results to improve the flexibility of their design. In a second cycle they might decide to introduce a rudimentary language with which they can generate data structures that change frequently in response to changing customer requirements. In a third cycle they might decide to expand the language so that it can be used to generate the majority of their code.

The incremental approach using small initial increments may apply particularly well to a domain that is new to a company. The company might not feel particularly confident about its ability to predict how its product family will evolve and may not have the resources for a large initial investment. In this situation you would like to build the smallest useful domain members first, both to validate predictions about variabilities and to bring in money quickly for added investment. If your predictions are wrong, there is less initial investment to be lost and less investment in retrofitting than if you had invested heavily in initial domain members with considerable functionality and complexity. This is true whether or not you use FAST, but using FAST is more likely to enable you quickly to see which predictions were wrong and to find the places in the design and code that are based on those predictions and must be changed.

Each cycle of domain engineering may require several months to several years, and the results appear as improved versions of the application engineering environment. While these cycles are proceeding, application engineering also proceeds, providing the feedback and the payback needed to maintain the domain engineering cycles. We find that after the initial cycle, subsequent cycles of domain engineering that change existing artifacts but do not add major new artifacts cost about 10% of the initial cycle.

14.7 Patterns of a FAST Organization

Applying FAST on a large scale in a software development organization requires changes to the structure of the organization—including the nature of the key organizational roles—and to the patterns of activities. In typical software development organizations, the software developer is at the center of development activities and communications.[3] Changes that must be made to the software to create new versions are channeled through the developer role. In a FAST organization, new family members are produced by the application engineer using the application engineering environment. The application engineer may never see the generated code or the family design. Much of what is now known as the enhancement part of maintenance—creating versions of an application that have different features—becomes application engineering and is based on generating the new family members.

When there are defects in the application engineering environment or there are new requirements that were either unforeseen or not incorporated into earlier versions of the environment, the domain engineer must correct the defects or enhance the environment. He or she uses current software development methods and engages in the types of activities needed to create and maintain families.

In addition to the changes in roles and activities, the interactions and communications among the components of the software production organizations change. Production becomes organized around domains, and the application engineering environment for a domain can be used to help produce a number of different products. Each of the product organizations must provide feedback to the domain engineering organization about how well the domain's application engineering environment is working. A new unit of management, called a domain, is introduced into the organizational structure. The traditional application-based, project-oriented software development organization splits into pieces: some pieces do domain engineering, and others do application engineering.

14.8 Applying PASTA

Whether an organization is transitioning to a new process or improving an existing one, it is useful and convenient to have a standardized way of describing the process and a standardized vocabulary for discussing it. PASTA provides the

---

3. See Chapter 6, reading [2], for a discussion of organizational patterns and examples of typical patterns.

means for standardized process description. You can think of PASTA as the application modeling language for the domain of process design and implementation. The application engineering environment for PASTA includes a PASTA editor and a generator. Together, they allow you to specify and analyze your process, generate process guidebooks in a variety of formats (such as PostScript files or Web pages), and generate an environment for enacting the process. You can apply PASTA incrementally, starting with a few process activities, artifacts, and roles and building to a sufficiently detailed description to support process automation. As you understand your process domain better, PASTA gives you the flexibility to describe it in as much or as little detail as you like.

Note that our PASTA model of FAST is incomplete in describing some aspects of the process. In part, this is to allow you to customize the FAST process to your environment and your methods of working. For example, the section of the model on configuration management of a family does no more than describe a process for filing change reports, specifying only a few key decisions about changes that are pertinent to family-oriented software development. You can modify this part of the process to accommodate your own change management procedures, but you may want to retain the family orientation as you move to a FAST process.

14.9 Transitioning to a FAST Process

It is a rare organization that can tolerate a jump to a radically different process. Our pattern for the FAST process allows a gradual, incremental change from a software development process to a software production process. Such an evolution can be structured so that each increment of the change brings immediate and long-lasting benefits to the organization. Early in the evolution, the members of the organization must learn to think in terms of families. The test is whether or not they can forecast the family members that they and their customers will need and want in the future. When they learn to do so, they can structure their software to easily accommodate the changes needed to produce new family members.

As pointed out by Edsger Dijkstra in 1968, such structuring is the key to designing software that is understandable.[4] Later in the evolution of its FAST

4. "... program structure should be such as to anticipate its adaptations and modifications. Our program should not only reflect (by structure) our understanding of it, but it should also be clear from its structure what sort of adaptations can be catered for smoothly. Thank goodness the two requirements go hand in hand." Edsger W. Dijkstra, *On Program Families.* See Chapter 1, reading [8].

process(es), the organization can build on such thinking to make its software easier and faster to produce. An evolving PASTA model of an organization's FAST process will help it to keep pace with and guide the evolution of its process, serving as a series of reference points for the evolution and a quick way of disseminating information about changes to the process throughout the organization.

One way to start the transition to a FAST process is to pick a few high-leverage, well-understood domains using the rules of thumb suggested in Section 14.5.1. Apply a simple version of the FAST process to them, creating your own process model as a guide to the process that you want to follow. Be sure it is a process that can be used effectively in your environment. Allow yourself several iterations through the process to be sure that you understand it and that you are getting the gains that you want. As you understand FAST better, let it spread to more of your organization and to more domains; gradually transition to more-effective forms of it, using your models as reference points and guides to your progress. Focus your initial domain engineering on a single product line and encourage reuse of your engineering across product lines. After some experience with opportunistic cross-product-line reuse, you can move to systematically engineering domains for cross-product-line use. You may find that it becomes necessary to reengineer your organization as you have success in sharing domains across product lines.

Try to keep the evolution as simple as possible, with the potential gains and risks clear at each step. Through the judicious use of process models and a clear understanding of the basic ideas underlying FAST processes, your software development organization can shift its thinking to a family-based process.

14.10 Readings for Chapter 14

[1] Bass, L., and Clements, P. *Software Architecture in Practice.* Reading, MA: Addison-Wesley, 1998.

See the section on CelsiusTech for an example of a company that adopted a FAST-like process in order to stay in business.

[2] Blum, Bruce. *TEDIUM and the Software Practice.* Cambridge, MA: MIT Press, 1989.

An early example of the application of a FAST-like process in the medical field.

[3] Brooks, Frederick P. "No Silver Bullet: Essence and Accidents of Software Engineering." *IEEE Computer* (April 1987): 10–19.

An eloquent essay on what makes software engineering difficult. Brooks distinguishes the essence of building a software system (determining what it should do and what capabilities it should have) from the accidental aspects (deciding how the essential decisions should be captured and represented).

[4] Cusumano, M.A. Japan's *Software Factories: A Challenge to U.S. Management.* New York: Oxford University Press, 1991.

A description of the Japanese approach to software reuse and process improvement in the 1980s in order to gain improved software productivity and quality.

[5] Levine, John R., Mason, Tony, and Brown, Doug. *Lex and yacc.* Sebastopol, CA: O'Reilly & Associates, 1992.

A description of yet another compiler-compiler (YACC) and how to use it and the lexical analyzer generator lex to create parsers for languages.

Glossary

Abstract interface For information hiding modules, an interface that provides access to the services of the module but hides how the secret of the module is implemented.

AML Acronym for *application modeling language.*

Analysis definition form Table used to specify a P-state that is an analysis.

Application engineer Engineer responsible for understanding a customer's requirements for a family member, creating a specification, and using the production facilities for the family to produce the new family member.

Application engineering A process for rapidly creating members of a family (applications) using the production facilities for the family.

Application engineering environment Set of tools used for rapidly producing members of a domain from application models. The toolset is specifically designed for the domain.

Application engineering process Process for using an application engineering environment to produce members of a domain. The process is specifically designed for the domain.

Application model Model of a domain member in an application modeling language.

Application modeling language A language for modeling a member of a domain with the following attributes:

1. the language allows you to specify a domain member by its requirements,
2. the language allows you to specify a domain member by the requirements that distinguish it from other domain members; common requirements need not be specified.

Artifact Work product of an activity in a software development process.

Artifact definition form Table used to define an artifact.

Artifact hierarchy Hierarchy of artifacts defined by the relation "is a component of," i.e., B is a subartifact of A if B is a component of A.

Artifact State The condition of the artifact, usually an indication of the progress made towards completing the artifact. Artifacts change state as the result of an operation.

Artifact Tree Representation of the artifact hierarchy as a tree.

A-state Abbreviation of artifact state.

C&R Commands and reports.

Commands and reports Domain whose members are definitions of executable commands, definitions of the reports associated with commands, and the customer documentation for commands and reports.

Commonality Assumption that is true for all members of a family.

Commonality analysis v. Process for defining a family.
n. Artifact resulting from a commonality analysis process whose key components are a dictionary of terms, a list of commonalities, a list of variabilities, a list of parameters of variation, and a list of important issues that arose during the process.

Composer Tool for generating members of a domain based on the composition and instantiation of templates.

Composition mapping A mapping from an application modeling language to a family design that specifies how to create a domain member from its specification in the AML.

Decision model A document that defines the decisions that one must make to specify a member of a domain.

Domain Family that has been engineered to make production of family members efficient.

Domain engineer Engineer responsible for creating a set of production facilities for a family to make the production of family members efficient.

Domain engineering A process for creating the production facilities for a family.

Domain model Specification and design of an application engineering environment.

Domain qualification Activity to decide whether or not it is worth applying FAST to a family.

Entry condition Condition that must be true in order to perform an activity in a PASTA process model.

Exit condition Condition that must be true for an activity to be completed in a PASTA process model.

FAGE Application engineering environment for the FWS domain.

Family A set of items that have common aspects and predicted variabilities.

Family design A design that accommodates rapid production of members of a family, usually by taking advantage of the common and variable aspects of the family members.

FAST A process for developing software families. Acronym for *Family-Oriented Abstraction, Specification, and Translation.*

FAST PASTA model Model of the FAST process using the PASTA process modeling approach.

FLANG Application modeling language for the FWS domain.

FOG Code generator for the FWS domain, taking as input FLANG specifications and producing Java code as output. FOG works by instantiating and composing code templates.

Fundamental law of family production The savings resulting from domain engineering are directly proportional to the number of domain members produced using the investment in the family, less the investment in the family. The constant of proportionality is given by the average cost savings per domain member.

FWS family A family of floating weather stations, each of which broadcasts the wind speed at regular intervals.

FWSSIM Acronym for *Floating Weather Station Simulator.*

Implement domain Activity to implement the specification and design of an application engineering environment for a domain.

Information hiding module A work assignment for a programmer or group of programmers that embodies a decision that is likely to change independently of other decisions. See [10], [11] for further explanation and examples.

Interface The set of assumptions that the programmers of one module may make about another module.

Operation definition form Table used to specify a P-state that is an operation.

Parameter of variation Quantification of a variability, including the decision represented by the variability, the range of values allowed in making the decision, the time at which the value for the decision must be fixed, and a default value for the decision.

PASTA A state-based approach to process modeling. Acronym for *Process and Artifact State Transition Abstraction.*

Process designer Person who defines a software development process.

Process environment developer Person responsible for developing the environment used to perform a process.

Process model A specification of a process.

Process state A group of activities that are performed in a particular situation to satisfy a particular concern, e.g., a design process state may consist of a set of activities that are performed when a requirements specification has been completed and whose concern is how to organize software into meaningful chunks.

Product line A family of products designed to take advantage of their common aspects and predicted variabilities.

P-state Abbreviation of process state.

P-state definition form Table used to specify a P-state that is not an operation or analysis.

P-state hierarchy Hierarchy of process states defined by the relation "is a subactivity of," e.g., P-state B is a substate of P-state A if B is an activity that may be performed as part of performing A.

P-state tree Representation of the P-state hierarchy as a tree.

Relation definition form Table used to specify the existence of a relation between two process elements.

Role definition form Table used to define a role.

SCR Software Cost Reduction.

Software cost reduction A family-oriented method for developing software that includes formal requirements specification, and the use of information hiding, the uses relation, and cooperating sequential processes as key elements of software design. SCR was developed at the Naval Research Laboratory. See Chapter 1, reference [2] for an overview.

SPEC Acronym for specification of executable commands. SPEC is the application modeling language for the commands and report domain.

Variability An assumption about how members of a family may differ from each other.

Bibliography

[1] Alspaugh, T., Faulk, S., Britton, K., Parker, R., Parnas, D., and Shore, J. *Software Requirements for the A-7E Aircraft*. Washington, D.C.: Naval Research Laboratory, 1978.

[2] Arango, Guillcrmo and Pricto-Diaz, Ruben. *Domain Analysis and Software Systems Modeling*. Los Alamitos, CA: IEEE Computer Society Press, 1991. 299.

[3] Basili, V. and Weiss, D. "A Methodology for Collecting Valid Software Engineering Data." *IEEE Transactions on Software Engineering* SE-10, 6 (November 1984): 728–738.

[4] Bentley, J.L. "Programming Pearls: Little Languages." *Communications of the ACM* 29, 8 (August 1986): 711–721.

[5] Blum, Bruce I. *TEDIUM and the Software Process*. Cambridge, MA: MIT Press, 1989.:265.

[6] Brooks, Frederick P., Jr. "No Silver Bullet: Essence and accidents of Software Engineering." *IEEE Computer* 20, 4 (April, 1987): 10–19.

[7] Britton, K., Clements, P., Parnas, D., and Weiss, D. "Interface Specifications for the A–7E (SCR) Extended Computer Module." NRL Memorandum Report 5502. Washington, D.C.: Naval Research Laboratory, 31 December 1984.

[8] Britton, K., and Parnas, D. "A-7E Software Module Guide." NRL Memorandum Report 4702. Washington, D.C.: Naval Research Laboratory, December 1981.

[9] Britton, K.H., Parker, R.A., and Parnas, D.L. "A Procedure for Designing Abstract Interfaces for Device Interface Modules." *Proc. 5th Int. Conf. Software Eng.* San Diego, CA (1981): 195–204.

[10] Cain, B. and Coplien, J. "A Role-Based Empirical Process Modeling Environment." *IEEE Second Int. Conf. Software Process*. Berlin, 1993: 125–133.

[11] Campbell, Grady H., Jr. "Abstraction-Based Reuse Repositories." REUSE_REPOSITORIES-89041-N. Herndon, VA: Software Productivity Consortium, 1989.

[12] Campbell, Grady H., Jr., Faulk, Stuart R., and Weiss, David M. "Introduction to Synthesis." INTRO_SYNTHESIS_PROCESS-90019-N. 1990, Herndon, VA: Software Productivity Consortium, 1990.

[13] International Telegraph and Telephone Consultative Committee. (CCITT) Yellow Book, Volume VI–Fascicle VI.7 Recommendations Z.311–Z.341. Geneva. 1981.

[14] Cleaveland, J. Craig. "Building Application Generators." *IEEE Software* (1988): 25–33.

[15] Clements, P. *Software Cost Reduction through Disciplined Design*. Washington, D.C.: 1984 *Naval Research Laboratory Review*. Available as National Technical Information Service order number AD-A1590000. July 1985: 79–87.

[16] Clements, P.C., Bass, L., and Kazman, R. *Software Architecture in Practice*. Reading, MA: Addison Wesley-Longman, 1998.

[17] Clements, P. "Interface Specifications for the A-7E Shared Services Module." NRL Memorandum Report 4863. Washington, D.C.: Naval Research Laboratory, 8 September 1982.

[18] Clements, P. "Function Specifications for the A-7E Function Driver Module." NRL Memorandum Report 4658. Washington, D.C.: Naval Research Laboratory, 27 November 1981.

[19] Clements, P.C., Parker, R.A., Parnas, D.L., Shore, J.E., and Britton, K.H. "A Standard Organization for Specifying Abstract Interfaces." NRL Report 8815. Washington, D.C.: Naval Research Laboratory, 14 June 1984.

[20] Coglianese, L, and Tracz, W. "An Adaptable Software Architecture for Integrated Avionics." *Proceedings of the IEEE 1993 National Aerospace and Electronics Conference-NAECON 1993*. Dayton, Ohio, June 1993.

[21] Conway, M. "How Do Committees Invent?" *Datamation*, (April, 1968): 28–31.

[22] Coplien, J. O. *Software Patterns*. New York: SIGS Books & Multimedia, 1996.

[23] Coplien, J.O. *Multi-paradigm Design for C++*. Reading, MA: Addison-Wesley, 1998.

[24] Coplien, J., Hoffman, D., and Weiss, D. "Commonality and Variability in Software Engineering." *IEEE Software* (November/December 1998): 37–45.

[25] Cuka, D., and Weiss, D. "Engineering Domains: Executable Commands As An Example." *Proc. International Conference On Software Reuse*, June 1998.

[26] Cusumano, Michael A. *Japan's Software Factories: A Challenge to U.S. Management*. New York: Oxford University Press, 1991.

[27] Dijkstra, E.W. "Notes on Structured Programming" In *Structured Programming*, edited by O.J. Dahl, E.W. Dijkstra, and C.A.R. Hoare. London: Academic Press (1972).

[28] Godefroid, P. "Model Checking for Programming Languages using VeriSoft." *Proceedings of the 14th ACM Symposium on Principles of Programming Languages*. Paris (January 1997): 174–186.

[29] Harel, D. "STATECHARTS: A Visual Formalism for Complex Systems." *Science of Computer Programming* 8 (1987): 231–274.

[30] Kang, K., Cohen, S., et al. "Feature Oriented Domain Analysis (FODA) Feasibility Study." Technical Report CMU/SEI-90-TR-21. Software Engineering Institute, Pittsburgh, PA, November 1990.

[31] Kirby, J. Jr., Lai, R.C.T., and Weiss D.M. "A Formalization of a Design Process." *Proc. 1990 Pacific Northwest Software Quality Conf.* October 1990: 93–114.

[32] Ladd, D.A., and Ramming, J.C. "A*: A Language for Implementing Language Processors." *IEEE Transactions on Software Engineering* SE-21. (November 1995): 894–901.

[33] Levine, John R., Mason, Tony, and Brown, Doug. *Lex and yacc*. Sebastopol, CA: O'Reilly & Associates, 1992.

[34] Neighbors, James M. "The Draco Approach to Constructing Software from Reusable Components." *IEEE Transactions on Software Engineering* SE-10 (1984): 564–574.

[35] Parnas, D.L. "On the Criteria to be Used in Decomposing a System into Modules." *Comm. ACM* 15 (December 1972): 1053–1058.

[36] Parnas, D.L. "On A Buzzword: Hierarchical Structure," Proc. IFIP Congress 1974, Amsterdam, North Holland, 1974

[37] Parnas, D.L. "On the Design and Development of Program Families." *IEEE Transactions on Software Engineering* SE-2 (March 1976): 1–9

[38] Parnas, D.L. "Designing Software for Ease of Extension and Contraction." *IEEE Transactions on Software Engineering* SE-5 (March 1979): 128–138.

[39] Parnas, D.L. "Software Aging" invited plenary talk, Proc. 18th Int. Conf. Soft. Eng., Berlin June 1994.

[40] Parnas, D.L., and Clements, P.C. "A Rational Design Process: How and Why to Fake It." *IEEE Transactions on Software Engineering* SE-12, 2 (February 1986): 251–257.

[41] Parnas, D.L., Clements, P.C., and Weiss, D.M. "The Modular Structure of Complex Systems." *IEEE Transactions on Software Engineering* SE-11 (March 1985): 259–266.

[42] Perlman, G. "An Overview of the SETOPT Command Line Option Parser Generator." *Proceedings USENIX* (1985): 160–164.

[43] Simos, Mark, and Anthony, Jon. "Weaving the Model Web: A Multi-Modeling Approach to Concepts and Features in Domain Engineering." Proc. Fifth Int. Conf. Software Reuse. June 1998.

[44] "Software Engineering Principles." Course Notebook. Washington, D.C.: Naval Research Laboratory, July 1980.

[45] Tracz, Will. "LILEANNA: A Parameterized Programming Language." *Proceedings of the Second International Work on Software Reuse* (March 1993): 66–78.

Index

CD-ROM Warranty

Addison Wesley Longman, Inc. warrants the enclosed disc to be free of defects in materials and faulty workmanship under normal use for a period of ninety days after purchase. If a defect is discovered in the disc during this warranty period, a replacement disc can be obtained at no charge by sending the defective disc, postage prepaid, with proof of purchase to:

Editorial Department
Computer and Engineering Publishing Group
Addison-Wesley
One Jacob Way
Reading, Massachusetts 01867-3999

After the ninety-day period, a replacement disc will be sent upon receipt of the defective disc and a check or money order for $10.00, payable to Addison Wesley Longman, Inc.

Addison Wesley Longman, Inc. makes no warranty or representation, either expressed or implied, with respect to this software, its quality, performance, merchantability, or fitness for a particular purpose. In no event will Addison Wesley Longman, Inc., its distributors, or dealers be liable for direct, indirect, special, incidental, or consequential damages arising out of the use or inability to use the software. The exclusion of implied warranties is not permitted in some states. Therefore, the above exclusion may not apply to you. This warranty provides you with specific legal rights. There may be other rights that you may have that vary from state to state. The contents of this CD-ROM are intended for personal use only.

More information and updates are available at:
http://www.awl.com/cseng/titles/0-201-69438-7